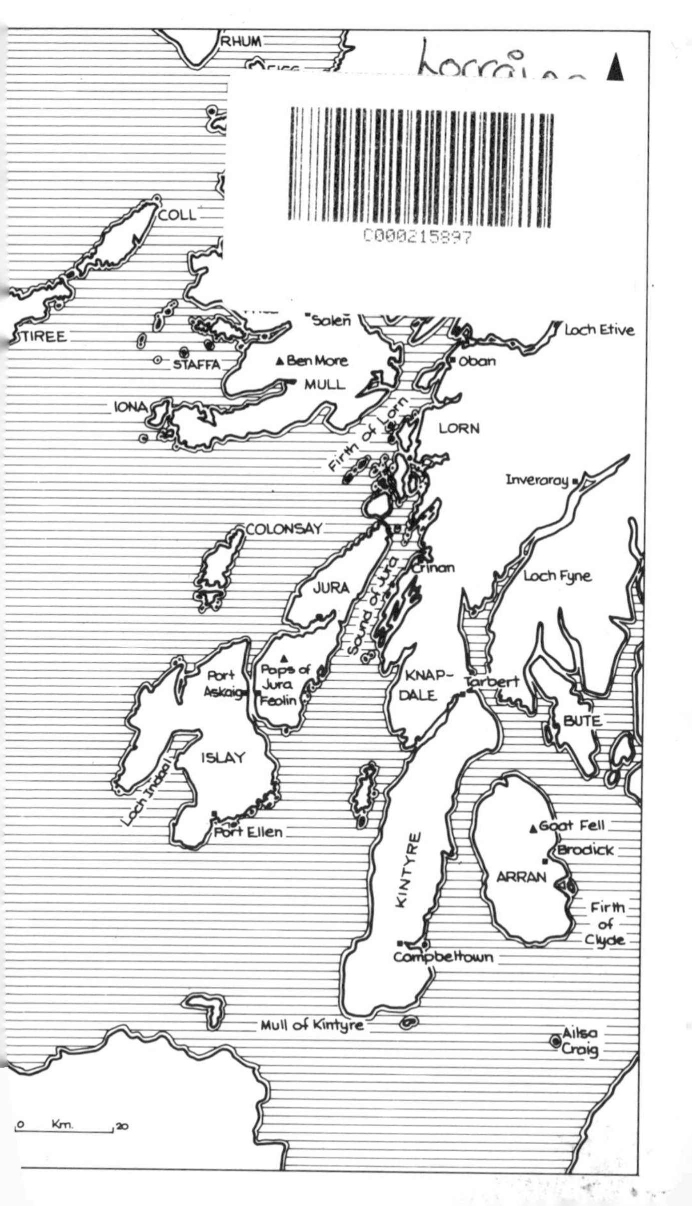
RHUM
COLL
TIREE
STAFFA
IONA
Solen
Ben More
MULL
Loch Etive
Oban
LORN
Firth of Lorn
Inveraray
COLONSAY
JURA
Crinan
Loch Fyne
Sound of Jura
Paps of Jura
Port Askaig
Feolin
KNAP-DALE
Tarbert
BUTE
ISLAY
Loch Indaal
Port Ellen
KINTYRE
Goat Fell
Brodick
ARRAN
Firth of Clyde
Campbeltown
Mull of Kintyre
Ailsa Craig
0 Km. 20

This guidebook is compiled from the most recent information and experience provided by members of the Scottish Mountaineering Club and other contributors. The book is published by the Scottish Mountaineering Trust, which is a charitable trust.

Revenue from the sale of books published by the Trust is used for the continuation of its publishing programme and for charitable purposes associated with Scottish mountains and mountaineering.

Skye and the Hebrides

Rock and Ice Climbs

Volume 2

The Outer Hebrides, Rum, Eigg, Mull and Iona

Dave Cuthbertson, Bob Duncan,
Graham Little and Colin Moody

Series Editor: Roger Everett

SCOTTISH MOUNTAINEERING CLUB
CLIMBERS' GUIDE

Published in Great Britain by the Scottish Mountaineering Trust, 1996

British Library Cataloguing in Publication Data
ISBN 0-907521-48-7

A catalogue record of this book is available from the British Library

Diagrams by Dave Cuthbertson, Donald Bennet, Bob Duncan, Al Matthewson and Colin Moody.
Maps by Jim Renny and Donald Bennet
Production by Scottish Mountaineering Trust (Publications) Ltd
Typeset by Elliot Robertson, Westec, North Connel
Printed by St Edmundsbury Press, Bury St Edmunds and GNP-Booth, Clydebank
Bound by Hunter and Foulis, Edinburgh

Distributed by Cordee, 3a DeMontfort Street, Leicester LE1 7HD

Contents

List of Diagrams and Maps

List of Illustrations

Prophesy of Drowning, Pabbay (Climbers, Kevin Howett and Graham Little) *Grahame Nicoll*

Stepping Out on the Main Wall of An Sgurr, Eigg (Climber, Dave Saddler) *Robin Wilson*

Between pages 228 and 229

Tystie, The Slab, Scoor, Mull (Climber, Davie Gregg) *Colin Moody*

Eat My Shorts, Horse Wall, Scoor, Mull (Climber, Mark Garthwaite) *Colin Moody*

The Incredible Dr Sex, Raven's Crag, Iona (Climber, Mark Garthwaite) *Colin Moody*

The Mission, Port na Cuilce, Colonsay (Climber, Graham Little) *Justin Finlay*

Back Cover

Paranoid Slippers, Mangersta (Climber, Grant Farquhar) *Gary Latter*

Acknowledgements

HARRIS AND LEWIS

Many people have helped with this section of the guide by contributing information or commenting on the text. These include Brian Davison, Johnny Dawes, Steve Meyers, Paul Pritchard, George Smith, Mick Tighe, Crispin Waddy and Adam Wainwright. Susan Cuthbertson and Joanna George helped with the typing and preparation of the text.

Dave Cuthbertson

MINGULAY, PABBAY, EIGG AND COLONSAY

Chris Bonington, Kev Howett and Grahame Nicoll helped with the Mingulay and Pabbay sections, while Jan Bertram kindly provided the details of a number of routes at Pabbay discovered by an enterprising German team. Dave Saddler helped with the Eigg section and Bill Skidmore and John Spencer added useful details and comments on the Colonsay chapter.

Graham Little

RUM

I owe several people my grateful thanks. To Hamish Brown for allowing me to use his material; to Andy Tibbs, Al Matthewson and John Mitchell for providing information and photographs; to Martin Curry, Reserve Manager, for commenting on my general notes, and to Nicci Campbell, Lyndsey Kinnes and Ann Murie for providing cheerful company - despite the midges - on visits to Rum.

Bob Duncan

MULL

Danny Brooks, Neil Horn, Rona Moody, Mark Shaw, Ian Stevenson, Dave Tindall, James and Nick Turner all helped with the preparation of this section.

Colin Moody

Introduction

The islands of Scotland are magical places, brimming with interest for all types of visitors. For the climber they offer uncrowded and adventurous climbing on both sea-cliff and mountain crag. The cliffs described in this volume include some of the most remote and challenging in Britain, including arguably one of the very finest, Sron Ulladale. They have drawn influential climbers who have made significant ascents over a number of decades, but until now it has been difficult to obtain detailed, comprehensive information. The lack of previous guidebooks to most of the regions described here has presented many difficulties to the authors of this volume, who have had to collate much of information for the first time. All of them are enthusiasts whose own climbs and explorations have made substantial contributions to the development of climbing on the Scottish islands.

The climbing described in this book includes small easily accessible inland crags and sea-cliffs, majestic inland cliffs including some of the largest in Britain, and remote sea-cliffs of difficult and serious access. A minority of the cliffs can only be reached by private charter boat. While the climbing on some of the islands, such as Mull, is fairly easily accessible from the mainland, the Outer Isles in particular are sufficiently remote to make weekend visits from the major centres of population unrealistic or uneconomic. These islands are best visited as part of a longer holiday, so that their cliffs and climbs can be explored to good effect. A relevant point here is that the weather can often be better than on the mainland, since there are no large upland masses to induce the rainfall which would otherwise fall in more mountainous areas. One thing is certain, a trip to the islands will always amply repay the effort required to get there, and we hope that this guide will allow many more climbers to share in the unique experiences that the Hebrides have to offer.

Roger Everett
June 1996

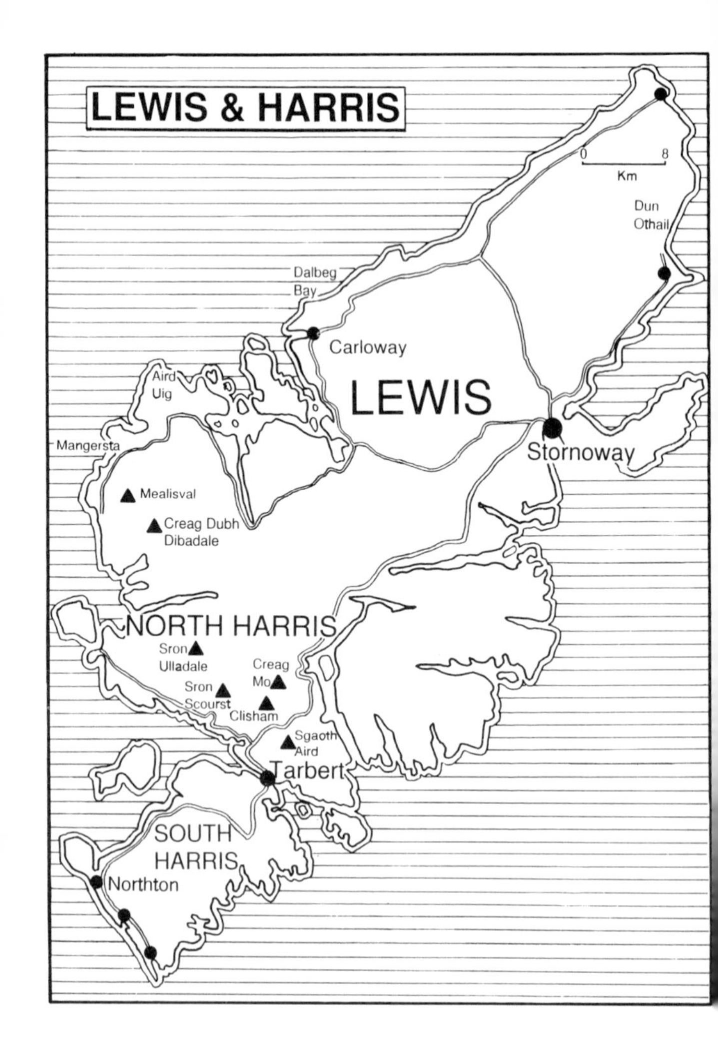
LEWIS & HARRIS
0
8
Km
Dun
Othail
Dalbeg
Bay
Carloway
LEWIS
Aird
Uig
Mangersta
Stornoway
Mealisval
Creag Dubh
Dibadale
NORTH HARRIS
Sron
Ulladale
Creag
Mo
Sron
Scourst
Clisham
Sgaoth
Aird
Tarbert
SOUTH
HARRIS
Northton

Lewis, Harris and the Uists

Introduction

Lewis and Harris form the northern half of the largest single chain of Scottish Islands, more commonly known as the Outer Hebrides or Western Isles, and in the past referred to as the Long Isle. Lewis and Harris are in fact one island, the deep incisions of Loch Resort and Loch Seaforth naturally forming its 10km border. Making up the remainder of the chain are the Uists, North and South separated by Benbecula, the Barra Isles, with Mingulay and Bernerary forming the most southerly points of the group.

Like so many of the Scottish Isles, the Outer Hebrides have their own special charm. The coastal scenery is quite breathtaking, where barren moorland of machair and inhospitable peat contrast against a rugged mountain landscape. There is a distinct feeling of remoteness and a sense of adventure. As far as you can see, there is a congestion of fresh water lochs and twisting burns. The smell of burning peat, and the now grassed-over remains of lazy beds and derelict black houses, paint a picture of a bygone way of life. All leave a lasting impression. In short, a trip to The Outer Hebrides is an adventure stepping back in time.

There is something here for everyone, novice or expert, and the choice of climbing in the mountains or on the sea-cliffs next to superb unspoilt beaches can make for a more holiday atmosphere.

A cautionary note however; visits to the Islands are infrequent, which basically means that a great number of the climbs have received very few ascents and in some cases there are no known repeats at all. In general terms, an attempt has been made to encourage visitors as opposed to scaring them off. Grades will always vary however, and the author certainly does not profess to have climbed all the routes in this section of the guide.

Travel

Caledonian Macbrayne runs a car and passenger ferry service from Uig in Skye to Tarbert in Harris, a crossing time of 1 hour 45 minutes, two to three sailings daily (not Sunday). This is recommended for those climbing in Harris. Caledonian Macbrayne also runs a service from Ullapool to Stornoway on a new ferry which takes 2½-3 hours, three sailings daily in summer, two in winter. For North Uist, the same company run a service from Uig in Skye, or from Tarbert in Harris to Lochmaddy, a crossing time of 2½ hours from Uig. In all cases, ferry times are subject to change especially during the winter. Booking is essential during busy holiday periods. There is also an air service from Glasgow to Benbecula, from where a post bus travels to Lochmaddy. There is an airport at Stornoway, with air services (British Airways), twice daily except Sunday from Glasgow, and twice daily Monday to Friday from Inverness. Private transport is advisable, especially if you intend to visit some of the more remote areas. In addition to a post bus and a taxi service which serves all three areas, it is also possible to hire a car in Stornoway.

A normal return fare for an average-sized car is about £110 plus £22 per person. A short break (3 nights only) is £93 plus £19 per person. These are 1996 prices.

Provisions

Stornoway and Tarbert provide all the usual amenities: banks, garages, guest houses, B&Bs, supermarkets, cafes, a post office, etc. There is also a cinema in Stornoway. Lochmaddy has, in addition to a tiny hospital, a bank, a garage and one hotel. There are also guest houses as well as a youth hostel (Map Ref 918 687), and a post office.

On Sundays, everything comes to a standstill in these parts.

Maps

OS 1:50 000 Sheets 8 and 13 cover most areas on Lewis and Harris
OS 1:50 000 Sheets 18, 22 and 31 cover North and South Uist.

Mountain Rescue

No mountain rescue service exists on the island. In case of emergency, call 999 and ask for police. This can be done on a public or private telephone.

Weather

Contrary to popular belief, the Scottish climate, unpredictable at the best of times, is often better than you might think. It is simply a matter of knowing where to go and when. The best and sunniest months are usually during late April, May, June, early July and early September. The climate on the island is generally a mild one with nearly always a fresh to strong breeze. Its geographical situation also allows climbing until the late evening during mid-summer.

Midges

What can I say - worse than the weather! Without doubt, midges will be plentiful from June until early September. One consolation is that the continuous sea breeze helps to combat this horrible little monster. Make sure you come well prepared.

Deer Stalking

Officially this starts on 15th July and ends on the 20th October. Hind shooting goes on until 15th February. If in doubt ask locally.

Winter

Due to low altitude, proximity to the sea and inaccessibility, virtually no winter mountaineering has been recorded. However, with a number of big dark cliffs in the area, the potential for winter mountaineering is definitely there.

Geology: The Lewisian Complex

Nearly all of the Outer Hebrides, as well as Coll, Tiree and South Rona, consist of rocks loosely described as Lewisian gneiss. Smaller outcrops also occur on Skye, Raasay, Rum, Iona and Islay. These rocks include some of the oldest so far known in Scotland or indeed in Western Europe.

Rocks belonging to the Lewisian complex consist chiefly of banded gneisses. These were derived from a variety of pre-existing rocks by deformation and metamorphism deep in the earth's crust. They incorporate various intrusive igneous bodies, including basic dykes, granite sheets and pegmatite veins. Although they form a very complex group, even the layman should be able to distinguish dark basic masses such as amphibolite, and broad, coarsely crystalline veins of pink pegmatite.

At least two ancient metamorphic episodes can be identified within these gneisses. The earliest, the Scourian named after the village of Scourie, has been dated by radiometric methods as 2,900 - 2,300 million years old. The subsequent episode, known as the Laxfordian (named after the nearby Laxford river), has been dated at 2,300 - 1,700 million years.

The entire complex was uplifted and deeply eroded before the deposition of Moine and Torridonian sediments began some 1,000 million years ago. The Hebridean region remained relatively undisturbed during the subsequent Caledonian orogeny, or mountain building episode, except for the development of the Outer Hebridean thrust zone. This zone is marked by a broad tract of eastward-dipping crushed rocks and extends for 200km along the eastern seaboard of the Long Isle from North Lewis to Barra. It accounts for the line of hills with west-facing scarps in the Uists.

History

St. KILDA

Allthough details of rock climbing on St. Kilda are not described in the text, a history of climbing in the Outer Hebrides would not be complete without a mention of St Kilda and its neighbouring islands and sea-stacks. Much has been written about the native tradition of climbing there. Birds and wool were the main resources (young puffins and gannets being the favourite), so climbing was done mainly for that purpose. The feathers were sold on the mainland and helped to pay for rent, the carcase was eaten and fulmar oil provided fuel for lighting. There is, however, abundant evidence to suggest that courage and skill as a cliff fowler were highly regarded as a test of manhood and in a practical view of fitness to support family, but also, as a natural consequence, a pastime in which the St. Kildans found great enjoyment.

Stac na Biorrach was reputed to be one of the hardest climbs in the group, and only a few St. Kildans could lead it. Charles Barrington (who made the first ascent of the Eiger) was on the island in 1883 partly to compare the methods of Alpine and Hebridean peasants as climbers. Barrington was the first 'amateur' to climb Stac na Biorrach, although an account by Sir Robert Moray written in 1698 is possibly the first description of any rock climb in Scotland. "After they landed, a man having room but for one of his feet, he must climb up 12 or 16 fathoms high. Then he comes to a place where having but room for his left foot and left hand, he must leap from thence to another place before him, which if hit right the rest of the ascent is easy, and with a small cord which he carries with him he hauls up a rope whereby all the rest come up. But if he misseth that foot step (as often times they do) he falls into the sea and the (boats) company takes him in and he sits still until he is a little refreshed and then he tries again, for everyone there is not able for that sport".

In 1900, Norman Heathcote (a member of the SMC) climbed Stac na Biorrach with Barrington. Heathcote noted that the islanders preferred to climb in bare feet or stocking soles, shunning the state of the art in footwear, which was worn by himself. The coarse wool stuck nicely to the outward-sloping slabs where the nailed boots would neither bite nor grip the hard surface of the granite. The St. Kildans used plaited horse hair ropes (preceded by rawhide) about an inch thick and protected by hide to prevent chaffing. On the biggest cliffs, they would usually top rope; otherwise, the techniques that evolved were similar to those developed in early Alpine climbing. In 1907, Bentley Beetham (the well known Lakeland climber) commented that rope management was only casual. However, the islanders must have been very proficient, for were it not for the fact that Barrington was the middle man on a rope with two St Kildans, his fall on the traverse of the second pitch on Stac na Biorrach would not have been stopped. Iron spikes were also used and sometimes left *in situ* to assist future ascents of the most difficult landings. One such climb is Stac Lee. Beetham noted that this was regarded as an initiation or passing-out test for aspiring cliff fowlers. The islanders considered Stac Armin (the highest Stac in the British Isles) to be more difficult; both stacks were climbed annually to harvest gannets. Heathcote commented that Stac Lee was easier than the Inaccessible Pinnacle on Skye.

Numerous other climbs abound, but sadly the native tradition of climbing was already in decline. Outside influence caused the younger people to turn their ideas elsewhere. Visitors to the island introduced diseases, and the community was forced to rely more on outside help. As a result, the government put pressure on the tiny community to conform to the norms of the society on the mainland, which led inevitably to the general evacuation in 1930. But to many, the lure of such a remote and hostile beauty still held great appeal.

Tom Patey visited the island with the view to climbing a direct route on the 400m cliff of Conachair. Unfortunately, he was marooned for three weeks of continuous gales, snow and rain. "Climbing was not an easy task, for during the nesting months many of the cliffs were plastered knee-deep in excrement, hence the quality of the underlying rock is a purely academic point. In winter, when the rocks are clean, it's too rough to land at the bottom. Anything really good (less than you might think), is too steep to provide any major free climbs. Pitoners would find a lot to do. Remember to take crampons and an axe if you go. Getting to any of the routes would probably involve traversing short cropped grass at an enormous angle. No wonder the original St. Kildans had prehensile, divergent toes!" Tom Weir and Douglas Scott had a similar experience when they were forced to use camera tripods instead of ice axes!

In 1969, M.Boyd with R.Balharry and C.Welsh made ascents of several of the major stacks for the first time since the departure of the St. Kildans. Their notes of the climbs, and in particular the difficulty which they encountered, makes the native achievements all the more remarkable. Of an ascent on Stac Lee, Boyd said: "According to the books, the St. Kildans lassoed an iron peg, then a man was hauled up from the boat. (The method with which Barrington made his ascent of Stac na Biorrach in 1883.) The tradition is of a difficult landing, and we had on our life jackets. When the boat was on the highest swell we stepped out, found slippery holds and began climbing. We didn't waste time. The first 100 feet was easy enough, but the bit beyond was a different story. It looked impossible. I banged in a piton for security. If I could traverse 15 feet of that wall to the far ledge ... I inched out on no more than balance holds, feeling I could retreat if necessary. But the last move could not be tested. The birds were screaming like an excited crowd at a football match. The next bit was actually overhanging, then in another 20 feet I was on a ledge with a good belay. We were now on a great bevelled roof of gannets, and walking up the ledges of slimy guano you sank in at every step. Now and again gannets would reach out and grip your arm in their beaks."

In September 1987, the National Trust for Scotland permitted an experimental visit by ten climbers which was headed by Chris Bonington and sponsored by Independent Television News. Included in the team were Pete Whillance, Brian Hall and Howard Lancashire. They successfully explored the northern cliffs of Hirta and made first ascents on the impressive face of Conachair. Inflatable dinghies were used to make unpredictable landings and a total of 19 new routes were climbed, from HVS to E6.

With the exception of Ministry of Defence personnel and the National Trust for Scotland's warden, the St. Kilda group is now uninhabited. It is owned by The National Trust for Scotland and managed by Scottish Natural Heritage as a nature reserve. There is no public transport, access being by private charter or boat, and permission is required for access.

THE LEWIS SEA-CLIFFS

The first climbs to appear on the sea-cliffs of Western Lewis were those made around the lighthouse at the Butt of Lewis by J.R.Cotterill and his party in the early thirties. Despite earlier reports by visiting members of the SMC, the only other record of any climbing was that done by the local cliff fowlers. No doubt other routes had been ascended, especially during the fifties and sixties (and certainly John Grieve and party climbed routes north of the Mangersta sands in the 1960s), but it was not until 1970 that the next routes were to appear and be written up in detail. These were the work of 'Lord John' MacKenzie, prolific new router of the most obscure Highland outcrops. John climbed the huge overlapping slab at Aird Fennish Head (Route Major; Severe) and on the Grey Tower at New Tolsta he climbed Look See Crack (VS).

However, the first prolonged period of development did not take place until the early seventies by members of the Lochaber M.C. and M.R.T. These visits (primarily to improve and practise the most up to date rescue techniques) became something of an annual event and ceilidh. As seen in the following list of first ascents, the temptation to explore such superb virgin rock obviously proved too much. Among the most prolific of the Lochaber team were Mick Tighe, Ian Sykes, Jim Paterson, Ian Donaldson, Bill Newton and Ian Sutherland. A small selection of climbs which stand out as classics today are Claymore (HVS 5a, 1970s), Atlantic Crossing (VS 5a, 1974), Flannan Slab (VS 4c, 1974), Flannan Direct (HVS 5b, 1974), Moac Wall (E1 5b, 1974), Star of the Sea (E1 5b, 1974) and Newton's Law (E1 5b, 1974). The latter two climbs were first done under the influence of a period when it was fashionable to carry an array of all the latest gadgetry and hang around in etriers. Realising that the routes were potentially excellent free climbs, honour was restored when first ascensionists Mick Tighe and Bill Newton returned to produce two of the finest free pitches on the coast.

These visits were by no means confined to the seventies. A seemingly inexhaustible and forever adventurous Mick Tighe, either as a professional mountain guide or in the company of his Lochaber friends, had been steadily developing literally hundreds of new routes right up until the publication of this guide. Unfortunately, a lack of detail has meant that a large portion of these climbs have not been mentioned in the guide. Just remember that the next time you think you have discovered a new geo or climbed a new route anywhere in the region of up to E2, you can be pretty well assured that Mick Tighe has been there. The following list represents a selection of the better routes climbed by members of the Lochaber M.C. from the early to mid-eighties, which will no doubt become classics in due course: Gravity Man (E2 5c, 1985), Northwest Passage (E2 5c, 1988), Cormorant Corner (E1 5b), Chicken Run Direct (HVS 5b, 1970s), Coloured Rain (E1 5b, 1988), Twelve Years On (E1 5b, 1986).

To join one of those infamous annual trips in 1985 were Gogarth veterans Dave Pearce and Jim Moran, although it must be said that one is slightly older than the other! Dave Cuthbertson and Gary Latter were also based in Lochaber at that time so they too were invited. Last but not least was big Jock the joiner whose job it was to ensure a hearty fire even when the dregs of the dreaded dram had been drunk completely dry!

In the Flannan area, Jim and Dave climbed the superb Magician (E5), Jim taking a 'nice one' when he pulled on a loose flake. While the remainder were piecing together latter day classics on the slabs of Griomaval, Cubby and Gary were busy putting up The Painted Wall (E4) and Whisky Galore (E5). That night, huddled around a camp fire, fuelled of course by that scourge of the Highlands, the team quietly recalled tall tales of a huge cliff the likes of which has never been seen. On the morrow, our search was in vain, so we settled for 100 Pipers (E3) and Penny Whistle (E3) on the Mangersta Slabs. The imaginative route-naming was inspired by the previous night's shindig! However, towards the end of the day, while on reconnaissance for the next day's plan of action, 'a wee donner roon the corner' from the Mangersta Slabs revealed all. That first breathtaking sight of the Screaming Geo left a strong impression on all of us.

Courtesy of H.M.G., Paul Moores and Cubby climbed the corner to the left of the Magician to give Queen's Freebie (E4 1985) while Gary Latter's Dauntless (E5/6) was probably the hardest undertaking on the coast at that time. It was not until 1988 that Cubby returned to settle the score, in the company of that well known Berwickian duo, Callum ('Hugo') Henderson and Lee (Van Cleef) Clegg. In the Screaming Geo, outstanding climbs such as Suffering Bastard (E4), Killer Fingers (E5) and Hughy's Cocktail Mixture (E3) provided ample inspiration for an attempt on the great hanging wall and roofed corner above the cave. The first sortie ended in a nocturnal aid extravaganza on the longest day of the year (fortunately for all those involved). On the next day, everything went without incident, except for a few falls on the final overhang, and the line was completed to establish a magnificent free route called the Screaming Ab Dabs (E6). In 1989, a number of different groups began exploration in the Dalbeg area, chiefly Brian Davison and Andy Cunningham, with Andy Nisbet, Andy Macfarlane, D.MacGimpsey and various friends. In the Dalbeg Buttress area, the Davison and Cunningham partnership discovered dozens of fine new routes; Limpet Crack (E3) has already established itself as a classic. The most impressive include Neptune a Calling (E5), The Black Hole (E4) and Endurance. Only time and more ascents will confirm the grades. Macfarlane and Davison climbed A Prophet's Doom in the Preacher Zawn and the 'unclimbed' lines on the Grey Tower at Tolsta Head to give Celtic Swing and Druid.

In the summer of 1993, tradition in the form of yet another southern raid provided Steve Mayers, Mike Tomkins and Jill Lovack with several fine new routes in the Screaming Geo. The best take two impressive lines up the left side of the big cave and are named The Crystal Maze (E6) and Distant Voices (E5). In the Aird Uig area on Geodha Gunna, Steve climbed the 'Separate Reality' type roof above the beautiful orange slab to give a hard climb called Brutal Reality (E6). The main event of the year was once again in the Screaming Geo, when Steve and Jill returned to climb the soaring arete to the right of Screaming Ab Dabs. The Shadow Dancer (E7), although well protected, is said to consist of very strenuous climbing of sickening exposure.

In North Uist, Chris Jex and Guy Jackson from Lochmaddy Outdoor Centre have been enthusiastically exploring the sea-cliffs in that area. All levels of difficulty have been climbed, ranging from Diff to E4/5. On Leac na Hoe Point, the combination route Bird on a Wire and Babe sounds particularly good at E4/5, as does Death Moves in Mysterious Ways on Rubha a' Duine. A large number of new climbs have also been done on Madadh Mor Island, which is situated on the south side of the Lochmaddy Loch entrance. Once again all levels of difficulty up to E4 have been climbed.

THE MOUNTAINS OF HARRIS AND LEWIS

The history of climbing in the mountains is a relatively short one, which can be attributed almost entirely to inaccessibility and a scarcity of public transport. However, the opening of the West Highland Line in 1894 was a major event in Scottish climbing, but in those days a Caledonian Macbrayne steamer crossed the Minch once fortnightly, in summer, with no guarantee of a landing.

Norman Heathcote (SMC) was a keen mariner and an enthusiastic explorer of these islands around the turn of the century. Heathcote recognised the wealth of climbing potential, made no less than four trips to the Outer Hebrides and wrote numerous articles of his exploits for the SMC Journal.

Although the Outer Isles witnessed considerable attention, little, if any, real climbing was done before the First World War. Toward the beginning of the thirties, new faces emerged and once again the Islands witnessed numerous exploratory visits. Hills were climbed and new scrambles were discovered, but the first real climbing possibilities appear to have been investigated by Botterill's party of the Yorkshire Rambler's Association. Botterill had already climbed on the islands of Rum and Eigg before focusing his attention on the big mountain cliffs of South Uist. From the summit of Beinn Mhor, Botterill's party descended an easy gully on the east side of Corrie Hellisdale, then proceeded to climb the third and fourth main gullies further west. The climbs were slimy and excursions were made onto the open face. They then went on to examine the cliffs of Sgurr Scaladale. Handicapped by rain, water, vegetation and snow, the first ascent of Central Gully was successfully completed.

In 1932, Macbrayne's launched their new steamer. The six and a half hour crossing from Kyle to Tarbert, coupled with the new Fort William to Mallaig line, radically improved access. The lure of the Outer Hebrides had attracted numerous leading lights, but no-one with more enthusiasm than James Alexander Parker (SMC). Parker's excellent photographs and the articles he wrote of his exploits did much to encourage climbing on Lewis and Harris. With E.Ewan and J.R.Symmers of the Cairngorm Club, a fortnight on the Island was spent obtaining information for the forthcoming Islands District Guide. On Sgorran Dubh Teinnasval they made an ascent of the Far South Buttress. Ewen and Symmers had already acquired a reputation as 'Masters of loose rock and vegetation - performing heroics in the Cairngorms'. Their speed and efficiency can be cited here: while on a visit to Mealisval they ascended the East Buttress on the North Face, and descended the Pala Glas in 3 hours 25 minutes. They then climbed the right bounding ridge of the Pala Glas and descended by a secondary gully within it. A traverse out onto the Eastern Buttress, and descent by it, took the same time. The first Islands Guide, published in 1934, was edited by W.W.Naismith and the Outer Hebrides section written by J.A.Parker.

Following Botterill's investigation of Beinn Mhor, J.Maclennan, D.J.Dawson and C.Ludwig (JMCS) climbed all the major buttresses in Corrie Hellisdale in April 1936. The two hardest buttresses, No.5 and No.6, were graded Severe, and pitons were used for protection. In July 1938, H.J.Irens, F.Solari and A.Kinnear of the Rucksack Club pioneered the first recorded climbs on Sron Ulladale, despite rumours by a local shepherd that two Germans had climbed the crag, unroped, prior to 1914 by nearly the same line. Irens's' route (Very Difficult) began under the prow of the North-West face and took a long left-slanting line, crossing the then unclimbed Great Gully. It was described as a "good mountaineering route". As the 'Golden Age' was reaching maturity in Glen Coe and Skye, activity in the Outer Hebrides was only just coming to light. Irens's climb on the Sron was sadly the last before the outbreak of World War 2.

It was a decade before development resumed. Mr and Mrs E.Rudge were among the first on the scene. In September 1947 they visited many different areas, exploring and climbing the occasional new route. It was of course Sron Ulladale which left a lasting impression on the couple, evident by this quote: "A ferocious and menacing promontory, is the most awe-inspiring individual mountain feature that I have seen anywhere outside the Alps". The most significant climbs during this period were the work of Bobby Folkard's party in 1948. Folkard and M.V.Wills (both London JMCS), Mrs Wills and Miss Fox spent a successful fortnight on the Island. On Sgorran Dubh Teinnasval, Folkard and Fox climbed a more direct version of the 1933 Parker route on Far South Buttress. Folkard (and Wills) donned plimsolls for an ascent of South Buttress (Severe) and again, with Wills, he pioneered a number of routes on the north-east face of Sron Ulladale, of which Amphitheatre Buttress (Severe) was possibly the best. An attempt to climb a route on Creag Dubh Dibadale ended 50m up, Folkard commenting "It is the most unrelenting wall of rock that we have ever seen anywhere". Less encouraging were the words of another Islands enthusiast "Like all previous comers, we were rather awestruck by this sight - pitoners might appreciate it!". Although many of these climbs are lacking the difficulty of their mainland counterparts, they are cited here as an indication of their boldness, pioneering spirit and big route feel.

An improved second edition of the Islands Guide was published in 1954, being more detailed and more informative but, despite these improvements, the fifties were a decade of little change. Mr and Mrs G.S.Johnstone described climbing on some of the Harris hills as a "wonderful rock playground". A few short routes of no real significance were climbed although N.Tennent and M.Tennent added Central Rib to Sgur Scaladale, but sadly no detailed description is available. The only other worthy addition before the sixties was the Amphitheatre Buttress Direct Route (Hard Severe 1958) by G.J.Fraser and Miss E.M.Baldwin.

During the early sixties, Mr and Mrs Evans of the YMC were to spearhead activity. Like Botterill 30 years before, they focused on the big cliffs, only this time it was on Sgur Scaladale, Creag Mo and Sron Ulladale. On the Sron's north-east face, Great Gully (VS 1961) and Tyke (Severe 1961) were the first to fall and on the west face they climbed South Buttress (Severe 1961). Their best effort was Miolnir (VS 1961), a steep climb bounding the left side of Sgur Scaladale's daunting black Central Wall.

The hills were generally quiet until 1965, when Marshal Reeves (JMCS) and Jack Ball set the ball rolling with Inversion (E1); the first route to breach the Sron's north-east wall was described as a "tortuous route of great character". On Creag Mo, Gollum (Severe) was climbed by the same party, the top half of which was taken by an earlier Evans route named Miny. Once again it was on the Sron where Reeves, this time with John Grieve (Grieve was one of a number of talented climbers from the south to settle in the Highlands) added further new routes called Aurora (HVS A2), and Eureka on the West Face. On Sgaoth Aird, H.Small and J.W.Graham climbed the prominent nose of Haudes (VS), a line first looked by G.S.Johnstone in 1952. The remote Sron Scourst (whose north flank Irens and Solari scrambled in 1938) saw the addition of the Direct Route (Severe 1966) climbed by Donald Bennet and Malcolm Slesser (SMC). Grieve probed around a line which was later taken by Stone on the west face of Sron Ulladale, and he also explored Creag Dubh Dibadale. Russel Sharp and Bill Sproul (Edinburgh Squirrels) followed a line of enjoyable grooves up the less steep South Buttress (VS 1969).

Aid climbing came to prominence by the end of the sixties, not just on Lewis and Harris but also in America and Europe. Climbers could get themselves into incredibly far-out situations and despite the slow methodical approach, a considerable amount of skill and nerve is required, particularly on the harder climbs where a fall would result in an entire pitch being stripped. Despite these trends, a few predominantly free routes were climbed. R.Sharp and W.Sproul opened up the Tealasdale slabs on Griomaval with Islivig Direct (VS 1969), an area previously dubbed as being "hopeless and manifestly unclimbable". On Creag Mo, Herbivore (HVS 1969) proved to be better than its name would suggest.

As is often the case, a number of teams had designs on a grand new route up the Sron's great north-west and west-facing walls. The rumours were out and the competition was on. No less so for Nottingham-based climber Doug Scott, well informed by Ken Wilson at the Mountain Info Desk, Scott was spurred into action after a visit to the Denny Moorhouse factory in North Wales to pick up the meagre remains of a mysterious large order of hiten pitons sent to Glencoe. MacInnes and Clough had already probed around the foot of the north-west face and Paul Grey's Sheffield team made a hasty retreat from what, only days later, became the Scoop's first pitch. With the Glen Coe Guides *en route*, Scott and his team feared the worst. On their arrival in Glen Ulladale whoops of joy bellowed from a group of hairy Scotsmen triumphant after completion of a fine new route on the west face. What Doug Scott forgot to realise was that his proposed new line was just one of dozens. After spending a night out, the talented team of Kenny Spence, John Porteous and Fergus Mitchell (Edinburgh Squirrels) hadn't climbed the steepest route on Sron Ulladale, but they had climbed the longest with Stone (HVS A2). Six days later, after retreating from the ramp-groove bounding the left side of the north-west face (later to become Moskill Grooves) and re-starting in the centre of the face, it was the Nottingham team's ascent of a direct *tour de force* named The Scoop which caught the attention of the climbing nation.

On Creag Dubh Dibadale, A.Ewing and W.Sproul discovered Via Valtos (HVS A2), while J.Ball and M.Reaves added a companion route with Solitude (VS A2), both climbed in 1970.

Consolidating on their Scoop success, Doug Scott and Guy Lee added another major line in 1971. Sidewinder (HVS A5) took 13 hours to prepare the initial wet A2 and A3 section, followed by 18 hours of continuous climbing, savouring the most difficult aid moves for the final barrier of overhangs. A year later the same team, this time in the company of one of America's top big wall climbers, Dennis Henneck, completed yet another major new route project which started two years previously with Tony Wilmott. The Nose (A5 1972) took 30 hours and two bivouacs to complete, and involved some extremely technical climbing on Crackn'Ups, Copperheads, Skyhooks and RURPs. Although Henneck never led on the most difficult pitches, he was nevertheless sufficiently observant to recognise the precarious nature of the climbing; and so it was concluded that the developments on the Sron rated highly amongst the world's most demanding artificial climbs.

Not all the developments centred around the biggest cliffs. On Sgorran Dubh Teinnasval, two independent parties led by T.Fletcher and B.Clarke climbed Flannan (VS 1972) and Nosferatu (VS 1972). Mick Tighe and Bill Newton discovered a new crag on Sron ri Gaoith called Hidden Buttress, where they climbed the fine central fault to give the Eyrie (E1 1974). The free ascents of Via Valtos (E1 1974) and Solitude (HVS 1974) by Geoff Cohen and Rob Archbold are worthy of note, but the most significant contribution, perhaps the most important free climb of the decade, was their new route Joplin's Wall (E2 1974). At last Dibadale's central wall had been breached.

A lull then hit the Scottish scene. It was as if one era was slowly grinding to a halt (in sumer at least) but the next generation was not quite ready. There were exceptions of course. The Scoop received it second ascent over 3 days in 1974 by a Plymouth team consisting of Deryck Ball, Andy Mahoney, Paul de Mengal and Gordon Briggs; loose rock being one of their main encounters. Paul 'Matey' Loyd, Paul Temple and Mike Brightwell made the second ascent of The Nose over 4 days in July 1976. They found the route as difficult as expected, although the A5 section was found to be A4, as the seriousness was lessened by two *in situ* wires. Paul Loyd returned with Terry King in 1977 to add his own highly technical Knucklehead (A4). This was an impressive addition, which went relatively unnoticed at a time when free climbing had really started to make an impact. Nevertheless it was still a contender for one of the hardest artificial climbs in the country.

In 1980 it was quite fitting, even traditional, that the next development should arrive in the guise of southerner Mick Fowler. Fowler's love for the Highlands and his appetitie for adventure was never ending. With the late Arnie Strapcans the most significant line yet was added to Creag Dubh Dibadale with Panting Dog Climb (E2 1980). Harder still is the impressive Big Licks (E3) climbed the following year. On the Sron, Fowler and Andy Meyers' free ascent of Stone ranked with the best in the country and introduced the E5 grade to the Scottish Islands. On a line of perpetual weep the same pair pioneered extreme climbing for the first time on Sgur Scaladale's Central Wall with Panorama (E3). Dave Cuthbertson and Paul Moores found Beyond the Ranges (E4 1985) on the west face of Sron Ulladale.

Once more it was an English party responsible for lifting grades to new heights (in the mountains that is). Hot shots Johnny Dawes and Paul Pritchard had their sights set on a free ascent of The Scoop, which at that time represented one of the finest challenges in British climbing. It was snatched from beneath the noses of the Scots, who were too busy talking about how they would attempt the route and not actually climbing it. Dawes and Pritchard were well versed in bold 'on sight' first ascents, but The Scoop was longer than anything they had done in Wales. Their determined traditional approach spanned six days of epic climbing using fixed ropes; a courageous and admirable performance which deserves much credit. With some variation to the original line, the end result was a magnificent free climb (E6 1987). A hard act to follow. Dawes and Pritchard returned to climb a line based on Knucklehead named Knuckle Sandwich (E7), a full grade harder than The Scoop.

Mick Tighe returned to Sron ri Gaoith, more often than not with a novice in tow, who no doubt wondered if all this adventure was normal for a first day out! Mick and various Lochaber friends added half a dozen or so routes, the best of which are Con John (HVS 1987) and Ventus (Hard Severe 1987).

In 1989 Ben Moon, Dawes and Pritchard climbed the fine groove-ramp on the left side of the north-west face of Sron Ulladale to give Moskill Grooves (E6). Pritchard and Dawes had certainly left their mark with The Scoop and Knuckle Sandwich, but over 1989 and up until the present it was Crispin Waddy and his friends that were to dominate nearly all the new development on Sron Ulladale. Their first major route, The Chisel (E7), follows a magnificent line much of which was the intended line avoided by Doug Scott's Sidewinder. The main centre of interest is the characteristic acute angled groove halfway up. Other routes to fall that same year include Kismet (E5) and White Dwarf (E5) which follow the obvious groove lines to the right of The Chisel's crux pitch. Cuinas (E4) takes the wall left of the Inverted Staircase while Palace of Swords Reversed (E5) and Big Luigi (E4) follow fine groove lines on the wall to the right of the Staircase. Also in 1989, Andy Macfarlane and Brian Davison added the fine Antipodean Exile (E2) on Creag Mo and Side Show (HVS) on Sgurr Scaladale. On the west face of the Sron, Davison free-climbed Flakeway to the Stairs and Andy Macfarlane added Borealis (E2), while on Creag Mo, Davison added a direct on Herbivore (E3). All three routes were climbed in 1990. In 1992 Crispin Waddy returned to piece together several partially completed projects, resulting in The Orphan and The Second Coming (E5). Both lie on the stretch of wall to the right of Stone. Crackhead (E4) was yet another worthy addition up the wall between Aurora and Big Luigi, and in 1993 The Missing Link was added.

The Scots remained slow to get it together on the Sron and yet again it took southerners to make an impression. Repeat ascents of The Scoop came from Bob Drury and Noel Craine in 1990, followed by Crispin Waddy and Andy Donson in 1992. Steve Meyers and Mike Tomkins alternated leads on another repeat ascent, flashing all but the'flying groove' and comfortably completing the climb in a day. On another visit, Steve and Jill Lovack completed a line on Creag Mo to establish a serious and intimidating climb (E6). The line had in fact rebuffed an earlier attempt by the highly respected Mick Fowler. Johnny Dawes returned in 1994 to climb a two-pitch direct on Stone called the Occasional Table (E6). He also made the best free attempt so far on The Nose (E7). Crispin Waddy, with George Smith, made the second ascent of his own route The Chisel, with Smith red pointing the acute groove. The same pair went on to add The Gloaming, a finer left-hand finish to The Chisel. Premonition (E6) is another very fine addition by the same pair, following a strenuous line of cracks and grooves in the left wall of Stone's crux corner. The Scoop at last received a Scottish ascent by Dave Cuthbertson and Glen Sutcliffe.

It could be said that these last 10 years have been the 'golden years' in Hebridean climbing, but where do we go from here? How much more adventurous can British climbing be than those routes which challenge the bristling, overhanging walls on Sron Ulladale? An admirable feature of the majority of the new routes climbed in the Outer Hebrides is the traditional 'on sight' approach.Let's hope the trend continues.

Lewis

Ardroil is 61km (38 miles) from Stornoway (about an hour's drive), and is normally the base for climbers intending to climb on the sea-cliffs and the Uig mountains. From Stornoway, take the A858, then turn off at Garrynahine on the B8011. Stay on this road *via* Miavaig and Glen Valtos. Go south, passing Timsgarry and go through Ardroil until a sign points 'To the Shore'. This is the camp site. which is marked as parking on the 1:50 000 map (Map Ref 049 329). From Tarbert take the A859 to Stornoway, turn left towards Achmore to join the A858 and then follow the above directions.

Accommodation
There is excellent camping at the above mentioned area, with toilets and cold running water. The cost is 80p per person per night.There is another camping and caravan site just beyond Valtos and Kneep (Map Ref 103 359). There are also several B&Bs and guest houses in the area, information of which can be obtained from a useful booklet titled *Discovering Uig*, which can be purchased locally.

Provisions
Fresh milk and bread can be purchased from the petrol station in Timsgarry. This is also a sub post office. However, it is recommended to purchase food on the mainland beforehand. There is also a doctor's surgery at the Valtos–Uigen road junction.

THE UIG HILLS

This fine cluster of little mountains is situated south of Camus Uig and is split into two lines of hills by the glens of Raonasgail and Tamanisdale. Mealisval (574m) is the highest peak in Lewis, but despite this rather modest altitude, these rugged mountains contain much character and always provide plenty of interest to the climber.

CREAG DUBH DIBADALE

Apart from Sron Ulladale in Harris, Creag Dubh Dibadale is the most important mountain cliff on the Island. It is never overhanging in the same sense that Sron Ulladale is, but for quality it is unsurpassable and arguably one of the finest mountain crags in Scotland. Almost a kilometre in length, the central wall drops in one dramatic sweep to the corrie floor some two hundred metres below.

To date there is only a handful of climbs ranging from Very Difficult to E4. The style of climbing is sustained, requiring a bold approach, particularly as protection is not always plentiful on the compact rock. The cliff faces north-east, catching the sun only in the morning so an early start is worth the effort. After prolonged periods of rain the cliff takes at least three or four days of good weather to come into condition. Once dry however, it doesn't appear to be greatly affected by shorter spells of bad weather.

The crag is on the flanks of Tamanisdale (467m, Map Ref 046 238). A new private road (unmarked on the OS map) runs from the B8011 and has been extended as far as Loch Tamanavay. On a recent visit this was found to be barred by a gate and padlocked. A mountain bike would be very useful.

From Ardroil go west and after 1½km turn left after the gravel pits (Map Ref 032 313). About 1km after the turn off, the road crosses the Stockgill River, and is barred by the gate. From the summit of Bealach Raonasgail, strike steeply left and head almost due east to a grassy col between Teinnasval and Tamanisdale before descending into the corrie. This is about 8km from the B8011; 2½ hours on foot. There is good camping in the base of the corrie with plenty of water.

In the centre of the highest part of the cliff, above an obvious tongue of red slabs, the wall is distinctly marked by black streaks (and features a prominent flying saucer-shaped depression high on the face). This wall is bounded on either side by the obvious crack lines of Via Valtos to the left and Solitude to the right. A ramp line to the right of Solitude is followed by Take Two and well to the right is the line of Peatsmoke. Marking the right-hand extremity of the cliff is the line of North Buttress. A feature of the left side of the cliff is an area of easier-angled ramps and grooves which provide the lines of South Buttress and 1948 Route. Descent is by way of a toe-crushing pad down either side of the corrie.

The climbs are described from left to right.

KEY TO MAP OPPOSITE

1 Creag Dubh Dibadale
2 Tealasdale Slabs
3 Creag an Tealasdale
4 Sron ri Gaoith
5 Sgorran Dubh Teinnasval

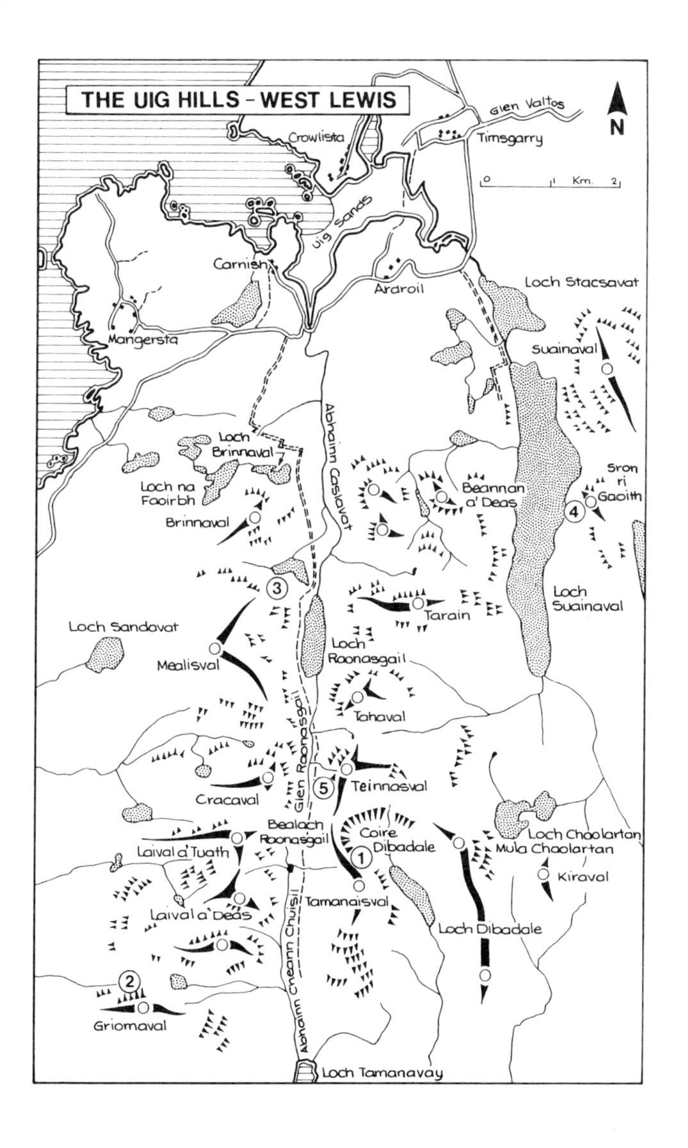
THE UIG HILLS - WEST LEWIS
N
0 1 Km. 2
Glen Valtos
Timsgarry
Crowlista
Uig Sands
Carnish
Ardroil
Mangersta
Loch Stacsavat
Suainaval
Loch Brinnaval
Loch na Faoirbh
Brinnaval
Abhainn Caslavat
Beannan a' Deas
Sron ri Gaoith
4
3
Tarain
Loch Suainaval
Loch Sandavat
Mealisval
Loch Raonasgail
Tahaval
Glen Raonasgail
Cracaval
5
Teinnasval
Bealach Raonasgail
Coire Dibadale
Laival a'Tuath
1
Loch Chaolartan
Mula Chaolartan
Kiraval
Tamanaisval
Laival a'Deas
Abhainn Cheann Chuisil
Loch Dibadale
2
Griomaval
Loch Tamanavay

1 South Buttress 155m VS * (1968)
With the exception of pitch 3, the standard is generally Very Difficult to Severe. On the left side of the cliff, left of Via Valtos, are two obvious slanting rakes. Left again is a less obvious slanting line starting up slabs.
1. 35m Climb slabs trending right to a ledge; flake belay above.
2. 30m Continue slanting right up the slabs to a thread belay under a bulging wall.
3. 25m Move up left of a prominent little overhang, step back right and climb the bulging wall, moving right at its top to a stance. Thread belay above.
4. 30m Move up to a corner, slanting right. Climb this and exit left at the top onto a heather ledge.
5. 35m Continue directly up a steep wall to easier ground.

2 1948 Route 180m VS * (1969)
This route takes a prominent crack system rising diagonally right, best seen from halfway down the side of the loch. Start beneath two slanting rakes left of Via Valtos and climb over slabs and grass to the overhung base with a grass-filled crack leading up right.
1. 40m Climb up and right to a peg belay.
2. 40m A continuation crack leads to twin cracks.
3. 25m Take the right-hand crack (2 peg runners) with a steep finish to another crack.
4. 35m Go left into a crack and climb up right to a slab and peg belay.
5. 40m Continue directly up broken rocks to finish.

3 Cold Start 180m E1 (1991)
Start 20 metres left of Via Valtos.
1. 5a Climb up and slightly right to a faint crack-groove. Ascend this to a belay below a smallish roof.
2. 5c Step right into a corner and go up to the right-hand side of a large sloping shelf.
3. 4c Move across to belay at the left side of the shelf. Traverse 5 metres left and climb slabby rock to belay left of a long roof.
4. 5b Move up and left to an obvious corner crack system. Climb this to a belay.
5. and 6. 4a, 4b Trend right and up to the top.

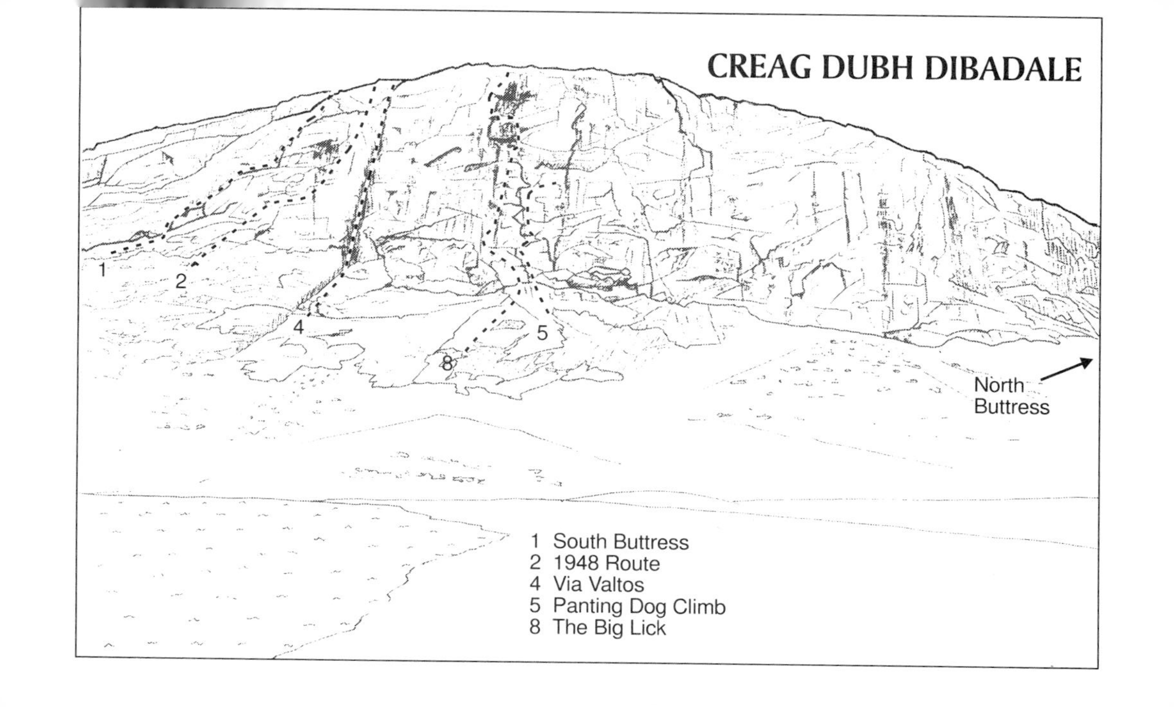
CREAG DUBH DIBADALE
1
2
4
5
8
North
Buttress
1 South Buttress
2 1948 Route
4 Via Valtos
5 Panting Dog Climb
8 The Big Lick

4 Via Valtos 150m E1 *** (1970)
The fine crack line on the left side of the steep central wall is often wet.
1. 40m 5a Climb straight up the crack to a grass patch.
2. 35m 5b Move out onto the left wall, then go up to an overhung corner with a sloping slab above.
3. 30m 5a Step up and right, then go left into a crack and climb straight up to a ledge.
4. 45m Go right then left to gain and climb an overhung corner, then move left into a crack. Continue by a chimney and finish more easily.

5 Panting Dog Climb 180m E2 ** (1980)
Another fine route, taking a direct line above the obvious tongue of red slabs and finishing up a series of prominent corners to the left of Joplin's Wall. Start on the highest grass ledge to the right of the tongue.
1. 35m 5b Step left onto the tongue and climb up to a short black groove, exit left and zigzag up the slabby wall above to a short groove. Climb this and step right from its top to an excellent rock niche.
2. 30m 5b Climb the black corner above and continue up an easy crack. Move right and climb up and under the slanting overhang until it is possible to traverse right to a prominent grass ledge.
3. 30m 5b Traverse horizontally right to a line of weakness in the wall above. Climb this to overhangs, move right onto a slab and pull through the bulges to a good stance at the foot of the obvious corner system.
4. 25m 5a Climb the corners to belay beneath a right-slanting corner with an overhanging left wall.
5. 30m 5b/c Ascend the corner, avoiding the large rocking block on the right (crux) to good ledges on the left. Step right and undercut and layback an easy-angled slab to belay on the next ledge.
6. 30m 4c Easier climbing leads to the top.

6 Joplin's Wall 200m E2 5b * (1974)
The line of this route in relation to Panting Dog climb is uncertain. Start at the top of the tongue of slabs. Climb to the left end of an obvious ramp which slants right across the upper section of the crag. Follow the ramp to the top.

7 Dominus Vobiscum 125m E4 (1995)
Start at the obvious groove low down and 30 metres right of Panting Dog Climb.
1. 45m 5b Climb the obvious curving corner into a short chimney and belay on ledges (spikes).

2. 50m 5c Climb a short corner, then go left and back right, heading for an obvious right-facing flake in a shallow groove (the right-hand of two flakes). Climb this to ledges, then move boldly up and right on slopers to a ledge. Continue up to a belay in a niche.
3. 30m 5b Step right, then climb easy slabs to a belay. Scramble off.

8 The Big Lick 175m E3 *** (1981)
This impressive and very sustained climb takes an almost direct line above the left side of the flying saucer-shaped depression.
1. 25m 5c Step right onto the front of the tongue and climb past the overlap. Trend left across groove lines to reach a good jug beneath a black bulge at the top of the most prominent groove. Thin moves lead left, then go up to a thin flake which leads to a ledge.
2. 20m 5b Climb the groove above the left end of the ledge to its capping overhang. Move round the right-hand side of this to a ledge, then move up to belay on the next one.
3. 45m 5b Surmount the overhang directly above the stance to gain the area of slabby rock. Climb this directly to a stance at the upper right-hand extremity of the black flying saucer-shaped depression.
4. 20m 5b Gain a pinnacle flake on the right and step left from its top to climb boldly up the wall of quartz. Continue more or less straight up to a good ledge about 10m below overhangs.
5. 25m 5c Step down left from the stance and traverse horizontally left on an exposed sloping ledge. Climb a corner for 4m, then move left again to belay on a ledge beneath a light-coloured area of rock.
6. 40m 5c Above are three groove lines. Gain a sloping ledge in the middle groove by an awkward move. Continue with difficulty until it is possible to move into the left-hand groove which gives easier climbing to the top. It is also possible to climb the left-hand line, which is cleaner and in a superb position.

9 Solitude 170m HVS (1970)
The right-hand crack is indefinite in its middle section. Scramble up to the foot of the crack.
1. 35m Climb the crack using holds on the left at the steep section. Eventually climb the wall on the left and move up to a belay at the foot of a large recess.
2. 35m Climb the right edge of the recess, then follow indefinite rocks and some grass to a vegetated ledge.
3. 20m Continue in the same line to a niche at the foot of the upper section of the crack. Poor stance and belay.

4. 15m Climb twin flakes just left of the crack. Step right and go up a steep crack line to a poor stance in a slabby niche.
5. 15m The crack now divides. Take the vertical left-hand weakness to a ledge. Move left and climb a short groove to the foot of a prominent chimney.
6. 50m Climb the steep chimney, then follow the gully to easier rocks.

10 Take Two 120m E1 (1981)
Start up slabs at the foot of the right-slanting ramp right of Solitude.
1. 20m 4c Climb the ramp until an awkward move leads left to a ledge. Climb a corner, move right round a bulge and go up to a narrow ledge.
2. 25m 5b Climb up and right to a black niche. Move round right, then go left and climb a steep quartz rib to a large sloping ledge. Climb a thin groove, then move left to a cramped niche.
3. 40m 5b Move left onto a pedestal, then make a strenuous move up to the top of the slanting crack line. Trend right over blocks and flakes to belay at the right end of left-slanting ramp line.
4. 35m 4c Move up the ramp and surmount an overhang. Continue to the foot of an obvious square-cut chimney corner. Climb this to the top.

11 Hitch Hiker 160m E2 (1990)
Start 10 metres right of Solitude and below and left of an obvious roof.
1. 40m 5b Start up the slabby ramp line as for Take Two, trending right to belay on a small ledge after passing a quartz band using 3 points of aid.
2. 40m 5c Move up a steep groove to a sloping ledge below the right-hand end of large roof, then traverse left to a ledge at the other end of the roof.
3. 40m 4c Hand traverse right to the arete, then climb a ramp line trending left.
4. 40m 4c Move left to finish up a corner and a left-trending groove.

12 Peatsmoke 115m E1 5b (1996)
At the right end of the main face of the crag a rib of rock extrudes below the line of the bottom of the crag. There is a left-facing corner on this rib and an area of extremely steep grass high up to the right. Scramble up the rib to the left of the corner to where it steepens and belay there.
1. 25m 4b Climb steep slabs to the left of the left-facing corner to an overlap. Climb over this at its left end, move right to easier climbing, then move left to belay on a narrow boulder-strewn ledge.

2. 25m 5b Step back right to climb grooves to a sloping ledge. Climb the obvious overhanging corner above, exiting right at the top, then step back left to an excellent ledge. A strenuous pitch.
3. 40m 4c Climb the obvious left-slanting ramp above and continue in the same line eventually to traverse slightly left to a belay in a wet groove.
4. 25m 4b Traverse about 5 metres right and climb a left-slanting ramp. Step right at its top and climb slabs to the top.

13 North Buttress 120m Very Difficult ** (1968)
This climb avoids any difficulty, but takes a more or less central line up the buttress. Runners and belays are relatively scarce. Start at a cairn and arrow on left edge of buttress, below a rib, about 3m up from the lowest point of the buttress.
1. 35m Climb the rib, first on its side, then on the front and again on the side where the angle is easier. Continue right along a rake to a belay.
2. 35m Move slightly left and climb the slab above (steep at first), then continue in a direct line to a grass ledge. Go left to another broad ledge and belay (cairn).
3. 35m Move right up the rake and continue up a right-trending crack line which continues to a belay on the right.
4. 15m Move left and climb directly up the wall.

TEALASDALE SLABS (Map Ref 012 220)

These slabs are set in a magnificent position and lead to within a few metres of the summit cairn of Griomaval (497m). The rock is clean and sound and gives climbing similar to that of the Etive Slabs at a Severe to VS level for much of their height. It is possible to climb virtually anywhere, and certainly the majority of climbers visiting the area tend to do so. The following descriptions are included as a pointer in the right direction. As usual with this style of climbing, protection and belays are at times a bit scarce.

From Ardroil, take the coast road going south through Brenish and Mealista. The road ends at a small fishing jetty. From there, head south-east to join the upper reaches of Glen Tealasdale before striking off to the foot of the climbs; about 1½ hours.

A steeply inclined grassy terrace (**Golden Gully**; Difficult) separates the shorter left-hand East Buttress from the Main Slab. The Main Slab is steeper in its lower part while the upper section is a tapering unbroken sweep. The cliff dries quickly after rain and even when there are weeps it is usually possible to weave around, connecting the available dry rock. The East Buttress appears to dry more quickly. Both the east and west shoulders of Griomaval afford easy descent routes, although the right-hand west flank is more convenient.

THE MAIN SLAB

Islivig Direct 240m Severe *** (1969)
This climb takes a direct line from the foot of the lowest slabs to the summit, following a crack and corner system. A good combination is to follow Islivig Direct for the first 150m to a point where Lochlan crosses it. The final 90m diverge rightwards, keeping right of Lochlan. A Hard Severe variation is possible by taking the obvious crack through the short steep headwall two-thirds of the way up the cliff.

Lochlan 240m VS *** (1970)
Midway along the lower area of the cliff, the slabs start with a series of black overlaps and directly below a slab corner starting 10m up. This is some distance left of Islivig Direct. Climb through the overlaps to gain the corner and follow this to the slabs above. Traverse right to a smooth white slab and climb this to a small ledge and peg belay left of a larger grass ledge (30m). Climb the groove behind the ledge and move right to the end of a ramp running left. Follow this, then climb a white scoop. Go left to a crack and climb this through several overlaps to a large grass ledge. Belay just to the right (40m). Climb the slabs and corners above, going right to take a belay in a sweep of white waterworn slabs (30m). Go right up slabs, crossing Islivig Direct, and finish up a crack through walls and slabs well to the right.

The Scroll 300m Severe (1970)
Some of this climb may be common to Lochlan. Scramble over grass and easy-angled slabs to a cairn at the foot of the steep band.
1. 35m Go right for about 10m, then follow a weakness trending left above the start to a small grass ledge.
2. 35m Continue trending left to good rock ledge.
3. 25m Go straight up to the end of a long grass ledge just right of Golden Gully.
4. 40m Move 10m right and down the grass to a small groove. Ascend the slab directly until the angle eases. Continue by trending right to a small ledge.

5. 40m Go diagonally right to a grassy ledge.
6. 45m Climb straight up to a rock ledge.
7. 40m Climb diagonally right to a crack line which leads to a small ledge.
8. 40m Climb a crack then more broken slabs to an abrupt finish a few metres from the summit cairn.

EAST BUTTRESS

Joint 120m VS (1972)
This route takes a line up the wall left of Golden Gully. Scramble 10m up the gully and start from a ledge at the foot of the slabs. On the first pitch pass a flake on its right. On the second, climb a corner groove at the left end of the overhangs and gain a recess with huge blocks. There is a chimney above, then easier slabs lead to the top.

Reefer 125m Severe (1972)
Start at the lowest point of the slabs left of Golden Gully, directly below a prominent square-cut chimney. Follow a crack system for 65m and finish by the chimney and slabs of Joint.

Twenty-Minute Buttress 60m Very Difficult (1972)
This route takes the furthest left buttress on the crag. Start at the lowest point and climb straight up using the left-hand V-groove. Finish on easier slabs.

CREAG AN TEALASDALE

These cliffs (easily reached by the new road) are situated on the north-east shoulder of Mealisal (574m, Map Ref 022 270), which is marked as Mula Mac Sgiathain on the OS 1:50 000 map. It has an impressive north-facing precipice almost 300m high overlooking Loch Mor na Clibhe. Unfortunately much of the rock is too broken and vegetated to afford any continuous climbing. With a modern approach however, the cliff should yield some short quality climbs.

Its eastern section above Loch Mor na Clibhe forms a narrow corrie where the face is cleft almost from the top to the corrie floor by a large fissure called the Palla Glas. On closer inspection this comprises a main gully and to its left a discontinuous lesser gully which starts about one third of the way up the main gully. The eastern side of the corrie gives cleaner rock and the buttress on this side, close to the gully, gives a moderate scramble with one short pitch, difficult in standard, about a third of the way up. To the right of the ridge adjacent to the Palla Glas, a grass terrace slopes up to the right. Below the terrace three shallow gullies divide the rock into three buttresses (and an insignificant buttress at the left end). Above the grass terrace the crags are rather broken, but they are more continuous above the right-hand buttress where the grass terrace virtually terminates.

The quickest descent is by a steep grassy and rocky gully which emerges onto the col just north of the summit of Mealisval. An alternative is by the north-west flank of Mealisval, skirting back under the north face and following a deep glen which runs east to Loch Mor na Clibhe.

Central Buttress 210m Difficult (1948)
Start in the centre of the buttress to the left of a black section of rock (cairn). Climb to a stance and belay below a small overhang (30m). Continue up the slab on the left to easier ground, then traverse right to a stance behind a block. Continue to traverse right and climb a slab next to a long greasy crack to a stance and belay (30m). Scramble to the terrace (45m). Walk right along the terrace to a small rock pinnacle just beyond a large area of overhanging black rock (cairn). Climb the pinnacle and traverse the ridge on the other side to a heather ledge at the foot of a vertical wall. Climb the wall on the right and continue directly by 90m of varied climbing ending in a grassy rake. Follow the rake to the left for a few metres to a 15m chimney with a large chockstone at the top. Climb this and finish by an interesting exit over the chockstone.

The Porker 85m Severe (1970)
This route lies on the same buttress as the 1948 Route. Near the middle of the buttress is a recess bounded on the right by overlapping slabs. Still further right is a just distinguishable waterslide. The climb follows the overlapping slabs. Start at an obvious ramp leading up right to the slabs proper (cairn and arrow).
1. 20m Move up the ramp, then go straight up the following grooves to a belay.
2. 20m Continue up cracks and slabs to a flake and a belay above.
3. 45m Climb the vertical crack behind the stance, and from the top of the crack step left onto a large slab. Traverse left and up across slabs above a recess to join slabs which initially bound the left-hand side of the recess, then climb directly over easy rock to the terrace.

SRON RI GAOITH (Map Ref 075 291)

This little mountain sports a number of crags on its west flank. The name Ardroil Buttress has been suggested for the most prominent of the cliffs overlooking Loch Suinaval, and Flannan Buttress for the outlying crag about 500 metres to the north. Of the three crags described, Hidden Buttress is by far the best and is well worth a visit.

Leave the main road about 1km east of Ardroil (Map Ref 057 323) and follow a driveable road to a weir at the north end of Loch Suinaval. Cross the weir and follow the east shore of the loch for about 1 hour; Hidden Buttress is a bit further along.

HIDDEN BUTTRESS (Map Ref 073 293)

This crag starts at water-level and, due to its south-west facing aspect, it cannot be seen from the approach. To reach the foot of the climbs first locate a suggestion of its outline, then follow a grassy ramp over the top of the crag and approach from the south side. All the climbs are on generally good rock with good belays and protection.

The crag is about 50m at its highest and 150m long, rising from left to right with a large boulder slope beneath it. Running across much of its length at half-height are a line of intermittent overhangs.

The climbs are described from right to left.

Election Special VS * (1974)
This is the obvious left-rising traverse line. Start towards the right side of the crag and follow the traverse in two pitches to the top.

Con John HVS * (1987)
Start at the same place as Election Special. Go first up and right, then move hard left into an obvious groove below overhangs. Pull out left beneath the overhangs to belay on a fine little ledge. Continue up the obvious line to the top.

The Eyrie 50m E1 ** (1974)
About 50 metres left of Election Special, in the centre of the crag, is a prominent fault line with small overhangs. Start by climbing left under double overhangs, then follow the fault directly to the top in two pitches.

Ventus 40m Hard Severe * (1987)
About 40m left of Eyrie is another fault. Climb the line of least resistance to the left of the fault.

Spike Fright 12m VS (1987)
Climb a left-rising line just before the crag peters out on the left. This is the only low-level way off and is a serious little route due to a rather large flake which sits just beneath the surface of the water!

ARDROIL BUTTRESS

This crag has only one recorded route to date.

Direct Route 90m Very Difficult (1971)
Start at a wide corner and go left beneath an overhang to follow the true crest.

FLANNAN BUTTRESS

Again, only one route has been recorded here.

Original Route 120m Very Difficult (1971)
Start at the lowest rocks, climb to an overhang and pass it by a groove on the left. Take the rib on the left and move back right until above an overhang. Follow the crest to the summit.

SGORRAN DUBH TEINNASVAL

This 150m west face is clearly seen high up to the left on the flank of Teinnasval (497m, Map Ref 041 254) near the head of Glen Raonasgail. The approach takes about 2 hours, initially following the walk into Creag Dubh Dibadale.

A stone shoot, which forks halfway up the face, splits it roughly into three parts: North Buttress to the left, Central Buttress between the forks, and South Buttress. Right again is Far South Buttress. Between South and Far South Buttress are three parallel gullies. North Buttress is broken and gives little more than a scramble. Central Buttress has a steep lower part, avoided *via* the stone shoot. The upper part also offers scrambling with harder variations, all leading to the summit. South Buttress offers the better climbing. The buttress features four narrow chimneys and, from a point a short distance up the main forked gully, rises a steep and deeply cut incision. On the right of this is a fine buttress after which the face is cut into by three parallel chimneys.

Descent is by way of the south-west shoulder, returning *via* Bealach Raonasgail.

North Buttress 120m Moderate (1952)
Follow the edge above the northern trifurcation of Great Gully. There are some good but easy slabs near the top.

South Buttress 145m Severe (1948)
Start at the lowest part of the main buttress overlooking the main gully.
1. 15m Climb a steep rib to a grass platform. Traverse left onto a triangular rock projecting over the gully and climb a slab to a small stance with a thread belay.
2. 25m Climb mainly on slabs to a platform.
3. 15m Either climb the crack above or the slab on the right, then continue to the foot of a grassy rake sloping up to the left.
4. 20m At the far end of the rake, climb another slab to a roomy niche.
5. 20m Go straight up to a heather and moss slope, then climb to a good stance and belay behind a pile of blocks. The slabs leading upwards from here are a fairly high angle and a huge overlapping slab blocks the way except to the right. Still higher there is a considerable overhang guarding the final exit.
6. 25m Traverse right and up until level with the base of an overlapping slab, then continue straight up, keeping a few metres away from its right edge. Halfway up it, traverse left and surmount the overlap by a delicate move and continue to a fine stance in a sheltered nook behind a pile of rocks.
7. 25m Climb out on the right and traverse left immediately below the final overhang to a small ledge. Surmount the overhang on good holds, then climb easier rocks until it is possible to scramble onto the roof of the overhang (cairn). Scrambling leads to the top.

Nosferatu 180m VS (1972)
Start by scrambling about 5m up to the right from the start of South Buttress to a peg belay below a slab.
1. 15m Climb the slab to a belay below a corner.
2. 40m Traverse right, climb a wall, then go up a slab and groove to a niche on the arete. Climb the arete to a stance and belay.
3. 40m Continue up the arete to a ledge.
4. 20m Climb a short corner to the terrace. Cross the terrace to the right; peg belay.
5. 30m Climb a groove just left of the arete, then take a short slab into a corner. Traverse right under an overhang and go up to a ledge. Move right and climb a slab on the arete to a grassy recess and peg belay.

6. 35m Step left and climb the slab above (peg runner) to a grassy niche. Traverse the slab on the left, move up a corner, then climb an overlap on the right to reach the top.

The three gullies, numbered 1 to 3 starting from that nearest Far South Buttress, are well defined for most of their height. No.2 is hardly a gully at all when seen close up.

No.1 Rib 140m Very Difficult (1948)
This is the loose rib between No.1 and No.2 Gully. Start at a tongue of rock coming down from the rib into No.2 Gully (cairn).
1. 30m Scramble up an easy slab to a stance, then climb the rib above to a small stance beside the gully.
2. 15m Climb a wall to a fine stance among a pile of immense blocks.
3. 15m Continue up the wall above, passing some large blocks, to a poor stance and belay just above a sloping platform.
4. 20m First climb a small rib, then ascend either a slab on the right (delicate) or a crack on the left (strenuous) and finish up the wall on the right to a small stance and poor belay.
5. 10m Near the top of the nose above, the holds virtually disappear but the angle soon eases. Stance and small belay. Traditionalists should note that on the first ascent the leader wore socks on this pitch, commenting that it would be at least Severe in boots!
6. 25m A small wall leads directly up a rib to a grassy stance.
7. 25m The rib is now easy and rather broken.

Flannan 120m VS (1972)
This climb takes a line up No.1 Rib. No trace was found of the cairn mentioned in the original No.1 Rib Route description, nor did the buttress fit the description of the route. Start at an earth ledge below the rib and at the side of No.2 gully. Climb a right-slanting groove onto the crest of the rib and climb this to a peg belay below an obvious corner (35m). Make a descending traverse to the right for 6m, then go straight up the overlapping wall overlooking No.1 Gully to a peg belay on a large grassy ledge below a steep slab with a prominent chimney above. Climb the slab and the chimney, then move left onto the crest of the rib and follow it to the top.

Far South Buttress 100m Very Difficult (1948)
The lowest portion of the buttress can be avoided by walking onto a grassy shelf from the right. Start just left of and a little above the lowest point of the lower section of the buttress (cairn).

1. 10m Climb a slab to a grass slope, then climb the overhanging chimney in the wall on the right on good holds to a stance.
2. 20m Traverse left along sloping ledges to below a black groove, then climb the groove on awkward holds until an escape can be made onto the rock platform on the left.
3. 25m Climb the corner above the belay for about 6m, then traverse left to a line of weakness going up to a grass slope and good stance.
4. 30m Continue up, trending slightly right and passing an overhanging rectangular block on the right, to a stance and belay just left of a small overhang.
5. 15m Step into and climb a small crack on the right, then continue up the slab to a grass platform. Easy climbing leads to a broad ledge.

OTHER AREAS

There is much exposed rock on Tarain (Map Ref 051 277) and the low-lying rocky hills to the north and east. Some rock climbing has been done here (no details) on the slabby north face of Beinnan a' Tuath and Beannan a' Deas immediately west of Loch Suainaval. Climbing may be found on the south-west ridge of the north-west flank of Tahaval to the south of Tarain. Another area which might offer potential can be found on the steep eastern corrie which splits the two summits of Laival a' Tuath and Laival a' Deas immediately to the west of Allt Bealach Raonasgail.

TAHAVAL
515m (Map Ref 042 263)

The following route lies on the west side of the south-west ridge.

All About Lewis 90m Mild Severe (1990)
1. 45m Climb the slab just right of the prominent corner (on the lower right side of the face).
2. 45m Trend leftwards and climb short walls to the summit.

Harris

North and South Harris are separated by the narrow neck of land between east and west Loch Tarbert. Almost all of the serious climbing centres around Sron Ulladale and Creag Mo and to a lesser extent Sgurr Scaladale, all in North Harris. Despite their magnificent situation and appearance, the majority of crags listed under 'other areas' are seldom visited although further investigation should reward those with a sense of adventure.

Climbers intending to visit the crags of North Harris usually camp or bivvi in their desired area. The ferry port of Tarbert offers all the usual amenities as well as a small number of B&Bs, guest houses and hotels. It is quite feasible to drive from the Uig area for the day (about 1hour 15mins).

SRON ULLADALE

(Map Ref 080 133)

The great overhanging north-west face of the Sron, which towers 270m above Loch Ulladale, is without doubt one of the most impressive rock features in the British Isles. The celebrated Scoop, a classic aid extravaganza and now also a magnificent free climb, follows a wild and unrelenting line close to its outer edge.

From Tarbert, initially follow the A859 to Stornoway. After 4km turn left along the B887 Hushinish road and follow this to a weir (Map Ref 053 078), about 1km before the gates at Amhuinnsuidhe. A private road leads to the hydro-electric dam at the southern end of Loch Chliostair. There is a gate shortly after leaving the main road which may be locked. From the dam, follow an excellent track first on the east side of the loch and then by the west bank of Loch Ashavat before dipping down to the Sron. This is about 1hr 10mins from the dam, about 1hr 45mins from the gate.

There is good camping a little above the loch and plenty of bivvi boulders at the foot of the Sron. Just be prepared to do battle with the mighty midge!

The north-east face lies out of sight around to the left of the prow which separates the north-east and north-west faces. The north-west face is the very steep recessed area to the right of the prow and contains a central deep-set line of roofed grooves which is The Scoop. The line of demarkation between the north-west and west faces is the

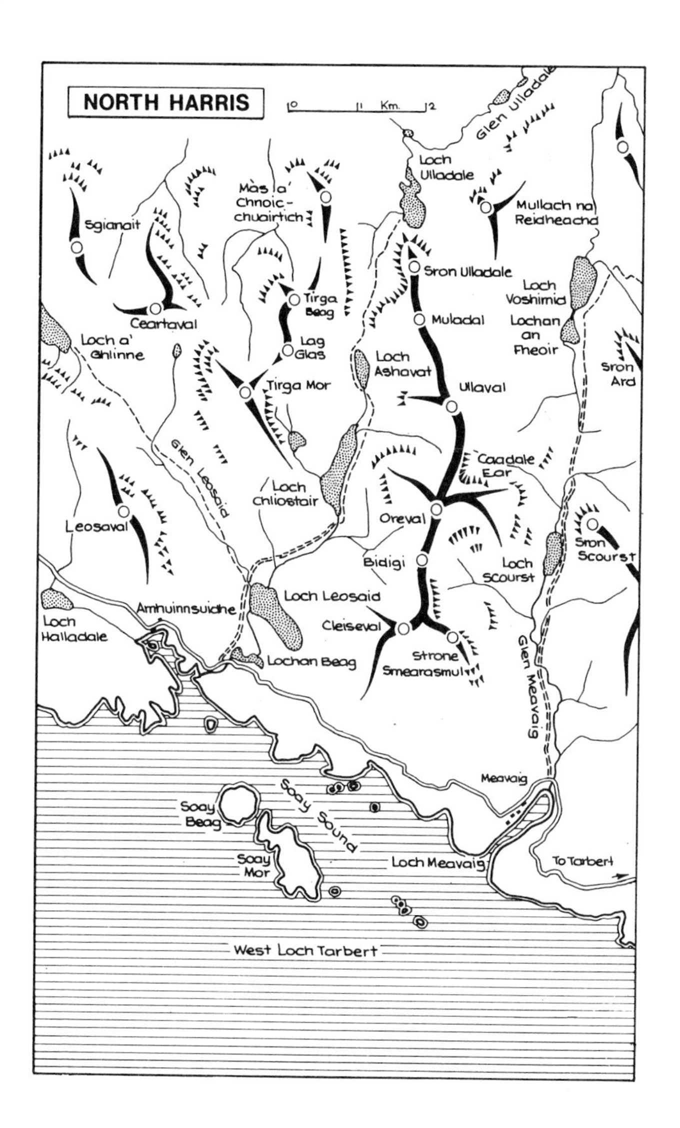

NORTH HARRIS
0
1 Km.
2
Glen Ulladale
Loch Ulladale
Màs a' Chnoic-chuairtich
Mullach na Reidheachd
Sgianait
Sron Ulladale
Loch Voshimid
Tirga Beag
Muladal
Lochan an Fheoir
Ceartaval
Loch a' Ghlinne
Lag Glas
Loch Ashavat
Sron Ard
Tirga Mor
Ullaval
Glen Leosaid
Caadale Ear
Loch Chliostair
Oreval
Leosaval
Sron Scourst
Bidigi
Loch Scourst
Loch Leosaid
Amhuinnsuidhe
Loch Halladale
Cleiseval
Strone Smearasmul
Lochan Beag
Glen Meavaig
Meavaig
Soay Beag
Soay Sound
Soay Mor
Loch Meavaig
To Tarbert
West Loch Tarbert

line of The Nose. Bounding The Nose to the right is an area of equally impressive yet less steep groove lines. The west face is at its highest just to the right of an obvious deep V-groove (The Chisel), recognisable in its upper third by the prominent corner crack of Stone. This massive wall extends rightwards for almost 1km, beyond a huge inverted staircase and an area of black-stained slabby grooves. It finally terminates at another slabby section of cliff, South Buttress, which is split by an obvious right-slanting gangway.

The rock is yet another form of Lewisian Gniess, mostly excellent but quite varied and sometimes a bit slatey in texture. Bands of mica schist and areas of quartz add further variety to the climbing which is most definitely 'Terrain Adventure'. The rock dries quickly after rain, particularly on the north-west face which appears to be virtually unaffected by even the most foul Scottish weather. The north-east and west faces require several dry days to come into condition, especially the obvious weep lines between the inverted staircase and South Buttress.

To descend, traverse right beyond South Buttress following intermittent deer tracks, descend a grassy gully containing a rocky rognon, and join the normal approach path where it ends its descent from Loch Ashavat. There is another more prominent gully to the right as you look at the cliff.

NORTH-WEST AND WEST FACES

The climbs are described from left to right.

1 Moskill Grooves E6 *** (1989)

This route takes the obvious ramp-groove to the left of The Scoop, starting up and left of that route.

1. 6b Pull over a bulge into a capped right-facing corner. Traverse right to a poor peg and move up into the huge right-facing corner. Climb this to nut belays at the top.

2. 6a Climb the overhanging crack and chimney line directly above the belay to a sloping ledge and small nut belay.

3. 5c Go right across slabs to join and finish up The Scoop.

Opposite: The Scoop, Sron Ulladale (Climber, Grant Farquhar)

Next Page: The Scoop, Flying Groove Pitch, Sron Ulladale (Climbers, Grant Farquhar and Rick Campbell)

2 The Scoop 205m E6 *** (1987)
A serious and committing climb of awe-inspiring steepness. Retreat could be complicated after Pitch 4, but it is still possible to abseil off after pitch 3. Start to the left of Stone by scrambling up some delicate slabs to an *in situ* peg belay.
1. 25m 6b A rude awakening! Step down from the belay and move up to an overhang. Climb this and a short wall (passing an old bolt) with a delicate pinch move onto a sloping ramp. Ascend the awkward overhanging wall above, then move right and climb a short steep crack in the back of the groove to a ledge with numerous pegs.
2. 20m 6a Step right and go up a cracked rib to enter the fine open corner above. Climb this to a comfortable ledge on the left.
3. 25m 6a If you think the rock on the pitch below was suspect, you had better hand the lead over to your partner! Climb the groove to a roof, make thin moves left and continue up to a hanging belay below the main corner.
4. 25m 6b Climb the flying groove out left by a series of wild layback and undercut moves. The groove above leads to an overhang which is turned on the left by means of an extremely exposed 'barn door' move round the arete (and you thought the pitch was finished!). Now continue strenuously up the thin crack and huge flake to the sanctuary of a lie down ledge and belay.
5. 15m 6a A well balanced pitch. Step down onto a huge flake and traverse left in a sensational position. Continue the traverse line with increasing difficulty to a hanging belay in a corner below the left end of the roof.
6. 25m 6a The welcome respite. An awkward move leads into the groove above. Take the left arete to a slab, then follow a slim undercut groove right to a good ledge under the capping roof.
7. 20m 6a A serious pitch. Move right and up to peg runners. Climb back down and traverse right to a bulge. Make a series of committing moves through the bulge to the sanctuary of a line of jugs leading to a belay on the lip of the overhang. Nuts, Friends and a peg belay.
8. 50m 5a Traverse left under the block overhang and go up to a ledge, turning any difficulties on the left. Now climb rightwards to the edge, which leads to top.

Previous page: The Chisel , Gloaming Finish, Sron Ulladale (Climber, George Smith)

Opposite: Flakeway to the Stairs, Sron Ulladale (Climber, Brian Davison)

2a The Scoop - Aid Version 170m A3 *** (1969)
Despite modern technology this is still a difficult climb. It is hoped that climbers intending to attempt The Scoop on aid will where possible make use of as many alternatives to pegs as possible. Pitches 1, 2 and 3 follow the line of the free version and are graded A3, A2 and A2/3 respectively.
4. 25m A3 Where the flying groove goes out left, climb the corner of red quartz to a big block overhang. Go out left and continue to the next roof and make a spectacular pendulum out left to a good belay ledge (shared with the free version).
5. 30m A3 Tension back to the corner and return to the roof. Turn a block on the left (handle with care), then continue up a smaller block overhang. Reach round horizontally right 2m and go up until the narrow crack peters out. Using the bolt, place a high peg on the right. Follow this line until it is possible to look up the final pitch, now vertical. Belay on the sloping slab on the right.
6. 45m HVS/A1 Climb up and right and follow a thin crack up a brown wet streak on the wall with a mixture of aid and free moves. Continue more easily over sloping blocks to the end of the climb, then scramble to the top.

3 Knuckle Sandwich E7 *** (1987)
1. 6b Climb the first pitch of The Scoop to a perched block belay.
2. 5b Traverse easily up right to a white ledge and poor bolt belay.
3. 6c Climb the overhanging thin crack directly above the belay to a tiny ledge. Climb up and right on big loose flakes to old bolts beneath an overhang. Pull desperately round this and go up to a hanging belay below the band of roofs.
4. 5a Traverse right to below the first big corner.
5. 6b Climb the corner to a difficult traverse right on overhanging quartz. Continue with difficulty to a small ledge.
6. 6a Climb perfect rock straight to the top.

3a Knucklehead 165m A4 (1977)
This aid route follows in part the line of Knuckle Sandwich, but it continues straight up to join The Scoop above the final overhangs.

The Nose 150m A5 (1972)
This famous climb takes a line between The Scoop and Sidewinder. In 1994 the line was partially freed at E7 6b.

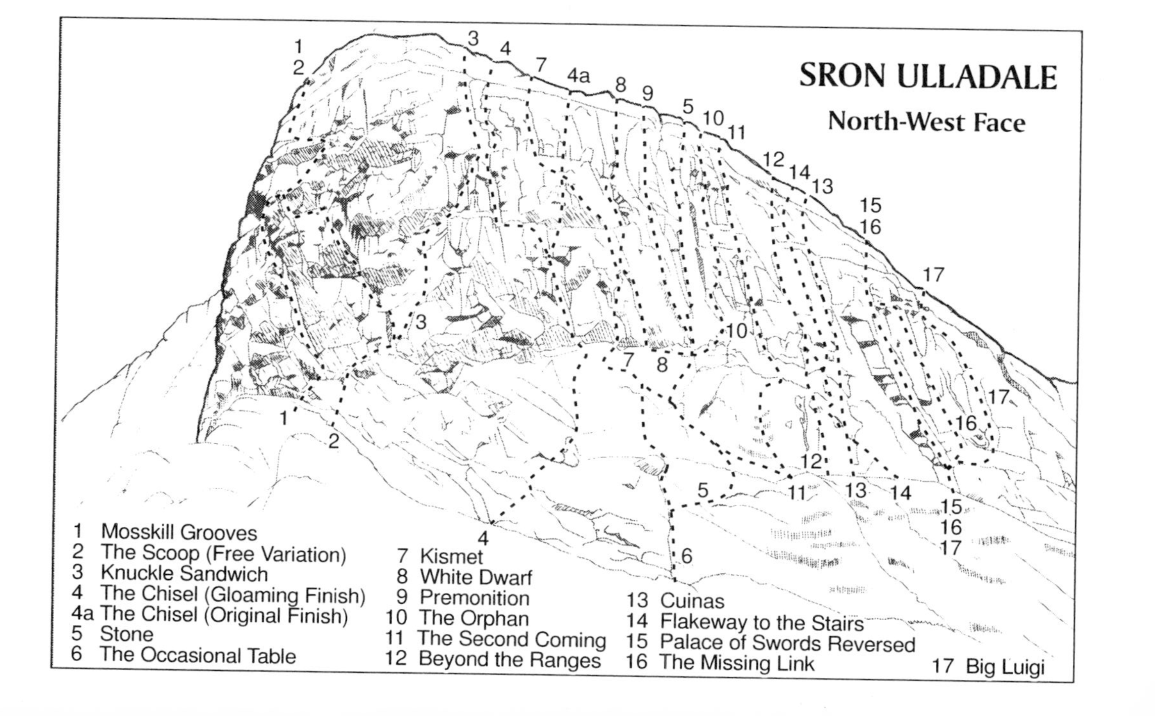
SRON ULLADALE
North-West Face
1 Mosskill Grooves
2 The Scoop (Free Variation)
3 Knuckle Sandwich
4 The Chisel (Gloaming Finish)
4a The Chisel (Original Finish)
5 Stone
6 The Occasional Table
7 Kismet
8 White Dwarf
9 Premonition
10 The Orphan
11 The Second Coming
12 Beyond the Ranges
13 Cuinas
14 Flakeway to the Stairs
15 Palace of Swords Reversed
16 The Missing Link
17 Big Luigi

Sidewinder 165m A5 HVS (1971)
A line to the left of The Chisel and right of Knuckle Sandwich.

4 The Chisel 130m E7 *** (1989)
Another fierce route which takes the widest corner at half-height with an obvious undercut flake on its left wall.
1. 20m 5b Start below and left of orange walls about 15m down and right of the start of The Nose. Move up and right through overlaps until a wide break leads down and right onto an obvious hanging wall. Continue right to a belay in a central crack.
2. 35m 6a Climb the crack until it becomes a groove. Follow this as it curves right. At its top, traverse right to an arete which leads boldly to ledges. A better protected variation (6a/b) is possible by taking a shallow groove to the ledge, starting about 3m before the arete.
3. 10m 5c Layback flakes on the left, then traverse right to a large ledge.
4. 10m 6a Climb up right to a break under the roof (this is the large horizontal break that is the most obvious horizontal line of the whole crag). Step left and pull steeply into the main groove and continue to a hanging belay.
5. 20m 6b Climb the groove of The Chisel with difficulty and continue left along the obvious undercut flake until it finally eases near the arete. Pull over the roof above to a foot ledge. Very strenuous and exposed, but well protected.

The Gloaming Finish (1994)
This is the left-hand finish.
6. 20m 6a Climb the short groove, then traverse left along a break until it eases, and belay in Sidewinder.
7. 20m 6a Step left and climb a roof into an obvious corner. Follow this until a short traverse across a hanging wall leads to a ledge. The grade allows for a wet section.
8. Mantel onto the slab above, and step right to a crack-groove. Climb this steeply into double narrow grooves. Climb these until a gritstone-like sloping rail leads to the top. (A rest was taken on this pitch, but it wouldn't be too hard in reasonable circumstances and conditions).

4a The Original Finish
An equally fine piece of climbing, starting after pitch 5.
6. 20m 6a Climb a short groove to a lichenous bulge. Move right and go up through this until a very exposed step right leads to a short open groove which leads to a crack. Climb this to a perfect square ledge.

7. 15m 6a Climb the corner above until it gets hard, then step right into a quartzy groove which leads to the top.

5 Stone 200m E5 *** (1969/81)
The fifth pitch is one of the finest on the island. Start at the lowest rocks on the west face, beneath an obvious open corner.
1. 25m 5a Climb the corner to a large flake on the right wall.
2. 35m 4b Descend a little, traverse right on the slab beneath the overlap, then go up an obvious break to a slab under a further roof.
3. 25m 5c Traverse left on a slab under the roof to a ledge. Go left again and climb an overhanging quartz groove. Exit left below its top to a ledge and belay.
4. 25m 4a An easy quartz ramp leads to a ledge beneath a big corner with twin cracks.
5. 45m 6a Climb the corner crack to a bulge which bars access to the upper crack. Either climb a wide crack on the left followed by a traverse right to gain the upper crack, or move right over the bulge and by means of a thin overhanging crack gain the upper section (harder). The upper section is sustained and strenuous but very well protected. Belay on the upper of two grass ledges below a corner.
6. 45m 5b Climb the corner until a small ledge on the right arete can be reached. This permits a right traverse into easier grooves leading to the top.
Variation to Pitch 3: HVS ** (1968)
Climb two short walls above, move left up a cracked wall and traverse into a large cave. From the left end of the cave climb down a corner and traverse a small ledge to a block belay below the long ramp pitch.

6 The Occasional Table E6 6b * (1994)
This is a relatively short route which climbs directly out of the first pitch of Stone. It could also be used as an alternative start to a number of the other routes in this area. Belay where Stone goes right. Continue steeply straight up to a sloping ledge (The Occasional Table). Make hard moves up and left to a dirty sloping ledge, continue up to the larger sloping ledge, then move right to a belay at a vertical crack. A serious route.

The next four routes all start with basically the same pitch which leads to the third stance of Stone.

7 Kismet 150m E5 *** (1989)
This route gets into the first groove line right of The Chisel's crux pitch and starts as far left as it is easily possible to go from the giant inverted staircase (this is some 60m above and right of the start of Stone, above the slabs). It is low in the grade and would be E4 with a point of aid on the roof of pitch 3.
1. 40m There are two ways of traversing left, either along an obvious break (6a), then steeply up a diagonal crack to a high niche, or climb immediately up a short wall past inverted flakes (5c), then continue easily left to the same niche. Step under the bottom right corner of an orange quartzy wall that forms the underside of the ramp of Stone, and continue until a thin crack leads up to the ramp. Belay level with a razor-thin flake which leads horizontally left.
2. 15m 6a Follow the flake left until it fades, then climb a groove to a ledge under a large roof formed by the main horizontal break.
3. 10m 6a/b Climb flakes across the roof and belay immediately in a large groove right of the main groove of The Chisel. These two pitches could easily be linked.
4. 25m 5c Step right and climb a crack in the arete between the two main corners until it joins the right-hand corner (White Dwarf). Follow this to its belay, then traverse right to a ledge and belay.
5. 20m 6a Climb the shallow groove above until it blanks out at 12m. Hand traverse round a blank pillar and pull up to a superbly appointed belay seat like a pew (with a view).
6. 15m 6a Step left into an open groove which leads to cracks and hence to the belay above pitch 6 of The Chisel.
7. 25m 6b Step down left onto a hanging slab and cross this to easier climbing. Continue left into Sidewinder's large top groove to finish.
Variation to pitch 7: 20m 5b
Traverse right for 6m past a large corner, then follow good holds up the arete of the groove to finish as for White Dwarf.

8 White Dwarf 140m E5 *** (1989)
This route takes the next groove to the right, heading direct for the top, and is very 'Comici-esque' after the first pitch.
1. 45m As for Kismet, but continue up the ramp to belay as for Stone.
2. 15m 5c Gain the large break which leads awkwardly left into the bottom of the large corner (the second corner right of The Chisel).
3. 20m 6a Climb the strenuous corner and belay at its top.
4. 20m 6b Climb up and left, then go up a little overhanging groove through a bulge. A steep crack leads to the pew stance on Kismet.

5. 15m 6a/b Climb straight up (footless initially), then go boldly into an acute-angled corner which leads to a ledge.
6. 25m 5c Continue directly until a wet mantel gains the top.

9 Premonition 115m E6 *** (1994)
Another excellent climb giving wall and groove climbing left of Stone.
1. 45m Climb the first pitch of White Dwarf.
2. 20m 6b Climb the cracks in the left retaining wall of Stone's crux corner until a traverse left leads to a rest in a hanging groove. Climb out of the top of this to a thin ledge, then go up to a larger one.
3. 25m 6b Move up into the left-leaning corner above. Climb this until it is possible to swing right into another corner. Climb this past a peg to its top, then step left to a short crack. Climb this, then hand traverse wildly right to a belay (bold in places; 2 rests were taken on this pitch).
4. 25 6a Climb a short crack-groove on the left to a ledge, and continue up cracks and grooves directly, and more easily, to the top.

10 The Orphan 115m E5 * (1992)
This route follows grooves to the right of Stone. Most of this climb was ascended in adverse weather, so the grade and description may not be entirely correct.
1. 45m Climb the first pitch of White Dwarf
2. 10m 5c/6a Traverse right along the lip of the roof below the right wall of Stone's crux pitch.
3. 25m 5c Climb various grooves until forced horizontally right to reach the third pitch of The Second Coming at an open groove. Move up and left and belay under a roof.
4. 20m 5c Continue up a groove to belay below a tower.
5. 15m 6a Climb steeply into a groove on the left side of the tower to finish.

11 The Second Coming 75m E5 ** (1992)
Start to the right of the previous routes but to the left of Beyond the Ranges, below an obvious black cracked arete. The description of this climb was written up at a later date and may be inaccurate.
1. 25m 5b Climb to the arete and go up it on quartzy cracks.
2. 10m 6a Traverse right along the lip of the roof, then go up and back left until above the previous belay.
3. 20m 5c Climb grooves and ledges to a tower of rock.
4. 20m 6b Climb a crack-groove on the right until it leans back and eases, then continue to the top.

12 Beyond the Ranges 110m E4 ** (1985)
This route lies on a slightly projecting buttress between Stone and Flakeway to the Stairs, but closer to the latter. It takes a line of right-facing corners and flakes just right of a pink quartz intrusion. Start near the left end of a terrace, gained after 60m of scrambling.
1. 45m 5c Climb the corner rightwards, then go back left under an overhang. Move up then back right to a ledge, climb through a break, then move left and make an awkward move left again to a large flake. Pull into a quartz crack above with a loose flake hold. Traverse right to a foot ledge, move up, then traverse back left across suspect but probably well keyed blocks. Now climb a quartz groove, pull out left in a superb position and continue to a fine ledge and belay.
2. 35m 5b Climb the groove above with a tricky move onto a ledge. Climb a short brown groove, then go right to belay at the foot of an obvious layback corner.
3. 30m 5a Climb the corner to a ledge with a block, then traverse left to another ledge with a block. Go back right and up to the top.

13 Cuinas 90m E4 (1989)
Start at a short corner in black rock about 30 metres left of the giant inverted staircase, and below an obvious small right-trending corner-overlap at 30m.
1. 40m 6a Climb up to the corner-overlap *via* cracks and flakes, then continue up it and belay on ledges beyond.
2. 25m 5c Climb an open groove to ledges and belay.
3. 25m 5b Continue up an open groove to the top.

The huge inverted staircase has been climbed to about two-thirds height, but it was found to be loose and nasty.

14 Flakeway to the Stairs 135m E2 * (1981)
This route climbs a line of flakes to the left of the obvious inverted staircase.
1. 35m 5a Climb diagonally left along a fragile ramp to overhanging and detached block flakes. Climb these to a small belay ledge beneath a roof.
2. 25m 5b Traverse right beneath the roof. Climb a crack on the right of the flake until it fades. Move left to a second flake, then climb a wide crack.

3. 20m 5c Descend left and around a corner. Move left and go up the wall to a ledge.
4. 55m 5a Climb the ramp and surmount the overhang. Continue to the foot of an obvious square-cut chimney corner. Climb this to the top. A more direct pitch goes up a corner left of the stance, which might be the same as for Beyond the Ranges.

About 15 metres right of the giant staircase lies a large corner, below which the following climbs begin:

15 Palace of Swords Reversed 90m E5 *** (1989)
1. 25m 5c Climb the large corner to a ledge on the right.
2. 20m 6b Climb the wall round an overhang above and left of the belay, then continue to a ledge (possible belay). Now climb the left-hand groove above (steeper than the right-hand one, but it has holds) past a peg runner to a belay on a ledge.
3. 20m 6a/b Step left off the ledge and go boldly up the wall round a roof into a groove that leads to a belay below a large roof.
4. 25m 6a Traverse horizontally right along a slab, then go up left above a roof and continue round an overhanging arete. Easy ground leads to the top.

16 The Missing Link 80m E5 ** (1992)
1. 25m 5c Climb the first pitch of Palace of Swords Reversed.
2. 20m 6a Step off the right side of the ledge onto an awkward ramp. This leads to a wide layback crack. Avoid this by an arete which leads boldly to a belay below a groove.
3. 20m 5c Climb the groove to belay at the right end of the traverse of Palace of Swords, pitch 4.
4. 15m 6a Follow the remainder of Palace of Swords Reversed to the top.

17 Big Luigi 75m E4 *** (1989)
1. 25m 5c Palace of Swords Reversed, pitch 1.
2. 25m 6a Follow the second pitch of The Missing Link onto the ramp, then continue right along quartzy rock into a groove. Climb this to cracks in a blank wall which lead *via* a short horizontal traverse to a belay.
3. 25m 5c Climb more or less directly in a straight line *via* grooves and cracks to the top.

18 Crackhead 65m E4 * (1992)
This starts some 45 metres right of the previous routes, directly below an obvious straight crack in the right side of a wall guarded by roofs.
1. 25m 5c Climb up to a break in the roof which leads to a narrow slab. This leads right to a belay in the base of the crack.
2. 20m 6a Climb the crack until near its top, where it becomes necessary to step left into a niche. Pull out of this to slabs.
3. 20m 4c Climb slabs to join Midgard, and so to the top.

19 Aurora 200m HVS *** (1967)
Start at a vague weakness of grooves 40 metres left of Prelude (arrow).
1. 35m Climb easily at first towards a small triangular overhang and move over this using a peg to reach good holds. Move right, then go straight up a groove to a sloping rock stance and peg belay on the right.
2. 10m Step back left across the groove to a steep wall. Climb this and exit left to an excellent rock stance (2 pegs and 2 slings for aid).
3. 10m Use a shoulder to reach a ledge up and right. Move right under the bulge, then go up and back left above it. Continue up a groove to a good rock ledge and peg belay on the left.
4. 45m Move a few metres right to a corner crack and climb this to a long narrow grassy rake. Cross this and climb steep slabs trending left towards an overhang-capped bay. On reaching bulges, pull up (peg runner) and traverse right to a small stance below large perched blocks.
5. 10m Traverse right to an overhanging corner-crack and climb this (2 slings), pulling out right beneath the roof to a good ledge.
6. and 7. 90m Follow slabs to easy ground.

20 Borealis 80m E2 (1990)
Start as for Aurora.
1. 20m 5a Climb the groove to a sizeable ledge directly below a triangular roof.
2. 30m 5b Traverse right to a right-facing corner. Climb this to a sloping ledge. Move left to another right-facing corner and climb this to a belay ledge, as for Midgard.
3. 30m 4c Climb a slab to a left-facing corner-chimney.

21 Midgard 180m Very Difficult ** (1961)
A fine route with exposed situations, taking the easiest line up this section of wall. Start about 25 metres left of The Gangway at the lowest point of a tongue of rock. Go up slabby rock on the left to a band of

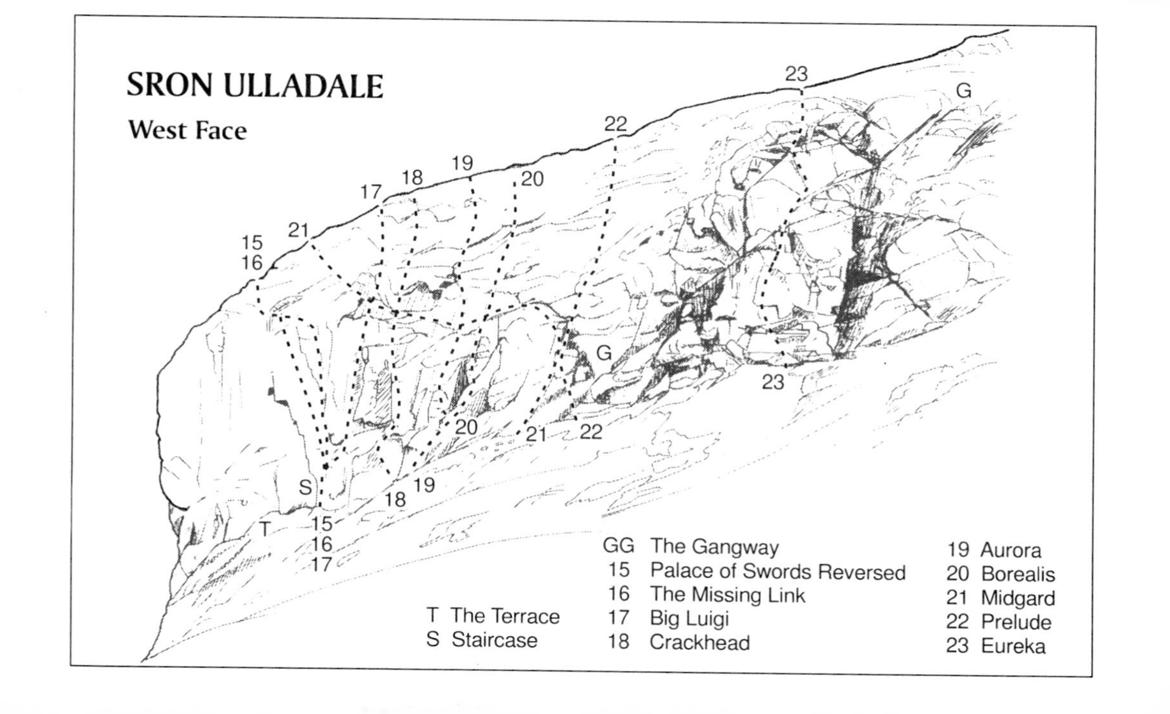
SRON ULLADALE
West Face
T The Terrace
S Staircase
GG The Gangway
15 Palace of Swords Reversed
16 The Missing Link
17 Big Luigi
18 Crackhead
19 Aurora
20 Borealis
21 Midgard
22 Prelude
23 Eureka

yellow rock. Move right along a ledge to a belay (20m). Move up right for 6m, then step left and traverse right again to belay below an overhang at the obvious traverse line (20m). Follow this left into a corner, then go up slabs and grass to a small flake belay (30m). Continue the traverse to the base of a second grass patch. Move down a little and go across to an easy gangway which leads to the top.

22 Prelude 170m Severe ** (1967)
This route starts in the same general weakness as Midgard, crossing it and taking a direct route up the wall. Start just left of the light-coloured tongue of rock about 30 metres left of The Gangway.
1. 35m Climb the obvious cracked groove left of a pillar, then go up right to ledges.
2. 35m Move up right a few metres, then go back left up a sort of gangway to a weakness in bulges above. Step up and traverse 10 metres horizontally right to an easy groove. Climb this and bear left on slabs.
3. etc. 100m Continue straight up with increasing interest, keeping in the centre of a clean ribbon of slabs. Belay as required.

23 Eureka 130m VS *** (1967)
This good route takes a direct line up the front of South Buttress, following a line of grooves on the lower tier and the bulging nose above the top of The Gangway. Start beneath this nose at a line of thinly defined cracks just right of a brown bulge at the left end of the lower tier.
1. 20m Go straight up grooves until a traverse leads to an overhung slabby ledge on the left. Belay on nuts and pegs.
2. 25m Move right from the stance and climb a short wall to a small ledge beneath a steep brown groove. Climb the groove to a heather gangway.
3. 45m Climb directly up the steep nose above and move left to pull over the bulge and gain a recessed slab. Climb this to its top right corner.
4. 40m Climb an alarmingly overhanging crack on magnificent holds. Finish up easy walls and ledges above.

South Buttress 110m Severe (1961)
The buttress at the extreme right end of the west wall is split into two tiers by The Gangway. Start halfway along the steep lower wall and climb 4m to a large obvious block belay. Move onto the slab on the left, then make a long traverse right under overhangs until a smooth wall

leads to a ledge and belay below overhangs. A broken gangway leads through the overhangs and scrambling follows to The Gangway. Climb the upper wall to a belay below a prominent overhang, and turn this by a groove on the right.

The Gangway Difficult (1961)
This is the obvious gangway which splits South Buttress from left to right. Start *via* a steep corner and a short traverse left, then 60m of pleasant slabs lead to scrambling. Belay as required.

NORTH-EAST FACE

This is divided by two huge gullies, Great Gully on the left, which cleaves the whole height of the cliff, and the Amphitheatre which starts halfway up. The floor of the Amphitheatre consists of a large grassy recess and splits the face to form a sort of lower and upper tier. The tapering buttress between the two gullies is Amphitheatre Buttress. To the right and above the grassy recess below the Amphitheatre is Rush Platform, above which is a steep clean wall where the line of Inversion finds a way. Two grassy rakes extend to the left from the Amphitheatre; the lower of these gives access to No.3 Buttress while the steep upper rake follows the base of the left side of Amphitheatre Buttress, and continues as far as Great Gully (the line of Irens's Route). To the left of the upper half of Great Gully, and starting at about the same level as the Amphitheatre are various routes on the buttresses. Numbered from right to left, No.1 Buttress is the one between Great Gully and the top left hand fork. No.2 Buttress is to the left of the fork. Separating No.2 and No.3 Buttresses is yet another branch of Great Gully. The buttress to the left of Great Gully starting from the base of the cliff provides the lines of Iron Butterfly and Tyke. Various lines have been recorded on the lower tier to the right of Great Gully, but most are too broken and vegetated to afford worthwhile climbs.

LOWER CRAG

Irens's Route 195m Very Difficult (1938)
This route climbs the full length of the face starting beneath the nose and taking a long leftward trend to finish up No.2 Buttress. It was described by Irens as a good mountaineering route. The exact line taken in relation to the Slab Start (Lower Crag only) climbed by Bobby Folkard's party in 1948 is uncertain. The 1948 route description has

been used here. Start from a grass platform (cairn) surmounting a small rock buttress and slightly right of the nose. A long tongue of slabby rock stretches down to the platform and gives a pitch of 30m. About 60m of easier climbing follows trending left. Climb the steeper rocks above to Rush Platform (35m). A short descending traverse left leads to the grass slopes of the Amphitheatre. From the left-hand base of Amphitheatre Buttress ascend a grassy rake to enter Great Gully. Cross the gully leftwards by steep grass to a buttress divided by two chimneys. Climb the right-hand chimney until a 'Severe' traverse leads across the left-hand chimney to another rib. The buttress above provides exposed but not difficult climbing on sound clean rock.

Amphitheatre Approach 95m Difficult (1948)
Start below and right of the Amphitheatre, and scramble to the foot of the rock and heather buttress immediately left of a wet black wall (cairn).
1. 35m Steep climbing, occasionally on rock, leads to a grass slope with a block belay.
2. 20m Starting at the back of a large grass recess, right of a gully, climb a steep slab until it is possible to step into the gully above a small cave, then go up the gully to a rock platform and belay on the left.
3. 25m Climb up left, then go straight up to a thread belay.
4. 15m Continue to a block belay (cairn) on grass slopes leading to the Amphitheatre.

Direct Route 355m Hard Severe (1958)
This is a direct line on Amphitheatre Buttress starting at the base of the cliff, crossing the 1948 Route about its tenth pitch but thereafter apparently taking a line somewhat to the right. It is said to be a fine climb and although vegetated in the middle, the final section gives beautiful clean climbing. In a grassy bay below the steepening of Great Gully, the buttress base forms a steep wall. Start at the middle of this wall beneath a corner crack.
1. 10m Climb the wall bearing left, then go back to a niche below the corner.
2. 25m Leave the niche on the right, then go straight up vegetation and a rock wall to a good ledge and belay.
3. 20m Follow a grassy rake to the right, then climb a steep clean wall until it is possible to move right to a ledge.
4. 10m Leave the right end of the ledge and climb a crack with a small tree alongside.

5. 20m Climb a crack and a broken groove leading right to a large platform.
6. 10m Ascend a small overhang direct, on the left.
7. 40m Easy grass leads to a short wall.
8. 20m Climb the wall around a large block and continue over slabs.
9. 20m Easy climbing leads to a belay in a gully 6m above the foot and to the right of the next wall.
10. 20m Move onto the wall above the belay, then climb straight up to beneath a V-chimney.
11. 15m Climb the chimney, pulling out awkwardly at the top onto a good ledge.
12. 20m Go up the slab above on small holds.
13. 20m Traverse up and rightwards to an exposed stance at the foot of the final tapering tower.
14. 20m Climb steeply just to the left of the rib on good holds; chockstone belay beside a protruding flake.
15. 15m Avoid the easy-looking groove, and move onto the face of the buttress. Climb close to its edge, then move right onto a sloping ledge.
16. 30m Continue straight up grooves from the right-hand edge of the ledge. At 15m, move right around a rib. Climb a quartzy block into a crack, and go up this to a platform under an overhang.
17. 40m Take the overhang at its right, then go straight up the narrow crest of the buttress, finishing up a wide chimney.

UPPER CRAG

Inversion 170m HVS *** (1965)
Start from Rush Platform which is gained by using the lower part of Irens's Route. The climbing begins at a cairn in the centre of a steep clean face.
1. 25m Go up steep rocks, then climb a shallow groove until it is possible to go right beneath a large overhang to a vertical black groove. Climb this, then follow a short rib on the right to a good ledge beneath the first great overhanging barrier. Chockstone belay.
2. 10m Traverse right beneath the roof to a cracked overhanging weakness on the edge. Climb this on surprising holds, then continue to a small stance with fine belays.
3. 20m The second barrier of overhangs is now above. Traverse left round a corner to a cracked overhanging groove. Climb this (difficult) to a roof, step down left, then reach over the roof to a hidden edge.

Mantelshelf up in a remarkable position to a slanting niche, then go awkwardly out right to an easier wall above. Climb the wall to a stance level with an obvious right-traversing line.
4. 25m Traverse down right, then move up to an edge at about 12m. Climb the bulge above to the left of a cracked chimney (loose blocks), then trend left awkwardly to a small ledge on the nose. Go straight up a slab for 4m, then climb diagonally right to a large grassy stance.
5. 35m Climb straight up the broad edge above, going slightly right on delicate slabby rock to a shallow black groove. Go up left, then move back right up a short grassy rake to a belay beneath very steep rock.
6. 25m Climb onto a large block, then a steep nose to easier ground.
7. 30m Easy rocks lead to the top.

Amphitheatre Buttress 150m Severe (1948)
This is the tapering buttress between the Recess and Great Gully. Start at its foot, reached by using any of the Lower Crag routes. Cairn.
1. 30m Climb a grassy rake to establish a position on the buttress, make an ascending traverse to a small cave. Poor stance and belay.
2. 45m Traverse right until the wall can be climbed to a grass ledge. The slab above leads to a heather ledge. Climb a 12m wall, first left then right, then heather leads to a small stance. It is possible to split this pitch.
3. 30m Climb the wall above to the left to below an overhang, then bypass this to the right. Regain the rock above the overhang as soon as possible, then continue to a good stance overlooking Great Gully.
4. 20m Climb the rib above to a commodious platform, which has a huge boulder at its back and overlooks Great Gully.
5. 25m The crux. Climb the wall on the right by combined tactics, then follow a short slab and the small holdless rib above until scrambling leads to a good stance. On the first ascent the leader climbed this pitch with one boot removed! Scrambling leads to the top.

No.1 Buttress 75m Difficult (1948)
This is the buttress between Great Gully and the top left fork. From the base of Amphitheatre Buttress climb the steep grass rake leading to Great Gully. Start in the gully fork to the left of the buttress and a few metres above its base. The gully above has two parallel overhanging chimneys; make a short traverse into a groove on the left, and ascend this to a grass slope above the overhang (20m). Now traverse right onto the buttress to some large blocks. Climb this to the top, keeping as much to the right as possible (50m of climbing then scrambling).

No.2 Buttress Very Difficult (1938)
This has been described above as part of Irens's Route.

No.3 Buttress 80m Difficult (1948)
Enter Great Gully by an airy walk along a ledge which starts from the lower grass slopes of the Amphitheatre. The departure on the other side is more awkward and involves two pitches of about Difficult. Now follow a grassy rake past the base of No.2 Buttress. The buttress begins from the grass on the left (cairn) which involves 45m of climbing followed by 35m of scrambling (somewhat artificial).

Great Gully 300m VS (1961)
This is a poor climb with more vegetation than rock. Evil-looking cave pitches are avoided on the left, but the crux (a square amphitheatre at one-third height) is unavoidable and is climbed in two pitches. The first goes up a left-slanting groove (10m); the second traverses right and up a groove through an overhang (25m).

Tyke 190m Severe (1961)
This route climbs the buttress immediately left of Great Gully. The rock is very good after a vegetated start. Scramble up 45m of steep heather to a small rowan. Gain the second rowan to the right, then climb slabs moving right then up over a bulge to a small stance and peg belay below an overhang. Traverse right below the bulge, then follow easier rock overlooking the gully to a good platform below a steep groove. From a gangway on the left, enter the steep groove and climb it to a terrace where the angle eases. Pleasant slabs lead to the top.

Iron Butterfly 270m HVS/A2 (1969)
The main difficulties are concentrated in the first 120m. The steep lower section is breached by an overhung left-slanting fault which leads to easier rocks above, which give excellent climbing. Climb steep and dangerous grass to reach the rock at 60m.
1. 30m Climb to a tree on a ledge, then move left and climb a short strenuous crack system to an eyrie below the overhung fault.
2. 35m Move down and right into the fault and climb it leftwards to a large ledge (8 pegs and nuts for aid).
3. 35m Move left to surmount the bulge (peg for aid) onto a slab, then go right into a corner, which leads to a belay. Easier rocks lead to the summit.

CREAG LEATHAN

This is the crag opposite Sron Ulladale. Only three climbs have been recorded, but all are worth doing. The best way off is down either end of the crag.

Little Red Rooster 65m HVS * (1981)
This route takes the obvious red streak of rock on the left side of the steepest buttress. Start from a grass ledge where the crag steepens, about 5 metres right of some piled blocks.
1. 35m 4b Climb the wall more or less directly until, at about 15m, it is possible to move right into an obvious wide crack. Follow this for 6m, then trend left to a rock stance below an easy left-slanting ramp.
2. 15m 5a Climb the ramp until it ends, then ascend wet broken-looking rock on the right to belay just left of a very wet corner.
3. 15m 4b Trend left and finish up a pink right-slanting groove.

Grey Rib 75m HVS ** (1981)
The obvious grey rib right of Little Red Rooster gives better climbing than that route. Start directly below the rib on a grass ledge.
1. 35m 5a Climb the rib to a stance.
2. 40m 5b Move back onto the front of the rib and, keeping to the crest, follow this to the top. A good pitch.

Windwhistle 90m Very Difficult (1961)
This climb goes up the most attractive continuous rock in the centre of the crag, finishing up an exposed wall.

GLEN SCALADALE

CREAG MO (Map Ref 172 097)

This interesting south-east facing cliff dominates the north side of the entrance to Glen Scaladale, and is clearly seen when driving north from Tarbert. Although the cliff is a bit loose and vegetated in parts, many of the climbs are a lot better than their appearance would suggest. There is also a lot of potential for single and multi-pitch routes.

The crag is easily reached in about forty minutes from the A859 where a bridge crosses the Scaladale River, about 1km south of Ardvourlie. Follow a stalker's path on the north side of the river for 1km before heading directly up the hillside.

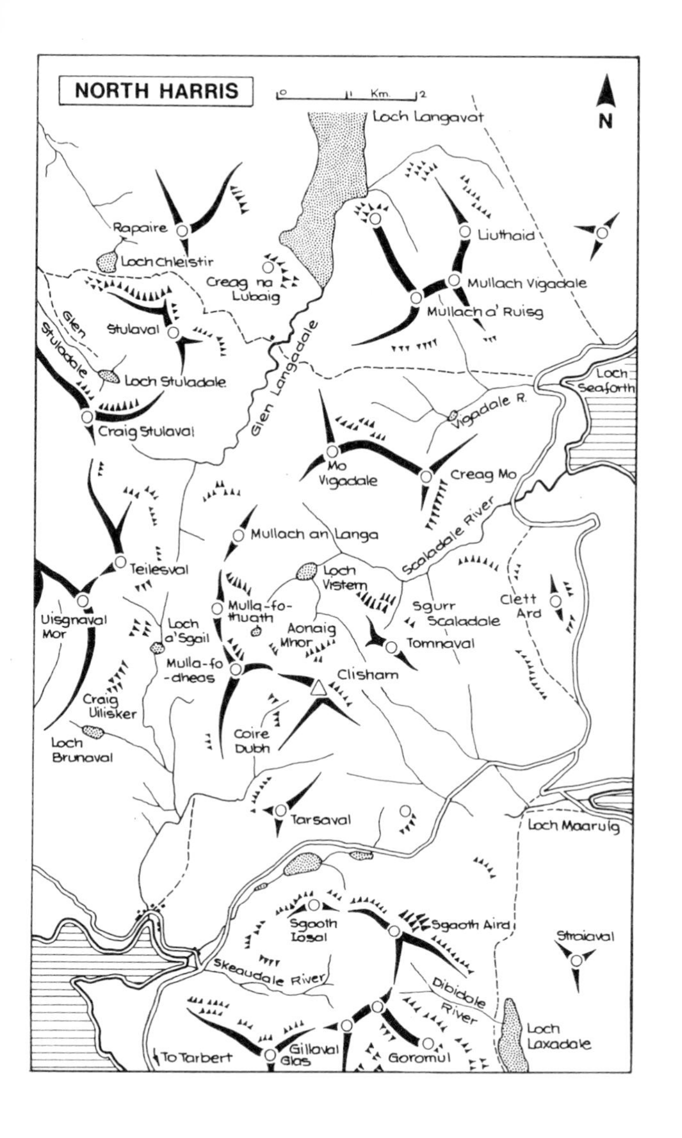

NORTH HARRIS
0
1
Km.
2
N
Loch Langavot
Rapaire
Loch Chleistir
Creag na Lubaig
Liuthaid
Mullach Vigadale
Mullach a' Ruisg
Glen Stuladale
Stulaval
Loch Stuladale
Glen Langadale
Loch Seaforth
Vigadale R.
Craig Stulaval
Mo Vigadale
Creag Mo
Scaladale River
Mullach an Langa
Teilesval
Loch Vistem
Uisgnaval Mor
Mulla-fo-thuath
Sgurr Scaladale
Clett Ard
Loch a'Sgail
Aonaig Mhor
Tomnaval
Mulla-fo-dheas
Clisham
Craig Uilisker
Coire Dubh
Loch Brunaval
Tarsaval
Loch Maarulg
Sgaoth Iosal
Sgaoth Aird
Straiaval
Skeaudale River
Dibidale River
Loch Laxadale
To Tarbert
Gillaval Glas
Goromul

The most obvious feature of the crag is an impressive central amphitheatre in the middle of which lies the prominent line of Central Grooves. A short grassy terrace runs right from here and splits the left side of the right wing into two tiers. Where the overhangs of the amphitheatre peter out on the left, a crack springs up towards the overhangs; this is the line of King Lear. About 40 metres left again, a long roof low down, crossed by Little Bo Peep, guards an area of slabby grooves above. The crag tapers down to the left, becoming more broken and vegetated. Marking the left-hand extremity is an obvious brown corner. Descent is *via* either side of the crag. The climbs are described from left to right.

1 The Corner 50m VS 4c

The obvious brown corner at the left-hand end of the crag. Start 3 metres right of the corner. Climb slabby rock trending left, then go up the corner to a ledge. Climb a series of short steep corners to a large ledge. Climb an overhanging rock band into a corner and continue to a grass ledge. Another short pitch can be made by ascending the steep wall above, or walk off left.

2 Little Bo Peep 75m E1 (1980)

This route takes a crack through the long wide overhang low down and the slabby rocks above. Scramble to an old peg below the overhang.

1. 35m 5b Move left and climb the crack through the overhang, climb up right more easily and surmount an awkward bulge to reach ledges.
2. 40m 5b Trend diagonally right, then follow a discontinuous crack up the centre of the buttress until it is possible to climb up left to belay on grass ledges. Grassy scrambling remains.

3 King Billy 50m HVS (1989)

1. 4c Start up the wall immediately right of the long low overhang of Little Bo Peep, and climb to a grass ledge.
2. 5a Climb the wall trending right into a corner. Follow this, then exit left through a roof.

4 Herbivore 110m HVS * (1969)

A good route despite its name. Start right of King Billy at a short slab.

1. 30m 4a Climb the right edge of the slab to a grassy niche below a small overhang. Step left and take this at an obvious weakness. Continue rightwards up grass and rock to belay at the base of a corner.

2. 20m 5a Move up the corner and go round a bulge to a ledge on the right. Carry on up the corner, using a thin flake, to reach a small ledge on the left wall. Continue up and left again to a larger ledge below a corner.
3. 15m Climb the corner for about 4m, traverse right to a shallow depression, step down and traverse a small grass platform and jammed flake to belay at the base of a corner.
4. 10m Climb the leaning corner and exit right over heather.
5. 35m Swing up left onto a slab, cross this to a corner and ascend an obvious scoop on the left wall to a ledge. Go left again and climb a short corner to finish up steep vegetation.
Direct Variation: E3 6a * (1990)
Follow Herbivore until it traverses right midway up the obvious corner. Continue up the corner with difficulty to a sloping finish.

5 Wee Gommie 75m VS 4c (1980)
Start about 10 metres left of King Lear. Climb a shallow pink groove, then trend left into deeper grooves and finish up the short slanting chimney.

6 King Lear 95m E1 * (1980)
This route climbs the obvious crack line and the steep wall above. Start about 5 metres left of the overhangs of the amphitheatre at a short groove with a mossy tree on its right wall.
1. 10m 4c Climb the groove and move right to belay beneath a corner.
2. 15m 5b Move diagonally right up the wall to gain the crack, then follow this until it is possible to move right to an excellent exposed stance above the overhangs.
3. 25m 5b Climb the wall above, trending right, to a ledge round the corner on the right. Pull through the overhang above the left end of the ledge and climb up left to a prominent short crack leading to a good stance.
4. 45m The grassy ramp on the right leads to a short wall and the top.

7 Central Grooves 75m E6 * (1993)
A difficult and serious climb which takes the obvious central grooves of the amphitheatre, to the right of King Lear.

1. 20m 5c Start up a loose black wall below a break in the roof and an obvious groove. Climb this to a poor peg (the high point of an attempt by Mick Fowler?), then move left over loose ledges to a worrying hanging stance on Friends.
2. 45m 6b Climb up right to make some difficult and committing moves past a peg into the base of the next groove. Follow this, moving slightly left at a sloping ledge, and finish direct.
3. 10m A short scramble gains the top.

8 Antipodean Exile 40m E2 5b ** (1989)
On the right side of the central overhanging amphitheatre a grass ledge leads rightwards to a blunt arete on the right side of a smooth clean wall. Start just left of the arete. Climb up to the incipient crack. It is possible to step left into the main crack and follow this, but if it is wet, traverse right and go up the arete. Climb the double cracks and a shallow chimney to the top.

9 Footpad 105m VS (1972)
Below and right of the amphitheatre is a white slabby arete. Scramble up steep grass and belay under a small overhang.
1. 40m Step left and climb the grooved arete, then climb a wall to a grassy terrace beneath the smooth wall left of Antipodean Exile.
2. 20m Descend slabby grooves and grass diagonally right until it is possible to step into a groove. Climb this to a grass pedestal on the right.
3. 20m From the right end of the pedestal climb a steep crack and a chimney to a small stance.
4. 25m Continue up the groove above, stepping out right at the top.

10 MacBeth 85m VS (1980)
Scramble up to belay beneath the grey-flecked buttress forming the most continuous and steepest piece of rock between Miny and Footpad.
1. 30m 4c Climb up to a shallow groove which leads to an overhang. Pass this on the right and move back left above it. A short wall of better rock leads to a grass ledge on the right.
2. 20m 5a Step left from the end of the grass ledge and climb a wall and a crack until it is possible to move left to another grass ledge.
3. 35m 4c The crack above the right end of the ledge leads to easier climbing and the top.

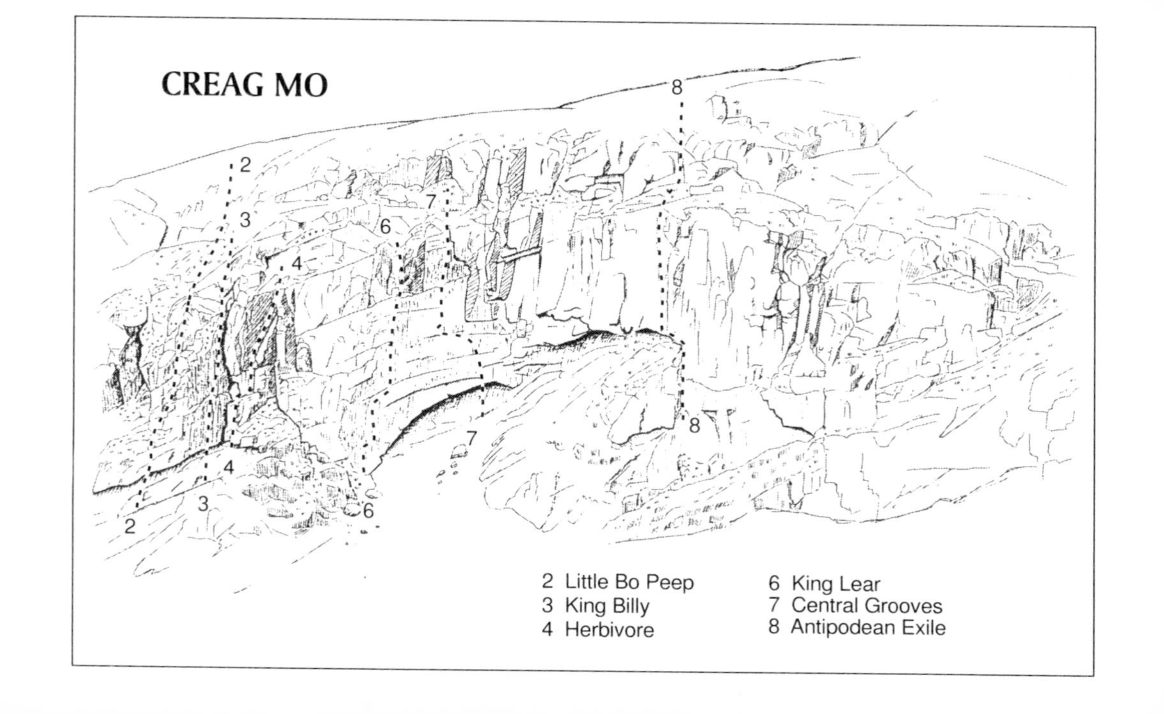
CREAG MO
2
3
4
6
7
8
2 Little Bo Peep
3 King Billy
4 Herbivore
6 King Lear
7 Central Grooves
8 Antipodean Exile

11 MacBeth Variation 85m HVS (1989)
1.35m 5a Start at the lowest bit of rock below a corner-groove. Climb the groove past loose blocks and a short overhanging wall. Continue until level with the first belay of MacBeth. Traverse briefly left, then go up a rounded edge to a belay below some roofs.
2. 15m Climb a chimney to the grass ledge below the third pitch of MacBeth.
3. 35m 4c Finish up MacBeth.

12 Miny 105m Severe (1961)
Start at the left side of the lower wall. Go up slabs past a small sapling to the grass terrace. From the right end of the terrace a steep groove (probably common with Footpad) leads to the top.

13 Smeagol 95m Hard Severe (1965)
This direct line on good rock leads to the prominent cracked corner of Gollum. Start at the clean right edge of a vegetated recess a few metres left of the start of Gollum.
1. 25m Trend up and left to a small ledge on an edge. Move right across a steep wall to a short groove which leads to a poor ledge and belay.
2. 20m Step left to a good rock ledge. Climb the interesting rock above directly, past loose blocks, to the left end of a large ledge.
3. 40m Move awkwardly left to a shallow bay and climb a groove on the left to a slab which leads to easy ground. Continue easily for 10m to the belay below the third pitch of Gollum. Follow this to the top.

14 Gollum 100m Severe (1965)
Start towards the right side of the lower wall at an obvious easy-angled slabby rib (cairn).
1. 30m Go up the rib to a steep groove which leads to a ledge on the left. Climb a slab to an overlap. Move over this and trend right to a steep little wall. Ascend this and move a few metres left to a stance on large detached blocks.
2. 35m Climb a slab on small holds, then go up a short groove splitting the steep wall above. Walk up a grassy rake to some large blocks and get onto the wall above at an obvious left traverse. At the end of this, go up right to a large grassy bay. Walk 10 metres left to a prominent cracked corner.
3. 35m Climb the corner to the top; not without interest.

SGURR SCALADALE (Map Ref 163 085)

This big north-east facing cliff, nearly 1km long and over 200m high, dominates the head of Glen Scaladale. Although there is a fair amount of unclimbed rock, the cliff is often dank and dingy with a lot of vegetation; this makes it less appealing than other crags in the area. The cliff needs a lot of fine weather for it to come into good condition and even then it is doubtful whether seepage ever dries completely.

Follow the approach path to Creag Mo, but continue up the glen for about another kilometre before striking up to the foot of the cliff. This takes about an hour from the bridge across the Scaladale River.

The main face rises above a terrace below which lies 60m of steep mixed terrain. It is bounded by East Gully on the left and West Gully on the right. To the right of West Gully the cliff is broken and vegetated. The steepest section of the main cliff is a black wall with a prominent line of overhangs slanting up from left to right. Bounding this section of cliff to the left is the gully-groove of Miolnir and Central Gully to the right. West Buttress is the obvious buttress to the left of West Gully.

The easiest way off is by following the north-west shoulder overlooking Loch Vistern.

1 West Buttress 225m VS (1969)

This climb takes a direct line up the buttress from the lowest rocks.

1. 35m Follow grass up left, then go back right to a stance at a pinnacle.

2. 35m Go straight up over rock and grass to a stance below a small overhang.

3. 20m Break out right and go up to a small stance below a long crack.

4. 30m Climb the crack for 12m, then trend right to a thin crack very near the right edge of the buttress. Climb this, step left, then climb the face to a grass stance.

5. 15m Move up to a greasy crack which leads (crux) to another grass stance. About 90m of scrambling remains.

2 Central Gully 230m (1930)

This is the first recorded climb on the face, climbed by Botterill and party. Apparently no difficulties were encountered until the diagonal grass traverse. At the penultimate pitch the party had to traverse out onto West Buttress.

Central Rib (VS, 1954) takes the area of rock between Central Gully and West Buttress.

3 Panorama 175m E2 (1981)
This route goes directly up the wall to the start of the diagonal overhangs. Start by scrambling up rock and grass for 75m to the highest ledge on the right of a wet groove-gully bounding the steep area on the right.
1. 25m 5b Move down left and cross the wet groove-gully to gain an ascending line of steps on the far side. Trend left to belay next to a large loose block.
2. 30m 5b Move left above the overhangs and trend up left to the obvious depression in the face about 30m below the start of the diagonal line of overhangs. Cross the depression leftwards on sloping holds and pass the overhang above on the left. Move delicately right above to a stance and dubious thread belay.
3. 25m 5b Climb steeply just right of the stance and surmount an overhang to gain the foot of a deep groove. Follow this until it is possible to move left on very wet rock to a wet stance and poor belays below dripping overhangs.
4. 25m 5c Move back right and ascend an exposed right-slanting ramp. From its end move up left to a sloping ledge with difficulty. Traverse delicately right for 3 metres to belay on nuts.
5. 35m 5b Move back left and surmount the overhang to gain a ledge beneath a deep long groove. Climb this and a short continuation groove to a ledge.
6. 35m 5a Ascend the grooves directly above and continue up short awkward walls to the top.

4 Miolnir 140m VS * (1961)
A good route up the obvious gully-groove on the left side of the main face.
Gain the gully after 30m of slabs on the left. Follow the steepening gully for 25m. Go up a groove on the right, then move back into a chimney to reach a boulder-strewn platform. Belay on the smaller ledge 4 metres to the left. Climb a steep wall above to below an overhang. Move right and climb the deep groove to a ledge on the left. Pull over the overhang (crux, 4c), then go left to a stance and belay. Finish up the steep corner above.

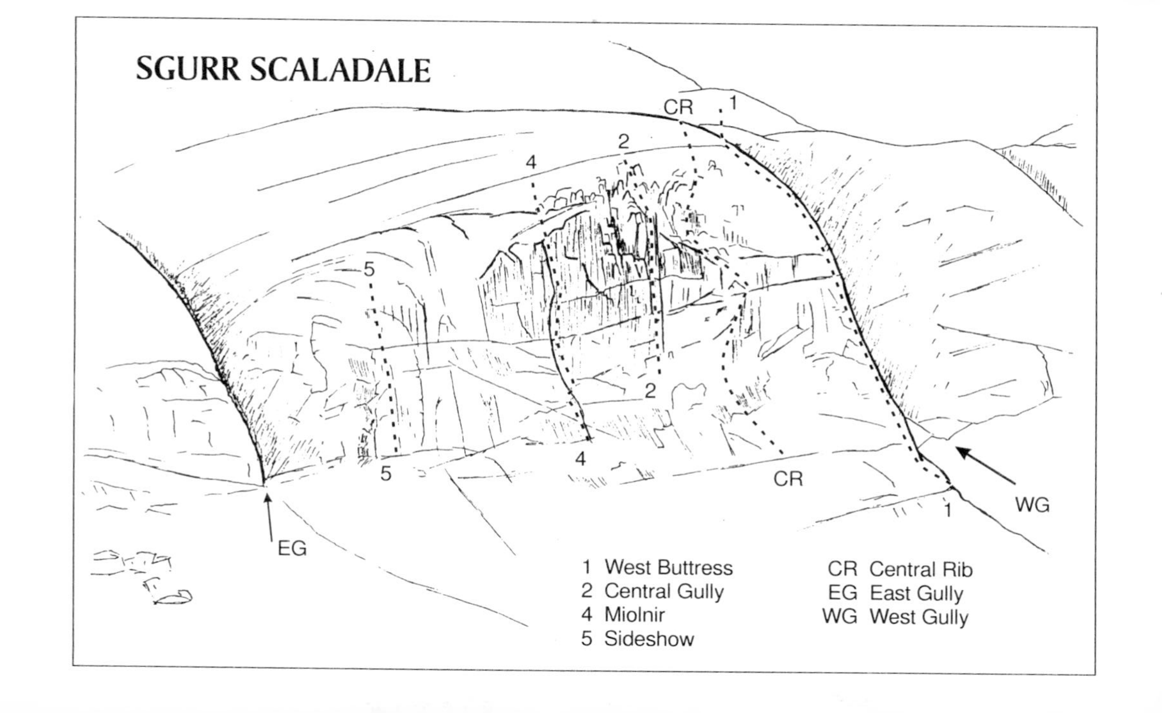
SGURR SCALADALE
CR
1
2
4
5
2
4
5
CR
1
EG
WG
1 West Buttress
2 Central Gully
4 Miolnir
5 Sideshow
CR Central Rib
EG East Gully
WG West Gully

5 Sideshow 105m HVS (1990)
Start below a roof immediately right of the East Gully.
1. 40m 5a Break through the roof and continue to a stance.
2. 25m 4c Climb up to a quartz vein and move right.
3. 40m 4c Move right to follow a continuous rib of rock to the top.

SRON SCOURST

At present no known climbing exists on Sron Ard (Map Ref 108 125). Other than a scramble on the north flank of Sron Scourst by Irens and Solari in 1938, only one recorded climb has been made on the impressive promontory overlooking Loch Scourst. Unsatisfactory routes have been climbed on the north-west face, and the gully system on the north has been used as a descent route.

Direct Route 90m Severe (1967)
A direct line up the west end of this great rock promontory. Under the steepest part of the cliff, an old fence ends at a smooth vertical wall. Start a few metres north of the fence. Climb broken rocks with a right traverse to a vertical chimney. Go up this for 5m, then traverse right to an exposed ledge. Climb more or less directly up steep rocks to a broad ledge 45m above the start. Continue slightly rightwards to a short awkward groove, above which the climb deteriorates.

GILLAVAL GLAS

The north-facing cliffs of Gillaval Glas overlook the Skeaudale River. The main crag, Cnoc Eadar Da Bheinn (known locally as Gillaval Dubh), is easily accessible from the Ardhasaig Bridge over the River Skeaudale (Map Ref 137 034) but offers climbing only high up on its east buttress, to which the ascent is tedious.

East of the summit of Gillaval Glas, below two small lochans on its north east shoulder, is the 75m Lochan Crag. There is one recorded route which is said to be on slabby, beautifully clean rock. There is another short but steeper crag a few hundred metres north-east.

Lochan Crag Climb 60m Very Difficult (1952)
Start on a ledge about 15 metres from the west edge of the buttress. Zigzag up to a rock recess surmounted by a prominent V-chimney, which slightly overhangs the recess. The traverse into the recess provides an interesting excursion on steep slabs.

The Sron a' Sgaoth crags on the south-west shoulder of Sgaoth Iosal (Map Ref 155 034) also overlook the Skeaudale River. Several steep slabs here offer climbing, while the northern extremity of these crags (overlooking the A859 and easily accessible from there) have three or four buttresses that give 60m or more of easy climbs and scrambles.

CLISHAM

799m (Map Ref 154 783)

This is the highest peak in the Outer Hebrides. The 250m slabs of Corrie Dubh appear to be too broken to offer much potential for serious climbing. They are bounded to the left by a narrow gully and on the right by a straight grassy gully. A rake rises from right to left across the slabs.

The only recorded climb begins at the bottom right-hand corner formed by the rake and the straight grassy gully. The route stays 15 to 30m from the grassy gully for 150m, then enters the gully. It then goes left to finish on slabs at a gentler angle. A better and harder route would bear left avoiding the gully.

Numerous possibilities for Grade II/III routes of 60 to 110m exist on Aonaig Mor Crag on the north side of Clisham. At least two routes have been climbed. **Pairc** (90m Grade III, 1989) follows the obvious icefall on the right hand side of the crag. **Leodhas** (110m Grade III, 1992) takes the right-hand buttress, immediately right of Pairc.

SGAOTH AIRD

559m (Map Ref 165 039)

The 150m crags on the north face are broken into numerous buttresses of which only three at the west end are of interest. From right to left, the first is Slab Wall, a belt of steep 75m slabs left of the parallel cracks which split this face. A narrow cleft separates Slab Wall from No.1 Buttress which has an obvious steep nose (visible from the road), with a semi-detached block forming the east wall of the gully. Left of No.1 Buttress is a gully with a scree cone, then follows No.2 Buttress which is divided by a left-slanting gully-shelf.

The crags are easily reached from Glen Laxadale or by a shorter approach from the nearest point of the A859 in about half an hour.

Haudes 40m VS (1966)
A bold route up the obvious nose of No.1 Buttress. Start in a narrow gully right of the nose and below a steep groove in the left wall.
1. 20m 4c Climb a steep groove (peg runner) to belay on top of a pinnacle.
2. 20m Climb the steep wall above to a block belay. Finish by a scramble up right *via* a small pinnacle overhanging the gully.
Variation Finish: Severe (1969)
From the top of the pinnacle, traverse 5 metres right and climb the edge of the buttress.

No.2 Buttress 150m Very Difficult (1948)
Scramble up the edge of the eastern section of the buttress overlooking the gully-shelf. After 75m the rock becomes continuous and steep. Climb the last short slab direct.

CNOC A' CHAISTEIL (Map Ref 143 101)

The crag at the north end of a spur which runs through Mullach an Langa has been climbed at its western end up a rib of square-cut blocks which leads to a sloping platform and a loose notched block at top. To the left the face is steeper and less broken.

TARAN MOR
303m (Map Ref 034 155)

The buttresses on the northern side of this hill, in the western group of Harris hills near the Loch Resort coast, are broken with ledges and grass rakes and feature slabs at a relatively easy angle. However, a deep almost hidden gully splits the mountain and its walls give a few pitches of steeper climbing.

Sundowner 135m Severe (1969)
Start at the foot of the buttress forming the left gully wall at a large boulder. Climb a diedre to a ledge with jumbled blocks. Climb up left into a chimney system. Some way above, climb a crack in a wall and finish up slabs.

SOUTH HARRIS

BEN LUSKENTYRE 506m

The eastern top of Ben Luskentyre has a rocky northern face overlooking West Loch Tarbert, well seen from the road just west of Tarbert. The face is broken by terraces, but at the right of the face the lowest tier forms a fine little buttress. There is a pleasant Severe taking a rising traverse, but harder more direct lines are possible, with fine slab climbing reminiscent of the Etive Slabs.

Another climb (60m, Difficult) starts 15 metres to the left of shallow grass on the right of the main buttress. Climb a 20m rib, then traverse right along the base of a broken slab and across a grass gully. Climb a corner and follow a groove up to the right, then climb a series of short walls and easy slabs to finish.

The Lewis Sea-Cliffs

Although much potential remains on the cliffs of Western Lewis, the main areas of interest are not very extensive. Most of the climbing is concentrated on the stretch of coastline south of Uig known as Ard Mhor Mangersta (spelt Mungarstadh in places), and the coastline running north of Uig Sands to Gallen Head. Dalbeg is situated toward the southern end of the coastline between Carloway and the Butt of Lewis.

With a high concentration of climbs in the E grades and many more routes at a slightly lower level of difficulty, these two areas now constitute one of the most important climbing grounds in the Outer Isles. Furthermore, the sea-cliffs are often basking in sunshine when the mountains are shrouded in mist.

The rock architecture here is most impressive, with many rocky islands, stacs, natural arches and great cavernous geos (the local name for a zawn). The rock itself, in some parts as good as any in the country, is a strange mixture of fine granite and striated Lewisian gniess, generally rough and gritty in texture but often buffed smooth and rounded through the action of the sea. Colourful intrusions of pegmatite and quartz are a common feature and in many cases they provide lines for routes to follow.

Generally speaking, the climbing is steep and exposed, even a little frightening, especially when the full force of the Atlantic is crashing beneath your feet!

Some useful notes

Due to the highly corrosive nature of salt water, the placement of *in situ* protection and belays has in general been avoided. Many of the climbs are tidal, so it is worth bearing this in mind when committed to an abseil approach. A rope especially for this purpose is recommended.

Another problem is sea-spray. The cliffs often appear to be dry but are in fact covered in a thin film of moisture. This usually evaporates as the day goes on, otherwise you can add at least a grade.

Opposite: *Paranoid Slippers, Mangersta (Climber, Grant Farquhar)*

Next page: *The Screaming Ab Dabs, Mangersta (Climbers, Dave Cuthbertson and Lee Clegg)*

PAINTED GEO (Map Ref 006 334)

So called because it resembles the Black Canyon of the Gunnison in the States, with a bit of imagination that is! This picturesque little geo offers a number of good quality climbs and boasts the shortest approach in the area. It is not greatly affected by tides and enjoys a sheltered south-westerly aspect.

Approach and Access

Continue west along the road from Ardroil, following signposts to Mangersta. On descending the hill into Mangersta, there is a phone box on the right. Shortly after this, follow a rough tarmac road going back right and continue to the radio station at the road end. Park in the area of the disused building immediately before the station. From the parking area, walk north and in a minute the wall is clearly visible, situated above an attractive tidal rock pool.

To reach the foot of the climbs, first descend a short grass gully and rocky ramp (often wet) on the south side of the geo, then traverse right (facing out) into the back of the geo and cross to the other side. Alternatively, descend by abseil from the top of the main wall.

The most obvious features on the wall are, from left to right, the right-facing corner of Director's Corner, the central crack of Motion Control, the right-slanting pink vein of Painted Wall and an obvious chimney line (VS/HVS; often wet) to the right where the back wall of the geo abutts the main face.

The climbs are described from left to right.

The first two routes are reached by scrambling down to the neck of rock between two gullies on the north side of the geo, left of Mick's Corner.

Gloss 20m E3 5b (1993)

Traverse awkwardly onto the pink undercut slab, then move up a series of breaks and footholds. Follow these rightwards to below an overhang. Exit with care up a quartz vein that forms a short corner on the right of the overhang.

Previous page: Director's Corner, The Painted Wall (Climber, Gary Latter)

Opposite: Singapore Sling, Mangersta (Climber, Lee Clegg)

Legalability 25m E1 5a (1993)
This route follows the right-hand side of the lower wall left of and down from Gloss. Start up a right-slanting crack through a bulge. Climb leftwards through a quartz band to ledges, then follow the crack on the left and climb a wall to the top.

1 **Mick's Corner** 25m VS 4c ** (1979)
Easy climbing on the lower half of the face leads to a good belay ledge beneath the line of Director's Corner. Trend leftwards on slabby rock to the base of an obvious shallow corner. Follow this to the top.

2 **Pink and Black** 20m E4 5c ** (1985)
This attractive climb follows the rib separating Mick's Corner from Director's Corner. Start as for Director's Corner. On entering the corner, swing leftwards from the left arete to twin diagonal cracks. Continue straight up, following a black seam to gain a good incut ledge. Finish more easily.

3 **Director's Corner** 20m VS 5a (1970s)
The obvious central corner is worth doing, although it is a bit loose in places.

4 **Dauntless** 21m E5/6 6a *** (1985)
A difficult and sustained pitch which is reasonably well protected. Start approximately 6 metres right of Director's Corner. Climb the quartz wall to a break. Continue to a second break, then go left into a scoop to the right of a flake at about one-third height. Now go back right, aiming for twin diagonal breaks near the top. Follow these strenuously to finish.

4a **Goodbye Ruby Tuesday** 20m E5 6a ** (1996)
A fine, sustained and strenuous eliminate taking a direct line up the wall. Small cams are useful. Start in the centre of the wall, 2 metres left of Motion Control. Go up the flaky white band to where the wall steepens. A series of powerful moves between breaks leads to good finishing jugs at the centre of the wall.

5 **Motion Control** 20m E2 5b/c *** (1985)
Belay on a light-coloured ledge at the start of the crack. The crack is steep and athletic, especially at half-height.

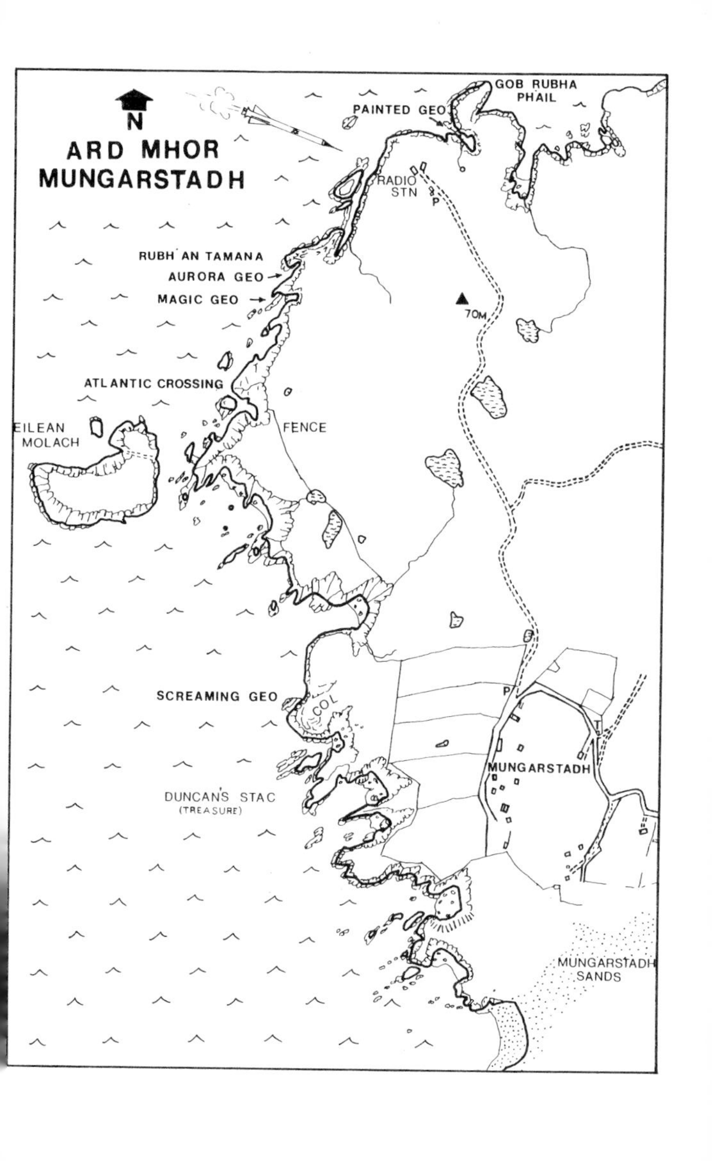
N
ARD MHOR
MUNGARSTADH
GOB RUBHA
PHAIL
PAINTED GEO
RADIO
STN
P
RUBH' AN TAMANA
AURORA GEO
MAGIC GEO
70M
ATLANTIC CROSSING
EILEAN
MOLACH
FENCE
SCREAMING GEO
COL
P
T
MUNGARSTADH
DUNCAN'S STAC
(TREASURE)
MUNGARSTADH
SANDS

6 The Painted Wall 20m E4 5c *** (1985)
From the belay on Motion Control, climb up and right into a scoop and follow the obvious pink quartz band, with tricky moves going right near the top; quite bold.

7 Whisky Galore 25m E5/6 6a ** (1985)
A necky lead. Start from a ledge about 8m down and to the right of Motion Control. Climb a slanting groove to a prominent niche on the right side of an overlap. Pull out of this and go leftwards above the overlap. Cross The Painted Wall and ascend to a good hold and some unreassuring protection. Climb strenuously up the bulging wall above to finish *via* a short crack (protection) on the left.

8 Dreaded Dram 25m E4 5c ** (1985)
Good climbing protected by small wires. Start to the right of Whisky Galore, beneath an obvious short black groove. Climb the black groove and the obvious continuation to the steep upper section. A series of short vague cracks leads to the final easy moves of Painted Wall.

9 Gneiss is Nice 25m E3 5c ** (1994)
Start on the highest ledge to the right of the black groove of Dreaded Dram. Ascend a vague crack in the wall to a horizontal break (protection). Pull onto the slab above and go up to the overlap. Traverse right and move up to the base of a prominent overhanging groove. Climb this strenuously to the top.

10 Broken Rib 25m VS 5a (1970s)
This route takes the line of an obvious prow at the back (east) end of the geo. Start by scrambling up to a large ledge. Follow the line of least resistance up the arete to the top. The start is bold.

Black Foot 30m E2 6a (1993)
This climb takes a right-slanting line on the black triangular wall on the south side of the geo, right of the main wide middle gully. It is easily seen from the top of the west end of the wall. Start from a small black ledge, reached by abseil. Climb a crack through a bulge, trending right, and up to a ledge with difficulty. Follow the obvious line left to the top.

The next route is in the geo east of the deep inlet of Torasgeo. From the parking place, walk right along the coastline past Painted Walls

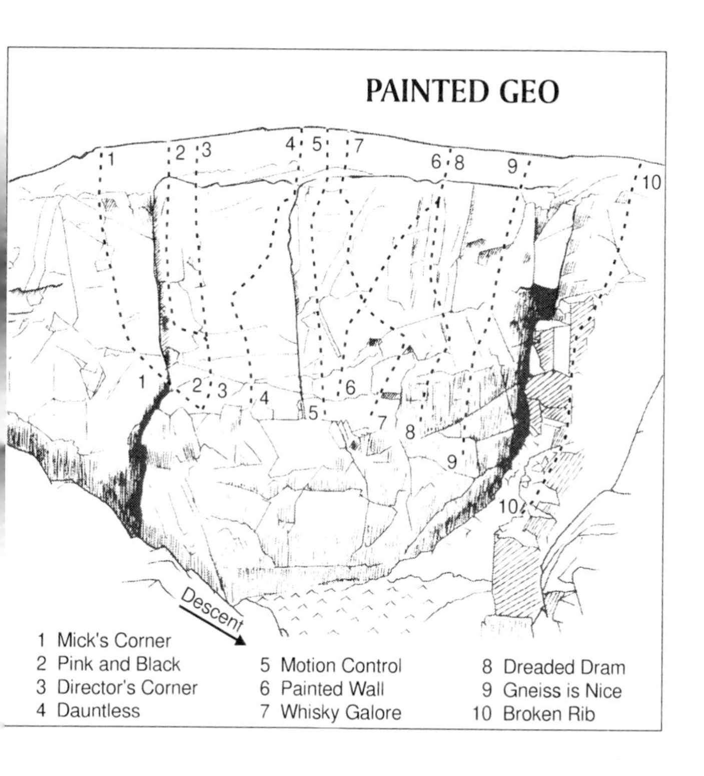

and Torasgeo to a geo characterised by an obvious pink quartz arete, the line of the climb. Approach by abseil to ledges above high tide level.

Ladies Who Lunch 35m E5 6a ** (1996)
From the belay, step left and climb through a small overlap, then move left again to the arete. Climb this for 5m to a rest. Swing back right and pull through a small overhang to beneath a gently overhanging wall. Place a high RP runner and make wild moves up the arete. Easier climbing on snappy ground leads to the top and a large block belay.

THE FLANNAN AREA

This is the name given to the two deep narrow inlets which are located south of Rubh' an Tamana, about 500 metres south of the radio station. The climbs are of the usual high quality, but due to a limited amount of light reaching some of the climbs, and being tidal, the starts are sometimes a bit greasy.

Approach and Access
From the parking area (see Painted Geo), go south and after a few minutes cross a small burn. At this point, if one looks down to the sea, an obvious rocky ridge will be seen which is separated from the hill side by a shallow depression or valley. The northern end of this ridge has a distinct black tail dipping into the sea; this becomes more obvious the further south you go.

AURORA GEO (Map Ref 002 329)

This is the first geo south of Rubh' an Tamana; it can be clearly seen by scrambling up some slabs (which make up the right flank of the valley when going south) to the highest point of the aforementioned ridge towards its northern end.

The west-facing wall, Cioch Wall, is tar black, generally less than vertical and characterised by a Cioch-shaped block situated towards its right-hand (southern) end. In the north-west corner of the opposite wall are the obvious lines of Newton's Law and Star of the Sea. The back (north) end of the geo forms an attractive arch over the sea and contains a distinctive quartz cross.

There are two ways to reach the foot of the first two climbs. One is to abseil directly down the line of the routes to belay on ledges above the sea; the other is to climb or abseil down from the top of the south end of this wall and traverse in along a slab (VS).

Newton's Law 30m E1 5b *** (1974)
Either start from a ledge at the foot of Star of the Sea and make an awkward traverse left to a slab at the foot of an open corner, or avoid the traverse by an abseil directly down the line of the route. Climb the prominent two-stepped corner direct, with some strenuous moves towards the top.

Star of the Sea 30m E1 5b *** (1974)
Despite being sometimes wet, this is one of the finest pitches at this grade on the sea-cliffs. Climb the impressive zigzag corner directly; well protected.

Romancing the Moose 30m E5 6a *** (1996)
A route of contrast in a committing situation directly above the sea-cave. Approach by abseiling down Star of the Sea. Teeter gingerly along the lip of the hanging slab to a good rest beneath the roof (RPs required). Jam wildly rightwards through the roof to gain an awkward crack. At its top move right to gain the headwall and climb steeply through the quartz bands to good finishing jugs in the centre.

Corner Climb 25m E3 5c (1996)
This route follows the corner right of the sea-cave. Climb up 5m to a hard move through an overhang. Continue more easily up the corner to the top.

THE CIOCH WALL

First locate the top of the Cioch-shaped block from above, then abseil to ledges at the foot of the climbs. To the left is the obvious President's Chimney. The first described route is reached by a tricky traverse around to the left of President's Chimney, passing under two flat walls, the line of Anonymous and the divergent cracks of Shag Crack to finally belay as for Cormorant Corner about 3 metres to the right of the obvious corner. Alternatively abseil directly down.

1 Cormorant Corner 20m E1 5b ** (1975)
Climb up and left into a hanging ramp below an overhang. Climb the overhang to reach a crack which gets easier towards the top.

2 Shag Crack 20m HVS 5a/b * (1975)
The left-hand of the divergent cracks sports one awkward move over the overhang.

3 Anonymous 20m VS 5a * (1975)
Climb the right-hand line to finish near the junction of two huge quartz veins which run across the wall.

4 President's Chimney 20m Very Difficult * (1970s)
Climb the deep chimney with some impressive back and foot moves towards the top. A Moderate escape route is possible by climbing the chimney until a move left leads onto the exposed blocky arete.

5 Immaculate Crack 20m Hard Severe ** (1970s)
The obvious and sustained crack to the right of President's Chimney; sometimes wet at the start.

6 Things Are Looking Up 25m E1 5c ** (1993)
Climb the vertical crack line and fault to the right of Immaculate Crack; at the upper limit of the grade.

7 The Roaring Foam 25m E3 5c *** (1994)
An excellent sustained route with good protection. Start 3 metres right of the chimney and follow the thin crack which veers rightwards in its upper half.

8 The Chicken Run 20m VS 4c * (1979)
Climb the wall to the right of the slimy wide crack; finish by a thin crack.

9 Chicken Run Direct 20m HVS 5b ** (1979)
This is the fine straight crack which starts 2 metres left of the Cioch block.

10 Look Back In Anger 20m E3 6a * (1993)
Climb the nasty thin crack, starting from the left edge of the Cioch.

11 Black Affronted 20m E2 5c * (1994)
Start directly behind the edge of the Cioch and climb a thin crack to a ledge. Step right to another crack and climb this to easier ground.

Don't Look Now 20m E2 6a ** (1993)
A lovely route up the intermittent thin crack at the right edge of the Cioch, which is gained by falling across the geo.

The next routes are located on the section of wall beyond the Cioch block. They are best approached by abseil, but they can also be reached by some awkward climbing through the gap.

The Vee 20m VS ** (1985)
Climb the prominent V-groove behind the step in the Cioch. A fine pitch.

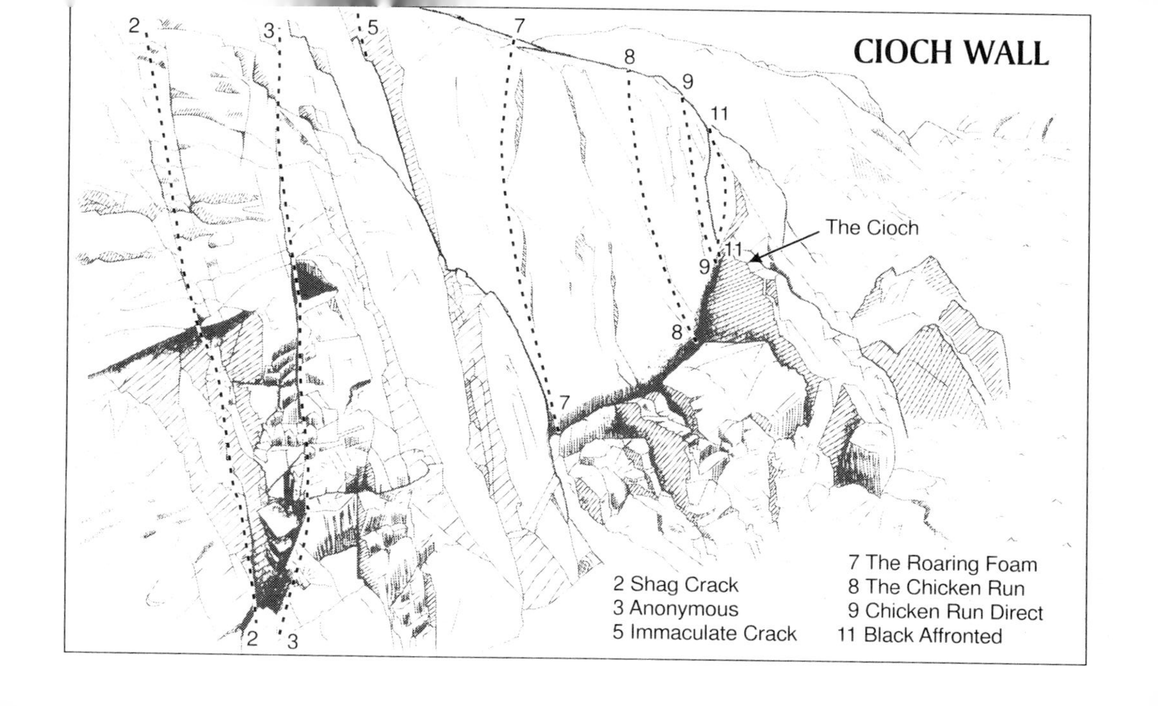
CIOCH WALL
The Cioch
2
3
5
7
8
9
11
2 Shag Crack
3 Anonymous
5 Immaculate Crack
7 The Roaring Foam
8 The Chicken Run
9 Chicken Run Direct
11 Black Affronted

The Zed 20m Hard Severe * (1985)
This is the zigzag line about 12 metres to the right of The Vee.

Both The Vee and The Zed can be reached by a 45m VS traverse from the Flannan Chimneys (see Magic Geo), making a fine expedition. Approximately halfway along this traverse is:

Gannet Crack HVS 5b * (1993)
A slab corner with an overhang part way up provides a well protected layback.

LANDLUBBER GEO

This is the geo just north of the Flannan area, formed by a gently-angled slab on its east side. The base of the Geo is easily reached by a walk down the gentle slab.

Dry Dock 25m E1 5b (1993)
An impressive route which takes the crack up the highest point of the steep wall. Start at the two large boulders at the end of the slabby tongue. Climb easily up a corner crack, then move up left and go over an overlap. Continue up the crack and finish up a corner.

MAGIC GEO

From Aurora Geo, continue south along the crest of the ridge for about 50 metres. The geo is easily recognised and features an impressive overhanging, west-facing wall of grey rock which is patchworked with long thin crack lines. In the north-east corner of the geo is the obvious line of Queen's Freebie, which is also a good abseil descent. The seaward east-facing wall, although impressive to look at, is much more slabby in nature and provides the lines of the classic Flannan Slab routes. The south end of this wall is known as the Red Wall.

THE RED WALL

This is the butt end of the promontory which separates Aurora Geo from Magic Geo. It is characterised by three diagonal crack lines, to the left of which are two chimney-grooves known as the Flannan Chimneys, best viewed from the top of the West Face. Access to these climbs is by either down climbing, with one awkward move from the top of the wall, or by jumping a narrow gap which is reached *via* the bottom of Magic Geo. See also the description for the descent to the climbs on the West Face.

Flannan Chimney Left-Hand 25m Severe (1979)
At half-height the chimney flares and protection is awkward to arrange.

Flannan Chimney Right-Hand 25m Severe (1979)
This sports a difficult move going right round an overhang at half-height.

Flannan Crack 25m VS 4c ** (1979)
The obvious right-slanting crack, starting on the left side of the wall.

Campa Crack 30m HVS 5a ** (1985)
Follow the next crack to the right directly throughout, with the main difficulties in the first 5m.

Limka 35m E2 5b ** (1985)
Start to the right of the previous route, then trend up and right following the obvious line. Finish up an easy arete in the angle between the east and south faces of the Geo.

EAST FACE

Flannan Slab Direct 45m HVS *** (1978)
This fine route starts at the bottom left-hand end of the wall beneath an open groove-chimney with an obvious slanting overhang.
1. 10m 5a/b Climb the groove to a tiny ledge and belay.
2. 35m 5a Hand traverse horizontally right for 6m, step up and gain another flake, then follow a line of good holds and left-facing flakes to the top. It is also possible to start direct, thus missing out the hand traverse at the beginning of pitch two.

Bubbles 40m HVS 5a *** (1993)
The relationship of this climb to Flannan Slab Direct and Flannan Slab is unknown. Start just left of Flannan Slab below a ledge, then move up left to the base of the groove. Move up easily (possible belay), then follow the groove to just below the traverse of the second pitch of Flannan Slab. Now traverse left to the arete and finish boldy up it.

Flannan Slab 50m VS *** (1978)
This route starts to the right of the centre of the face, beneath the line of a thin crack. It is also possible to start further right; neither way is well protected until the first ledge is reached.
1. 25m 4c Climb the thin crack up the wall on the right to a ledge. Now go up and left to another ledge. Belay on the ledge above.
2. 25m 4c Gain the prominent short left-facing corner above. Climb this and traverse left (crux), then go up to good holds at an obvious traverse line. Follow this leftwards under the overhangs to finish.

In the Pink 40m E1 5b ** (1985)
This is the fine corner at the right-hand side of the face. Protection is good, although the crux is blind and high up. Go up and right and climb a short overhanging corner to a ramp. Climb this to a quartz band, move left into another groove, then continue to the top.

WEST FACE

Queen's Freebie 40m E4 6b (1985)
The corner at the left-hand end of the wall sports a desperate move over the bulge at half-height.

The Magician 40m E5 6a *** (1985)
This impressive route, high in its grade, climbs the crack to the left of a long thin crack which almost touches the ground, and to the left of a short corner-ramp in the centre of the face. Start about 7 metres right of Queen's Freebie. Climb boldly up and left to gain a red band and the start of the crack. Climb the sustained and strenuous crack (thankfully well protected), veering right towards the top.

The Sorcerer 40m E5 6a *** (1985)
Another bold route. After the start of The Magician, climb a ramp on the right then go back left to a flakey corner. Pull over this, then traverse right to finish up the groove above.

Am Burrach 50m E3 5c * (1993)
To the right of The Sorcerer is a steep undercut crack. Reach this from the start of The Sorcerer and climb a steep flake-filled groove to the right of the crack. Finish up a right-facing corner.

The Alchemist 50m E4 * (1996)
This route takes the groove and bottomless chimney on the right side of the steep landward wall.
1. 20m 5c Climb the prominent deep black V-groove which soon eases. Above, head diagonally right to belay on the large ledge directly beneath the steep leaning groove.
2. 30m 6a Strenuously climb the innocuous-looking groove with difficulty to better holds on the left wall at 6m. The chimney-groove above provides a pleasant easier finish.

The next routes are situated in the bay immediately to the right of the West Face of Magic Geo. Approach by down climbing, or abseil down the line of two parallel chimneys (**Solitary Chimneys**; Difficult). An attractive feature of the chimneys is the appealing south-facing wall to their left. The right side of the bay consists of a black mitre-shaped wall which contains two obvious crack lines. About 6m down and right of the right-hand crack is a slim corner, the start to A Night at the Opera. Further right, an obvious groove system has been climbed at HVS; approach directly by abseil.

The Black Crack 30m E1 5a * (1970s)
This is the left-hand of the aforementioned cracks. There is often a water-filled hold at about mid-height.

A Night at the Opera 35m HVS * (1985)
Traverse right and belay on a small ledge at the foot of a corner. (Probably the last accessible line before the sea).
1. 10m 5a Climb the awkward corner to a ledge and belay.
2. 25m 4c Move up and right, then go left to a quartz seam at the edge of the slab. Finish up this.

HUNTER'S SLABS

To the south of Magic Geo, at the southern end of the rocky ridge, is a prominent Aiguille block feature. Behind the Aiguille (on the south side) lies a broken gully, but to the right of this and sweeping down to the sea is a lovely area of pink slabs (visible from the top of the Red Wall), which is about 30 metres wide and 45m high. Several routes have been climbed here in the Very Difficult to Severe grades, mainly on slabs with one central chimney line. Approach is by abseil down the line of an obvious crack on the north side of the Aiguille.

HIDDEN GEO

This is immediately to the south of Hunter's Slabs. Go across the top of a broken gully behind the Aiguille by the line of an obvious traverse for 60m. At this point the geo is still out of sight. Then descend by abseil.

Spiney Norman 35m HVS 5b ** (1983)
Climb the obvious, superb, and well protected open corner.

Hidden Gem 35m Severe ** (1983)
About 12 metres to the right of the previous climb is an obvious sloping corner crack. Climb it direct.

ATLANTIC CROSSING AREA (Map Ref 991 324)

From the parking area at the radio station (see Painted Geo), go south and contour the hillside above the coastline. Go beyond the Flannan Area to the remains of an old fence with a small lochan just before it. The pointed triangular headland block which is girdled by Atlantic Crossing is obvious. This is almost 1km from the car park. To reach the foot of the climbs, scramble along a north to south connecting ridge, which is slabby on the seaward side and overhung on the landward side. From a notch, descend an obvious ramp and a boulder field. This takes about 15 minutes from the carpark.

1 **Atlantic Crossing** 100m VS ** (1979)
This is effectively a rising girdle of the headland block. The climb begins where a boulder choke abutts the main face and forms an obvious V.
1. 40m 5a Climb awkwardly down the smooth boulder (on the left, facing in) and step onto the main wall. Either ascend a metre or so to an overhang and traverse left, or go left almost immediately (steep) on good holds, and bearing in mind that your second is potentially in for a big swing! Continue left across a series of grooves to a prominent spike (possible belay). The traverse line terminates in an exposed position on the buttress edge. Belay above a bottomless corner.
2. 15m 5a Make an awkward step round the corner on the left onto a slab, (a belly flop seems to be the most common method). Climb a bottomless chimney on the left to a small ledge and belay in a sentry box.
3. 45m Climb the cracked wall and slab above, trending left near the top.

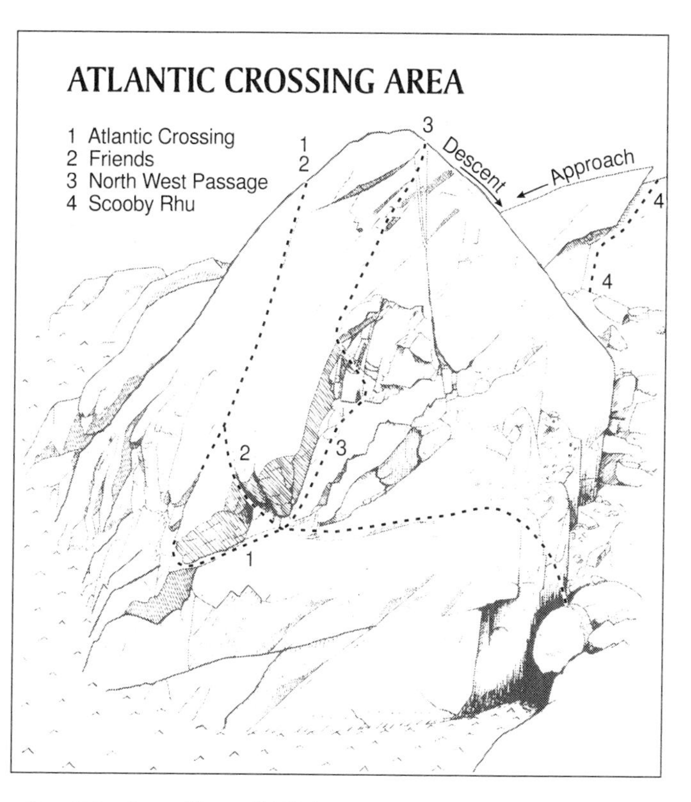

2 Friends 15m E1 5b * (1986)
A short but sensational variation to Atlantic Crossing. Belay as for North-West Passage. Climb the crack which springs leftwards out of the niche to the left of North-West Passage to join Atlantic Crossing.

3 North-West Passage 35m E1 5b ** (1988)
This takes the line of an obvious hanging right-facing corner situated about two-thirds of the way along the first pitch of Atlantic Crossing. Belay beneath the corner. Pull into the corner with difficulty and continue to some block overhangs (suspect). Turn these on the right,

then traverse back left to exit onto the slabs at a point where the overlap begins to go back right. Follow the line of least resistance to the top.

4 Scooby Rhu 15m E1 5a ** (1979)
The wonderful layback which starts from the foot of the descent ramp is short but well protected.

SEAL BAY

About half a dozen routes have been climbed on the slabs opposite the start to Atlantic Crossing, of which the following are the best.

Sunset Ridge 65m Difficult ** (1978)
The pleasant ridge opposite the start to Atlantic Crossing. From the top of a quartz pedestal, step up and right to a belay on a ledge. Take the easiest line up the slabby rib above to a belay before the top. Easier climbing leads to the top.

Photographer's Corner 60m VS 4c * (1986)
This is the line of left-facing corners on the right-hand side of the slabby wall which faces Atlantic Crossing. The approach is *via* a long sea-level traverse from the right. Climb the corners direct in two pitches.

Sholmaru Difficult
This is a very fine low-level girdle of the slabs, starting from the foot of a broad slab-ramp immediately south of Seal Bay and finishing at an obvious feature called the Neck. Sholmaru can be linked with **Lonmaru** (VS/HVS) which starts at the Neck and takes a natural fault line 20m above sea-level and goes right to an exposed corner where a tricky descending traverse leads into a rock bay, whence there is a choice of exits.

SCREAMING GEO (Map Ref 002 317)

This is the pride and joy of the area, with climbs ranking with the best in the country. Although most of the climbs are in the middle to upper grades, there are some fine E2s, an excellent HVS (Claymore), an incredible two pitch Severe (Lighthouse Arete), and If All Else Fails, a pleasant Very Difficult. The Mangersta Slabs enjoy a sunny south-westerly aspect as does the Screaming Wall, but the north-west face catches the sun only in the late afternoon and early evening.

Approach and Access
From the Mangersta/Painted Geo junction (see approach to Painted Geo), walk along the Painted Geo road for about 20 metres to a rusty steel gate on the left. When parking, care should be taken not to cause any obstruction. Go through the gate and follow the fence going west and at right-angles to the road. Cross the fence at the far end, then head south-west aiming for a small circular stone which sits just above a grassy col (this is on the left side of the long flat summit of Buaile Chuido). Go straight on from the col for about 30 metres, at which point the middle platform can be seen. This is about 10 minutes from the car. Go down a small rock ramp (slightly to the left, looking out) to reach the platform which in turn provides access to the climbs.

The cliff is arranged in two main sections. The right-hand section forms an impressive sweep of granite-like slabs, The Mangersta Slabs, which are visible from the southern end of the platform. Round the corner from the northern end of the platform is the daunting North-West Wall. The upper tier is obvious while the superb lower tier is hidden directly below. The impressive Screaming Wall (West Face) is the stupendous face above the cave. The ridge at the left side of this is taken by Lighthouse Arete. Closer in on the left wall of the corner formed by the north-west and west faces, the attractive pink crack of Hughys' Cocktail Mixture can be seen, with the arete of Shadow Dancer just to the left.

THE MANGERSTA SLABS

The first route starts from a superb ledge at sea-level, which can be reached by making a right-slanting diagonal abseil from the corner at the right end of the middle platform.

Penny Whistle 45m E3 5c ** (1985)
Unfortunately the top third of both this climb and Hundred Pipers involves some quite serious climbing on rock which is suspect. From the right end of the ledge, climb a groove straight up to a broken band. Then go leftwards to finish up Hundred Pipers.

Hundred Pipers 45m E3 5c ** (1985)
Start directly below a large open groove which is high up on the face above the horizontal band. Pull over the bulge and follow thin cracks up the slab on superb rock. Weave through the horizontal band and climb a slim quartz groove to gain the easier finishing corner.

Claymore 30m HVS 5a ** (1970s)
This excellent route climbs the obvious line of slim corners and cracks just to the right of the abseil. Ascend the right-facing corner to a ledge at about 6m. Step right into the thin crack (often wet) and climb an awkward bulge to a ledge on the left (sometimes full of water). Move back right and go up a shallow groove to a small foot ledge, then traverse left (crux) to better holds which lead to a small left-facing corner. Climb this and trend left over a bulge to finish.

Moscow Mule 30m E2 5b ** (1988)
Start as for Claymore. From the ledge at 6m, follow an obvious hand traverse line to the left edge. Climb a crack for a metre or so, then make a trying move left across an overhang to a jug. Finish up an easier groove above.

Singapore Sling 30m E2 5c ** (1988)
A fine eliminate based on the previous climb. Belay on a ledge round to the left of Claymore, reached directly by abseil. After a couple of metres, move right around the edge and climb a thin crack with some difficulty to join the crux of Moscow Mule. Climb this and a tricky wall above, going slightly left to finish.

The following routes are gained from the same belay ledge as Singapore Sling.

Let's Go Down to the Water Line E1 5b (1980s)
From the belay, take a rising left traverse to reach a prominent platform ledge. Continue along a flake crack and the line of least resistance. Belay before reaching the middle platform to reduce rope drag.

From the prominent platform ledge, two routes at about E1 have been climbed. The first more or less climbs directly above the ledge to enter a prominent groove, while the other works back up and right.

I'll Try up Here Again 30m E1 5b (1993)
Approach by abseil down an obvious corner below ledges, about 15 metres left of Claymore. The route takes an improbable line up some steep ground, and may share sections with the previous climbs. Climb an easy wall to a steep crack. Pull onto a small slab left of an overhang, then step down to a crucial foothold at the bottom of the slab. Climb round the overhang and follow the nose to the top.

The next two routes are on the upper tier and are passed just before rounding the arete on the platform that leads to the north-west face. **Pinky** (10m, HVS 5a, 1993) takes the left-hand crack just right of the arete, and **Perky** (VS 4c, 1988) takes the corner about 2 metres further right. Many of the groove lines further right have been climbed on a top rope.

NORTH-WEST FACE, LOWER TIER

The approach is by abseil from a choice of good belay boulders and cracks on the middle platform. The climbs are described from right to left. Note that these climbs are affected by the tide.

1 If All Else Fails 25m Very Difficult * (1988)
From the right end of the obvious raised shelf, climb up to the left end of a slab (good belay). Climb this *via* a short vague crack on its right side, then continue rightwards along a series of narrow ledges to finish up a fine little exposed wall.
Direct Finish: E1 *
Climb into a short hanging crack in a groove about halfway along the traverse of the normal route. Short but steep.

2 Hullaballoo 20m E6 6b (1993)
This hard and serious route takes the intermittent cracks just right of the left-facing corner, moving awkwardly into this at 7m. Follow the corner and the wall above more easily to the top.

3 Suffering Bastard 25m E4 6a *** (1988)
The prominent crack system to the left of Hullaballoo gives a brilliant well protected pitch. A Friend 4 is useful for the final groove, but not essential. An undercut start leads to the base of the overhanging cracks. Climb these with an awkward transfer into the left-hand crack. Finish up a superb bomb-bay groove.

4 Killer Fingers 30m E5 6a *** (1988)
Immediately right of the central overhanging face sits an obvious slab with a layback crack above. A fine pitch. An undercut start and a two-stepped corner lead to a crack on the right side of the slab. Climb the crack and arrange protection. Now step down and hand traverse left. Make a difficult move to reach the layback which leads to the top. The boldness of the climb depends on how far up the crack protection is placed before the traverse left.

5 Salty Dog 30m E5 6a *** (1988)
The twin crack system on the left side of the central overhanging face, immediately right of a smooth black slabby rib. Climb the undercut left-hand groove and continue up the crack with some deviation. Reach the final small bottomless groove with some difficulty (small wires); this leads to the top.

6 The Screaming Ab Dabs 75m E6 *** (1988)
A magnificent and committing climb which follows an impressive line up the right side of the big cave before attacking directly the overhangs above. The crux is short but hard and in an intimidating position. Start at the left end of the lower tier on the left wall of a corner.
1. 20m 5c The Yosemite Crack. Climb an undercut groove, then move left to the obvious white crack. This leads to a perfect ledge and belay.
2. 25m 5b Traverse of the Gods. Traverse left along the horizontal break with lots of exposure, then move up to a ledge on the right. Make a rising left traverse across an orange/brown-coloured wall to a small ledge at the girdling break. Large Friends are useful for the belay.
3. 30m 6b/c The Moonlight Cooler Pitch. Move right over a bulge and follow a line of black pockets going left to a large but secure block under the roof (possible belay). Traverse right and use undercuts to gain the obvious ramp hold above the lip (Friend under the roof and a Friend 00 in a small diagonal quartz crack above the roof). Pull over the roof with difficulty and continue slightly left to better holds beneath the next overhang. Climb this by means of a horizontal crack and finish up the quartz corner above. Beware of rope drag.

6a The Prozac Link 50m E4 *** (1996)
A serious undertaking, difficult to retreat from.
1. 20m 5c Climb The Screaming Ab Dabs, pitch 1.
2. 25m 5b Screaming Ab Dabs, pitch 2.
3. 50m 5c Climb pitch 3 of The Screaming Ab Dabs as far as the the large block under the roof. Move left round the front of the block onto large holds, then continue traversing left beneath a curious down-pointing flake (possible belay) and onto a pink quartzy wall with difficulty (junction with Distant Voices). Climb directly up the quartzy wall as for Distant Voices and climb the ramp rightwards to finish.

SCREAMING GEO
Northwest Face
X
Y
7
1
2
3
4
Y
7
5
X
2
1
3
4
5
1 If All Else Fails
2 Hullabaloo
3 Suffering Bastard
4 Killer Fingers
5 Salty Dog
7 In the Shop on the Hill
XX and YY
unclimbed cracks

NORTH-WEST FACE, UPPER TIER

7 In the Shop on the Hill 20m E3 5c * (1988)
A short but difficult climb up the crack and scoop left of the arete. Climb the crack to a horizontal break, then go left and up with difficulty to the base of a scoop. After a difficult move, the scoop eases slightly and soon the top is reached.

7a It's Raining Rocks! 15m E3 6a * (1996)
Climb the steep initial crack of In the Shop on the Hill, then follow the prominent vertical crack above at the point where that route escapes up the easy scoop-groove on the left.

The next three routes are approached directly by abseil. This has the advantage of both avoiding a long traverse to reach the belay and avoids disturbing nesting birds. Large Friends are useful for the belay.

8 Hughy's Cocktail Mixture 25m E3 5c ** (1988)
The fine pink crack in the left wall of the corner. From the belay at the girdling break, pull round the overhang in a fine position and layback the crack above. Sustained but slightly easier climbing follows, with some deviation to finish.

8a Paranoid Slippers 30m E4 6b ** (1996)
This route takes the wall between Hughy's Cocktail Mixture and Shadow Dancer. Start up Hughy's Cocktail Mixture to pull over the roof. Traverse left on the lip (crux), then move up and left to better holds. Continue up and left to a sentry box. Finish up and leftwards past a horizontal break, left of a wide crack and on the arete overlooking Shadow Dancer.

9 Shadow Dancer 40m E7 6b *** (1993)
A wild and strenuous route taking a line of sickening exposure up the hanging arete to the right of Screaming Ab Dabs. So named because once the leader was on the arete the belayer could only monitor progress by watching his shadow. Start as for the previous route, but on pulling over the overhang make technical moves out left to good holds. Another committing move left leads to the line proper, an overhanging flake crack. Climb this ever leftwards to eventually reach a brief respite under a roof. Pull directly over this, then trend right past a peg to the base of a corner. Follow this easily to the top. A double set of Friends and some long extenders are helpful.

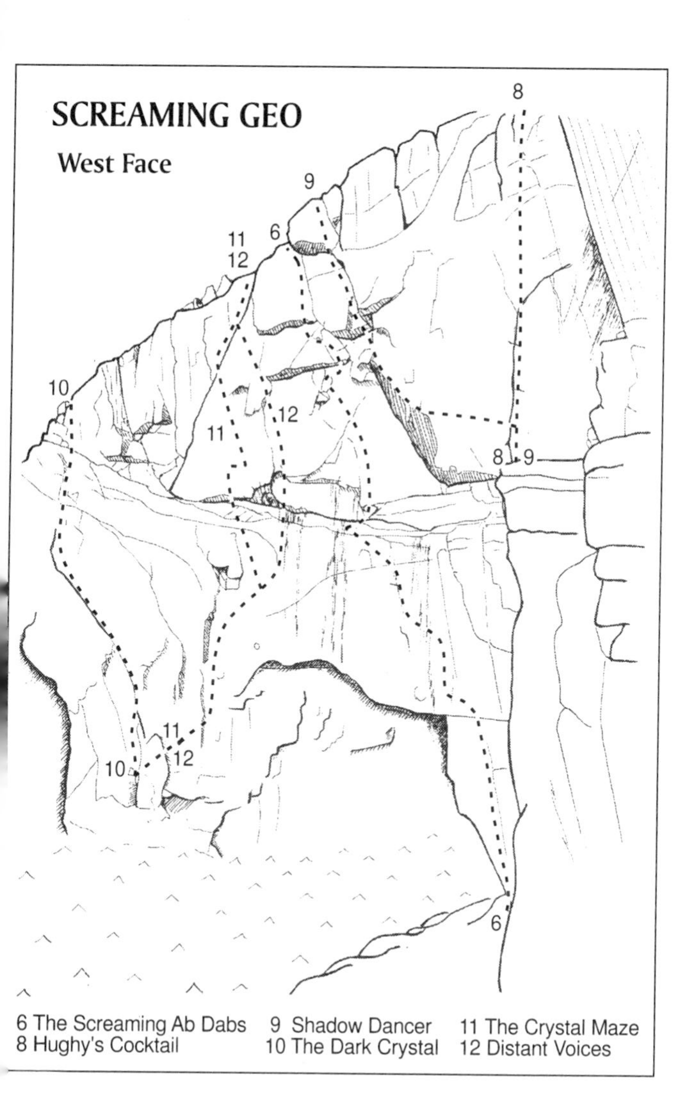
SCREAMING GEO
West Face
8
9
6
11
12
10
12
11
8
9
11
12
10
6
6 The Screaming Ab Dabs
8 Hughy's Cocktail
9 Shadow Dancer
10 The Dark Crystal
11 The Crystal Maze
12 Distant Voices

THE SCREAMING WALL

This is the west face of the Geo. The following four routes take the area of rock left of the cave, to the left of The Screaming Ab Dabs. They all have a common start on good ledges reached by a 45m abseil from large blocks above the centre of the wall.

10 The Dark Crystal 50m E2 ** (1993)
1. 25m 5b Trend up and left from the stance to reach the base of two grooves. The left-hand groove leads to blocky ledges and a belay.
2. 25m 5b Continue up and slightly left to finish up an obvious corner.

10a Grant's Bad Hair Day 50m E2 * (1996)
1. 20m 5a Start on ledges as for Dark Crystal. Traverse right until below a shattered corner, move up this and onto the front face of a precarious block. Move up to a ledge and belay.
2. 30m 5b Follow fault lines easily up and left, aiming for the left-hand end of a big overhang. Move left round the arete beneath the overhang in an exhilarating position and continue easily up and left to finish up a cracked corner, as for Dark Crystal.

11 The Crystal Maze 45m E6 *** (1993)
1. 20m 5c Take a line up and right to a stance about 5m above the lip of the cave on a small ledge.
2. 25m 6b Climb the overhanging black wall above the stance (just right of the black corner) to the roof. Cross the roof to the right of the pink quartz, moving slightly right at a horizontal break, then climb the wall above to a small overhang. Pass this on its left to a white quartzy wall, then climb this to an easy right-slanting ramp and the top.

12 Distant Voices 55m E5 ** (1993)
1. 20m 5c The Crystal Maze, pitch 1.
2. 20m 6b Climb easily up right to a break in the roof, then go back left above the roof to the comfort of some good holds on the rib. The next roof is easier and leads to a good stance above.
3. 15m 5c Trend left, then move up to reach the easy ramp of The Crystal Maze.

Lighthouse Arete 45m Hard Severe ** (1987)
This is the obvious ridge at the left end of the cliff, where it turns to face north. Abseil to the foot of the arete and climb it in two pitches.

Conundrum 50m E4 6b (1996)
This climb is on the continuation of the north-west face of The Screaming Wall, probably to the left (facing in) of Lighthouse Arete. The wall is characterised by a steep lower section and a slabby upper wall. Two dog-leg cracks split the face. Abseil from large blocks marked by a cairn to ledges at sea-level. Start 5 metres right of the right-hand dog-leg.
1. 25m 6b Follow an easy blocky right-facing open corner to below a groove. Tricky moves lead up the groove to an overhang at 10m. Move right under the overhang with hard moves up the steep wall, continuing up the overhanging groove. Move right to a small ledge and belay.
2. 25m 5a Move left from the belay and follow a right-trending quartz band towards increasingly easy ground and the top.

The following two routes are on the fin-shaped headland forming the north-west side of Leiregeo, the deep bay just north of The Screaming Wall, easily seen from Screaming Geo. The triangular pink wall has several quartz lines, and the routes are to the right of a prominent corner system which splits the face at its highest point. Approach by abseil from a large block to a small ledge just above high tide level.

Rick Campbell's Motorway Adventure 30m HVS 5a (1996)
A tricky move leads to a corner. Climb this and the slab above to reach a steep crack. Trend right past a quartz flake to the top and belay well back.

Crab Sunday 30m E2 5a (1996)
From the belay, move up and left for 3m, then go directly up the slab to a large flake corner crack at half-height. Climb this (crux) until the angle eases. Block belay well back.

RUBH'AN TAROIN (Map Ref 002 299)

Immediately north of the northern tip of the promontory which forms Rubh' an Taroin, and south of Lag ma Leatha, is a fine little bay. On the north side of the bay a short but excellent wall faces south-west. The first two routes are best approached by abseil, down the left-hand (western) side where the cliff just begins to fall back.

From a rough layby (Map Ref 005 298), walk across to the north of Mullach an Taroin (not shown on the 1:50 000 map, but it is the highest hill at this point), climbing down a dip and rising back up again to reach the short cropped grass at the top of the Rubh' an Taroin promontory.

A word of warning. Do not be taken in by the non-serious ambience and short length of the climbs here (particularly in the area of the Taroin Chimneys). It is not uncommon to experience freak waves which appear to roll out of virtually nowhere and engulf the entire cliff!

Moac Wall 30m E1 5b *** (1974)
Start at the left side of the superb wall. Climb gently overhanging pock-marked rock, then trend left, crossing some small overlaps at two-thirds height. Well protected.

Twelve Years On 30m E1/2 5b *** (1986)
Climb the crack line just to the right of Moac Wall (almost the same start), through some overhangs, then more or less direct to the top.

Just south (on the west side) of the northern tip of the Rubh' an Taroin promontory is another shallow bay which contains four routes on its north side, also facing south-west. A prominent block on the cliff edge is an identifiable feature. Approach by abseil. **Sea Star** (VS) is located towards the left side of the wall. **Ken's Dilemma** (E1) is left of centre, and **Red Ramp** (Very Difficult) is next to the right. In the back of the bay is **Bay Back Crack** (Severe).

The southern tip of the promontory contains another fine little bay with lots of fun routes, mostly in the lower grades. Between this bay and the bay containing Red Ramp are the prominent **Taroin Chimneys**. Both chimneys are climbed at VS, but they are serious due to a lack of protection. On the rib to the right of the right-hand chimney, a line of shallow grooves has been climbed at E2, taking the line of least resistance cutting back leftwards.

AIRD FENISH HEAD (Map Ref 991 295)

This can be reached in about 15 minutes from the road at a point about 6½km from Ardroil and 1½km north of Islivig.

Route Major 60m Severe (1971)
There is a gigantic overlapped slab on the southern side of the Head. Tide permitting, climb from its foot *via* an obvious left-hand corner crack, crossing an overlap (crux). Then follow a vertical corner on huge loose holds, and finish by moving right to the centre of the slab.

AIRD UIG AREA

This region encompasses the coastline between Camus Uig and Gallen Beag, Gallen Head being out of bounds according to the RAF. For convenience of access, the coast has been split into two sections. Going from north to south, Chapel Head includes all the crags between Gallen Beag and Geodha Nasavig, while Camus Uig covers the crags running north from Sheilavig Skerry to Ceodha Gunna.

The whole coastline provides a wealth of little (some not so little) coves and crags, most of which have been explored over the past 15 years. However, due to a lack of documentation and with much of the information written up from memory, not all of the crags are described with as much detail as some might like, so be prepared to experience some difficulty in finding a number of the geos in this section.

CHAPEL HEAD

From Ardroil, go north passing Timsgarry and go through Aird Uig village. Enter the disused radio station, immediately turn left at Smuggler's Restaurant, go through a gate and follow a land rover track which ends at a building overlooking Loch a' Beannaich.

BLACK WALL (Map Ref 037 380)

South of Gallen Beag (and 100 metres north of Chapel Geo, level with a Lochan; see map) there is a 20m black wall with a prominent corner on the right-hand side. Higher and to the right again are some brown-coloured rocks, below which is a fine tidal pool.

Chapel Crack 20m Hard Severe * (1986)
Climb the corner direct, with a through-route to finish if required.

Diving Board 30m Severe * (1986)
From the bottom of Chapel Crack, climb diagonally left to a prominent traverse line. Follow this to a belay at 15m. Climb up 6m and take a narrow broken slab on the left to the top.

Colonel Huff 15m Severe * (1986)
Start left of Diving Board. Climb a prominent short V-shaped cleft and move onto a ledge. Climb a prominent crack to the top.

Around the Bend 30m Very Difficult * (1986)
Follow the line of Diving Board, but keep 6m higher all the time and take a broader and higher gangway to the left to finish.

Sallie's Dilemma 12m VS * (1986)
Break out right halfway up Chapel Crack and follow a short curving groove, with a mantelshelf at the top. A broad ramp leads off to the right and a hard direct finish on the left, *via* a small overhang, where one runner was used for aid.

To the right the crag falls back into a small rocky bay. The first corner line around the corner is:

Coloured Rain 25m E1 5b ** (1988)
Climb the corner direct, with hard moves at about 10m and 20m; well protected.

Right again around another corner the crag becomes undercut and there is a square-topped sentry box high up. Just to the right again is another corner with small overhangs at two-thirds height.

Shadows in the Sun 35m E1/2 5b ** (1988)
Traverse into the corner from the right for about 12m to avoid the undercut start. Climb the corner and its overhangs direct for a strenuous finish.

To locate the following climb, look for a cairn which is about 150 metres north of the boundary wall beside the outlet from Geodh a' Bheannaich. From the cairn, continue for a further 100 metres. The cliff is unappealing to look at, and if there is any doubt, the back wall of the geo is directly in line with a lochan and the radio masts of Gallen Head.

Here Today Gone Tomorrow 35m E4 6a ** (1993)
This route takes the unattractive sea-facing wall at the back of the geo. Follow a vague crack until it becomes easier to move onto the wall on the right at about 25m. The whole of this buttress is severely undermined and may not be there for much longer!

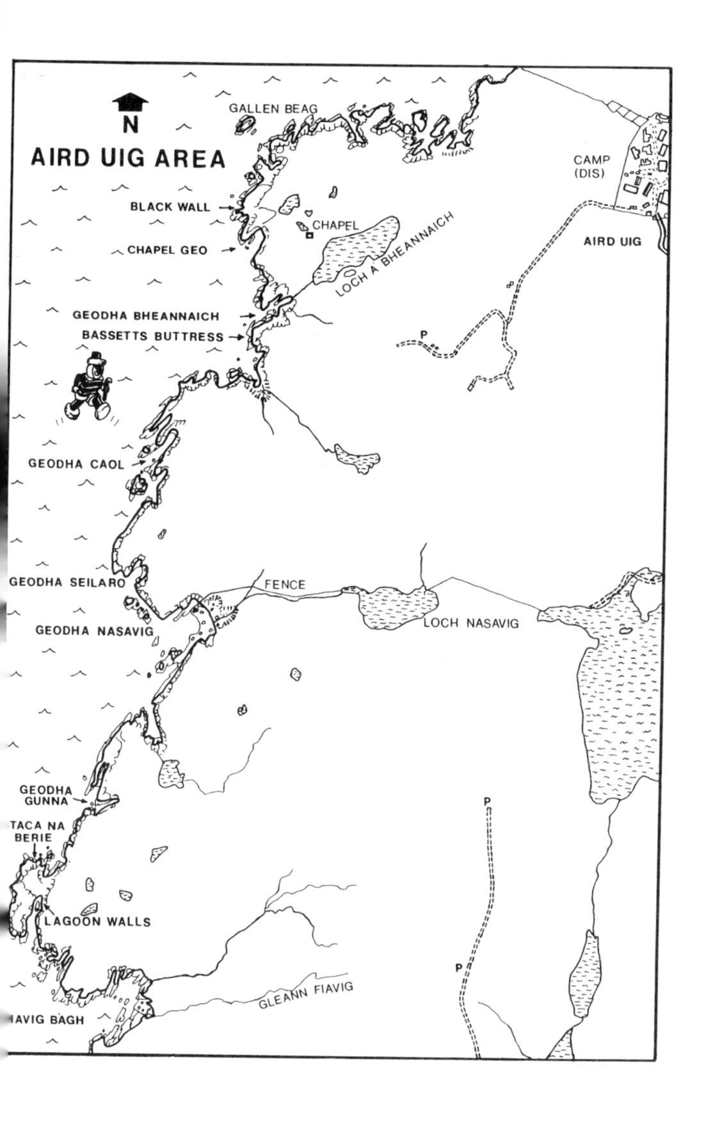
N
AIRD UIG AREA
GALLEN BEAG
CAMP
(DIS)
BLACK WALL
CHAPEL
CHAPEL GEO
LOCH A BHEANNAICH
AIRD UIG
GEODHA BHEANNAICH
BASSETTS BUTTRESS
P
GEODHA CAOL
GEODHA SEILARO
FENCE
LOCH NASAVIG
GEODHA NASAVIG
GEODHA
GUNNA
TACA NA
BERIE
P
LAGOON WALLS
P
GLEANN FIAVIG
AVIG BAGH

There is some uncertainty regarding the location of the following climbs. They may be immediately south of the entrance to Here Today Gone Tomorrow. To reach the climbs, scramble diagonally down from the south, seaward side. There are good ledges at the bottom of the climbs. One identifiable feature is an obvious large flake which gives the line of Whimp's Chimney. The descent is just to the south of this (or by abseil). The climbs are described from right to left (facing the cliff).

Whimp's Chimney 40m Severe * (1986)
Climb the prominent chimney direct, surmounting the chockstone at half-height with difficulty.

'Cor Blimey Corner 30m VS 4c * (1986)
Climb the prominent corner to the left of Whimp's Chimney, which can be reached by climbing some black rocks to gain the upper corner.

Scoosh Case 30m HVS 5b * (1988)
The stepped rib between Whimp's Chimney and 'Cor Blimey Corner is hard to start, then trends left. It is possible to escape right at half-height into Whimp's Chimney, but this spoils the fun.

Cuthron 25m E1 5b * (1986)
Left again from 'Cor Blimey Corner, there is a prominent slightly overhanging crack high up. Reach this *via* a short corner; there is an opportunity to break out left partway up.

Hitman 35m E2 ** (1988)
Follow Cuthron for about 12m, then move out left and make some trying moves to a ledge. Continue the left trend and make a sensational pull up around the corner to a very fine and airy left traverse to finish.

GEODH' A' BHEANNAICH (Map Ref 037 377)

This is easily reached from the parking place by walking due west for 5 minutes. It lies immediately north of an old boundary wall and the outlet from Loch a' Bheannaich, and is best viewed from the south side of the outlet. The cliff is a long projecting slabby buttress of reddish rock and features an obvious crack line near the left end, below which is a convenient belay ledge above high water, next to a little cave.

Juggy Crack 25m Severe * (1993)
Gain the ledge by abseil and follow the crack in its entirety.

BASSETT'S BUTTRESS (Map Ref 037 376)

This buttress lies about midway between Geodh' a' Bheannaich and Geodha Chruidh, about 200 metres south of the former. When viewed from the west side of Geodha Chruidh, an impressive and deep narrow inlet borders its south side. Look out for a square-cut projection covered in yellow lichen when locating the top. The buttress sports a handful of pleasant climbs, all of which are easily approached directly by abseil. The right edge, finishing up a corner is VS; the crack to the left is Severe, and the wall about 20 metres to the left again is 'Heel Hooker's Wall, a pleasant though not over protected Severe.

GEODHA CAOL (Map Ref 034 373)

This fine atmospheric geo lies about 200 metres south of Geodha Chruidh. It consists of two parallel inlets which are separated by an 10m wide promontory. The climbs are on the south-east (landward)-facing wall of the inner inlet. The wall is easily identified and features a prominent right-facing corner (Into the Sea), and a quartz rib which juts into the north-west corner at the back of the geo.

1 Spike Fright 40m VS 4c * (1985)
From the belay of Into the Sea, traverse out left and climb a crack through the overlap. Continue up the enjoyable wall above to the top.

2 Into the Sea 40m E1 5b ** (1985)
Gain the foot of the corner by abseil. Depending on the state of the tide, there is a good square-cut ledge. Climb up and right to a thin crack, then follow it into the upper part of the slabby corner. This leads to the top.

3 Scoopy Do 40m VS
About 30 metres to the right of the above two routes, a right-facing corner ends halfway up the cliff where a diagonal crack-fault cuts across it. To the left of this corner, a shallow line of weakness runs diagonally left and up, giving quite a bold climb.

About 500 metres to the south, a number of short fine routes have been done in Geodha Seilaro (Map Ref 034 369).

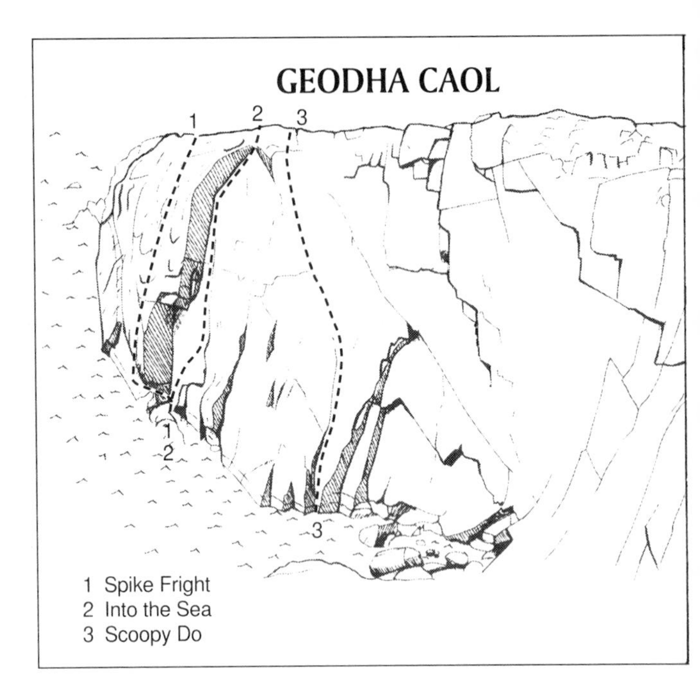

CAMUS UIG

Go north, passing Timsgarry on the road to Aird Uig, and take the last turnoff to the left (the first after the school) towards Crowlista. After 1km, the road turns sharply south. Just before this bend, go north on a landrover track, past a disused quarry on the left, and park the car opposite the crag of your choice.

The small crags opposite Sheilavig Skerry (Map Ref 026 343) provide some good climbing on short clean rock, as does the area around Geodha Ruadh (Map Ref 027 347). Just north of here, at Map Ref 029 353, is Torcaso (not shown on the 1:50 000 maps) which lies just north of Sgeir Fiavig Tarras and south of Fiavig Bagh. To the north of the area is a lovely tidal pool flanked by several low grade routes of about 20-30m. A few metres south is a deep 40-50m geo with a steep north wall which provides two VS/HVS routes up obvious fault lines.

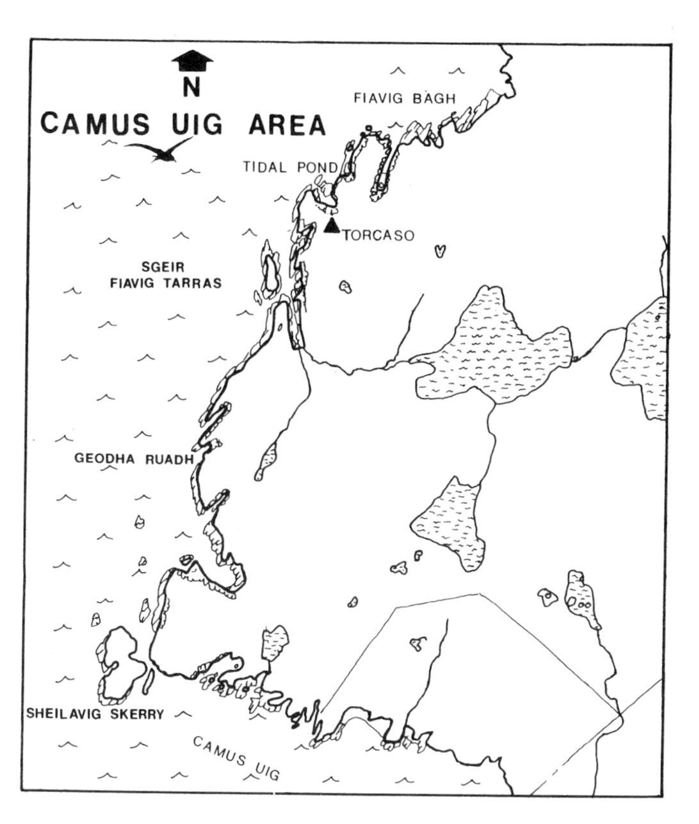

Approach is by a big abseil, with no easy way out. South again for a few metres there is a lovely little inlet running almost north-south, the southern end being almost opposite Sgeir Fiavig Tarras. Four or five climbs have been found here up to HVS, one being a fine crocodile fault line with a steep finish. There is good clean rock throughout this area, although none of it is very high. This is not a place to be with a big sea running, although on a fine day it is glorious.

North again is the lovely little headland of Staca na Berie (Map Ref 031 359), which has been explored fairly extensively over several years. Although the routes are fairly short, there are plenty of them and the situations are superb. The rock is good to nearly perfect.

The area itself takes the form of a waisted headland with a small inlet to the north and a bigger one to the south. The headland itself is penetrated by a hole or 'gloop', the bottom of which can be reached by a difficult traverse around to the north at low tide; otherwise you can abseil in. Either way there are three routes back out of the hole from Very Difficult to VS, all up obvious fault lines, and all making fine expeditions.

The inlet to the south is correctly named Sail na Berie, but has been named the Lagoon, with the flanking walls called the Lagoon Walls. The 20m west wall of the lagoon has yielded several brilliant little climbs in the VS to E1 bracket, reached by abseil or traverse. A nice-looking diagonal fault has been climbed (a bit loose) and so has a steep little crack, and there is a superb corner crack of excellent rock. On the steep west wall proper, the left wall has been top-roped at VS. The eastern side is good but not steep, and several short routes have been climbed. Apart from some climbing on the promontory of Staca na Berie, there are some chimneys worth doing on the south-west (seaward) side of the Berie.

Just a few metres to the north of Staca na Berie (midway between Berie and Geodha Gunna) is a fine little bay of clean, gently overhanging rock with some fierce little crack and fault lines at around E2. This includes a central crack which succumbed only after pulling on a few runners. Another fine line to the left was climbed at about HVS with a couple of ramps lower down going at Difficult to Very Difficult.

GEODHA GUNNA (Map Ref 033 363)

This geo can be reached by a 30-minute walk from the Aird Uig car park or in 15 minutes from the Camus Uig carpark. It is distinguished by the beautiful orange slab and 'Separate Reality' crack through the headwall above on the north wall of the geo.

Brutal Reality 30m E6 6b *** (1993)
The pleasant slab is followed by a brutally overhanging hand crack which, with a bit of luck, leads to the top.

Going north again there are some fine climbs to be found on Geodha Nasavaig, which has a fiendish-looking overhanging wall on the south side. There is also a brilliant little black slab and corner hidden away somewhere between Geodha Nasavaig and Geodha Seilaro. Other individual gems may be found in the Geodha Seilaro area.

THE DALBEG AREA

Dalbeg is about 30 minutes drive from Stornoway. Take the A857 north to Barvas, then follow the A858 south towards Bragar and Carloway. Dalbeg Village is about 2km from South Shawbost and 500 metres off the main road. A more scenic route goes *via* the famous Callanish Standing Stones (cafe) and doesn't take much longer.

There is a camping and caravan site at Dalbeg Bay with a number of B&Bs and guest houses in the area. Provisions and fuel can be purchased in Dalbeg and nearby Shawbost.

Approach and Access
The headland north of Dalbeg beach is split by an obvious deep slot. A large boulder sits prominently at the top of this. Walk through the fields to the top of the headland. The seaward side of the slot forms a narrow buttress with an arch through it at the bottom. The seaward wall of this buttress offers several fine routes on good rock.

Topography
The wall itself is split by an obvious quartz crack running diagonally right to left (Limpet Crack) and there are two groove lines further right, not visible from above. Access is by abseil or by scrambling down a gully towards the sea before traversing left (as you face the sea) onto easy-angled slabs.

The left end of the wall has a ramp line up its side which forms a stepped corner where it meets the wall; this is Rampling (Very Difficult). The left edge of the ramp, finishing up a short crack, is VS.

On the wall proper are two slanting crack lines, the right-hand one and higher of the two (Limpet Crack) offers the better climb. To the right, starting at half-height in the centre of the wall, is a groove line running to the left (Neptune). The arch at the right-hand end of the wall has two groove lines above it, one starting to the left of the arch the other a few feet to the right. The routes are described from left to right.

Damp Down 35m E3 6a (1989)
The lower of the two crack lines is a bit artificial as it is possible to step down onto the ramp in a few places. Start up Rampling until it is possible to pull onto the wall using a flake. Make hard moves left along the crack under a small roof to a foothold, then go up the left-hand of two cracks to a flat handhold. From this, reach right into the right-hand crack and follow it to the top.

Limpet Crack 40m E3 5c *** (1989)
The impressive diagonal quartz crack line running left from the middle of the wall gives an excellent pitch with the crux at mid-height.

Neptune a Calling 35m E5 6b (1989)
Start up a blunt rib left of Neptune which leads to a small roof after 7m. From there, make difficult moves left to a small horizontal slot, then go left again to a vertical crack before moving up to a large flake. Now climb right into a shallow corner and go up to the finishing grooves of Neptune.

Neptune 40m E2 5c (1989)
There is a left-slanting groove line starting at mid-height in the centre of the wall. Start up the wall below this (5 metres right of Limpet Crack), enter the groove and follow it to the top.

Wave Watcher 45m E4 (1989)
1. 25m 6a Climb the left-hand of the two grooves left of the arch, with a strenuous start.
2. 20m 4c Finish up the left arete of the buttress.

Underneath The Arches 45m E4 (1989)
This climb is affected by high tide; be warned, this sea has a big swell on it. The climb takes the front of the buttress, but the crux is getting to it.
1. 20m 6a Start at the left side of the arch and climb the right-hand groove rightwards under the roof to the slab.
2. 25m 4c Finish up the left arete of the buttress.

Dalbeg Buttress 60m HVS (1989)
1. 15m 5b From just above the sea, lean across the gap to the right side of the arch. Using an RP1 as a handhold, step across the gap and heelhook to get onto a ledge; this can be very slimy, and may have to be timed to miss the waves. Once on the ledge, climb up a few metres and belay below an overlap.
2. 20m 5a Go onto the front of the buttress and climb up, weaving through three overlaps. Take the top one by its left arete.
3. 25m 4a Climb the slab above, then the corner in the middle of the slab.

THE EAST WALL

On the east (landward) side of the black slot, there is an easy-angled slab with a wall facing to sea with two corners. The next three routes are on this wall. **Celtic Ray** (20m VS 4b, 1990) takes the first corner, **Don't Break My Raybans** (20m HVS 5a, 1990) takes the wall between the two corners, trending right to the arete to finish, and **Born to Fly** (20m HVS 5a, 1990) takes the second corner.

CAVE SLAB

From the descent to the Dalbeg Buttress, turn right (facing out) at the top of the descent slab. The left end of the slab is undercut by a large cave, whereas the right side runs to a series of steep grooves below an orange-coloured slab with a crack line running up its center. The routes are described from left to right.

The Black Hole 45m E4 6b (1989)
This route takes the crack in the overlap at the far left-hand end, starting by moving into a wide undercut niche. Hard moves over the next overlap lead into a short steep corner. Swing right and follow the crack in the slab left of the overhang to finish up a short corner.

Simple Jim 35m E3 6a (1989)
Start by hard moves up the crack 3 metres right of the last route. Follow the red slab up to a roof, then traverse left and pull over the overlap at a quartz vein. Move up and traverse right to the base of a steep corner. Climb this past a huge block and finish leftwards.

Beam Me Up Scotty 30m E1 5b (1989)
Follow a left-trending black ramp line to pull into a niche at the base of the final crack (crux), then climb the wide crack in the easy red finishing slab.

Bones 30m Severe (1989)
Start just right of the previous route and climb up to gain the thinner right-hand crack in the red finishing slab.

King on Corner 25m E1 5a (1989)
The smooth groove at the right side of the red slab is a bit loose in places.

The next routes, at the extreme left end of the slab above the sea, are reached by walking round the headland of Cave Slab and abseiling down a short sea-facing wall to a sloping platform. An overlap at the right side gives access to the extreme left end of Cave Slab. Left of the overlap are two grooves which provide the lines of the second and third routes. The routes are described from the abseil point rightwards.

Warp Drive 15m VS 4c (1989)
The pocketed wall which is the line of the abseil has a crack and a shallow groove running up it 3 metres left of Dilithium Crystals. Climb the wall.

Dilithium Crystals 20m HVS 5a (1989)
Climb the second groove left of the overlap on good cracks and pockets.

It's No Good Captain, She's Breaking Up 20m HVS 4c (1989)
Start up a ramp, harder than it looks, then move into the first groove left of the overlap.

Captain's Log 30m HVS 5a (1989)
Cross the overlap at its lowest point, move over two small overlaps onto the top slab, then head towards a groove capped by an overhang. Climb the crack on the left of this to the top.

BLACK ZAWN

The next zawn north to Cave Wall is marked by two large cairns at its top. There is an easy slab on its northern side and a steep back wall split by Old Salt, a left-slanting quartz crack starting from a ledge halfway up the wall, above a cave. The black south wall has a ledge running up left from the sea and ending by some large flakes, used as a belay point. The top of the wall has three prominent corners, the largest (left-hand) one being taken by Sea Shanty. The middle shorter one is Briny and to the right of this is the left-facing corner of Salty Old Sea Dog.

The routes are reached by abseiling down the wall to the right of center, and moving along the ledge. They can also be reached by climbing down at low tide from the bottom of the abseil into Warp Drive (described above).

Sea Shanty 40m HVS 5a (1989)
From the left end of the ledge, move up and left to light coloured rock and a ledge system trending left. From the bottom of the corner move up and exit right at its top.

Briny 35m E1 5b (1989)
From the same start, move up a faint blunt rib above the belay (directly below the V of the corner) to some overhanging unstable-looking blocks. Weave left through these to the start of a good crack, then move into the top corner.

Salty Old Sea Dog 30m VS 4c (1989)
Start 5 metres right of the previous route. Climb a short corner to a ledge, then go up a crack until it is possible to move left into the bottom of the corner. Follow this to the top.

Sea Monster 30m Hard Severe 4b (1989)
Immediately right of the last route is a corner facing the sea. A steep start leads to a ledge at half-height, then climb a crack at the left side of the ledge to a final steep finish.

Navy Cut 30m HVS 5a (1989)
Follow the two-tiered corner at the right end of the black wall.

No Fags for Christmas 15m VS 4c (1989)
This route takes the groove at the seaward end of the west-facing wall, about 7 metres right of Navy Cut.

The back wall of the zawn has a quartz crack running from a ledge above a cave at its bottom right side. Abseil down to the ledge, a full rope length with the belay well back.

Old Salt 40m E3 5c (1989)
From the left end of the ledge follow the quartz crack diagonally left for about 30m to a ledge. It would be possible to finish up a groove above here. However, the crack continues at ledge level, so step down and follow it left to its finish.

Parting Shot 45m E3 ** (1996)
This is a direct line up the back wall. Approach down the slab.
1. 20m 6a Start at the right-hand of two grooves. Gain the pod by awkward moves, then move right at its top, go round the overhang and climb the groove to a fine cave belay.

2. 25m 5b Move up and left for 3m, then go straight up *via* a down-pointing fang into the final groove. Take care with the rock.

SMALL WEST WALL

From the headland north of the black zawn, drop down (moving away from the black zawn) to a black rock platform with a pool in it about 20m above the sea. To the right of the pool is an easy-angled wall with an overhang at the bottom. This has been climbed at Hard Severe, starting from the right or with a 5c direct start. This is bounded on its right by two corners, Original Route and Solitude, and 10 metres further right is the wide overhanging crack-chimney of Mongrel.

Original Route 10m Very Difficult (1989)
The obvious corner right of the slab. It is possible to move out onto the wall near the top at Hard Severe.

Solitude 10m VS 4c (1989)
To the right is another corner with an awkward start.

Sunday Stroll 10m VS 4c (1990)
Start as for Solitude, then swing right onto the nose of the arete and go round to a ledge. Finish up the wall at the back.

Hang It 10m HVS 5a (1989)
To the right, a short overhanging crack leads to the ledge.

Mongrel 10m VS 4c (1989)
Ascend the overhanging squeeze chimney right of Hang It.

The centre of the wall below and left of the rock platform has a groove capped by an overhang with a hanging plaque of rock to its left. The bottom of the wall can be reached by abseil or by scrambling down stepped ledges from the platform. The routes are described from right to left.

Tea For Two 15m VS 4c (1989)
Climb the shallow corner right of the overhang, starting up a crack. A variation start up the slab to the left is possible at 5b.

Down Under 15m E2 6a (1990)
Climb the groove to the left to the overhang, then move over this on good finger jams

Gleaning the Bone 15m E2 5c (1989)
Climb the narrow pillar with a hanging plaque of rock to the left of the groove.

Flying Teapot 15m HVS 5c (1989)
Climb the groove left of the narrow pillar.

Left of Flying Teapot past a blunt arete is an easy-angled wall, **Henry's Hard Times** (Severe). The corner to its left is Difficult. Left again is an overhang with cracks going to its left and right sides.

Endurance 15m E4 6b (1990)
This takes the corner and crack through the right side of the roof. Climb the corner to the bottom of the groove. Awkward moves up the groove lead to the overhang. A foothold on the right helps progress through the overhang to the headwall and a sloping finish.

Ruth's Lazy Day 20m Hard Severe (1989)
Climb the groove left of the overhang.

Clean Hand Gang 20m E3 5b (1990)
This takes the wall to the left as directly as possible. Start at the right side of the wall, then make moves up and left to a good hold. A long reach to a flat incut leads to good holds trending right to a ledge. Climb the edge of the groove to the top.

Jessie James 20m E2 5b (1990)
Climb the right side of the arete forming the left end of the wall to a good hold. Move left to good but spaced holds on the arete to reach a ledge. Finish by moving up and left into Outlaw.

The next three routes take the three grooves to the left.

Outlaw 20m HVS 5a (1989)
Climb the groove immediately left of the arete, exiting up the corner.

Robbery Under Arms 20m E1 5b (1989)
Climb the middle of the three grooves, starting up the left-hand series of cracks and small ledges. Continue up to the hanging nose, then step right to finish.

Thuggery 20m HVS 5b (1989)
Climb the left-hand groove, starting up a corner past a flake to continue through the roof.

BIG WEST WALL

Immediately after the groove of Thuggery, the wall gains height and is capped by an overhang with a corner running through it at either end. The wall curves round into the next zawn where a recess offers two corner climbs up either side.

New World 25m E1 5b (1990)
Start up a steep groove left of Thuggery, just right of the overhang which runs along the bottom of the wall. At the top of the groove move right to a ledge, then climb the wall to the prominent corner at the right end of the top roof.

Island of No Return 35m HVS 5a (1990)
There is a square-cut groove capped by a small roof about 7 metres left of where the overhang running along the bottom of the wall ends. Move up to the top of the groove, then hand traverse right to a foothold and ascend the cracks to a basalt intrusion. Move to a ledge on the right, then go up to another ledge. Traverse left into the bottom of the corner which marks the left end of the top overhang.

Chew the Route 30m E4 6a ** (1996)
This route takes the hanging arete leading rightwards from New Addition. Start as for that route and climb its flake chimney to the ledge. Move right onto the arete to reach a big undercling. Gain the crack and groove (crux), then make sustained moves using the arete to a fine belay ledge.

New Addition 40m HVS 5a (1990)
Climb the right-hand corner of the recess about 5 metres left of the previous route, then take a flake chimney which leads to a ledge. Climb the corner to the top.

First Born 40m VS 4c (1990)
Climb the left-hand corner of the recess to a ledge, then go up a wall before stepping left into a shallow chimney and corner leading to the top.

Crow Road 35m E2 5c * (1996)
Start 3 metres left of First Born at the base of the right-trending groove. Follow the groove trending right onto the arete. Move steeply through the small roof split by a crack (crux) to gain the groove above that leads to the top.

PREACHER ZAWN

The next zawn north has a large block leaning against the wall and a fence ending at its top. The center of the north wall is cut by the wide crack of Red Hand Gang.

Blessed Are the Weak 45m E4/5 6a *** (1996)
This brilliant route takes a direct line up the face left of Red Hand Gang. Climb Red Hand Gang for about 6m, then make a long step left and climb up and left aiming for the centre of a horizontal overlap. Cross this and go up direct to a good ledge. Climb the hanging flake above, then go up slightly right on pocketed rock to a crack and finish at the highest point of the cliff.

Red Hand Gang 35m E2 5b (1989)
Ascend the prominent crack near the collapsed block. Loose.

Mr Big Comes Clean 30m E2 5c (1989)
To the right of Red Hand Gang are three corners. Climb the one furthest to the right.

A Prophet's Doom 20m E3 6a (1990)
Climb the sustained crack line 3 metres right of the previous route.

GEODHA NA MUA

A ten-minute walk south from Dalbeg Bay leads to a wide valley with a stream which runs down into the head of the zawn. The zawn is characterised by a large spire which splits its centre; there is an easy scramble down at the back of the zawn.

Prawn in the USA 40m E2 5a/b (1996)
On the left-hand side of the zawn (facing out) a large block rests against the wall. Just beyond this is a cave with a chimney rising out of its left-hand side. Start just left of the cave. Move up until it is possible

to step right onto the slab above the cave. Climb up right into a corner and ascend this for 4m before moving right at a striated area onto a bulging buttress of light grey rock. Follow good holds up right to protection under a bulge. Climb directly through the bulge and go up a left-trending crack to where it becomes horizontal. Move straight up past horizontal breaks to the right edge of the pinnacle by a pink intrusion, then trend left to the top.

STORM ZAWN

This zawn is about 15 minutes south of Dalbeg Bay at Map Ref 218 459. There is an area of cliff between the sharp inlet of Geodha Sporain and the promontory of Rubha na h'Airde. Descend by abseil down easy-angled ground at Rubha na h'Airde and traverse left (facing in) into the bay. At the left-hand end of the bay is a wave-cut platform below the most compact area of cliff.

The Storm 50m E5 6a *** (1996)
A brilliant route. Start at the far left-hand end of the wave-cut platform where an overhang ends in the left-hand of two cracks. Climb the crack for 15m to a ledge. Climb straight up for 3m before moving left to climb a vague flake. Move back right and go up to the notch in the overhang. Exit rightwards over this into a slabby groove and follow this to broken ground and a ledge on the right. There is an inadequate belay at the end of a 50m rope. On the first ascent a rope was left some 25m down the cliff and was used to abseil off. However an easy traverse right of some 6 metres leads to the finishing cracks of the next route.

It's HVS Glen, but not as we know it 50m E4 5c ** (1996)
Start from the top of a raised blocky area at the right-hand end of the platform. From the centre of the platform go slightly left up a corner-groove to a good ledge beneath a down-pointing spike at 12m. The spike becomes a hanging right-facing corner. Make a few moves up a ramp on the right, then step left into the corner and layback up to a ledge. With hands on the ledge step left to the foot of a crack, then follow the crack with difficulty to a capping block. Chimney up the left-hand side, then continue more easily to a belay at the horizontal cracks just below the top as the rope runs out.

DUN OTHAIL (Map Ref 544 515)

From the end of the road from North Tolsta to Garry beach, continue up the peat road until it veers inland, then head north and after 20 minutes walking the castle-like crag is easily seen on the coast.

The Bay just north of the tower offers a few climbs. About 400 metres north of the tower is a wall with four large boulders at the bottom. The following two routes can be reached by abseil down this wall.

Haar 15m Severe (1989)
Climb the slabby wall immediately above the four large boulders.

The Milky Bar Kid 20m VS (1989)
North of the four boulders is a large arched roof, then a south-facing corner. Start up a ramp on the right of the corner, then move into the main corner-chimney.
Direct Start: E1 5c
Start up the steep jaming crack which forms the bottom of the chimney.

THE GREY TOWER

From the last routes it is possible to see two obvious corner lines on the grey tower.

Celtic Swing 65m E1 (1989)
This climb follows the right-hand corner.
1. 4a Climb the wall and corner to belay on a ledge with some loose rock.
2. 5b/c Step up from the belay, then traverse left to a short corner and go up right to a large ledge. Alternatively, climb straight up a crack from the belay, then go left to the large ledge. From the ledge, take the left-hand crack to a belay.
3. 4c Follow the corner until below a large pillar. Traverse left to exit.

Druid 65m E2 (1989)
A companion route which follows the left-hand corner line.
1. 10m 5a Climb the wall to the right of the corner and belay on the ledge.

2. 35m 5b Step around the corner and climb it to an obvious large ledge and belay.
3. 20m 5a Continue up the corner to finish.

To descend from these two routes, climb up about 15m and traverse east on grass ledges. Move a few metres onto the north wall, then go down heather followed by some delicate down climbing. Alternatively, descend by abseil.

On the south side of the tower, below the grass, are three obvious open corners at sea-level. **State of Mind** (20m E1 5a, 1989) takes the one on the right and **Cloud Burst** (20m E2 5b, 1989) follows the one on the left.

North and South Uist

NORTH UIST

North Uist presents a number of small sea-cliffs with many climbs in the lower to middle grades. The climate is similar to that of Lewis and Harris but the island, or rather the cliffs, are free from the agonising midge. Go and see for yourself! Access to Lochmaddy is *via* ferry from from Uig in Skye or Tarbert in Harris.

LEAC NA HOE POINT (Map Ref 980 725)

This collection of crags is on the north-east tip of North Uist. From Lochmaddy, take the road to Solas, then turn off to Loch Portain. Before reaching Cheese Bay, turn right to the east and park the car at Map Ref 973 732. Go past a white cottage, then contour the coastline about 30m up to reach the crag after 15-20 minutes.

In general the rock is good but requires some care. The first crag to be reached, a 20m black wall, is steep and does not seep after rain, making it an ideal bad weather option. A scramble down the right side of the crag at low tide gives access to the climbs. A shelf also leads to the next crag at low water. Routes are described from right to left.

The King of the Swingers 20m E1 5b
Start beneath a set of parallel cracks at the extreme right-hand side of the cliff. Climb the cracks, then make some bold moves on friable rock to gain a ledge. Climb the final steep section and finish leftwards up the slight arete.

The Babe 20m E3 5b *
Follow the central crack line direct with difficult moves at half-height and at the top.

Bird on a Wire 20m E4 6a **
The left arete is the steepest part of the crag and requires a certain amount of stamina and imagination. Follow the arete for the first couple of moves, then arrange good gear in the crack to the left. Step right and climb steeply to a good rest on the right. Regain the arete and a good ledge. Continue on good holds to a left-slanting crack which leads to the top.

A better and more sustained route follows Bird on a Wire to the bottom of the diagonal crack, then traverses right into The Babe.

The next cliff around from the black wall sports the most adventurous routes in the area. The rock is also the most friable but still worth climbing on. Either abseil from two metal stakes set about 10m back from the edge of the cliff, or walk left around the ledge from the foot of the previous cliff. The crag faces east and features an obvious corner-gully on the left. Some care should be taken during the nesting season. The climbs are described from right to left.

The Spark Severe 4a
This route follows a line of vertical broken cracks. A steep section at half-height is not that difficult but protection is not forthcoming.

The Flame Severe 4a
Start as for The Spark but instead of going straight up follow the left-slanting crack line to the rounded arete on the left. Continue winding your way to the top.

Jex's Midnight Runners VS 4c *
On the left side of the rounded arete is an obvious straight crack. Follow the crack to half-height, then step right and continue to the top.

The Sock That Got Away Hard Severe 4b *
Climb the steep broken crack line on the other side of the gully in a wild position (unusual rock). At half-height pass a small overhang, then continue up and right; at the top bridge the groove-gully for a good rest.

The next cliff is around the corner from the platform and is easily recognised by two large stakes. The crag is south-facing and offers a variety of features and climbing styles. The only approach is by abseil from two stakes (backed up by wires). Care should be taken when the rope is running over the edge.

Minnie the Mooch 25m VS 5a
Around the corner from the platform area is a hidden recess with a black slab on its left, a steep wall and crack on the right and two obvious crack lines in the middle. Follow the left, shorter, crack line to the junction with the slabby arete on the left-hand side; belay. Follow a rugged groove and a short steep right-slanting crack to the top.

The Arete 12m Difficult
The next area of cliff around to the left has the same top section. The bottom 12m sports three separate lines. The left-hand line is a broken crack and the arete, which is very obvious from the top.

The next set of cliffs can be easily seen from the vantage point near the top of the Leac na Hoe. Two obvious ramp lines are an identifiable feature. From the top of Minnie the Mooch, walk around the top of the cliffs to an obvious gully and ramp line going down to the sea. Alternatively, starting 30 metres further round, descend the upper ramp line to a stake (large sling to back it up). A short abseil leads to the start of the routes.

The crag faces south-east and is quick drying. It is characterised by three main cracks. The climbs are described from right to left.

Arms Like Twiggy 15m E3 5c **
The steepest route in North Uist. Follow the well protected crack on good jams.

The Hole with the Mint in It 15m Hard Severe 4b **
Climb the first and obvious corner easily at first, with some problematic moves near the top. Well protected.

Cearn Dusgaidh 15m VS 4c ***
Climb the second and steeper corner crack with good moves near the top.

The Lonely Runner 20m E1 5a *
Walk along the ramp as far as possible and traverse to the start of shattered cracks. Go up and left of the cracks to finish in an exposed position on solid ledges but with little gear.

The Ramp 12m Moderate
Follow the ramp from its lowest point to finish through a gap at the top. This is commonly used as a descent route.

RUBHA AN DUINE (Map Ref 974 718)

This crag is easily identifiable from the north of the bay. It features a large damp vegetated crack left of centre and a dark-streaked wall with a ledge halfway up on the right-hand side. The crag faces north-east and is usually wet after prolonged periods of rain, but note that the dark peat-stained streaks often appear to be wet even when dry. The climbs are described from right to left and start on the ledge which can be gained with ease by a scramble down the right-hand side.

The first five routes are about 12m in height and offer a good introduction to the area.

First Steps Very Difficult
Starting from the very end of the ledge, follow the winding line up right of the wall.

The Dentist's Extraction Severe 4b
Starting about 2 metres left of the previous climb, go up to the right-hand side of a small cave and continue past a good ledge to the top.

Captain Caveman Hard Severe 4b *
Follow small edges on steep rock to a small cave. Pass the cave directly and trend left after the exit from the cave.

Death Moves in Mysterious Ways E2 5b **
The hardest route on the cliff has a wild set of moves in its upper half. Start in the centre of the wall above the blank overhanging section. Move up razor sharp holds to a blank section below the overhang. Climb the steep section on small but positive holds, very little gear and a lot of nerve!

Jamiroqui Hard Severe 4c
From the left side of the ledge climb a steep wall to the start of a set of cracks and the corner left of the overhang. Finish by a pull on good jams (usually wet).

The next two climbs start from the bottom of the cliff and can be gained by scrambling down the gully from the right.

The Long and Winding Road 20m Hard Severe 4c
Start at barnacle level below an obvious black cleft. Climb the crack and exit to a good ledge. Follow a slabby section to a vague pinnacle, then finish steeply on the right at the highest point of the crag.

Dreams of Chamonix Granite VS 5a *
Start 3 metres left of the previous climb. Climb steep rock on good holds to some slabs which lead to a steeper section on the left. Make a tricky move and continue to the top.

The next cliff (Map Ref 971 736) is to the south of Rubha an Duine in a big bay which contains a wall on each side with a host of walls and corners to the north of the bay. The first climb is before the bay and approached by abseil from a stake (wires to back it up). The 20m cliff faces south-east and is characterised by a stunning corner which contains a crack line on its left wall.

Psychosonic Cindy 20m E4 6a **
The climb is hidden from view until standing at the bottom of it, and gives a sustained and progressively difficult lead. Follow the crack on the left wall of the corner (well protected) to a layback move at 10m. From this point protection is sparse and the climbing is a lot more strenuous and sustained. Finish the last 4m in a wild position with a jug at the top.

An area called the Wailing Wall is situated on the north side of the bay. This south-facing crag can be approached by either an abseil from a stake and numerous belays nearer the edge, or from a ledge located 500 metres north back along the coast line where it is possible to scramble down to a platform *via* a channel on the right-hand side. Walk around to the right (looking out) passing under a small crag (described later) and continue to the bottom of the wall. The wall is about 25m high and has a cleaned line up its middle. Another section to the left features some impressive cracks and a striking crack on the right which connects the Wailing Wall. The climbs are described from right to left.

Northern Exposure 25m Hard Severe 4c
Start to the right of centre by the edge of the overhang. Climb steeply for 4m, then traverse right and up to the right-hand side of a ledge at half-height. Continue keeping to the right of the wall and finish up a corner. Protection is spaced but adequate.

The Commitment 25m VS 4c *
Start in the centre of the wall and climb steeply to the ledge at half-height. Follow the cleaned area to a good undercut and continue

with some unnerving moves to a good ledge 4m from the finish. Step left and follow the crack line 3 metres left of the corner of Northern Exposure.

Guys and Dolls 25m VS 4c
Start at a hidden crack line just right of the large crack which splits the wall from the next section. Follow the crack to a steepening, then step right and up to a vague corner-groove below a steep crack. Finish on steep ground above a ledge which contains the remnants of a nest and droppings.

The next routes are situated on the small crag which is passed on the alternative approach to Wailing Wall. From the bottom of the Wailing Wall, walk back right (facing in) under overhangs and around to the short steep wall. The routes are described from left to right.

Jelly Fish 12m HVS 5a
Layback the obvious hanging flake to gain cracks, then continue up and right towards a square-cut block and the top.

The Depth Charge 15m E1 5b
In the middle of the wall is an overhang with a crack above it. Surmount the overhang and climb the steep crack to a narrow ledge. Continue on large flat holds to the top.

The KSB Boot 10m Very Difficult
The route is on the right-hand wall next to the exit gully. Start up the wall to reach a good ledge just left of the exit gully and follow the crack to the top.

The U Bend Very Difficult
An unusual excursion. Look for a pot hole on the ground in front of the steep wall and go down (tide permitting) into a tunnel. Go through it and climb up the wall on the other end back to your original position.

The Invisible One Severe
The obvious crack in the centre of the wall leads to a steepening near the top.

Sammy the Seal Severe
Climb the wall on large edges and breaks to the top.

Sukiyama Severe
Climb a crack to start, then follow a more vague crack to the top.

Jemima Puddleduck VS 4c *
Follow a left-trending feature and break through a small overhang halfway up. Continue to some good holds and exit through an overhang.

Hurdy Gurdy VS
Start 2 metres right of the above route and climb the wall on small holds to a large break. Continue through the roof on good holds.

Benjamin Bunny HVS 5a
Although short, this route provides some puzzling moves. Follow a slightly right-trending line up the wall 2 metres right of the last route.

The next two routes are 5 metres to the right and can be found by locating an obvious quartz chimney.

The Log in Motion Severe *
Follow the crack line left of the quartz. At half-height it steepens and trends slightly left.

The Gneiss Chimney Hard Very Difficult
Climb the crack line to the right of the quartz and continue up a chimney through the overhang at the top.

CREAG SCALAN (Map Ref 965 706)

The crag is situated halfway down the coastline from Leac na Hoe point. Access is not easy due to the wild terrain; either walk from Leac na Hoe point at the end of the road from Loch Portain (1 hour), or take a boat from the village of Lochmaddy (15 mins). The crag faces east-south-east and is obvious due to some large boulders and corner lines. The rock is very loose in places. The first route lies 5 metres left of the bad step in the walkway under the crag.

The Squidgy Sandal 15m VS 4c
Start left of a large overhang at the foot of a steep corner containing a distinctive crack. Climb the well protected corner, then follow the right-trending crack towards the arete. Pull over the lip to gain steep but easier ground leading to the top.

The next route is short and is situated to the left of the crag. A difficult start leads to an obvious crack which leads more easily to the top.

GRIMINISH POINT (Map Ref 735 768)

Access to this area can be made in two different ways: (i) Follow the North Uist ring road as far as the junction with the turn-off to Griminish. Follow the track around to the left to some ruined buildings. Walk towards the beach, then follow the fence along the coastline. The crag is situated in a small bay just below a hill fort (marked on the map). This is the quickest and easiest way; about 20 minutes. (ii) Follow the ring road and take the turn-off to Scolpaig Bay, passing a ruined castle, and continue to a farm building. Go beyond the building and park above the small beach. Follow the coastline around to the right, passing a spectacular sea-arch and numerous inlets, to arrive at the hill fort.

The crag is north-facing and about 60m long and 15m high. It dries quickly if the wind is coming from the north, otherwise some of the routes seep for a couple of days. The tide does not directly affect the climbing apart from reducing the length by a couple of metres. Access to the bottom of the routes is by abseil or by scrambling to the routes on the right-hand side *via* an obvious ramp. The routes are described from left to right, facing the crag.

The Smudgy Budgie E3 5b *
Climb the smooth and unprotected slab without using the crack to the right.

Chaplin Crack Difficult
Climb the obvious easy crack.

The Fornicating Cherubs Very Difficult
Climb the crack line close to Chaplin Crack, finishing two metres to its right.

Arachnaphobia Severe 4b
Climb a crack to a junction with Amnesia at half-height. Finish up this.

Amnesia Severe 4b *
Follow the left-trending layback crack.

Barney Rubble Severe 4a *
Follow a set of cracks up the centre of the wall, steeply at first, then go up to the overhang. Climb awkwardly through this to finish.

Slippy When Wet Hard Very Difficult
Follow the rightmost crack to the overhang, then squirm up the chimney on the right to a welcome finish.

The next two routes traverse the entire length of the crag, starting at the bottom of the ramp on the right-hand side near the start of Log in Motion.

Riders on the Storm 60m VS 4c **
Start at water level and traverse left with tricky moves at barnacles to reach a good horizontal crack. Follow the crack to a shattered area at the start of The Invisible One. Belay. Follow the left-trending crack lines that eventually lead to the top of The Smudgy Budgie. Finish up this.

The Black and White Minstrels 30m VS 4c ***
This traverse starts slightly higher than the other and follows a higher line one metre down from the ramp line. Follow the crack line until a step down has to be made. Follow a slightly lower break under the overhang and continue on bigger holds to The Invisible One.

Culicoidiphobia Hard Severe 4c
Take a direct line up the centre of the wall following two small vertical cracks.

MADADH MOR ISLAND (Map Ref 955 673)

The Island of Madadh Mor is situated on the south side of the Lochmaddy Loch entrance. The rock is a good quality gritstone-like basalt. The cliffs are about 40m high at their highest point and face west so they catch the sun from midday until sunset. Being an island, access can be something of a problem and the only way is by boat. Wind speed and the size of the waves are other factors which have to be taken into consideration. The crags comprise many aretes and corners with superb crack climbing. Belays can be made well back on the east side of the island so an extra rope is useful. Nearly all the climbs are gained by abseil. Access is much easier when the tide is out because a ledge runs around the majority of the climbs. The routes are described from left to right when facing out to sea, starting from a corner-groove left of a small wall which sports two good cracks.

The Jellyfishing Very Difficult
A steep start up broken grooves leads to an easy pull through a small roof.

Convincing Karen Very Difficult
The left-hand crack follows various ledges up the wall which contains an obvious crack on its right.

Layback or Be Jammed Hard Severe **
Layback or jam the obvious straight crack line in the wall.

How Much Very Difficult
Climb the crack between the wall and the arete.

Contortion on Camera Severe 4a
The arete provides good holds in a good position.

Why Difficult
Climb the corner-groove and wall just left of the obvious corner.

Lemming Sandwich Very Difficult
The corner left of the steep wall.

Sticky Toffee Pudding Severe 4b
The steep crack to the left of the wall.

Why Ever Not VS 4b
Climb the steep wall on good holds and ledges.

Just Like Grit VS 4c *
Climb the arete passing two overhangs in a wild position.

About 10 metres to the right, a corner-groove has been top roped, but this section suffers from seepage. The next route starts on the obvious arete which has a small archway under it. The wall to its left is obvious from the water and is square-cut with a steep section at half-height.

Life on the Edge 20m HVS 5a **
The left arete of the square-shaped wall passes through some steep and impressive ground. Start at a square-cut ledge on the arete. Climb the arete passing two roofs and continue in a wild position to the top.

The Wave of Elation 20m VS 4c **
Start two metres right of the arete and follow a crack in a corner-groove to the centre of the wall. Cross the roof at its easiest point and make intriguing moves through it. Mantel up ledges and follow a thin crack to the top.

Ringing on Heaven's Doorbell E4 5c
Start in the centre of the wall and follow crack lines just right of the previous route. At the overhang, break off to the right on good undercuts. This section is not well protected. Gain the right-hand arete and follow a crack line using small holds to the top.

The next route, situated on the longest part of the cliff, is fairly easy to find due to two large overhangs on each side of it at the top. Neither this nor the previous route have been led, so the grades are speculative.

Riding on the Crest of the Wave 35m E3 6a ***
Start from the platform at low tide and follow the obvious soaring crack line up the wall to a steep and balancy section at half-height. Enter the right-hand groove, then continue up a corner crack to an exit on superb jams on the right of the corner.

The next routes start close to the triangular-shaped roof on the right-hand side of the crag. There are tell-tale signs at the top which mark the start of the abseil.

Mr Jaffa 25m E1 5b
Start 3 metres left of a low triangular roof below a curving black groove. Start up the groove, then step left onto the rib. Follow the rib up through small steps and climb the crack on progressively smaller holds to reach good holds near the top.

Far from the Maddy Crowds 20m VS 4c
From the abseil line, traverse right up ledges for 4m to below a rib on the right of the triangular overhang. Follow the rib, avoiding the

overhang on the left, and reach a ledge. Continue to the top on poor rock.

The next routes start 3 metres to the right around the corner from the abseil.

The Crucifix 20m E1 5b ***
Start in the far back corner and climb the impressive crack to the large roof at 5m. Tackle the overhangs in an awkward position and gain a small slab between the two overhangs with an obvious triangular foothold in its centre. Traverse right around the corner and follow a crack in a superb position to the top.

Sea Fury 25m E1 5b ** (1995)
In the centre of the west face right of the highest section is a prominent roof. Climb up the chimney and go over a small roof to undercut right under the main roof and reach a fine easier finishing crack up the slab.

The Grinning Juggler VS 5a **
Start at an imposing corner crack just right of The Crucifix. Climb the crack to a roof, traverse right under it on massive undercuts to the corner of the roof, step right and continue up the crack as for the next route.

Monkey Business VS 5a **
Start at the crack line in the wall which is also part of an arete. Follow the crack to a junction with the corner of the roof, turn another roof on the right and continue up another crack to a ledge on the right and a delicate finish.

Further right the cliff features some roofs low down and cracks above. These have been top-roped but neither cleaned nor led. The next routes start in the obvious corner-groove 5 metres to the right. A notch in the skyline is a good reference point.

From the Bottom 15m Very Difficult
Climb the corner easily to the notch in the skyline.

The Downfall Hard Severe 4b
Starting just to the right, climb a crack passing a rock scar halfway, and make an airy finish.

Chalkbags and Sadrags VS 5a *
An eliminate between the two cracks of Downfall and Tom's Diner. Start below a small overhanging niche. Pull through this and continue up the wall on excellent edges, making sure not to stray onto either of the cracks.

Tom's Diner Severe 4a
The crack to the right of The Downfall is similar but less sustained.

A Sudden Gust of Gravity Hard Severe 4b **
The next crack to the right is more continuous with a tricky move at the top.

Foot Loose and Fancy Free HVS 5b **
Climb a crack at the start, then go up to a roof. Step wildly onto the hanging pillar and reach through the next overhang for a good hold. Follow the perfect crack line on the right of the slab to the top. A tricky climb.

Fried Green Tomatoes VS 4c *
Start on the right-hand side of the hanging pillar, ascend on good holds through the overhang, then follow the crack line to the top. Not quite as bad as it looks!

Layed Back in Lochmaddy VS 5a *
Start up a slab below the right side of the roof and traverse round the corner of the overhang in a good position. Continue more easily to the top.

The Real McCoy Hard Severe 4b *
Climb the corner and difficult crack on pinches and insecure holds.

The Phileas Fog Finish VS 5a
Start up the previous climb for 3m, then break out left onto the steep wall and traverse across using the steep undercut flake. Continue up the right arete to the top.

The Yellow Melon VS 4c *
The obvious yellow wall can be climbed but the crack is out of bounds. Protection is spaced but a good climb none the less. Finish in the square recess.

Sky on Fire Severe
Follow the right-hand arete to the top of the yellow wall.

Sploosh Very Difficult
Climb the crack line to the right of the arete with an obvious chockstone in it.

The Postman HVS 5a *
This steep climb faces south. Start from the corner, climb the right-hand groove for a couple of moves, then attack the centre of the wall *via* the obvious slots and square-cut holds. Mantel to finish in a good position.

Redwing Hard Severe 4b
Around the corner of the sharp arete is a deep corner; climb this on awkward holds to a good layback finish.

The Lobster Pot Hard Very Difficult
Climb the easy crack line and ledges to the top.

SOUTH UIST

BEINN MHOR

620m (Map Ref 809 311)

The north-facing Hellisdale Buttresses of Beinn Mhor can be reached in two hours from Loch Dobhrain over the Bealach Hellisdale. There are six gullies and seven distinct buttresses. The gullies tend to be slimy and vegetatious. All the buttresses have been climbed, but few details were recorded. The gully furthest right (when seen from below) provides the only recorded winter climb on the island, which was lined with water ice after two weeks of cold easterly winds.

BEN CORODALE

527m (Map Ref 819 329)

Chimney Buttress 50m Hard Severe
The west face of the peak contains a chimney. The route climbs the pink buttress immediately left of the chimney. Climb up cracks for about 20m until the angle eases, then continue to the top, finishing up a steep off-width crack if desired. The approach walk takes about 90 minutes.

LEAC SHLEAMHUINN (Map Ref 775 147)

There is an area of discontinuous granitic-gneiss slabs on the southern slopes of Easaval on the very south of South Uist. Approach from near the jetty at Ludag and walk up to the slabs in 10 minutes. They stretch across the hillside and unfortunately the majority of the longer lines are too easy-angled to afford anything but climbs of Difficult and below. The one area that is distinctly steeper is a diamond-shaped slab well seen on the approach and roughly centrally placed in the slab mass. The rock belies the Gaelic name slippery and is of top quality. It is not worth a special visit, but it is easily accessible for short routes whilst waiting for ferries. Protection is entirely lacking on most lines.

Slippery Slab 25m VS 4c
A fine climb with an intimidating initial section. Start in the centre of the diamond-shaped slab 2 metres left of a slanting crack. Step over an overlap and continue straight up.

Eriskay Crack 20m Difficult
Climb the pleasant slanting crack right of Slippery Slab.

Ludag Slab 25m Very Difficult
Climb the slab right of Eriskay Crack.

Saltavik Slab 20m Very Difficult
Near to the left of Slippery Slab is another slab set lower down. Climb this with an interesting middle section.

There is another crag about 300 metres around the hillside to the east which offers a 30m slab of around the same steepness. There are 3 or 4 lines of about Difficult or Very Difficult. About 20 metres right of the slabs (which are clearly seen from the road) is a short steep wall about 40m long and about 10m high. It has a crack up the left arete and an overlap near the right-hand end. The top of the slabs slope back, giving rounded and often difficult finishes.

Arete Crack 10m VS 4b
Climb the crack at the left end of the crag.

Flakey 10m HVS 5a
Climb the line of flakes right of the last route.

Flakey 2 10m E3 6a
Climb the line of flakes right again which end before the top of the crag, with a long reach for small holds at the top.

Crack Route 10m E2 5c
Right of the last route is a crack with heather in it. The crack branches at the top; follow the left branch.

Wall and Crack 10m E3 6a
Climb the wall right of the crack and cross the right branch of the crack to finish up flakes at the top.

Wall and Crack 2 10m E2 5c
Climb the wall to finish up the extreme right-hand crack line of the right branch. There is a long reach in the middle.

Crack and Roof 10m VS 4c
Right of the cracks and at the left end of the overlap is a vertical crack running through the left end of the overlap.

Roof and Crack 10m E1 5b
Right of the last route, in the middle of the overlap, is a vertical line of flakes. Climb to the overlap, then go through it and follow the crack. Avoid stepping left at the top.

Ledge Route 10m E2 5c
Climb the wall to the right end of the overlap, then pass this, step left onto a ledge above the overlap and finish directly (rounded).

Ledge and Crack 10m HVS 5a
Follow Ledge Route to the ledge, then move right along a diagonal crack.

Mingulay and Pabbay

The remote island of Mingulay, rising to a height of 273 metres, is the second most southerly of the Outer Hebridean isles, which extend from Lewis in the north to Berneray in the south. Measuring 4km by 3km, it once supported a population of over 100, but it is now uninhabited. The western seaboard presents a continuous line of cliffs to the Atlantic, reaching a maximum height of 235m at the Builacraig. Mingulay supports large colonies of puffins, razorbills and guillemots and many other seabirds. The best campsite, with running water, is on the flat sward adjacent to the ruined village at Mingulay Bay.

The maps that cover the island are Ordnance Survey 1:50,000 Sheet 31 and 1:25,000 Sheet 260 (NL 58/68).

Access

There is no public transport to Mingulay. The nearest island with a regular ferry service from the mainland is Barra, 15 kilometres to the north (Caledonian MacBrayne run a regular service from Oban to Castlebay, crossing time 5 hours. There are also flights to Barra from Glasgow). Boat charter from Barra to Mingulay is a possibility, but access by private yacht from the mainland is perhaps the most satisfying approach. Mingulay Bay in the east is the safest anchorage and landing point although this is obviously weather dependent. The best months for access are likely to be May to August.

Rock Climbing

Although many sections of the cliff-line are vegetated or heavily colonised by sea-birds, there is also much clean rock. At its best the gneiss of Mingulay offers the highest quality of rock climbing, being largely solid, furnished with generous holds even on the steepest walls and having superb friction. In particular, the magnificent 100m wall of Dun Mingulay must lay claim to being one of the finest rock faces in Britain. For sea-stack enthusiasts, Mingulay offers some impressive specimens including the formidable Lianamul and Arnamul (both probably unclimbed since the native population left).

Although there are rumours of earlier activity, only three rock climbing sorties to date have been recorded. The first in 1993, was initiated by Graham Little with Kevin Howett, Chris Bonington and Mick Fowler sharing the adventure. In 1995 and 1996 Little and Howett returned with other friends and a well matured addiction.

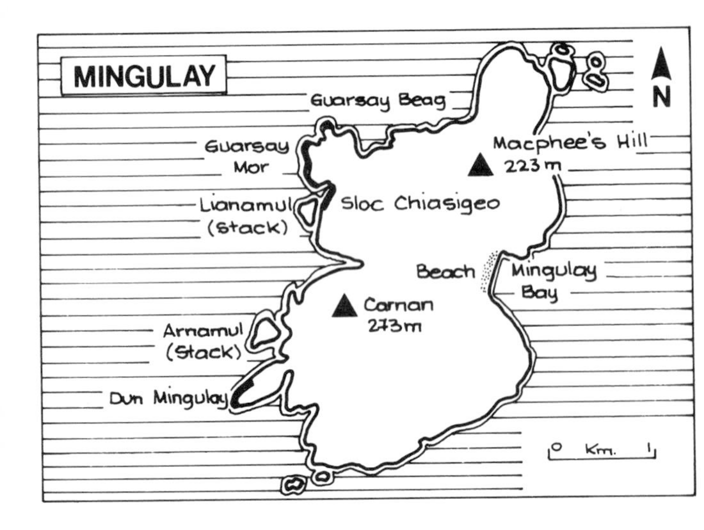

Despite the wealth of unclimbed rock, the sheer remoteness and problematic access should keep Mingulay as one of the great under-developed gems of the Hebridean seas for many years to come.

Access to the start of all routes is by abseil and 100 metre non-stretch ropes are strongly recommended.

DUN MINGULAY (Map Ref 534 820)

Dun Mingulay is the nearly isolated cliff-girt headland in the south-west of Mingulay, joined to its parent island by a narrow neck of land (the remains of a defensive rampart are still visible). A west-facing section of the cliff at Sron an Duin forms a superb 90m wall of clean, vertical to overhanging rock providing climbing of an exceptional quality and situation. Access to the base is by abseil (an exciting experience in its own right) and is very much dependent upon calm seas. Very little loose rock is evident and there are few nesting birds.

Opposite: Under the Pink, Guarsay Mor, Mingulay (Climber, Bob Reid)

Next page: A Word with the Bill, Guarsay Mor, Mingulay (Climber, Andy Cunningham)

Near the extreme nose of Sron an Duin a wide ledge runs just below the top of the cliff. It can be gained by a short scramble and provides abseil access to the following three routes.

Fifteen Fathoms of Fear 50m Severe ** (1995)
An intimidating route for its grade. Abseil from the ledge at a cairn 5 metres north of some boulders. Belay on a small ledge above the undercut base of the wall. From there climb up leftwards into a vague corner crack, the rightmost of several, then continue straight up passing the left end of a long roof (with guano below). A wide depression leads to a steeper finish at the abseil point.

Done Mingulay 70m E2 ** (1995)
Abseil from a bay near the northerly termination of the ledge, about 10 metres north of the cairn marking Fifteen Fathoms of Fear. Belay on a ledge in an alcove at sea-weed level (low tide desirable!).
1. 50m 5b Climb up and right on the initial black wall, then trend left into an obvious groove line heading for a small prominent roof (well right of the bigger ones). From the top of the groove climb right into a flake crack leading to the roof. Pull rightwards through the right end of the roof and into a corner leading to belay ledges.
2. 20m 4a Climb straight up a right-facing flake crack to the top.

Dun Moaning 75m E2 ** (1995)
This climb takes a line just to the left of Done Mingulay, starting as for that route.
1. 25m 5b Climb the initial black wall, then trend left into a triangular niche. Exit from this and climb to a ledge on the left under a bulge.
2. 25m 5b Climb the short corner on the left of the bulge with difficulty, then step back right above it to gain a groove line heading up left to the right side of the huge upper roofs. Belay below the roof at a tiny ledge.
3. 25m 5b Move up to the roof, pull left over it to gain a corner which leads up to the upper larger roof. Traverse right below it to pull over its right edge at an obvious hanging groove. Ascend a black wall on the left to finish at the abseil ledge.

Previous page: Prophesy of Drowning
(Climbers, Kevin Howett and Graham Little)

Opposite: Stepping Out on the Main Wall of An Sgurr, Eigg
(Climber, Dave Saddler)

The central and highest section of the wall holds two routes. The abseil descents to the starts of these routes are marked by two small cairns just back from the cliff top.

The Silkie 100m E4 *** (1993)
An impressive, direct line with sensational exposure on the third pitch. Abseil from a point adjacent to the southerly of the two small cairns to a rock plinth a couple of metres above tidal slabs.
1. 15m 4c From the rock plinth climb a groove to distinctive red bands. Traverse left along these to a small ledge and belay.
2. 30m 6a Climb straight up to below a black diagonal arching overlap and follow it rightwards to below its widest point. Move up, then pull through into a small scoop on the left (crux). Step back right across the lip, then climb flakes trending left up a wall of compact rock to belay on the right below a square roof. A magnificent pitch.
3. 45m 5b Turn the square roof on the left, then take a quartz corner breaking out right through a second roof. Step left onto its lip, then go directly up a juggy wall to another small roof. Cross this to gain a cracked block ledge. Ascend slightly rightwards to a better ledge and belay.
4. 10m 4a Climb steep but easier ground to the top.

Voyage of Faith 120m E3 *** (1993)
An outstanding, intricate and sustained line with much atmosphere and stunning exposure. Abseil from a point adjacent to the northerly of the two small cairns to the base of a short square-cut corner immediately above tidal slabs.
1. 25m 5b Ascend the short square-cut corner to a small ledge at the base of an open groove. Climb the groove, then pull out left to belay on a small ledge.
2. 30m 5b Move out left from the ledge, then follow a line of flakes trending left until a vertical flake crack leads to an obvious horizontal fault. Hand traverse left along the fault, then move up to a very exposed belay on a small nose of rock at the base of a slight corner (this whole area is undercut by a large sea cave).
3. 30m 5b Climb the corner to a small ledge, then traverse a couple of metres left to a short parallel groove. Ascend this, then step left and slightly down to a very narrow ledge. Follow this leftwards until the overlap can be bypassed giving access to a traverse line back right above the overlap. Belay at blunt rock spikes adjacent to an obvious break in the main band of overhangs.

4. 35m 5c Traverse out right through the overhangs (lower line), then climb directly up on steep rock *via* a groove to the base of a short hanging corner. Climb this with difficulty and thence to the top.

Children of Tempest 95m E1 ** (1995)
This is the pillar bounding the north side of the clean main wall of Sron an Duin. Abseil to a commodious ledge at the base of the pillar from a collection of large blocks (small cairn) about 30 metres north of the cairn marking the abseil point for Voyage of Faith. Start at a flake at the left end of the highest ledge.
1. 25m 5a Trend left up a black slabby wall to enter a short slim groove with a cracked left wall. Climb this to a horizontal break. Pull up the wall above, step left, then climb another short groove to reach a small triangular rock ledge. A fine intricate pitch.
2. 40m 5c Ascend the diagonal crack rightwards, with a thin move at its end, to gain ledges above. Climb easily to below the base of a deep flake crack in the steep clean pillar above. Follow this on grand holds to a large ledge.
3. 30m 4a Climb trending right up rock steps to belay at the abseil point.

SLOC CHIASIGEO (Map Ref 551 838)

Liverbird 125m E1 * (1993)
This route lies on the north-west facing wall midway between the stack of Lianamul and the head of the narrow geo (inlet). It follows a fairly obvious crack and groove system. The best access descent is by abseil to the south of the line, gaining slabs overlooking the narrow channel between Mingulay and Lianamul. A scramble northwards leads to the start at the right-hand end of a wide platform with a small pool just above high water.
1. 50m 4b Climb easily up to a ramp, then go diagonally up the ramp into a steep corner. Climb this to a small ledge.
2. 35m 5b Continue straight up the crack system and at about 20m enter a black overhanging groove. Climb this to a point about 6m below capping overhangs. Step up and pull rightwards round an arete to gain a small stance in a corner.
3. 40m 5b Climb through the overhang above, using the left-hand crack, then pull across and round a rib to the right-hand crack to reach a horizontal break. Move slightly left into a steep deep-cut groove and follow this on excellent holds to the top.

GUARSAY MOR (Map Ref 548 842)

This, the most north-westerly headland on Mingulay, lies to the north of Sloc Chiasigeo. Its 500 metre long west face is composed of superb clean rock with a distinctive inlet halfway along. The first two routes described lie to the south of this inlet, and the others are to the north.

Stugeron 105m HVS ** (1993)
This route climbs the groove line to the immediate left of the crest of the buttress on the south edge of the inlet. Start from a cave immediately above high water at the foot of the groove line (abseil access).
1. 30m 4c Step left and climb a subsidiary groove until it is possible after about 10m to gain the main groove. Follow this to pull out onto a ledge on the right.
2. 45m 4c Move up and right through a bulge, then carry straight on to a ledge system below the headwall.
3. 30m 4c Move left to a deep V-groove, pull over a small roof, then continue to the top.

Pressure Band 100m HVS ** (1993)
1. 45m 5a Start as for Stugeron. Follow the groove line of that route for 5m, then pull left out of the groove and round a rib to follow the obvious steep crack line to a good ledge.
2. 25m 4b Step up and right, then go back left to the ledge below the headwall. Traverse left for 5 metres to the foot of a steep groove.
3. 30m 4c Climb the groove to the top.

Grey Rib 70m Severe ** (1993)
Abseil to the highest point of the ledge, just above high water mark, at the foot of the buttress on the northern side of the inlet.
1. 35m 4a Climb 3m leftwards to gain a ramp leading up into a short corner. Move up and left out of the corner onto the crest of the buttress and continue up for 12m to a stance.
2. 35m 4a Climb straight up steeply on superb holds.

No Puke Here 65m VS ** (1993)
This climb follows the rib to the immediate right of a recess roofed by a huge overhang, to the left of Grey Rib.
1. 30m 4b Climb the slabby rib on excellent rock, then move left from a short crack to a good ledge.
2. 35m 4b Continue straight up on good holds.

The west-facing northern extremity of the Guarsay Mor headland, north of the roofed recess, presents an immaculate wall of clean vertical rock skirted by a big rock ledge at a comfortable height above the sea. This ledge can be accessed by abseil, the best starting point being a huge semi-detached block near the cliff edge. The routes are described from south to north and all are of very high quality.

Lost Souls 55m E5 *** (1995)
Bold, blind and poorly protected yet superb! From the right end of the big ledge traverse 10 metres right to a small ledge which marks the start.
1. 30m 6a Climb rightwards off the ledge, then move up to a higher ledge. From near its right end make thin moves up to a small flake. Further thin moves on small quartz holds lead up under a small roof. Step left to the edge of a second small roof then pull through the break between the two to gain 'Thank God' jugs. Move up to a small roof, step right under it, then climb to a horizontal crack. Follow it leftwards to belay in a niche.
2. 25m 5b Climb the slabby wall above, trending slightly right to reach the right-hand end of a horizontal breach in the capping roof. Gain and follow the hand traverse line out left in a spectacular position, then at its end climb straight up to finish.

Taxing Macphee 55m E2 *** (1995)
Start at the right-hand end of the big ledge at a dark flake crack.
1. 30m 5c Climb the flake crack to its top, then pull up and move left across the wall into a slight scoop. Climb up through the cleavage in the roof above to a ledge.
2. 25m 5a Follow a right-rising line to a glacis. Move up to a distinctive quartz flake. Pull over this, then step left and climb straight up to finish.

Crystal Daze 50m E3 *** (1995)
Start at a thin crack below a wide, vertical pink crystal band.
1. 25m 6b Sustained climbing up the thin crack leads to a pull out right to gain a big pocket. Climb the wall above trending left to belay on a small ledge below a bulge (as for Ossian Boulevard).
2. 25m 5b Move right under the bulge, then climb up to a short dark quartz corner. Ascend this, then follow the curving arch continuation until a big pocket over the lip on the left allows a pull out and the wall above to be climbed.

Ossian Boulevard 60m E1 ** (1995)
Start about 5 metres right of the left end of the big ledge at a slightly right-slanting groove.
1. 35m 5b Climb the groove until moves right above an overhang lead into a series of corners going right across the wall. Belay under a bulge at the top corner (as for Crystal Daze).
2. 25m 4b Climb left through the bulge, then go directly to the top with one move left to cross a patch of quartz-feldspar.

A Word with the Bill 50m E3 *** (1995)
1. 30m 5c Climb the thin crack just to the left of Ossian Boulevard with a hard pull up into an easier-angled scoop. Step left and climb another crack for a few moves, then head right and up to an overlap. Traverse right under the overlap, then climb straight up to a ledge.
2. 20m 5a Follow the right-curving crack above and pull left through a quartz-feldspar bulge to finish straight up.

Okeanos 50m E1 *** (1995)
Start at the left end of the big ledge.
1. 25m 5b Gain a good spike, then make hard moves up and left to holds leading back right into a steep crack.
Climb the crack, then move left along a juggy break to twin diagonal cracks leading to a ledge and belay (in common with Under the Pink).
2. 25m 4b Climb slightly rightwards, passing to the right of a big blotch of pink quartz-feldspar, then go up a left-facing corner to finish.

Under the Pink 50m E1 ** (1995)
Traverse leftwards from the left end of the big ledge to a small stance on a black slabby wall.
1. 25m 5b Move up and left to the base of a smooth scalloped groove. Ascend this (crux), then follow a flakey fault line rightwards to belay at a small ledge at its end (in common with Okeanos).
2. 25m 4b Climb directly upwards to pass a big blotch of pink quartz-feldspar on its left, then finish straight up.

The base of the following two routes can be gained by climbing down the ridge leading to the tip of Guarsay Mor (Difficult). From the base follow seaweed-covered platforms back towards the cliff to reach a slabby ramp. Belay at the top of this. A 45m abseil from the appropriate position would also reach this point.

Oh No, Norman's Due Back Tomorrow! 50m E3 ** (1995)
1. 30m 6a From the belay descend a little and move back right onto a slabby wall. Move up into a layback corner crack and climb this to a good ledge on the left. Climb up, then go right into a diagonal crack under an overlap. After a few moves pull onto the wall above and make hard moves left into another diagonal crack. Follow this into a right-trending corner leading to the right end of a belay ledge.
2. 20m 4a A corner and easier ground leads to the top.

Port Pillar 45m HVS *** (1995)
1. 25m 5a Climb into a short crack in the bulge above the belay, then go right below the base of an obvious large corner to climb the face of the fine pillar forming the left side of the cliff face. Belay on a ledge at the top of the pillar.
2. 20m Climb easily directly to the top.

GUARSAY BEAG (Map Ref 551 845)

A clean west-facing wall lies at the north-west extremity of the Guarsay Beag promontory, directly below an obvious cairn. The face is characterised by a shield-like section of rock, lichenous in its upper part and defined by grooves on either flank. At the base of the shield, about 5m above the sea, is a curious hole in the rock much favoured by seabirds; guano cascades from the hole with an attendant pungent odour. The start of the following three routes is on a ledge below the hole (accessed by abseil).

With a View to a Shag 35m Severe 4a * (1993)
Ascend the groove bounding the left-hand side of the shield.

Easy Day for a Shag 35m Severe 4b * (1993)
Climb the groove bounding the right-hand side of the shield.

From the Hole to Heaven 35m VS 4c ** (1993)
Climb the centre of the shield on excellent holds in an impressive situation.

PABBAY

This small, uninhabited, rocky island, rising to a height of 171metres, lies between Sandray and Mingulay some 12 kilometres to the south of Barra. The ruins of a small settlement lie above the beach in the east. This is the best campsite with fresh water.

The appropriate maps are the Ordnance Survey 1:50,000 Sheet 31 and the 1:25,000 Sheet 260 (NL58/68).

Access

As with Mingulay, a private boat or charter is required to reach the island. The best anchorage and landing place in most conditions is the bay and sandy beach in the east.

Rock Climbing

The west coast of Pabbay displays some grand cliffs rising to a height of over 100 metres. Much of the rock is clean and solid gneiss affording excellent climbing. Apart from some minor cragging on the first cliffs to the south of the beach (I.Davidson and P.Heneghan in 1989) the only recorded rock climbing visits have been in 1995 and 1996. Within a period of two weeks in 1995 two independent parties visited the

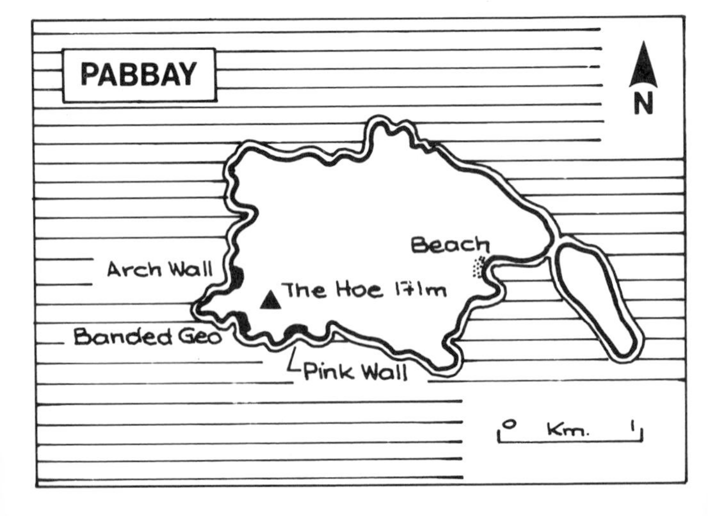

island putting up a series of fine routes in the south-west, the highlights being Spit in Paradise (E3) and U-Ei (HVS) by a German team and the impressive The Priest (E2) by Graham Little and Kevin Howett. Much scope for exploration remains.

ARCH WALL (Map Ref 592 873)

Just to the north of Rubha Greotach, the most westerly headland on Pabbay, lies a great rock arch which is spectacular even by Hebridean standards. To its left lies a 100m open corner. Between these two features is a massive pillar, narrow at its base, widening with height and holding twin corners capped by a big roof near the top. The left edge of the big open corner is bounded by another pillar. To the north of this the cliff gradually becomes lower and less steep.

The Priest 110m E2 ** (1995)
This route climbs the pillar between the great arch and the big open corner, finishing up the left-hand of the twin roof-capped corners high on the crag. It is has great character and atmosphere with big route commitment. The base of the route is reached by abseil with 100m rope, starting above the right wall of the corner (left looking down).
1. 50m 4b From a tiny ledge some eight metres above the sea, climb the slabby right wall of the corner just left of the edge to gain a small ledge and belay on the very edge.
2. 25m 5c Move up into a groove, step right, then enjoy sustained and intricate climbing *via* cracks and grooves, well right of the edge, leading to a belay on a rusty slab under a roof.
3. 35m 5b Move up to the roof, step right, then climb to the base of the left-hand corner. Climb this fine corner to the big roof, then make a short difficult left traverse to finish.

THE HEADWALL

This 25m high slabby wall of immaculate rock lies above the right side of the great arch and can be accessed by traversing along a grassy ledge from the right. The routes are described from right to left.

Shortbread Fingers 20m Severe 4b * (1995)
Start at the first obvious groove and scramble up to a ledge. Starting close to the edge, climb straight up for 8m, then move left to a ledge. Climb the slabby wall above to the top.

Orang-Utang Klaus 25m Severe 4b * (1995)
This route starts below two distinctive roofs. Climb a corner for 7m, outflank the roofs on the right to gain another corner. Follow this to a ledge, then climb the slabby wall above on good holds.

Pat and Patachon 25m Severe 4b * (1995)
Start 5 metres left of Orang-Utang Klaus. Climb the centre of the wall, passing a curved horizontal break, then go straight up to a block belay.

Telephonmann 30m Severe 4a * (1995)
Make a 6 metre traverse left along a ledge from a short distance up Pat and Patachon to gain a corner. Climb straight up to reach a small roof, cross this, then follow the continuation line above.

Geniestreich 30m Severe 4b ** (1995)
Start at a large flake. Climb the distinctive crack to the ledge above.

Katzenklo 30m VS 5a * (1995)
Start at the lowest point of the Headwall, 5 metres left of the large flake. Climb the wall for 10m (poor protection) to a small darkish corner. Climb this, then head for a small overhang. Easier ground leads to the top.

Es Gibt Reis Baby 30m HVS 5b ** (1995)
Start 5 metres left of Katzenklo, close to a block. Follow the black groove to the top on slabby rock.

Das Ist Doch Die Situation Heir 30m Severe 4b * (1995)
Start to the left of the aforementioned block. Follow a slab for 5m, then traverse right to a corner. Follow the corner to the top.

Leftie 30m VS 4c ** (1995)
Start at the left end of the grass ledge. Climb the wall (crux) for 6m, then go straight up to a roof. Pass the roof at the right-hand edge, then climb easier ground to the top.

BANDED GEO (Map Ref 592 870)

Just to the south of Rubha Greotach, the most westerly headland on Pabbay, lies a geo (inlet) holding a 60m high west-facing wall with a quartz-feldspar band running across it. The routes described below are on the cleanest section of the wall which has a long overhang at two-thirds height and a deep corner above a slab on the right. The routes are described from left to right and are all accessed by abseil.

Spring Squill 65m E1 ** (1995)
From the right end of a long ledge move up and right to a smaller ledge with a flake and thread belay.
1. 40m 5b Follow a flake line rightwards to a ledge, then trend steeply back left and into the right-hand of two short cracks leading to easier climbing. Move up a vague depression, past a huge down-pointing flake, to climb a crack through a bulge (crux) and go up to belay on the left under the long overhang.
2. 25m 4b Pull through the narrowing in the overhang and continue directly to the top.

Oh No, Norman's in Reverse! 65m HVS * (1995)
Abseil from a point about 10 metres south of Spring Squill down the line of a prominent chimney-corner. Belay on a tiny ledge at the base of a black slab.
1. 40m 5a Climb leftwards up the slab to an obvious break in the left arete of the corner. Swing left onto the wall and climb past an awkward little overhang to a ledge on the right.
2. 25m 4a Move left and climb an orange ramp to easy ground and the top.

Corncrake Corner 65m HVS * (1995)
This route climbs the line of the obvious chimney-corner, which is the line of the abseil (as for the previous route).
1. 40m 5a Climb up into the deep chimney. Follow this, then move up the right wall of the corner to pass an overhang. A quartz-feldspar bulge above leads directly to easier ground and a ledge in common with the previous route.
2. 25m 4b Climb directly up the wall above to finish.

Spooky Pillar 65m HVS ** (1995)
This route tackles the pillar to the right of the prominent chimney-corner (and left of a less well defined unclimbed corner). Abseil to the tiny ledge as for the previous routes.
1. 40m 5a Climb straight up through the bulges, keeping slightly left of the edge, until a move round the edge at the top bulge leads into a crack. Follow this to a good ledge and belay.
2. 25m 4a Easier climbing leads straight up to finish.

The following two routes lie to the right of the main wall of Banded Geo.

Warm Up 40m Severe 4b * (1995)
This route lies at the right-hand side of the main wall. Climb a crack line to gain a corner. Step left below the obvious roof, then climb a slab for 7m to reach a ledge. Climb darker rock to the top.

Steife Brise 40m VS 4c ** (1995)
This route climbs the third corner system to the right of Warm Up. Climb straight up to a roof. Negotiate this on the right, then climb the corner above, using flakes, to reach easier ground.

PINK WALL (Map Ref 596 869)

This 90m high wall is divided by a terrace at about mid-height. The upper section is much cleaner than the lower one. The following two routes lie in a slight recess immediately right of the wall. They can be accessed by a 100m abseil.

Spit in Paradise 105m E3 ** (1995)
Start on a platform to the right of an overhanging crack.
1. 45m 5c Climb the wall by a direct line. After about 15m move left to gain the overhanging crack. Climb this to somewhat easier ground (bird hazard). Ascend another 7m to reach a good ledge.
2. 35m 6a Trend left towards a wide overhanging crack. Climb this to a ledge. Step right to climb the wall right of an obvious corner system to a huge roof. Trend left through overhanging cracks (crux) to reach a ledge and good thread belays.
3. 25m 5b Climb straight up, passing small roofs on a slabby wall to gain a corner. Follow this to the top.

U-Ei 110m HVS *** (1995)
Start on a platform (in common with Spit in Paradise).
1. 50m 5a Climb a slabby wall on perfect holds for 25m, then traverse left to a small overhanging corner. Follow this corner straight up towards a roof. Bottle out left to a comfortable ledge.
2. 30m 5a Climb an easy corner to an overhanging block. Pass the block on the right to gain a ledge and a luxurious belay.
3. 30m 5a Ascend to an overhang, cross this, then climb a fine overhanging corner system. Finish by a left-slanting ramp.

MINGULAY AND PABBAY ADDENDUM

DUN MINGULAY

Rory Rum the Story Man 100m E5 *** (1996)
This meaty route takes a line to the left of Dun Moaning. Start by abseiling into the wall as for that route and gaining a small quartz ledge just over the lip of the lower water-washed bulge left of Dun Moaning. Pendulum to the left end of the ledge and belay.
1. 25m 6a Climb the obvious left-slanting diagonal overlap to its end, then make hard moves to a small ledge above. Follow the thin flake above to below a bulge. Teeter left under it to gain an obvious block ledge at the base of a small groove.
2. 30m 6a Climb the groove and make a hard move up and left to good holds under the big roof. Traverse left under the roof with increasing difficulty past a deep slot, then follow sloping holds to a jug. Pull directly through the roof above by a large projecting hold and take a hanging stance on the lip.
3. 15m 5c Climb directly through the roof above into a curious hole. Belay on the big ledge above.
4. 30m 5a Traverse 5 metres right and follow easy ground to the top.

A Few Fathoms More 50m VS * (1996)
Abseil as for Fifteen Fathoms of Fear to a low ledge.
1. 30m 4c Climb straight up to another ledge. Ascend a flake crack on the right, then go straight up until a few metres below a wide slot rising above a horizontal break (holding a colony of guillemots). Traverse left (crux), then move up to belay on the horizontal fault.
2. 20m 4c Climb a groove immediately left of the wide slot. Step right, then climb directly through bulges to finish.

RUBHA LIATH

This is the headland in the extreme south-west of the island overlooking the small offshore islands of Geirum Mor and Geirum Beag.

Rubha Soul 30m E2 5b * (1996)
Abseil from the very tip of Rubha Liath to a ledge above the sea. Move up a little, then traverse left on jugs across an overhanging wall to pull up into a groove. Follow this to below a roof, traverse left, then pull up into the final groove to finish.

The Power of the Sea 40m E3 ** (1996)
This atmospheric route lies on the south side of the narrow inlet to the north of the point of Rubha Liath. Abseil from a small cairn at the top of a fairly obvious clean-cut corner to a tidal ledge well above the sea.
1. 25m 5c From the left end of the ledge climb a sustained flake crack. From its top step right to enter a narrow slot breaking through overhanging rock, then climb this to a horizontal fault.
2. 15m 4c Enter and climb the fine corner above.

ARNAMUL PROMONTORY

This is the long west-facing wall opposite Arnamul Stack (Map Ref 547 828). Access is by abseil off the west end of the promontory onto a huge ledge running below the crag and about 10m above the sea. Towards the left end of the ledge (just to the left of the abseil line) is a buttress cut by grooves on either side. The line of the next route roughly follows the groove systems to the right of the buttress.

Lament to the Abyss 75m E1 ** (1996)
1. 35m 5a Climb steeply into the right-facing corner and follow this line to the base of a detached pillar. Move right and climb cracks to the middle ledge.
2. 40m 5b Climb the crack directly above the belay into a right-facing corner, over overlaps, and continue to the top in an exposed position.

GUARSAY BEAG

Here We Go! 35m Very Difficult * (1996)
Start to the left of the Shag routes on a sea-level ledge. Climb the centre of the vague pillar to the left of With a View to a Shag.

BLACK GEO

This is the complex geo between Guarsay Mor and Guarsay Beag which ends in a cave with a black slabby headwall. To the left of the cave are impressive hanging grooves.

Black Slab 50m VS 4c (1996)
Abseil to the ledges at the mouth of the cave. Climb the slab to a left-facing corner, then continue up easy ground to finish up a corner formed by the headwall above the cave.

The following three routes are all on a black wall to the west of the hanging grooves in the edge of the cave. Abseil directly down the wall to a ledge.

Depth Charge 50m VS ** (1996)
Start 3 metres left of the right end of the ledge at a prominent crack that issues directly from the ledge.
1. 25m 4c Climb the immaculate crack to the point where it ends beneath a small overlap. Step left, then go up and right through a small bulge and groove to belay on a prominent ledge.
2. 25m Ascend directly up flakes right of a small roof to a point where a swing left above the roofs leads directly to the top.

Don't Forget the Rope 50m VS 4b * (1996)
From the right end of the ledge, climb a gnarly crack through a stepped roof. Above, climb up and slightly right to a groove through a bulge. Climb directly to the top.

The Wreck of the Edmund Fitzgerald 55m HVS * (1996)
Belay as for Don't Forget the Rope.
1. 25m 5a From the extreme right end of the ledge climb rightwards up a scooped wall, then go straight up to belay in an alcove.
2. 30m 4c Continue more easily to finish up a wide quartz groove.

GUARSAY MOR

Alzheimer's Groove 70m HVS ** (1996)
This climbs a line starting from the lowest ledge under the start of No Puke Here.
1. 40m 5a Move left into grooves running up to the right end of the roofed recess. Switch from the right to the left-hand groove, then trend right and up to belay above the right end of the roof.
2. 30m Step left and trend left and up above the roof to the top.

Oh No, Archie's Going Around in Circles 50m HVS 5a ** (1996)
From the small ledge at the start of Under the Pink, climb straight up the wall to the right-hand groove. Climb this for a few metres, then go leftwards into the middle of the wall crossing the groove of Under the Pink. Climb more or less directly up the middle of the wall through a small quartz recess to easier ground above.

SLOC CHIASIGEO

This is the huge geo that cuts into the back of the gap between Guarsay Mor and the stack of Lianamul. Its south-facing wall contains a very small indented sub-geo approximately halfway out from the back. To its west is a clean orange wall sitting above some huge ledges about 50m above the sea. The orange wall is bounded on the left by a distinctive black right-facing corner. Abseil to the base of the corner for the following route.

Morning Glory 70m E1 ** (1996)
1. 30m 5a Climb the wall on the right of the corner *via* an obvious short but steep crack, then climb a black wall through bulges heading leftwards to a ledge below the orange wall.
2. 40m 5b Climb the superb orange wall diagonally rightwards to a bulge. Pull through directly and climb the wall above, again slightly rightwards, to the top.

ARD NAN CAPUILL

This is the headland that lies at the north east tip of the island and faces the small island of Solon Mor. The next route lies on the black slabby wall near the north end of the channel separating Mingulay from Solon Mor. Abseil down the black corner demarcating the south side of the slab to belay on a sloping ledge tucked away in the corner.

Loose Living 30m HVS 5a (1996)
Move out right from the corner and climb the black slabby wall by the line of least resistance, finishing just left of a short corner crack. There is some dubious rock.

PABBAY

THE ARCH WALL

Out of the Womb 100m HVS 5a (1996)
This route essentially climbs the big open corner to the left of the Great Arch, initially climbing the wide slabby right wall. Abseil down the big open corner as for the entry to The Priest and belay at the lowest possible ledge approximately 10m above the sea.

1. 45m 4a Climb easy ground heading for an obvious square-cut block. Go up and left into a curving groove. Good holds lead out of the groove and up left to a belay.
2. 20m 5a Traverse up and right to a large footledge. Make hard and exciting moves up steep flakes to get established above a roof. Traverse right, then go left and climb up to belay in the large corner.
3. 35m 5a Climb the chimney-corner of the main corner to the top.

Prophesy of Drowning 115m E3 *** (1996)
This magnificent route, one of the finest routes in the Hebrides, climbs a line parallel and to the right of The Priest. Start by abseiling down the large corner as for that route to a belay on the lowest small ledge on the right side of the slab.
1. 40m 5b Climb the right edge of the slab passing to the right of a larger ledge to reach a small block about 10m above. Swing wildly round the overhanging right arete into the base of a hanging groove with a distinctive projecting ledge in its base. Climb the groove and the larger continuation above in an excellent position to exit right onto shattered ledged rock, level with the lip of the great roof of the arch.
2. 20m 5a From the edge of the roof climb up and right across an immaculate wall to enter a small right-facing groove which becomes a ramp. Belay at its top below the main corner line.
3. 30m 5c Climb the superb corner with hard moves through its steepest section. Climb the easy corner above to a roof and exit left onto a large ledge below the final corner.
4. 25m 5b Follow the final corner to the capping roof and exit right.

The cliff continues north from the area around the arch itself for 200m but it is very lichenous, gradually diminishing in height and angle. However, there is a fine clean slab opposite a long skerry at the north end of the face. The following two climbs are found on this. Access is by abseil to ledges at high tide level.

Nothing to Declare 45m Very Difficult * (1996)
Climb to the apex of a triangular slab. Pull leftwards over the overlap and continue easily up the slab above.

Customs and Exercise 45m E1 5b * (1996)
Start left of the previous route and climb a corner leading towards a short steep crack. Go up this (crux), then gain the niche above. Pull out of this and climb the easy slab above.

BANDED GEO

Stretch it Out 60m VS * (1996)
1. 40m 4c From the base of Warm Up swing left round the edge, then go up and left into a corner. Follow the corner and continue left onto a large ledge.
2. 20m 4a Climb straight through the bulge above to reach easy ground.

To the right of Warm Up is a black chimney leading to a hanging groove. Just right again is a nasty looking off-width chimney and flake crack, the most obvious feature on this part of the crag.

Squat Thrust 60m Hard Severe * (1996)
1. 40m 4b From the base of Warm Up traverse right over low-tide barnacles into the black chimney. Climb this and the groove above to a ledge. Break rightwards across the wall and go up to a ledge.
2. 20m Easy ground leads to the top.

Blo' na Gael 50m E1 *** (1996)
1. 35m 5b Climb the right edge of the wall right of the off-width groove. Pull through the undercut and climb up and left into a curving crack. Move right into a thin crack and climb this to a bulge on the edge. Go right through the bulge and back left into deep cracks on the wall leading to a ledge.
2. 15m 4a Climb through gnarly ground and corners to finish.

Right of Blo' na Gael is a wide corner crack leading to an unstable bulge, the next corner system to the right being the Steife Brise.

Wind Against Tide 50m E1 5b ** (1996)
Climb the right wall of the wide corner crack right of Blo' na Gael to gain a large horizontal break. Traverse the break rightwards until level with large roofs and climb a thin crack, then go up and right to a good ledge. Finish more or less direct.

RUBHA GREOTACH

The most southerly tip of the island presents an area of immaculate wave-washed rock and two short walls facing due south. The first encountered when heading out to the tip is The Galley. Beyond this the headland terminates in a sheer wall dropping into the sea at its east end. This is called The Poop Deck.

THE GALLEY

Access to the base of the Galley is by descending a choice of two ramp-corner lines near the west side of the headland (the left-hand side of the wall looking in), the one furthest west being the easier. The wall increases in height to the right where its base forms a gully descending into the sea.

The features are described from right to left. Above the tidal section on the right is a conspicuous roof at three-quarter's height. To its left are two parallel overhanging corners. Left again is a clean wrinkled wall bounded on the left by two larger corners.

Winos in a Barren Land 25m E3 6a ** (1996)
This climbs through the roof at the right-hand side. Traverse the obvious break along the base of the wall (low tide preferable) to a belay in the base of a small right-facing corner directly below the roof. Climb the corner to below the roof. Pull left through the roof with difficulty and go up the wall above to the top.

Wiggly Wall 25m HVS 5a ** (1996)
This route takes the clean wall in the middle of the crag. Start on the right side of a projecting buttress at the base of the wall. Make hard moves on flat holds to gain a ledge below the main wall. Superb climbing leads first rightwards then direct to finish up a crack forming the left side of a huge block.

The Abridged Version 25m Severe * (1996)
This route climbs the large corner left of Wiggly Wall. Start on the left side of the lower projecting buttress and go up steeply onto the ledge below the corner, then follow it steeply on jugs.

The Complete Works 25m Severe ** (1996)
Start as for The Abridged Version and climb the left-hand corner, finishing up a ramp and an overhang (crux).

THE POOP DECK

Access to The Poop Deck is only possible *via* abseil from any point along the crag top. At the right end is an immaculate wall seamed by cracks, whose base is sea-washed at high tide. This is bounded on its left by a projecting grey buttress which terminates at a ledge at two-thirds height. This buttress has a slabby corner defining its right side and a steep corner its left side. To its left is a steeply overhanging wall which develops a long roof further left. Below the roof is a colony of guillemots. The routes avoid the birds and are described right to left.

In the Pink 30m E2 5b ** (1996)
This route climbs the pink quartz corner near the right side of the wall. Start directly above a beautiful rock pool under the overhanging base of the wall. Climb a slight groove through an overlap with difficulty to the base of the quartz. Go up this and the corner above to pull out left at the top.

The Craik 30m E3 6a *** (1996)
This climb takes the stunning vertical crack left of In The Pink. Start at the base of a small right-facing corner below the centre of the wall (Illegal Alien). Step into the corner, then climb steeply up and right through a small hanging niche with difficulty to better holds below a deep crack. Go up this to a footledge and climb the superb thin crack above with further difficulty.

Illegal Alien 30m HVS 5a *** (1996)
Start at the small corner of The Craik. Climb the corner to a small ledge on the left. Continue up cracks to finish up the twin cracks at the top.

Wetter Than a Day at the Beach 30m E1 5b * (1996)
This climb follows the hanging corner which essentially bounds the left side of this wall. Start below the isolated roofs near the top of the crag. Climb a crack line leading into the corner which leads to the top.

The Immigrant 35m Severe * (1996)
This is the corner forming the right side of the projecting buttress.
1. 15m Go up the slabby corner-ramp to belay on a ledge at its top.
2. 20m Walk left to the end of the ledge and climb steps up and rightwards to the top.

Geovannie 30m E1 5b * (1996)
Climb the arete of the slabby corner to the ledge. Follow the crack line directly above to finish.

Human Cargo 30m Hard Severe ** (1996)
Climb steps rightwards up the front face of the projecting grey buttress, then go left to the highest point. Step left and climb the steep juggy headwall.

Bogus Asylum Seekers 30m E3 6a *** (1996)
Start 4 metres left of the corner bounding the left side of the projecting buttress. Climb a left trending groove-ramp. Above it, step right and attack the overhanging crack in the headwall. A superb and well protected route.

ALLLANISH PENINSULA

This is the large area of land forming the north-west end of the island. Its southern boundary is the deeply incised geo of Sloch Glansich. Its westerly wall forms a continuous grey and black slabby wall whose most obvious feature is an impressive large black open book corner rising out of the sea about halfway along the headland. On the east side of the northern tip is an un-named geo whose east wall presents a splendid steep face. This has been nicknamed Hoofer's Geo.

Wee Free 25m Very Difficult ** (1996)
This climbs the open book corner. Abseil down the corner to the lowest pedestal at the base of the slab, then climb the cracks in the slab just right of the corner.

Corncrake Chorus 30m Hard Severe ** (1996)
From the pedestal belay, step out right onto the slab and climb directly up the centre. Much easier than first impressions would suggest.

Zen and the Art of Corncrake Management 25m E3 5c ** (1996)
The left wall of the corner is overhanging and sports a fine dogleg crack. Start from a higher ledge in the corner and climb the crack on the left onto a large ledge below the dogleg. Climb this with difficulty to the top.

HOOFER'S GEO

The climbing is on the east face of the geo and the routes can be conveniently viewed from the west side. Near the back of the geo is a deep gully cutting into the east face. Just to the left of this is an immaculate wall containing a hanging crack and a groove. The routes are described from right to left, as one approaches by the Very Difficult scramble descent down the gully.

Hoofer's Route 25m E1 5b ** (1996)
The first steep wall encountered sits under a beak-like overhang. Belay left of a deep cutting. Step right at a blunt rib to under a roof. Pull over and trend right to link up with a fine rising crack line. Jugs lead to the top.

Bint There Dun it 25m HVS 5a * (1996)
Start as for Hoofer's Route and follow the blunt rib to the roof. Pull over direct and follow a groove to the top.

Sugar Cane Country 35m E4 6a *** (1996)
Technical sustained climbing up the centre of the smooth wall, essentially tackling the right-hand and thinner crack. From a belay on the ledge left of a stepped corner, climb on good edges to gain a ledge and the start of the flake crack. Follow this with difficulty to a ledge. Step left and climb a steep crack to exit.

As Sound as Mr JA 25m E2 5b ** (1996)
This route climbs the obvious hanging groove to the left of Finesse. Start as for that route and trend up and left to the base of the groove *via* steep moves. The groove is straightforward but the direct finish through the off-width above is not.

Squeeze Job 35m HVS 5a * (1996)
A few metres to the left the last route a steep corner crack leads through a bulge into a chimney which narrows into an off-width above. Climb this line, finishing up the left wall after the leaning off-width.

Further left again is a bay set back with slabby grooves, cracks and chimneys on either side.

The Ramp 40m Hard Severe ** (1996)
In the middle of the bay is a shallow groove and crack line. Follow this to its end and finish up the headwall on surprising jugs.

Rum

More so than almost any other place in Britain, with the possible exception of a few other locations described in this guide, Rum offers the climber an opportunity to experience the past. There are strict controls on the number of visitors to the island, many of whom are there to see the wildlife. Of those who visit Rum to explore the hills, the overwhelming majority are intent on a traverse of the Rum Cuillin ridge. This means that there is very little chance of seeing other climbers on the same mountain, perhaps even at all during one's stay. Those who relish solitude and the sense of exploration and discovery that climbing on deserted cliffs can offer will find much to commend Rum.

The climbing itself is not of the highest technical standard and the routes tend to be on the short side, especially when the logistical problems of the approach are taken into account. However, the cliffs are generally much more compact than their distant appearance might suggest and the climbing is often of a high quality.

The greatest enjoyment climbing on Rum can offer for most people will be to climb several routes of modest difficulty in a wonderful and almost unique position. Such qualities do not tend to receive much emphasis these days, but it can be said with confidence that those who make the effort, and it is not substantial, will enjoy a rich experience which may well be more rewarding than they might expect. A few spring days on Rum should be on the wish-list of all who enjoy being on mountains in splendid situations.

Rum was privately owned by the Bullough family from 1887 until 1957, when it was sold to the Nature Conservancy Council, now Scottish Natural Heritage. It is run by SNH as a National Nature Reserve, and was designated a Biosphere Reserve in 1977 as part of a UNESCO programme. As such it is of international importance and is the site of much interesting work, including extended studies of red deer, and the project to reintroduce the Whitetailed Sea-Eagle, started in 1975 and enjoying considerable success. Many other birds and animals draw large numbers of people to Rum, including the large colonies of Manx Shearwater, which nest in burrows on or near the tops of several Rum mountains, particularly Hallival.

One particular species found on Rum should not be underestimated. This is the biting midge, the Rum variety being exceedingly vicious and present in vast swarms from May until October. Campers are advised to take suitable precautions, including taking mosquito coils and having midge netting on their tent doors.

As an aside, Rum now appears to be the preferred spelling, as it was until the late 19th century, and this is used on the latest Ordnance Survey maps. Some of the Rum mountains have also changed their spellings, including Allival to Hallival and Trollaval to Trallval.

Maps

The Ordnance Survey 1:50,000 Sheet 39 covers the whole island. The relevant 1:25,000 maps are OS Sheets 233 (NG 30/40) and 261 (NM 38/40).

Access

Rum is most easily reached by passenger ferry, the Caledonian MacBrayne steamer *Lochmor* running a service between Mallaig and Kinloch on Rum, also visiting Canna, Eigg and Muck. The service runs approximately four times weekly (for further information, telephone CalMac on 01687 462403). The passage time to Rum varies between 2 and 3½ hours, depending on whether Eigg or Canna is visited first, or Rum sailed to directly; all variations arise in the course of the year. The SNH flit boat *Rhouma* meets the *Lochmor* in Loch Scresort and transfers passengers to the jetty, at no charge. *Rhouma* has a limited capacity and two trips are frequently necessary at busy times. The ferry leaves Mallaig very early on Fridays during the summer.

Non-scheduled sailings are run by Arisaig Marine (tel. 01687 450678), who can also arrange charters. Charters from Mallaig are also available (Bruce Watt Cruises: tel. 01687 462283). Those fortunate enough can sail their own boat to Loch Scresort. There are no other good anchorages on Rum.

There is no need to seek permission to visit Rum, but overnight accommodation must be arranged. It is also not necessary to get permission to climb, in the sense that climbing is permitted if an area is 'open'. However, particular restrictions do apply to climbing parties. The reasons for these are mainly to prevent major disturbance to research work and wildlife.

KEY TO MAP OPPOSITE

1 Barkeval, South Crags
2 Hallival, South-East Face
3 Askival, The Prow, Coire nan Grunnd
4 Askival, The Prow, Clough's Crag
5 Askival, North-West Face
6 Trallval, Triangular Buttress
7 Trallval, Harris Buttress
8 Trallval, Longship Crag
9 Ruinsival, North-West Face

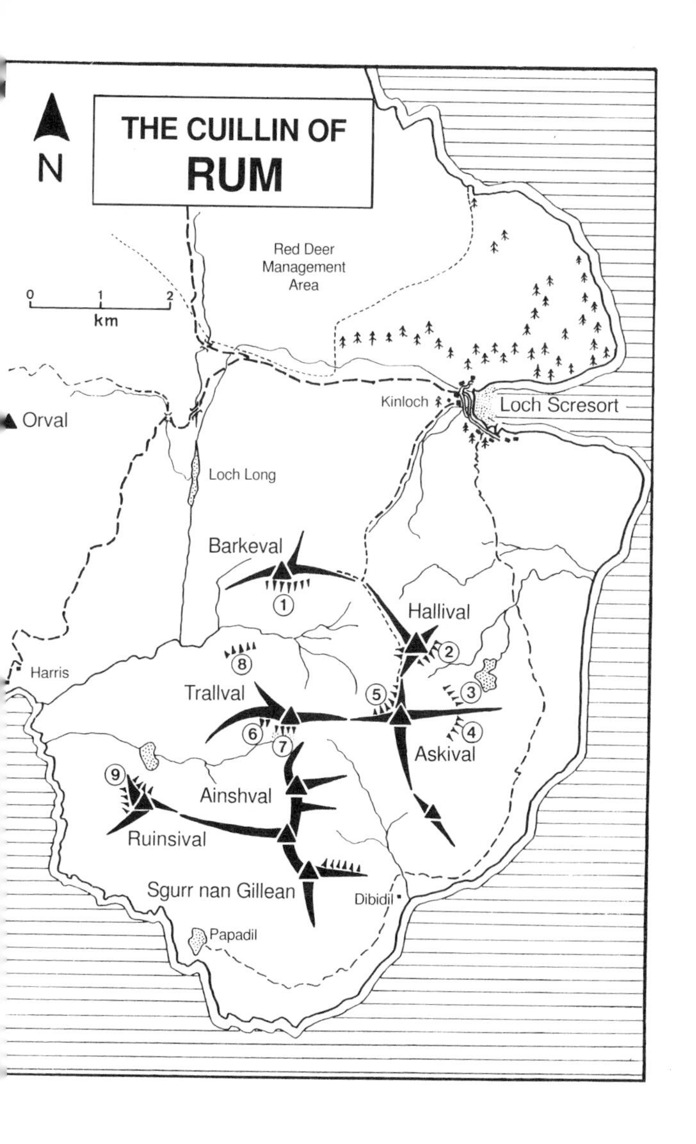

THE CUILLIN OF
RUM
N
0
1
2
km
Red Deer
Management
Area
Orval
Kinloch
Loch Scresort
Loch Long
Barkeval
1
Hallival
2
8
Harris
3
Trallval
5
4
6
7
Askival
9
Ainshval
Ruinsival
Sgurr nan Gillean
Dibidil
Papadil

The red deer study area at the northernmost tip of the island is closed throughout the week, but it is open at weekends, excluding June and October. Other areas of the island will be closed at certain times of year, often due to breeding birds. Some areas may be closed at very short notice. Maps are displayed at the Reserve Office showing which areas are affected and these should be consulted on a daily basis by parties on the island, but anyone intending to visit to climb should telephone and discuss their plans. The staff are very helpful and it is in your interests to do so. You would not be the first to go and only then discover that the area where you intended to climb was closed. SNH has an increasing interest in recreational land use and genuinely wishes to encourage responsible visitors, including climbers, but completely unrestricted access is simply incompatible with SNH's wider roles and responsibilities.

SNH staff are not liable to provide assistance in the case of accident; mountain rescue services are provided by Lochaber MRT. As a consequence, climbing parties must be a minimum of four people and a maximum of fifteen.

Note that neither gardening nor the use of pitons or bolts is permitted. Information sheets on all these matters will be provided to climbers by contacting the Reserve Office (01687 462026). It is recognised that the above could be somewhat off-putting, but the reality is that visits can be arranged easily at most times of year and a little forward planning (anathema to many, to be sure) is all that is required. Parties should nominate a single person (who should be one of the party) to contact Reserve staff; this makes life easier for all.

Accommodation

There is limited accommodation on the island, consisting of (in increasing level of comfort):

1. Camping on the southern shore of Loch Scresort (note the comments on midges above!). Wild camping is not permitted anywhere on Rum.
2. Two open bothies, at Dibidil (Mountain Bothies Association) and Guirdil (Gatliff Trust). There is understood to be a rat problem, at least at Dibidil, at the time of writing. This may reduce its attraction to those who are not rodent-lovers. Neither bothy is provided with deadwood and Dibidil has no driftwood either.
3. There are several bothies at Kinloch run by SNH, provided with heating and cooking facilities.
4. Hostel accommodation at Kinloch Castle, with heating, drying and cooking facilities provided (meals available April-September).

5. Hotel accommodation at Kinloch Castle in genuine period Edwardian surroundings (April-September). Accommodation at the hostel and hotel should be arranged with the hotel (01687 462037). All other accommodation should be arranged with the Reserve office.

There is only a small Post Office shop on the island, so bring in all essential supplies.

HISTORY

Mountaineering in Rum dates back to the 1890s, when the first visits by what we would recognise as climbers began. Probably all of the hills had been ascended before, and quite possibly some of the more precipitous ridges, but with the increasing interest in mountaineering in the late 19th century the island started to receive visits purely for this purpose. Sir Hugh Munro, in Volume I of the SMC Journal, describes a visit resulting in ascents of Hallival, Askival, Ainshval and Sgurr nan Gillean. In the following years several SMC Yacht Meets (grand affairs, no doubt, as befitted a gentleman's club) saw ascents and descents of the major ridges by the likes of Pettigrew, Raeburn, Bell and Brown.

The first recorded rock climbs date from the 1930s, with Oxford University parties climbing the East Ridge and the striking Oxford Groove, both on Hallival, and two routes on the Askival Slab. A couple of other climbs were made in the late 1930s, but visits to the island were few and do not seem to have been encouraged, Hodge in the SMCJ of 1939 having observed that in those days it was "not usually possible to obtain even milk".

In the immediate post-war years access to Rum eased somewhat, perhaps at least in part due to the death of Sir George Bullough in 1939. In the period since then development has been patchy, with occasional flurries of activity coinciding with the visits to the island of particularly energetic groups, and relatively long periods when nothing new has been recorded. In 1945-46 the Junior Mountaineering Club of Yorkshire made the first such foray, recording several climbs on Ruinsival and Askival, then in the following year it was the turn of an Edinburgh University team, which included Geoff Dutton, Hamish Nicol, Gordon Parish, Iain Smart and Malcolm Slesser. In a visit of four weeks, one five-day period saw fourteen new routes climbed on a range of cliffs which included Ruinsival, the Triangular Buttress of Trallval and the West Face of Askival. Mike Ward and Bill Murray visited in May 1948 and climbed on Harris Buttress and Triangular Buttress, Trallval, adding the island's first VS, Bloodstone Crack.

Two years later, Dan Stewart and Donald Bennet, with others, climbed half a dozen routes, including the (by all accounts excellent) Central Rib on Harris Buttress. In 1959 Anne Littlejohn first appears in the records. For a number of years, with companions from the LSCC, she climbed extensively over the island, recording over twenty new routes. Her last new climbs date from 1966, a particularly busy year, when Hamish Brown, with a party from the Braes o' Fife MC, made the first of his many ascents. He in turn was also to put up over twenty new routes over a period of twenty years. Rum was again busy for a few May days in 1967 when Ian Clough and party visited.

So development continued spasmodically through the late sixties, seventies and into the eighties, the majority of climbs being in the middle grades. Of note was Bob Barton's Guillotine (1979) on Harris Buttress, Trallval, the first VS on the crag.

As the eighties advanced the average grade of new climbs rose gently, but Rum remained far from the cutting-edge. In 1985 Graham Little did his bit to add something for the more ambitious, but Orval Pinnacle (E3) stands out as quite untypical of the island, both in terms of difficulty and in the poor quality of the rock (although perhaps what he left behind is more solid).

New routes continue to be found, with the West Face of Hallival being developed by John Mitchell and party in 1990. Further development of Harris Buttress on Trallval in 1994 saw this cliff begin to realise its potential, reinforcing its reputation as the finest on Rum.

THE CLIMBING

The location and description of climbs on Rum have been the source of considerable difficulty over the years and have still not been fully resolved, despite the efforts of many. The particular efforts of Anne Littlejohn of the LSCC and Hamish Brown of the SMC (to whose excellent little guide, now sadly out of print, this section on Rum owes much) should be noted here. As a consequence, this guide focuses attention on the approaches to the climbs and to describing major features of the crags. If you can get there, then you can hopefully find something to climb! The presence of cairns referred to in the descriptions may be taken as positive evidence towards one's correct location; the converse, however, does not hold true.

No quality star gradings are given. The climbing, as observed previously, is rather better than first impressions might suggest, but there is insufficient information to attempt rating the climbs in order of merit. In any case, such an exercise would seem rather out of place.

Approaches

There are three main approaches of interest to the climber. The first is the Allt Slugan path to Coire Dubh and thence Bealach Barkeval (Bairc-mheall). This is found by crossing the stile just over the bridge before the castle. It then runs through a field beside the castle, through a small gate and past the power house to another gate at the edge of the wood. The path is well marked to a broken dam at Coire Dubh. From here the best approach is to head slightly left and then up, heading south-east, before striking out right and descending slightly to the bealach. More direct approaches are possible but they require more effort. Allow about 1½ hours from Kinloch.

The second approach is *via* the road to Harris. This is easily found by following the main road past the castle to the Kinloch River, taking the road to the left there. Harris is about 2½ hours' walk.

The third approach is the Dibidil path which is found most easily by walking towards the castle from the jetty. Just before the first house a faint path runs up beside a burn. Follow this to the back road and the path to Dibidil is signposted. Allow 1½ hours.

THE CUILLIN TRAVERSE

The traverse of the main Rum peaks gives a superb day out with magnificent views to all sides. Readers are referred to the SMC District Guide for a detailed description.

BARKEVAL

591m (Map Ref 376 972)

The climbing on Barkeval is on the south face, directly below the summit. The rock here is peridotite, very rough and weathered to give a very fissured and pocketed surface. To an early climber it was "perhaps the best rock in the world for climbing" (Harker, SMCJ Vol. 10, p26), although it may not be entirely to contemporary tastes.

Approach *via* the Coire Dubh path, ascending from the Bealach Barkeval to the summit; about 1½ hours from Kinloch. Seen from the south and west, Barkeval has a long, straight and very distinct scree chute, the upper end of which stops abruptly at a point about 150m directly below the summit. The square edge at the top of the chute is the 'Rectangle'. This is a useful reference point for locating the climbs and can be found quite easily from the summit. Some 30 metres south of the summit and directly above the Rectangle is the top of Broad

Buttress. This is bounded on its left, looking down, by a wide gully. Left again is a narrow rib - Narnia Arete. The best approach to the climbs starts down this. Follow Narnia Arete for 15m until another broad, broken rib drops from a shoulder on the left, separated from Narnia Arete by a V-gully. This is Honeycomb Arete. Descend this to the Rectangle.

SOUTH CRAGS

The most distinctive feature is Narnia Arete. This and Honeycomb Arete merge at the top right-hand corner of the Rectangle and form the West Edge which drops down into Glen Harris. Right of this is the East Edge, the east flank of which has some of the steepest, most continuous and impressive masses of rock on Barkeval, if not on all of Rum. However, they are composed of a most unusual but unfortunately very dubious-looking rock, the surface being liberally tiled with large rectangular flakes.

Left of Narnia Arete is a gully, then the large and broken Broad Buttress. Left of Broad Buttress is a large overhang above the Waterslide, itself directly above the Rectangle. Left of the Waterslide is Western Isles Buttress, beyond which is a prominent Green Patch.

Rangail Route 105m Severe (1971)
Down left from the Rectangle is a dark gravelly band of rock which descends and tapers to the left. Above its left end is a steep prow, just right of a dyke. Climb the prow to easy ground (20m). Beyond, a fault rises from a black grassy bay. Climb the steep rib to the right of the bay with the crux at the top (25m). Scramble to the top.

Rose Root Slab and Crack 75m Severe (1967)
To the left of Western Isles Buttress, above and set back from the deepest part of the gravelly band referred to previously, is a 20m slab. Climb this and continue in the same line to an overhanging nook. Break out right over this to grassy ledges just left of the Green Patch. Move right up a small slab under a face to the base of a deep-cut chimney (15m, crux). From the stony shelf above continue straight up for about 20m to finish.
Variation: Severe (1982)
Climb the obvious curving corner on the right of the main chimney pitch.

Western Isles Buttress 105m Difficult (1967)
The buttress left of the Waterslide. Start at the top left corner of the Rectangle and follow the best line to the top.

The Witness 60m Very Difficult (1989)
Above the Waterslide an obvious crack splits the big overhang. Start down and left of the crack's base at a rib formed by two slabs. Climb the rib and move right to belay (20m). Make an exposed step right across the top of a poised block and continue up the crack line (40m). The lower section of Broad Buttress can be used as an approach.

Broad Buttress 120m Moderate (1967)
The buttress whose base forms the top of the Rectangle can be climbed anywhere.

Black and Tan 50m Mild Severe (1975)
Start well up the gully between Broad Buttress and Narnia Arete (cairn?). Climb a black-streaked slab to a corner with a grass ledge and poor belay (15m). Take the paler slab above, crux at the start, to a good stance (20m). Follow a slab and the corner above to a cairn (15m).

Christopher 45m Severe (1975)
This climb on the gully wall of Broad Buttress may be the same as one recorded as Guinness. Gain a chimney and follow this to a ledge (15m). Move up right, make an exposed step up and left (crux), then follow a crack and a chimney, ending high on Broad Buttress (30m).

Half a Gale Slab 60m (1989)
The slab forming the left side of Narnia Arete is said to be reminiscent of climbing the dried-up wall of a reservoir.

Narnia Arete 105m Moderate (1967)
Climb the distinctive and conspicuous arete east of Broad Buttress, keeping to the sharp crest.

Honeycomb Arete 105m Easy
The usual descent route.

Aficionado 50m Severe (1982)
The wide gully to the east of Honeycomb Arete has a subsidiary gully on its left with a chimney at the back. This route takes the prominent

crack running up the right-hand slab from the subsidiary gully. Belay at a large overhung niche (25m). Take the overhang direct, then traverse to easier ground following an obvious intrusive band of rock (25m).

HALLIVAL

723m (Map Ref 395 963)

Climbing is found on Hallival on the south-east and west faces. The easiest approach for both is from Coire Dubh, traversing the slopes to reach the base of the south-east cliffs, or crossing the broad ridge to traverse in below the crags of the west face. Allow about 1½ hours from Kinloch. The south-east face can also be approached *via* the Dibidil path, which is quit at the Allt Mor na h-Uamha, but the going is difficult and it is not recommended, except for the views of the cliff if one traverses into Coire nan Grunnd on the way up.

Hallival has given its name to 'allivalite', a rock associated with gabbro. A distinctive feature of the rock on Hallival, and much of it on Askival and Trallval, is the distinctive banding of the light grey allivalite and orange-brown peridotite, the latter often eroded into a honeycomb of pockets and breaks.

SOUTH-EAST FACE

This is split into three tiers, the Bottom, Middle and Summit Tiers. Unfortunately, the tiers were not all named at the same time and this has given rise to some confusion, which may not yet be completely resolved. The Bottom Tier gives climbing only at the right-hand end, where Oxford Groove starts and continues up through the Middle Tier. There are several good, steep routes up to 25m. The Middle Tier provides the bulk of the climbing, with routes the length of the cliff and reaching 70m. Most conspicuous is Allival Slab at the right end. The Summit Tier stands well back from the Middle Tier, diminishing to a rocky step at the right end above the Allival Slab.

Descent Routes
Easy ascents or descents can be made of the Bottom and Middle Tiers by the gully bounding the left end (looking up) of the Allival Slab, and by traversing lines on the slab (see below). To the right (again looking up) one can descend easy ground beyond the East Ridge, but take care as the green, hummocky slopes are riddled with Shearwater burrows.

The big scooped V-gully left of the centre of this face, above the large wide scree chute, is not a descent. For routes further left, a descent can be made just left of Ashes, Difficult at most. Start at a large block at the top of the gully (cairn) and bear left then right. This is steep at the foot, but there is a good spike at 4m. Alternatively, it may be just as quick for most to use the South Ridge. One can escape from the V-gully at the bottom of the Middle Tier by moving right up easy slabs to gain a green gully leading to the top of the tier.

BOTTOM TIER

Choochter Rib 70m Very Difficult (1967)
This actually climbs up to the Bottom Tier, following a blunt rib with a slabby right wall leading to the foot of Oxford Groove. It can be used as an approach to the climbs, if you can find it. Start from the lowest rocks and keep close to the rib. Climb a 3m slab on the right, gain a shelf on the left and mantelshelf onto a flake on the nose. An awkward move lands one on a ledge in an overhanging recess, belay (20m). Climb a short chimney, then go right and climb the crest (15m). Follow the ridge above to the top.

East Ridge Difficult (1931/32)
The description and history of this route is unclear. The Bottom Tier was originally climbed *via* a groove to the right of a small overhang at the foot of the ridge. The following year a gully to the north of this was taken to the grass terrace, and the Middle Tier ascended by a short, narrow chimney a few metres to the right.

Breeze 20m Severe (1967)
The right wall of the lower section of Oxford Groove is a smooth slab which breaks into cracks higher up. Start at the extreme right and climb straight up.
Variation: 20m Severe (1990)
Climb Oxford Groove for 3m, then make a right-rising traverse onto a wall for 5m. From a broad ledge climb a short arete, then traverse left to a crack line. Follow this to the terrace.

Oxford Groove 60m Severe (1933)
This is the obvious stepped V-groove which cleaves both Bottom and Middle Tiers at the right-hand end.

Relish 20m HVS (1984)
Climb the rib between Oxford Groove and Gargoyle Chimney by following the left-slanting line in the wall to an obvious crack in the pocketed wall. Finish up the rib above.

Gargoyle Chimney 25m Severe (1966)
The obvious chimney left of Oxford Groove, with a projecting chockstone at the base. Pull over the gargoyle and climb the chimney.

Honky Tonk 25m HVS (1992)
This route follows the obvious line just left of Gargoyle Chimney. It may share some climbing with the next route:

Salad Days 25m VS (1984)
Starting 4 metres right of Diamond Corner, climb a steep cracked wall to blocks, then traverse briefly right and go up corners to the top.

Diamond Corner 20m Severe (1967)
This route lies some 10 metres left of Gargoyle Chimney and comprises a groove with a squarish diamond-shaped overhang at a little over half-height. Climb the corner, passing the overhang on the right, then bear left to the crest and follow this to the top.

Haddie 20m Severe (1974)
This follows an obvious line up the wall left of Diamond Corner. Start at a sentry box and follow the crack to the top.

Sunny Side 20m Severe (1967)
Left of Haddie is a big dirty corner-chimney with an impressive left wall, then an overhanging arete left again, then some cracks springing from a roof. Start left of these. Climb to a pedestal, move onto a pock-marked band, then bear left for a few metres before finishing up a crack slightly right.

MIDDLE TIER

Thumbs 20m Severe (1974)
Climb the smaller groove on the right of the upper pitch of Oxford Groove, passing a pinnacle at 7m.

Cambridge Arete 25m Severe (1951/52)
The arete left of the upper pitch of Oxford Groove. Move up blocks left of the overhang, climb a deep 4m groove, then traverse to the arete and follow it to finish by an awkward crack.

Red Brick 20m Difficult (1961)
Start as for Cambridge Arete but, instead of traversing right, go left onto the edge of the Allival Slab. Move up the edge for a few metres, then slant left up an obvious series of ledges to finish easily beside the top of Cambridge Arete.

Allival Slab 45m Difficult
This slab is bounded on the left by a gully which gives an easy line of ascent or descent. A 4m crack in its right wall gives access to the bottom left corner of the slab. An easy right-rising traverse leads to the top of the slab, whence a short steep crack in the wall above leads to the crest of the East Ridge some 20 metres left of the top of Oxford Groove. Alternatively, the slab may be traversed at a lower level until it steepens, with small holds and fine exposure. Climb up and slightly right to end near the top of Oxford Groove.

Flake and Crack Route 35m Very Difficult (1966)
A third of the way along under the overhangs below Allival Slab there is a corner. The flake up which the route used to start now lies on the corrie floor. An alternative start (1990) traverses in from the bottom left corner of Allival Slab to an obvious small pinnacle; junction with the original route. Climb up the slab above to an obvious steep crack.

Allivalhalla 35m Very Difficult (1990)
Gain the bottom left corner of Allival Slab and make an easy rising traverse into a vegetatious crack heading to an obvious corner. Where the slab steepens before the corner, move 3 metres right and follow a thin crack to the left of a detached block, exiting onto an easier-angled slab to the left of an obvious block which forms a horizontal overhang.

Helen's Horror 45m Very Difficult (1966)
About 4 metres left of the Allival Slab there is a deep chimney. Bridge this to the overhang, make an awkward step right, then climb grass and easy rock to a small cave. Leave this by crawling along a small ledge on the right, then finish up a short wall.

Nice 'n' Easy 20m Hard Severe (1990)
About 20 metres left of the gully bounding the left edge of Allival Slab is a small pyramid-shaped buttress. Climb the well defined left-bounding arete, with an entertaining finish.

Asphodel 50m VS (1966)
Round the corner to the left of Allival Slab are three deep grooves. This is the middle one, about 30 metres left of Helen's Horror. Traverse onto the arete on the right, then follow a slanting crack to the foot of a vertical 4m crack in the right wall. Climb this strenuously to good finishing holds on the right and continue to a stance among piled blocks (35m). Continue up a crack formed by two of the blocks to a rocky hollow. Finish up a crack directly ahead, passing an overhanging block on the left.

Lotos 70m Mild Severe (1966)
Climb the leftmost of the three grooves mentioned for the previous route. Pass an overhang on the right at 8m and at the top traverse left by a rocky ramp and go up into an amphitheatre of loose earth and rocks. Finish by traversing piled blocks on the right and climbing the second groove beyond, or better (Hard Severe) by a layback crack immediately above the line of the groove.

Ashes 25m Very Difficult (1966)
The central section of the east face, between Allival Slab and the big scooped V-gully, is divided by two streams. Start a few metres to the left of the right-hand stream. Climb a steep groove with an overhang about three-quarters height.

Amaranth 30m Severe (1966)
This climb lies several buttresses to the right of the big V-gully. A crack runs up the middle of a wall which is set back in the crags. A small projecting block in the crack is a distinctive feature. Start at a small cave (cairn) beside an arete right of a line of easy slabs. Climb an overhang and a small slab, then move easily to a ledge below a crack. Follow the crack up the wall, past a projecting block, to finish just right of a triangular recess containing a square block.

Moly 30m Very Difficult (1966)
This route follows a wide, obvious groove situated midway between the V-gully and the Askival col. Start by a dyke behind a flake on the

right wall. Step into the groove about 6m up and when this becomes a deep crack move into the chimney on the right. This has a loose protruding flake at the bottom, more large blocks and a capstan above; it sounds like a delicate tread might be an advantage.

Midge 25m Very Difficult (1966)
Start about 65 metres right of the South Ridge of Hallival. Climb a V-groove with an obliquely-jammed block halfway up and a large square-cut overhang at the top, avoided on the left.

Midgeless 20m Difficult (1966)
Starting 15 metres left of Midge, climb a steep corner crack to an awkward finish on the right.

SUMMIT TIER

Frustration 15m Severe (1967)
Climb the first obvious double-decker incut corner on the tier, right of the top of the escape route from the V-gully.

Corner Crack 10m Severe (1966)
Above Ashes the tier is cut by an obvious steep corner. Scramble from a cairn and climb the corner.

WEST FACE

The climbing is on a compact crag high on the west face, just below the summit and overlooking Atlantic Corrie. It looks scrappy from below but (according to the pioneers) it offers some fine routes. Viewed from below the most prominent feature is the Western Slab, to the left of which is Western Wall. Right of Western Slab is Hourglass Buttress, easy-angled in its lower part but with a fine steep slab above the grassy ledge at the buttress waist. Right of this is a broken area of ribs, the Central Ribs, ending in a prominent V-groove which bounds the left edge of Western Ridge. To the right of this the rocks become lower and more broken. There are easy descents at both ends of the crag.

To the left of Western Wall is a chockstone-filled gully. The first two routes lie on either side of the gully.

Wander 20m Severe (1995)
Climb the right-hand edge of the wall left of the chockstone-filled gully.

Dog Day Sunrise 20m VS (1995)
Climb the bulging crack immediately to the right of the chockstone gully, and exit right at the top.

Grendel 20m VS (1990)
From the left end of Western Wall, climb a black-streaked wall and groove to ledges. Climb steeply up the right wall, mantelshelf onto an overhanging ledge and finish up an overhanging crack.

Fugazi 20m VS (1990)
Starting 10 metres left of Troll Corner, climb a blunt nose to gain an obvious niche. Climb the steep right wall to a small ledge, then bridge up to a mantelshelf onto an overhanging block. Move left and climb the steep headwall, traversing right to a break, then climb a corner to the top.

Troll Corner 20m VS (1990)
At the junction of Western Wall and the side-wall of Western Slab, climb a steep corner crack with an overhanging direct exit. Continue up a slab to finish left of a rock gargoyle.

Left Edge 25m Very Difficult (1995)
Climb the extreme left edge of Western Slab.

Slab Direct 25m Very Difficult (1990)
Climb straight up the centre of Western Slab, finishing to the right of the rock gargoyle.

Cullie's Route 25m Very Difficult (1990)
This route climbs the right side of Western Slab, to the right of the scrappy groove.

Atlantic Highway 25m Hard Severe (1995)
Climb two slabs from the lowest point of Hourglass Buttress with increasing interest to reach a sloping grassy ledge. Move left and climb up to below an overhanging crack. Climb the crack on good holds.

Moss Slab 10m Severe (1990/95)
This lies on the upper section of Hourglass Buttress. Climb from the bottom left corner, traverse onto the slab and climb it to the top.

Direct Start:
This makes the best use of the slab. Scramble from the right-hand side of Hourglass Buttress to reach a sloping grassy ledge. Start by the left-hand corner as for the normal route, but traverse across a niche to gain the bottom left-hand side of the slab and climb it directly.

Bishop's Groove 20m Severe (1990)
This route takes the obvious V-groove to the left of Western Ridge. Scramble up some loose blocks to belay at sound rock. Climb the groove to the top.

Pandora's Box 35m Severe (1990)
Start at the left edge of Western Ridge. Climb a narrow slab and a left-facing corner to a large overhang which is turned on the right. Climb a V-groove to a steep wall, which is climbed using the left side crack to an overhanging prow and belay. Traverse 5 metres right and climb an easy open V-groove above.

Western Ridge 45m Severe (1990)
From the lowest rocks, climb directly to a belay at an overhang. Climb this to the end of continuous climbing at 25m. Continue over two short walls separated by grass ledges.

ASKIVAL

812m (Map Ref 393 952)

This is the highest and arguably the finest of the Rum mountains, and it offers magnificent views. There is climbing on all sides, although only a limited amount is on the upper part of the mountain, and that mainly on the North-West Face. The remainder of the climbing is found on crags on the east flank. The ridges provide some airy scrambling.

Approach *via* the Allt Slugan path and a traverse along the west side of Hallival to reach the bealach between Hallival and Askival.

NORTH RIDGE

This was first climbed by Munro in the 1890s. It provides the most interesting section of ridge on Rum, giving about 180m of scrambling with a 10m step, the so-called 'Pinnacle'. The lower section includes a very striking and narrow grass arete. Above, the Pinnacle bars the way;

climbed direct it is Moderate. The gully to the west is the same grade, while the east face offers the easiest line. The steep west flank is difficult of access and has one recorded route:

Zigzag 40m Severe (1966)
After climbing the Pinnacle the ridge levels for a bit. At the next steepening, descend the gully to the west (right). Facing the ridge again, the route climbs the buttress to the south (right), ending on the top of the step. Start at the lowest rocks by right-bearing cracks to avoid an overhang. Move up and traverse left to climb up the edge of the gully to a stance at the end of a ledge. Either climb the groove above or follow the ledge to the right until it is possible to climb up. Continue to the top of the step.

EAST RIDGE

Before being climbed as an ascent, this ridge was descended by J.H.Bell and W.Brown at the SMC Easter Meet of 1897. All the difficulties can be avoided, but more sporting possibilities exist. At the top the ridge steepens. Climb over a jammed block to a sandy shoulder a little below and to the north of the summit.

SOUTH-EAST FACE

This face is broken by a number of ridges which all end on the small summit plateau. Locating climbs here has proved to be beyond all current authors, and the two descriptions will provide a challenge to those so inclined.

Ogilvie's Ridge Difficult (1938)
South of the East Ridge is a shallow gully and beyond this and about a third of the way across the face is a steep, well-defined ridge. The rock is good. About halfway up, 4m short of the top of a 20m chimney, finish right on a steep exposed slab. Climb the narrow pinnacle above on the right to the neck beyond. Follow the exposed edge and traverse several easy pinnacles to finish about 40m from the summit cairn.

Rouma Route Very Difficult (1976)
This is probably a variation on the previous route. South of the East Ridge are some scree-filled gullies, beyond which lies a prominent slab split by a chimney (cairn). Climb the chimney, or harder, the slab, then

two small steps leading to a steepening (25m). A chimney above leads to a serrated crest with a vertical step (20m). Ogilvie turned this on the right, but either of the two corners on the left is better. If the first corner is chosen, it should be quit before its top to step right onto a narrow crest which ends the route. Scrambling lands one about 12m from the summit of Askival.

THE PROW

The East Ridge flattens as it drops eastwards and forms a distinct prow at about 500m, which has cliffs on both facets, those on the north-east side overlooking Coire nan Grunnd, and those on the south-east side overlooking Coire nan Stac. The latter cliffs have been given the name Clough's Crag, which extends for over 750 metres in two well defined tiers on the long, right portion. On the left (southern) part, they jut forward in a big bulge of rock before a definite break where there is a grass slope with a burn.

CLOUGH'S CRAG

Consolation Crack 20m Difficult (1961)
At the extreme right end are two small buttresses, the right one having several conspicuous overhangs in its upper part. To the left of this buttress is a large grassy bay. Start at the top of this. A rough slab on the right leads to a ledge, from the left end of which a steep 8m crack leads to the top.

Right-Hand Buttress Direct VS (1961)
Start at a cairn at the bottom right-hand corner of the frontal wall. Traverse left at first, then go straight up to an awkward position close under the overhangs. Move delicately left (crux) to a large slab; belay high on left. Re-cross the slab to the right and climb a steep 6m corner.

Dribble 40m Very Difficult (1967)
About 45 metres left of the previous route, a cairn and an arrow mark the start of an obvious corner, which is normally wet.

Eyrie Arete 40m Very Difficult (1967)
A cairn and an arrow mark the start, about 12 metres left of Dribble. Climb slabs and a crack on the right flank of the arete to a small overhung ledge. Go round the arete and climb to a grass ledge and block belay (25m). Go right and up a left-slanting gangway to the top.

Satisfaction 25m VS (1982)
About 8 metres right of Eyrie Arete there is another prominent ridge. Traverse onto the ridge from the right-hand side and climb onto the arete (crux). Move up the arete to a good block, then move back right and take the obvious line, finishing by a prominent hand crack.

The Candle 40m Mild Severe (1967)
A short distance left of Eyrie Arete, a tall pillar is set in a niche in the wall. Climb the left-hand crack of the candle to its top, move right and climb a crack to a ledge and belay (20m). Avoid the obvious corner directly above by climbing left to a grass terrace (20m). The Upper Tier continuation gives 30m of Difficult climbing.

On the Upper Tier, above Right-Hand Buttress, there are two routes up twin buttresses, separated by a grass gully. The starts of both routes were originally cairned. **Amble Arete** (30m Moderate, 1967) takes the right-hand twin up the crest on good holds and **The Ramp** (30m Very Difficult, 1967) takes the left twin, going up the ramp, then moving right to climb the crest.

The next routes are on the bulging buttress just before, and right of, the break in the cliffs.

Trap Chimney 55m Difficult (1967)
A cairn and arrow mark the start at an obvious chimney near the right end of the buttress. Climb the chimney to a ledge on the left (20m). Continue up the fault, passing under two large chockstones.

Fluch 60m Very Difficult (1967)
Start about 10 metres left of Trap Chimney at a cairn below a big corner. Follow a strenuous crack to a ledge and belay (12m). Continue up the corner to a grass ledge under twin cracks (20m). Take the right-hand crack, then climb into a bay on the left (15m) and continue up a corner to the top.

Fuarr 65m Difficult (1967)
Start 10 metres left of the previous route; arrow. Climb a slab to a corner, then take the right-hand crack to a large grass ledge (30m). Above, trend leftwards over slabs to the top.

Gemme 90m Very Difficult (1980)
Start on the far left of the lower tier, marked by an arrow at a crack. About 4 metres left of this, climb a slab to an arrow on the right wall. Climb a crack up the wall to a grass ledge and belay. Climb a steep slab to a belay, then make a short traverse left to a slab, and climb to the top.

COIRE NAN GRUNND

The crags here are on the north-east flank of Askival Prow, overlooking Loch Coire nan Grunnd. At the left end of the long escarpment is an obvious buttress split by two prominent cracks. In the middle is Central Buttress, which has several fierce-looking cracks of over 30m (mostly unclimbed). To the right is a prominent roof-capped corner.

Calder Chimney 35m Very Difficult (1967)
Start at the left end of the buttress, at the left-hand crack with an arrow at the start. Climb the chimney to a ledge on the right, then traverse left across the chimney to climb the left arete to big blocks (20m). Follow the chimney to the top.

Valhalla 20m VS (1975)
This climb follows the steep crack immediately round the arete to the left of Calder Chimney. Traverse left at the edge at 10m and finish up cracks above.

Fylde Crack 40m Very Difficult (1967)
Start at an arrow right of the left end of the buttress, at the right-hand crack. Climb up, then left by a narrow slanting crack to join the main chimney. From the top of this climb the slab on the right.

Striding Edge 30m Very Difficult (1967)
Start at an arrow 20 metres right of Fylde Crack. Climb the slabby arete and cracked wall above to a ledge (20m). Climb the overhanging crack and the awkward groove above.

Grunt 15m Severe (1967)
Climb the slanting crack up the smooth wall just right of Striding Edge.

The following routes are in the Central Buttress Area: **Tyke Arete** (20m Very Difficult, 1967) takes the arete left of the roof corner; **Layback Crack** (20m Severe, 1967) follows a prominent crack in the middle of a shallow bay right of the roof corner; **Trundle** (20m Severe, 1975) climbs the corner just left of the previous route; and **Grease Crack** (20m Very Difficult, 1967) takes a chimney-crack a few metres right of Layback Crack.

On the left end of the main face of Central Buttress, well left of the above routes, is an arete on which the following routes have been recorded:

Skrymir 35m Severe (1975)
Start on the arete, move up to a prominent left-slanting crack and follow it to a ledge (20m). On the wall above are two cracks; climb the left-hand one (15m).

Asgard 20m Severe (1975)
Climb the obvious groove right of the arete.

The Pink 30m VS (1975)
Take the second corner to the right of Asgard, just right of the highest part of the face. Climb jamming cracks to a ledge, then follow the right-hand corner-cracks to the top.

Below Coire nan Grunnd, between the two main burns draining the corrie, is a crag facing roughly north-east, the most notable feature of which is a big blank slab. At the extreme northern end is a short wall, then a grassy gully, on the left of which is a north-facing wall taken by the following climb:

Pineapple Wall 35m Severe (1991)
Start at the base of a wide, greasy oblique crack. Once off the ground, traverse left a short way to the next crack where it widens into a scoop. Climb the wall above to broken ground, then step right and continue up the arete.

Rum and Pineapple 20m Severe (1991)
Start about 8 metres left of the end of the wall below a skyline boulder and a vague groove. Climb the groove, then step right and follow the obvious thin crack to the top.

WEST RIDGE

This easy ridge starts from the Bealach an Oir (*Pass of Gold*) and gives some scrambling at the top which can be turned on the south.

NORTH-WEST FACE

This impressive face can be seen from Barkeval, Hallival, or Trallval. It rises above steep and broken slopes and so gives fine situations, with routes up to 105m. The best approach from Kinloch is probably *via* Bealach Barkeval, crossing Atlantic Corrie to the Bealach an Oir, and going back up the West Ridge to the easy rake below the crags. Allow about 2 hours. The ground below the crags is steep, loose and broken, and while a high-level traverse from the north is possible, leaving the North Ridge at the very toe of the Askival Pinnacle, it is not really recommended as a slip would be very serious.

The North-West Face lies to the right of the big amphitheatre on the right of the west flank of the North Ridge. The climbs described are those which have been located following their first ascent, but several which have failed that test have been omitted. Edinburgh Climb and Askival Slab start at a higher level than the climbs to the right, the approach being up particularly steep, mossy and gravelly ground which, following wet weather at least, is extremely dangerous. It is not known how much attention these routes have received since their first ascents.

Edinburgh Climb 105m Severe (1947)
This route lies on the part of the face which looks almost north and can be seen from the North Ridge. There is a cairn at the start, an obvious defect in sheer cliffs. Easy rocks lead to the crux groove, which leads to a traverse to a shelf and belay. Follow the easiest line to the top rocks, which are Difficult.

There are two routes on Askival Slab, both 60m and done in 1935. The **Left-Hand Edge** is Very Difficult and the **Right-Hand Corner** is Severe.

Rolling Pin Route 60m Very Difficult (1951)
Start in a gully 8 metres right of Askival Slab. The gully is broken at 25m by an overhang, then it becomes a chimney. Go about 20m up the

gully and belay on the left. Climb straight up a slab, often wet, to the overhang. Move up and right, crux, to a corner. Traverse slightly right and go up to a niche. Exit right with difficulty to an easy traverse leading to a chimney with a narrow exit. An easy final 10m lead to a ledge.

No.1 Gully
This gully lies about 25 metres right of the previous route and has one or two pitches, Difficult if taken direct. Escapes are possible throughout.

One-Two Buttress
The third, most southerly, of the ribs of the face has a few Moderate pitches.

Shearwater Rib 55m Very Difficult (1957)
About 10 metres left of One-Two Buttress a sound rib protrudes. Climb 12m to a platform, sling belay(!). Swing right from a hold and go up a nose to a large platform at about 25m. Continue above, or detour on the right, and finish by the top section of One-Two Buttress.

No. 2 Gully is a wide, rotten gully with no real climbing, although the rocks beyond it to the south give good scrambling.

Atlantic Ridge 105m Very Difficult (1948)
The right-hand of the long ridges on this side of the face has a distinctive steep 15m wall at about 30m. Start a few metres right of the sharp left-hand edge. Follow a shallow crack for 25m to a platform on the edge. (Round the left corner is a steep demarcating groove). Continue a few metres to the right up the steep 15m wall. Thereafter the route goes all the way to the top, ending suddenly at the summit.

Atlantic Slab 100m Very Difficult (1974)
Seen from Atlantic Corrie, there is a prominent slab running from the foot of the crag to finish slightly left of the summit. This route follows the slab, starting just right of a large overhang about 90 metres left of Atlantic Ridge. Climb a crack to a stance (20m) and continue up the crack system to a slab with a small arete to its right (35m). Climb the slab to a bay (10m), then climb the wall leading to the big slab above by a deep crack (large chockstone). Follow the slab to the top (35m).

BEINN NAN STAC

546m (Map Ref 396 941)

Much of these crags are very steep, or wet, but they may repay investigation. Seen from Dibidil bothy there are three areas of tumbled rocks below the lowest and nearest line of cliff.

Wet Crack is a route of uncertain grade and provenance; it is hidden above the top right corner of the middle area, where there is a deep-cut chimney with chockstones. Go under these and climb the 15m dripping chimney at the back of the chasm.

Brown Trousers 55m VS
This route takes the slab right of the previous route, leading to the obvious grassy corner. The crux is the exit from this along a wide, exposed and sloping ledge, until holds above can be reached. Pull round the corner and go up to grass.

Ankle Very Difficult (1986)
This route takes the left skyline, as seen from Dibidil, following the last of the rocks on the flank of Beinn nan Stac. Start at a cairn. A slab left of a hanging V of rock leads left to the edge, then break back and go up steeply to a bouldery ledge and grass terrace (25m). Easy ground follows with odd bits of scrambling up the ridge to the top of the hill.

TRALLVAL

702m (Map Ref 377 952)

This, the most central of the Rum Cuillin, is slightly lower than its neighbours and gives a particularly fine viewpoint. It has twin summits, the western top being slighly higher. The ridge between the two tops provides an airy scramble. Although the summit rocks provide little climbing, on the southern flanks of the West Ridge lie Triangular Buttress and Harris Buttress, the latter the largest cliff on Rum with routes of up to 135m. These cliffs are hidden from all viewpoints to the north and east, being best seen from Ainshval. Despite some attention in recent years, scope for further exploration remains. Indeed, a number of new climbs were found in 1995 on Longship Crag, low down on the north face.

To get to the summit from Kinloch, go over the Bealach Barkeval and traverse Atlantic Corrie to Bealach an Oir, then follow the East Ridge to the top. For the Harris and Triangular Buttresses, from Bealach an Oir traverse under the south-east face to Bealach an Fhuarain which provides easy access to the summit and both buttresses. Alternatively, follow the Harris Road, possibly taking the Long Loch fault, to cross Glen Harris until the south-west corrie (Fiachanis, known as The Sandy Corrie), can be followed to the foot of the cliffs.

The most scenic, interesting and quickest approach from Kinloch is *via* the Bealach an Fhuarain. For the return journey the Harris road may be preferred. Allow about 2 to 2½ hours *via* Bealach an Fhuarain, 3 to 3½ hours *via* Harris.

SUMMIT BUTTRESS

There is one route recorded on the walls below the summit.

Malindarra 60m Difficult (1984)
This follows a line of short corners on the wall flanking the south side of the west peak, directly below the summit. Start in a grassy bay to the left of the gully descending from between Trallval's twin peaks. A prominent band of lighter rock skirts the base of the wall. Climb the corner system, without deviation, to the top.

TRIANGULAR BUTTRESS

The West Ridge runs out for about 500 metres before dropping towards Harris. Triangular Buttress lies under the western end of this almost flat section of ridge, facing south-east. It is best seen from Ainshval. It has an obvious triangular shape, with a right-slanting slab on the left and a left-leaning chimney-crack on the right. Easy descent is possible *via* slabby ground a short distance to the west.

Ptarmigan Crack 45m Difficult (1947)
This route was called Fat Man's Agony by the first ascent party, but it was renamed by the second ascent party the following year and has been known by this name since. It follows the left-leaning chimney-crack forming the right edge of the triangle. Start to the left of its foot, climb up to a prominent window and go through a very small manhole. Grooves on the right lead into the chimney which is followed until lack of space forces an exit; a variety of finishes are possible.

Fat Man's Evasion 45m Severe (1947)
Start 25 metres left of the previous route. Climb up to a platform level with with the foot of the chimney. A fine airy traverse to the right leads across into the chimney above the manhole.

Botany Crack 40m Severe (1950)
Start at a cairn in a rectangular recess guarded by a fine 6m pinnacle at the foot of the slab. Go up the recess to a good platform, move slightly left and follow the crack to the top.

Zigzag Route 35m Severe (1950)
A few metres to the right of the previous route is a peculiar serpentine crack. Climb this, then move up left to a belay. Continue up right to a conspicuous overhung recess; passing the overhang proves awkward.

The Wandering Botanist 35m Hard Severe (1982)
Climb Zigzag to the recess, then step left onto the wall and climb it to an overhang. Traverse left under this and finish up Botany Crack.

Bloodstone Crack 30m VS (1948)
To the left of the gully in the centre of the buttress is a short steep crack; cairn. The start is strenuous, on dwindling holds on the right wall. There is a good stance above.

HARRIS BUTTRESS

This is a big 120m broken wall of gabbro. First impressions are of a broken, wet and repellent wall, particularly when approached *via* Sandy Corrie. However, the reality is fortunately rather more favourable, there being some very good climbing here, perhaps including the best on Rum.

At the centre of the buttress is an indefinite rib, Central Rib, below which there is a poised capstan-like rock. The rib is bounded on both sides by shallow gullies, each with a large overhang. About 12 metres right of the right-hand gully is a vertical 75m crack, the line of Guillotine. The routes are described from left to right.

1 Lucky Eddy 30m VS (1986)
Start 30 metres left of Hagar at an obvious left-facing corner. Climb the crack to a ledge below a steep corner, then climb this direct or *via* the arete to the right. Finish up right.

2 Hagar 30m HVS (1986)
This climb starts at a small cairn 30 metres from the west end of the cliff. Climb a thin crack, then move into an obvious niche (crux) and go up this to the top.

3 Peer Gynt 115m VS (1994)
Left of Central Rib, the crag's most obvious feature is a small grey buttress low down, seamed by right-slanting cracks and bounded on its right by a big corner which fades higher up (Doric). Start at the toe of the grey buttress. Climb a crack to a slot, step left, then go up to an easing (15m). Continue on slabs, heading slightly rightwards to a blocky ledge (50m, 4c). Take the inset corner on the right for 3m until a move left gains a bigger ledge with a huge block. Work up to a right-facing corner which leads left to a ledge below a Y-groove, well seen from below (25m, 4a). Climb the groove, smear into the right-hand branch, and continue more or less directly up the nose above (25m, 5a). Scramble to the terrace (15m).

4 Doric 130m E1 (1994)
On the western sector, left of the gully on the left of Central Rib, is a prominent right-facing corner and crack which fades into the face. Above is a rib between two overhangs. Climb the crack. Where it peters out at a ledge, step left to a wall and a cracked flake and continue up to a ledge and belay shared with Peer Gynt (50m, 5b). Climb the short corner above before breaking out left and moving up to a ledge and block (as for Peer Gynt). Trend right to the foot of the rib (15m). Climb the rib *via* a crack, blocks and bulges. Finish to the left, passing a large block to enter a large corner and ledge. There is a better belay 5m higher in a corner (40m, 5a). Continue up the rib and wall on the right to the terrace.

5 Central Rib 90m Hard Severe (1950)
This is one of the best routes on Rum. Start at the lowest point of the rocks, a few metres above the capstan. After the initial overhang, a groove and easier slabs lead to the foot of the rib where it becomes a definite and almost vertical arete. Climb the crest, or just right of it, for two pitches to a small, finely-placed platform. Cairn. Two further pitches up slabs and steep corners finish on a sloping grass terrace, cairn. The upper slopes can be reached by a short wall directly above, or easier slabs to the right.

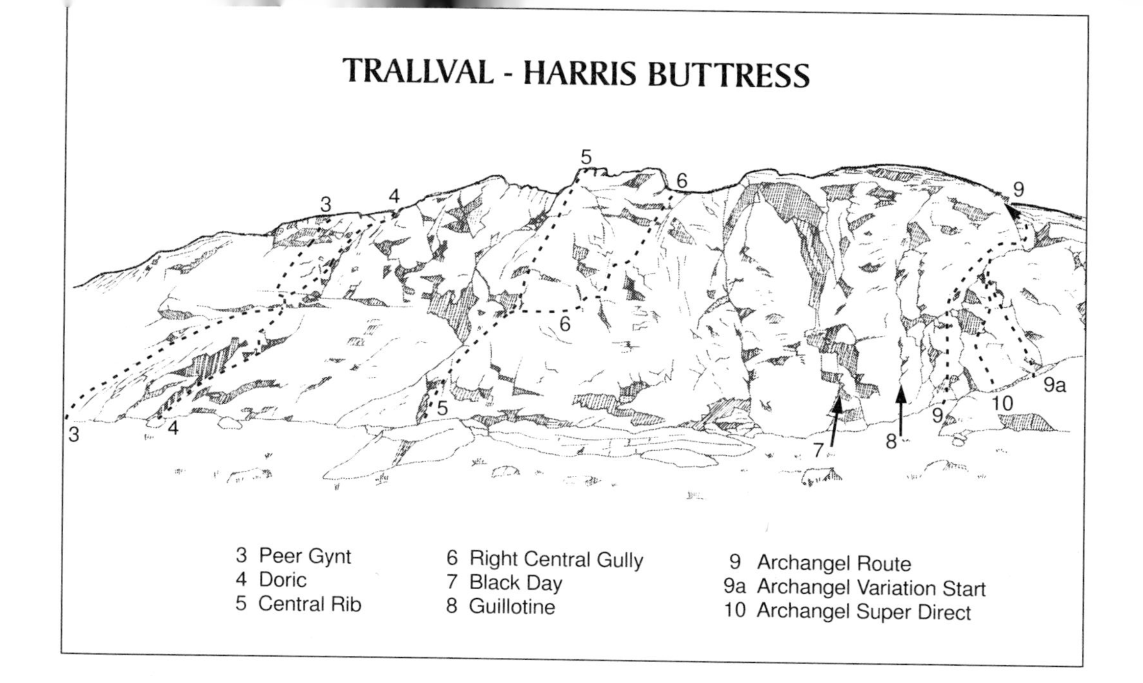
TRALLVAL - HARRIS BUTTRESS
3
4
5
6
9
6
3
4
5
7
8
9
10
9a
3 Peer Gynt
4 Doric
5 Central Rib
6 Right Central Gully
7 Black Day
8 Guillotine
9 Archangel Route
9a Archangel Variation Start
10 Archangel Super Direct

6 Right-Central Gully 90m Very Difficult (1951)
This is the straight black gully slanting right, just right of Central Rib. Start as for that route but where it steepens go right over easy ground to the foot of the gully. This is awkward to start. After two further pitches, the gully divides into two chimneys; the one on the right is Severe. Follow a steep crack with a useful flake on the right wall, then climb various cracks for over 30m to a chimney with a prominent chockstone and the finish.

7 Black Day 120m VS (1983)
This may be a variation on Guillotine. Climb the black central corner to the top section, then escape by a traverse right to join Archangel Route. There is a hard section at 25m, moving right to avoid some steep loose ground.

8 Guillotine 125m VS (1979)
This route follows the crack mentioned above, which becomes twin parallel grooves in its upper reaches. A good and sustained climb. Climb the crack and move right to a good ledge below the right-hand groove (12m). Climb up to the bulge guarding the groove, avoid this by following the left-hand groove for a short way, whence a delicate traverse leads back into the original groove and a ledge on its right (15m). Move left to a small pinnacle perched between the grooves. Climb into the bay above and escape by a steep crack on the left, then move left to a large block ledge (25m). Move back right under the Guillotine and use it to surmount the short steep corner. Follow pleasant ramps and grooves to belay below a large white slab (35m). The slab now leads easily to a junction with Archangel Route (35m). Escape is also possible leftwards.

9 Archangel Route 120m Very Difficult (1948)
A route of interest and character. Some 13 metres right of Guillotine a wide, open chimney leads to the left end of a broad ledge. Climb rocks left of the chimney to a block pinnacle, then "spread wings of faith, and take a short, bold flight across the gap" to a corner crack which leads to the broad ledge (belay). From the right end of the ledge a wide crack leads to a large corner. Climb this for 6m before exiting to the ridge on the left. Turn the final overhangs on the left.
Variation start: Very Difficult (1951)
Start 12 metres right of the original route at a small cairn. Climb a steep groove. Trend right and up for 45m to the foot of the great groove.

10 Archangel Superdirect 30m HVS 5a (1994)
Start a few metres right of Archangel Route and climb to the centre of the big traverse ledge by a short capped groove and a big flake.

Return Call 25m E1 5b (1994)
At the extreme right-hand end of the buttress is a small subsidiary buttress with a steep west-facing wall separated from the main buttress by a gully. A diagonal overlap runs from right to left, with a steep crack splitting the wall above. Start in the middle of the overlap, break through the roof (delicate blocks) to gain a platform on the right. Climb the crack above to the top (crux).

The Dwarfie 35m HVS (1994)
Above the terrace and directly above the finish of Peer Gynt is a small two-tiered buttress of impeccable rock which offers this excellent short route. Climb the wall between a roof and thin crack on the left, and a steep flaky crack on the right (20m, 5a). Continue up the middle of the cracked slab behind the ledge (15m, 4b).

LONGSHIP CRAG (Map Ref 371 962)

Situated low on the north face of Trallval, just 70m above the Abhain a' Ghlinne, this cliff is ideal for days of low cloud. The rock is a very rough peridotite and where clean of lichen it is climbable in the wet. Access from Kinloch is *via* the Bealach Barkeval or (longer, but less ascent) by following the Harris road to Long Loch, then following it and the Abhainn Sgathaig to Glen Harris.

From across the glen the crag can be said to resemble, without too much imagination, a Viking longship, with two 30m high buttresses connected by a stretch of lower crags some 200 metres wide. Useful reference points, from the left, are a left-facing wall veined with thin dykes; a prominent arete, the lower half of which has broken away and slid down to form a detached pillar; a triangular slab leading up to several short, vertical cracks; a stretch of low-level overhangs followed by a recess and then a jutting triangular overhang high up. To the right again are two left-facing slabs, one behind the other, then a horribly vegetated gully.

The high buttress on the right (containing a birch tree) has a curious domed overhang, then develops into a face, lichenous on the right, split by several crack lines and, in the upper half, by a cleft which reaches right through behind the buttress to the vegetated gully. Right of this face is a right-angled niche, after which the cliff leans back somewhat. An almost heart-shaped slab in the centre of the face is a feature of this area which gradually becomes more broken and peters out. Descents can be made at either end of the crag.

Phew! 30m VS (1995)
Start up the left-bounding crack of the veined wall just to the right of the black rock. At the overhangs move one metre left, then go up to a sloping ledge. Continue up the corner above, then move round onto a left-facing slab on the left and thence to top.

Heartwork 30m E1 5b (1995)
About 2 metres right of the previous route is a bold fault line up the veined wall. Follow this to a ledge, then move left to a bulging right-trending layback crack. Climb the obvious corner on the right.

The Light Fantastic 30m VS (1995)
Start up the obvious V-groove to the left of the detached arete (common to Breenge) and break away by a crack on the left wall leading to a deep cleft. Climb this to the top.

Breenge 30m VS (1995)
This route follows the obvious V-groove to the left of the detached arete. Climb the groove and corner, turning the overhang at the top on the right.

Cruise Control 30m E1 5b (1995)
Climb the clean open corner right of the detached arete to the overhang. Turn this on the left, then finish up an easy slab. A superb line.

Vanishing Point 20m Very Difficult (1995)
Climb the left-hand crack up the obvious triangular slab easily to the vertical cracks at the top. Climb these, stepping right to finish.

A Bit on the Side 15m Very Difficult (1995)
To the right of the triangular slab is a vertical arete, and right again is a deep wide crack. Climb this using holds on right wall to a halfway ledge. Move right to a crack splitting the wall and climb this to the top. Low in the grade.

Rum Doodle 25m Hard Severe (1995)
Climb the corner crack to the left of the triangular overhang using holds on the slab and jamming in the crack until the angle steepens and the crack splits in two. Take the left-hand crack (the right is chossy) and climb past a possibly detached flake to the top, stepping right to finish.

On the Greener Side 25m VS (1995)
Climb the arete below the triangular overhang to below the roof, then turn the overhang by a crack on the right.

Slab and Arete 20m Difficult (1995)
Follow a broken crack line on the right edge of the large left-facing slab, then climb the arete to the top.

Feersum Endjinn 30m VS (1995)
Start up the black vertical flake crack in the centre of the right-hand main face and continue leftwards to gain a slab. Climb this to an apex and make an awkward move through a bulge to gain the bottom of the cleft. Squirm up through this to gain a ledge, then go up the centre to the top. A varied and interesting route.

Shadowlands 30m VS 4c (1995)
Climb the obvious black groove to the right of Feersum Endjinn past a steep crack and follow the corner above through an overhang, finishing up the left-hand ramp.

Atlantic Breeze 30m HVS (1995)
Scramble to the foot of the bulging heart-shaped slab and climb it by the central crack. At the top of the slab go through small overhangs and follow the continuation of the crack to the top.

Across the Lines 30m Very Difficult (1995)
Climb the deep crack on the right of the heart-shaped slab directly to the top.

Doric Direct 30m Severe (1995)
About 10 metres right of the heart-shaped slab, a 6m pillar of lighter coloured rock leans against the face. Climb this, then go through the small overhangs above and slightly to the right. Go over the bulge above, then climb the flake crack and finish through a recess to the left of a large rectangular block.

RUINSIVAL

528m (Map Ref 356 940)

This, the most distant of the Rum peaks with worthwhile climbing, has several north-west facing crags. The cliffs are relatively low and may offer a reasonable alternative if higher crags are out of condition, although it is a fair way to go to find out!

Approach either *via* the Harris road, with the option of a shortcut through the Long Loch fault, or *via* Bealach Barkeval, descending Atlantic Corrie and skirting the northern slopes of Trallval until Loch Fiachanis and the foot of the cliffs can be gained. The latter approach is shorter; allow about 2½ hours from Kinloch. When approaching *via* Harris, cross the Rangail River a few hundred metres from the beach. From Dibidil, approach *via* the Bealach an Fhuarain, or along the Leac a' Chaisteil, or go round the coast *via* Papadil.

The cliffs have been split into three tiers, each being subdivided into a number of buttresses. Locating them all can be confusing. A useful reference point is the Giant's Staircase, which descends directly from the summit in a series of nine rock steps. Down and right of the Giant's Staircase are the crags of the Lower Tier, while to its right at about mid-height is the distinctive Highlander Buttress of the Middle Tier. On the left side of this is a smooth wall, the right side sporting a series of grooves and ribs. Right (west) again, across the wide stone chute and distinguished by large green platforms in the centre, lies the Green Wall, the remaining crag of the Middle Tier. Above this and overlooking the stone chute is the Summit Tier.

The Fiachanis Face is a two-tiered corrie lying to the east of the Giant's Staircase, immediately south of and above the loch.

1 Giant's Staircase 180m Very Difficult (1947)
This gives a good climb. The second, fourth and fifth steps are Very Difficult; the climb is Moderate to Difficult thereafter. Against the fifth step and seen from afar is a pinnacle which is Severe by the face, followed by an unpleasant step off it onto a steep 6m wall. The ridge ends near the summit plateau.

LOWER TIER

This is a line of buttresses, which have been named North Buttress, Woden's Wall (behind and to the right of North Buttress), Thor's Buttress, Frigga's Buttress (across a break), and South Buttress.

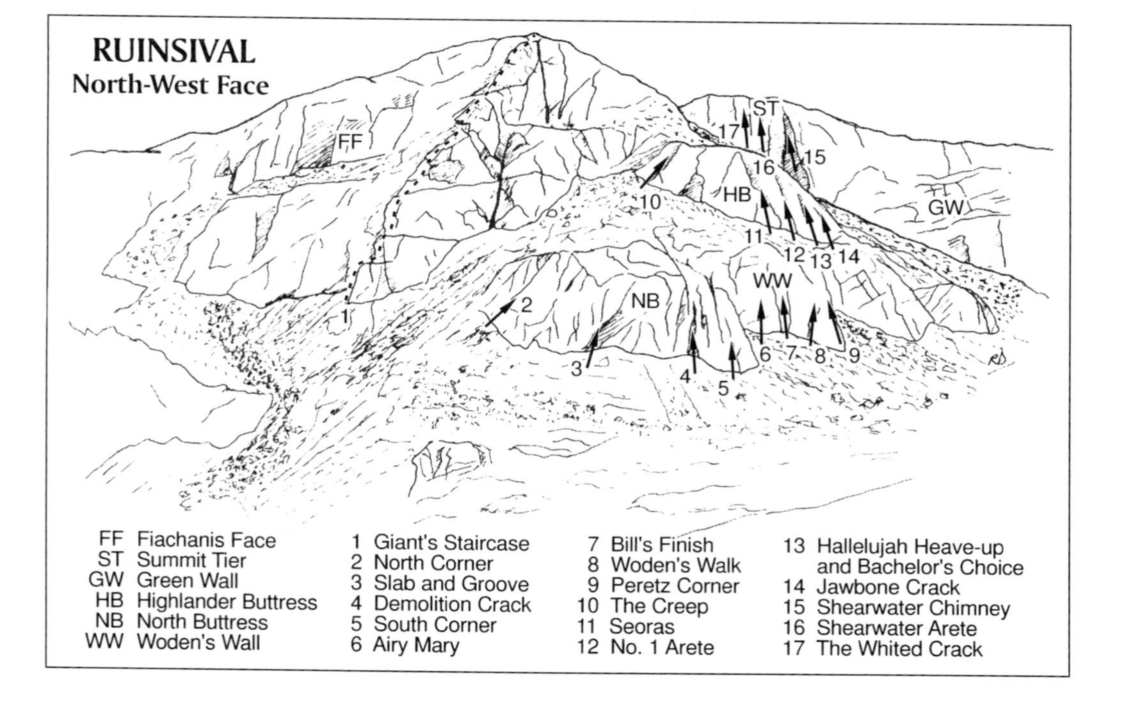
RUINSIVAL
North-West Face
FF
ST
GW
HB
NB
WW
1
2
3
4
5
6
7
8
9
10
11
12
13
14
15
16
17
FF Fiachanis Face
ST Summit Tier
GW Green Wall
HB Highlander Buttress
NB North Buttress
WW Woden's Wall
1 Giant's Staircase
2 North Corner
3 Slab and Groove
4 Demolition Crack
5 South Corner
6 Airy Mary
7 Bill's Finish
8 Woden's Walk
9 Peretz Corner
10 The Creep
11 Seoras
12 No. 1 Arete
13 Hallelujah Heave-up and Bachelor's Choice
14 Jawbone Crack
15 Shearwater Chimney
16 Shearwater Arete
17 The Whited Crack

NORTH BUTTRESS

2 North Corner 35m Moderate (1945/6)
Climb a chimney just right of the north corner.

Riona 35m Severe (1959)
About 30 metres right of North Corner there is a 12m flake with a damp gully to the left and a wet overhang high on the right. Climb from a cairn up the most prominent part of the flake to a stance at 12m. Move left, and swing round by a perched block to a large, possibly unsound ledge. Go up the steep wall above, moving slightly right, to finish directly above the start.

3 Slab and Groove 45m Very Difficult (1945/6)
A few metres left of the centre of the buttress there is an obvious break in the rock wall. Follow a slab rightwards, then climb an awkward groove left to a triangular grass ledge. Quit this by the slab on the right, or (harder) straight up.

Cracked Rib 45m VS (1950)
A few metres left of Demolition Crack is a rib with an overhanging base and split by a vertical crack. Cairn. Go up 20m past a heather shelf to a recess under and just right of the rib; spike belay. Traverse to the rib and follow it on the right to a shelf and belay. Climb the final part on the left of the rib.

Perdita's Traverse 40m Very Difficult (1959)
Left of the start of Slab and Groove is an arete and two grooves. Climb the left-hand groove to a broad ledge. From its right end, climb down round an airy corner and go right into the right-hand groove. Take the projecting staircase on the right side of this groove, crux, to a large stance on the arete. Finish up the right side of this.

Perdita's Groove 30m Mild Severe (1960)
This route takes the groove to the right of the previous route. Follow the groove straight to the top, with a good stance halfway. If the stance is reached from the broad ledge on Perdita's Traverse, then the standard is only Very Difficult.

4 Demolition Crack 35m Severe (1947)
To the left of the south corner of the buttress is a deep groove, V-shaped in its lower part, which cuts the face. Climb a subsidiary groove 6m further left to a flake at 15m. Traverse right to enter a corner in the main groove and ascend directly.
Variation: 20m Very Difficult (1950)
Climb the main groove direct.

5 South Corner 30m Moderate (1945/6)
Climb up just to the right of the corner.

WODEN'S WALL

Sloping Ledge 25m Very Difficult (1947)
Start directly above Demolition Crack at a cairn. Ascend to a sloping ledge beneath a large funnel of slabs. Either enter the funnel at the end of the ledge (Severe), or continue right over a groove and go up to the top.

6 Airy Mary 35m Very Difficult (1947)
Start at a cairn and climb a corner crack 12m left of the rib on the left of Bill's Finish. Continue very steeply thereafter, then the angle eases and the rock becomes loose. Finish by a slab and rib to the left.

Sentry's Sortie 30m Very Difficult (1959)
Between the central break in the face and the south corner there is a large shattered arete. Start 4 metres to its left (cairn) and take a steep 6m crack over two ledges to the crest of the arete. Follow this a short way to a grassy platform and block belay. Cross the groove to the right, then climb up, enter a sentry-box to the right and exit by the corner above it (crux).

Groove and Chimney 30m Difficult (1959)
Take the groove right of the shattered arete to the grass platform of Sentry's Sortie. Climb up 4m as for that route, then traverse left over a flake to a ledge, from where a short chimney leads to the top.

7 Bill's Finish 30m Difficult (1945/6)
This goes up the very broken slab to the right of the central break.

8 Woden's Walk 35m Very Difficult (1947)
Ascend the obvious crack to the right of the previous route. After the first pitch, traverse 25 metres right to near the top of Peretz Corner. Exposed.

Woden's Crack 35m Very Difficult (1950)
Start as for Woden's Walk, but continue straight up the crack.

9 Peretz Corner 35m Difficult (1945/6)
The big ridge to the right of the wall appears tower-like from below. Start round the corner to the right.

THOR'S BUTTRESS

Chuckiestane Groove 35m Severe (1959)
Start at a cairn at the highest point of the grass and scree between Woden's and Thor's Buttresses, below a wet groove between two overhangs. Climb the left wall until forced into the groove, the last few metres being the crux. Easier ground leads to a good stance at 20m. Continue up the groove at an easier angle and finish up a steep wall.

Right-Hand Chimney 35m Very Difficult (1961)
Far back on the left flank of Thor's Buttress, to the right of previous route, are two obvious chimneys. Take the narrow, steep right-hand one throughout.

June Jigsaw 25m Very Difficult (1961)
At the right flank of the buttress is a cairn at a large dissected slab. Follow the deep crack to the left, then go right by a ledge to a vertical crack. Climb this to blocks, then follow easy ground to the top.

FRIGGA'S BUTTRESS

Gothic Crack 20m Very Difficult (1961)
There is a wide crack edging the huge frontal flake of this buttress. Climb from the top of the arch up the centre to the top.

Yellowstone Chimney 25m Difficult (1961)
This is the chimney between Frigga's Buttress and South Buttress, with a yellow wall on the left. The crux is at the top.

SOUTH BUTTRESS

Curving Chimney 25m Difficult (1961)
On the right flank, a deep damp chimney curves up right. Climb this on the left wall to chockstones and continue to an awkward exit.

South Crack 20m Very Difficult
Go beyond Curving Chimney past a grassy overhung corner to a first weakness. Follow the steep crack above a big block, then climb the wall on the right and the steep nose.

MIDDLE TIER

This comprises Highlander Buttress and Green Wall.

HIGHLANDER BUTTRESS

10 The Creep 15m Difficult (1945/6)
The face on the left of the buttress is bounded on the left by a grassy gully. Climb a crack in the gully and continue over a narrow exposed slab. The rest of the wall is vertical and intimidating.

11 Seoras 45m VS (1966)
Seen from afar, towards the right of the face is a dark triangular depression. Climb to the apex of the triangle, then go over this, crux, to a groove. Follow the groove and take the right fork to end at a cairn at the top of No.1 Arete. "The first chink in the defences of a fine wall" (H.M.Brown).

Right of the face, a series of grooves and aretes gives good climbing. No.1 Arete is the one edging the face, No.2 Groove is to its right, then No.2 Arete and so on.

Fingerless 40m VS (1974)
Climb the prominent crack 12 metres left of Seoras to a right-trending ledge. Follow this to the base of a crack and climb it to the top.

12 No.1 Arete 50m Mild Severe (1966)
Start at the lowest point and scramble to a steepening and belay. Climb the crux overhang onto a surprising pedestal, then finish up grooves.

13 Hallelujah Heave-Up 55m Severe (1947)
This is in No.2 Groove. Difficult rocks lead to a wall. Climb this at the corner by a loose block. From the large shelf, traverse 3 metres right onto the left wall of No.3 Arete, then ascend the crux groove. Traverse left around the corner and go up a slab to the heave-up.

14 Jawbone Crack 35m Hard Severe (1947)
Climb No.3 Groove until forced by the overhang onto the right wall, crux. A delicate move leads back into the groove above.

Bachelor's Choice 50m Very Difficult (1947)
Follow the first two pitches of Hallelujah Heave-Up, then traverse left to No.2 Arete around a sensational corner to a prominent ledge. A 25m rising traverse across a vertical wall, astride a long flake, leads to the top of No.1 Groove. Exposed.
Variation Finish: (1959)
After going round the sensational corner to No.2 Arete, follow this for 4m, then traverse left along an exposed ledge for 7m and descend slightly, with difficulty, to belay in the corner. Climb this for 3m and continue the traverse left to an exposed corner. Descend to a broad exposed ledge, then follow it to a long narrow slab forming its continuation. Climb this to the top.

GREEN WALL

Campion Slab 20m Very Difficult (1966)
This is the rough, steep, diamond-shaped slab on the left side of Green Wall. Climb the curving crack, or go up from the flake to the right.

Face Route 60m Severe (1966)
Start 8 metres left of the rake running up to the green platforms, at the foot of a dyke; cairn. Climb up left by a crack to a ledge, and follow cracks straight up the wall over two further ledges to finish up a wide 15m crack.

Very Well 30m Very Difficult (1970)
This follows the rib bounding the right side of the chimney-gully right of Face Route.

Claymore 70m VS (1967)
Start at a cairn 5 metres right of Face Route. Move right on a dyke to a small platform. Climb the left face by a crack, strenuous, to a perched block on a terrace. Cairn. Continue up cracks in the wall (24m, cairn). An easier 15m wall leads to a larger terrace where escape is possible, but the best finish is up the crack on the nose for 25m.

Right Corner 45m Very Difficult (1966)
The far right of Green Wall has a tongue of slabs with an undercut crack to the right. Climb up beside this, on the slabs or the corner, with the difficulties in the top section.

Right Corner Chimney 40m Difficult (1966)
The tongue of slabs is bounded on the left by this chimney.

SUMMIT TIER

15 Shearwater Chimney 50m Very Difficult (1947)
Above and to the left of the buttress, this chimney rises out of a wide gully, the upper section overhanging. There is a chockstone belay at 35m. Finish over a hanging block and through the window above.

16 Shearwater Arete 45m Difficult (1947)
Climb the arete to the left of the chimney, moving to the right from its top up a vertical wall.

Avalanche Avenue 20m Severe (1947)
This route is on a small buttress left of and up the stone chute from the above. Ascend the prominent groove, traverse left to the terrace and go up a rather loose funnel above.

17 The Whited Crack 35m Very Difficult (1947)
This is the obvious white crack, often greasy, in the peridotite wall of the gully above Shearwater Arete.

FIACHANIS FACE

Well across the top tier, going east, is a steep unclimbed wall; Bulging Wall. About 45 metres east of this is a 25m spikey wall at an easier angle; Fork Slab. In its centre a crack forks at 4m into three prong-like cracks. These were all climbed at Very Difficult (1966).

PINNACLES AND STACKS

STAC NAM FAOILEANN

There are two stacks here, about 1½km before Dibidil coming from Kinloch. The first can be climbed by a groove on the landward side (12m Difficult, 1967). The second is more shapely, also Difficult, and lies a little to the south. It can be climbed after descending the sea-cliffs for 30m.

STAC NAM FAOILEANN CLIFFS

Tidal Exit Cracks 25m Mild VS (1983)
Start in a recess directly opposite the rear of the stack and climb the corner to exit round the overhang onto a ledge. Step left and go up steep diagonal cracks to a small niche, 5m from top. Climb up the niche on small holds (crux) and mantelshelf onto the top.

Big Boots and Trainers 25m HVS (1983)
This route takes the deep-cut chimney at the landward side of the point. Abseil down to flat rocks at the base of the chimney. Climb this to a sloping ledge on the left. Climb the left-hand crack to a bulge, go over this, and continue up the centre of the chimney to the final mantelshelf.

STOATIR POINT

This is the obvious point about 20 minutes from Dibidil on the path to Kinloch. The routes are on the light-coloured south face. Abseil from a block to a large shelf at the foot of the climbs.

Isoamylase 20m Severe (1980)
Follow the big left-trending crack near the abseil to a large shelf. Walk right to a corner and climb this, then step right and finish to the right of the abseil bollard.

The Rozzer 25m VS (1980)
Traverse just above sea-level to an obvious niche at the left edge of the crag. Step left onto a slabby arete, then climb the corner and awkward bulge above. Traverse briefly right on a large shelf, then climb a crack up leftwards to finish on thin holds.

Ocean of Mercy 20m VS (1980)
Start as for Isoamylase. Go up the wall, heading slightly left to a crack with a chockstone at 4m. Go right on small holds to a corner with sloping shelves, then move up to a large ledge and belay. Move left along the ledge and finish up Isoamylase.

Morning Tide 25m VS (1980)
Start 3 metres left of and slightly lower than Isoamylase. Move up about 2m, then traverse left across the wall on small holds. Go up to a small ledge, then traverse to the top of The Rozzer corner. Mantelshelf as for The Rozzer, then move right and go up a wall to a ledge. Move left along this to an obvious flake, climb this, finishing on loose blocks left of The Rozzer.

The obvious stack off this point is Difficult on the seaward side (1980).

PAPADIL PINNACLE

This 10m pinnacle is at the seaward end of the loch. The easiest line is a scramble.

FIST AND FINGER STACK

South-east of Sgorr an t-Snidhe, 3km south of Harris, there is a striking double stack joined by a neck to the shore and requiring low tide for the approach. Cross to the south end of the stack and go up to a pedestal. Follow weaknesses left, then go right to the final wall and overhang. Take the curving 'pinky crack' up left (Very Difficult, 1970).

SGORR AN T-SNIDHE

On the main point, visible from Harris, is a small stack which needs low tide to get to the seaward side. From there, scramble up to a sneck at the north end, then climb onto the 'sea roofs' - two steep slabs, the first being crossed to its top right to gain the upper slab to the summit (Very Difficult, 1970).

ORVAL

571m (Map Ref 334 991)

This has an impressive 30m pinnacle at the foot of its northern cliffs. It is loose, and was originally ascended by lasso and Tyrolean traverse. The first conventional ascent included some flying time, due to the unreliable rock.

Orval Pinnacle 30m E3 5b (1985)
Start at the slight groove on the right-hand side of the pinnacle, just down from the neck. Climb the groove to a small ledge on the outward face. Climb the face, with a move left to gain another small ledge (5b). Continue up the face, with a move onto the left edge to gain the small flat-topped summit (5b). A long sling should be carried for an abseil anchor.

LATE NEWS

Information about the following route on The Prow of Askival was received almost too late for inclusion:

Golden Rib 100m Severe (1996)
Two-thirds of the way along the southern extension of Clough's Crag (heading south-west) is a yellow rib, with a wet shattered gully on its left and a wet wall on its right. This point is at the southern extremity of the large boulder field which runs below the cliff. The rib has an overhung base, several clean slabs and an open groove at its top.
1. 20m Gain the rib using the lip of the slab on its left side. Follow the crest to an overhung grass ledge and belays.
2. 20m 4a Move up and round the left side of the overhang (crux) to regain and follow the crest of the rib to a grass ledge.
3. 35m Move up towards a hanging V-groove and pass this *via* some loose blocks on its left side. Move up the fine rib above to belay below a leaning roof.
4. 25m Gain the hanging slab above, moving right to avoid the roof. Finish up the open groove above, or better, by the blocky wall on its left.

Eigg

Although in relatively close proximity to its higher and larger neighbours Rum and Skye, the island of Eigg's unique skyline gives it disproportionate prominence in the Hebridean seas. A visit to Eigg more than confirms this distant impression; the scenery is magnificent and varied, its flora and fauna diverse and the fringe activities numerous. Indeed it is possible to spend a very good holiday on Eigg without actually doing any rock climbing.

In simplistic terms Eigg can be split into two parts; to the west of the road, a swelling moorland (now partly afforested) culminating in the monolithic pitchstone ramparts of An Sgurr; to the east a moorland plateau fringed by crumbling basalt crags (reaching a maximum height of 130m in the east). The whole island offers spectacular coastal scenery, that in the north and west being particularly grand and penetrated by deep caves and lonely boulder-filled coves. The deep cave of Uamh Fhraing and the nearby cathedral cave of Uamh Chrabhaidh in the south are easy to get to and a useful diversion on an off-day. The fine sands of the Bay of Laig and the 'singing sands' of Camas Sgiotaig, in the north-west, offer an even more relaxing alternative with the possibility of good windsurfing at the former. During the summer, lively ceilidhs are held at the village hall (Map Ref 478 840).

Rock Climbing

Few rock features in the British Isles can equal the grandeur of An Sgurr. Its near 100m high vertical nose dominates the island and provides a distinctive landmark when Eigg is viewed from the mainland or adjacent islands. That it has attracted such little rock climbing attention over the years is probably due to a combination of its formidable appearance and a largely undeserved reputation for poor rock. In fact, the columnar pitchstone porphyry, when divested of loose blocks and poised pillars, ranks with gabbro and gneiss for quality, providing a wealth of friendly rock features and protection. With the exception of a couple of routes mentioned in the text, the rock dries quickly after rain. The majority of the coastal cliffs of Eigg are composed of basalt, which tends to be loose and vegetated and is best left as a challenge for future generations of route-hungry pioneers.

Rock climbing on Eigg is possible throughout the year, being relatively low-lying and possessing a favourable climate. In late summer and autumn, mist and midges can greatly detract from the experience.

There is a potential conflict between the activities of climbers and the rich and diverse plant life that has colonised the ledges of An Sgurr. This is also true of predatory birds during the nesting season. A responsible attitude to cleaning routes and to climbing during the spring months is essential.

History

Other than the peripheral probings of Professor Norman Collie early this century, and the pioneering presence of M.Botterill in the early 1920s, Eigg was largely neglected until Ian Clough and friends climbed the obvious fault and chimney lines in the late 1960s. They named the two most prominent features after the early pioneers. The open faces were still regarded as unjustifiably loose. However, the challenge of The Nose proved irresistible, and a raiding party from south of the Border picked this formidable proboscis in 1970 with the aid of six bolts and an unspecified number of pegs. Other than the enigmatic Purphura by Paul Moores, the 1970s saw no further action. The next wave of development came in the late 1980s when Graham Little and friends put up a selection of fine routes on the open faces of An Sgurr's south-facing walls and buttresses. Although Psycho (1987) pointed the way to a new wave of development on the steeper walls, this has largely failed to materialise. Two hard routes on the short but immaculate upper west section of Ocean Wall, courtesy of Kev Howett and Graham Little in 1994, will perhaps herald renewed climbing interest in this beautiful island. Much unclimbed rock remains, with scope for many new routes, particularly in the higher grades.

Access

There is a passenger ferry (which will also carry bicycles) from Arisaig (*M.V. Shearwater*) operated by Murdo Grant (tel. 016875 224 or 678); crossing time, 1 hour. Alternatively, take the ferry from Mallaig (Caledonian MacBrayne, tel. 01687 462403). The crossing time is 1½ hours if direct, but it can take up to 5½ hours if the other Small Isles are visited *en route*. Passengers are transferred to and from the island by a small ferryboat at a supplementary charge. A taxi usually meets the ferry. A bicycle is the ideal form of transport if the whole island is to be explored.

Maps

Ordnance Survey 1:50,000 Sheet 39 and 1:25,000 Sheet 261 (NM 33/48)

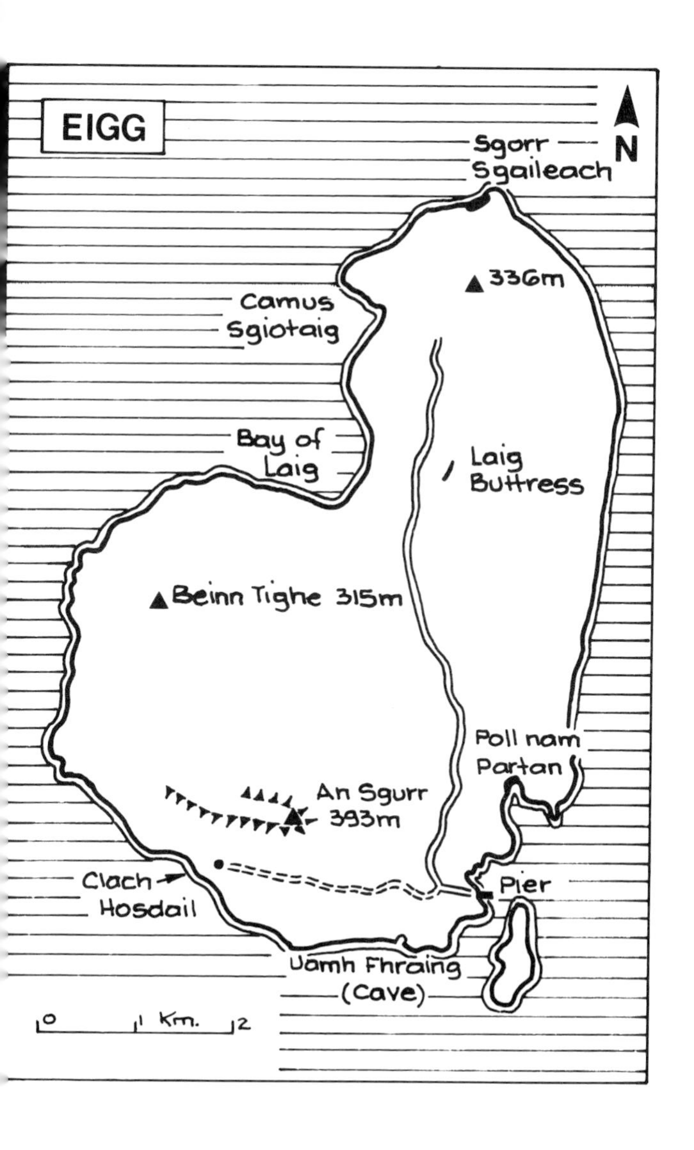
EIGG
N
Sgorr
Sgaileach
336m
Camus
Sgiotaig
Bay of
Laig
Laig
Buttress
Beinn Tighe 315m
Poll nam
Partan
An Sgurr
393m
Clach
Hosdail
Pier
Uamh Fhraing
(Cave)
0
1 Km.
2

Accommodation
There is a hotel at Kildonnan in the south-east (tel. 01687 82446) and a guest house at Laig (tel. 01687 82437). Several self-catering, bothy-type cottages are available for rent; the bothy at Grulin being particulary convenient (tel. 01687 82413/23/28). Caravans are available for hire at Cleadale. Wild camping around An Sgurr is discouraged. The official site (perhaps the least attractive spot on the island) is at Map Ref 477 847. Camping in the north of the island is generally accepted; ask locally.

Provisions
The island's only shop (and post office) is located at the centre of the island at Map Ref 479 865. Excellent home baking can be purchased from the cafe at the pier.

AN SGURR

393m (Map Ref 463 847)

From The Nose, at the abrupt eastward termination of An Sgurr, a great south-facing pitchstone wall extends to the west to an obvious break. The descent routes lie on either side of a small broken buttress. This face is known as Main Wall, and is divided into three sections by the great faults of Botterill's Crack and Collie's Cleft. Beyond the break lies Big Cave Buttress with The Slab above and Minor Buttress to the west. Next comes Chimney Buttress, with its distinctive grassy chimney, and then the fine dome-shaped Beehive Buttress. After a wide gap in the crags, a boulder-filled gully delineates the east flank of Ocean Wall, with its long, slabby upper face extending north-westwards. The final rock feature is Village Wall, separated from Ocean Wall by steep, broken ground.

Characteristic of all these rock faces is a vegetated ledge line that girdles the crags at around half-height. All the climbs described lie on the clean upper tier, the lower tier being, in general, loose and vegetated. Banding the base of the upper tier, just above the ledge, a near-continuous band of friable basalt presents problematic starts to many of the routes.

The climbs are described from right to left, starting at The Nose.

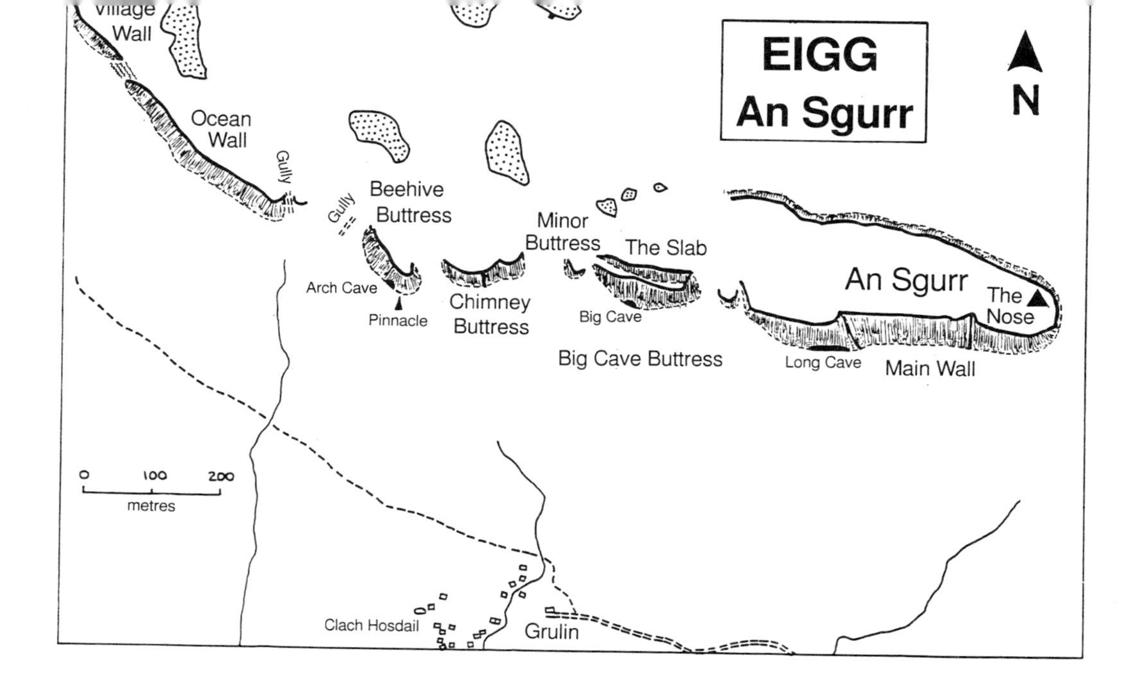
EIGG
An Sgurr
N
Village Wall
Ocean Wall
Gully
Gully
Beehive Buttress
Arch Cave
Pinnacle
Chimney Buttress
Minor Buttress
The Slab
Big Cave
Big Cave Buttress
An Sgurr
The Nose
Long Cave
Main Wall
0
100
200
metres
Clach Hosdail
Grulin

MAIN WALL

With the exception of The Nose and Purphura, all the routes on Main Wall start from Long Ledge. This can be accessed *via* a number of routes, the easiest being the vegetated gully below Botterill's Crack. A more direct access route to the central section of the wall starts directly below Collie's Cleft and involves a few tricky moves up a rock edge on the right side of a shallow chimney.

1 The Nose 90m A3 (1970)
The abrupt eastern termination of An Sgurr is probably the most impressive inland rock feature in the Hebrides. This route, which gains and climbs the obvious bulging green flutings, can be comfortably inspected from a grassy plinth below the face (accessed by a pleasant heathery ridge). It is unlikely that a second ascent has been completed, although at least one attempt has been made. The triangulation pillar on the summit provides the only reliable final belay and a convenient abseil point for abseil inspection. A free ascent of The Nose presents one of Scotland's great rock climbing challenges. Start at the foot of a steep left-slanting groove, directly beneath the central overhanging section and well below the heathery ridge that abuts the face.
1. 30m 5c/Aid Climb a thin crack in a steep wall past a small overhang (poor rock). Continue past loose flakes to a small stance.
2. 30m A3 Move right along the obvious ramp for 6m, until it is possible to aid up green flutes, trending slightly right, to a stance and bolt belay on a steep wall (tied-off knife blades, 6 corroded bolts).
3. 30m 5b/Aid Step left and climb directly up the wall above on improving holds (two points of aid).

2 Psycho 60m E3 ** (1987)
This route takes a very impressive and sustained line up the vertical wall just west of The Nose. It is only slightly less frightening than being stabbed to death in a shower! The start can be identified by a pale rock scar, outlined on its left by a reversed number seven, with a small cave at its lower right-hand corner, just above Long Ledge. Start below the cave.
1. 30m 5b Climb trending slightly right, then go directly up the wall to a small heather ledge *via* hollow-sounding columns.
2. 30m 5b From the left end of the ledge climb up for 8m, make a short left traverse, then follow cracks to the top. An excellent pitch.

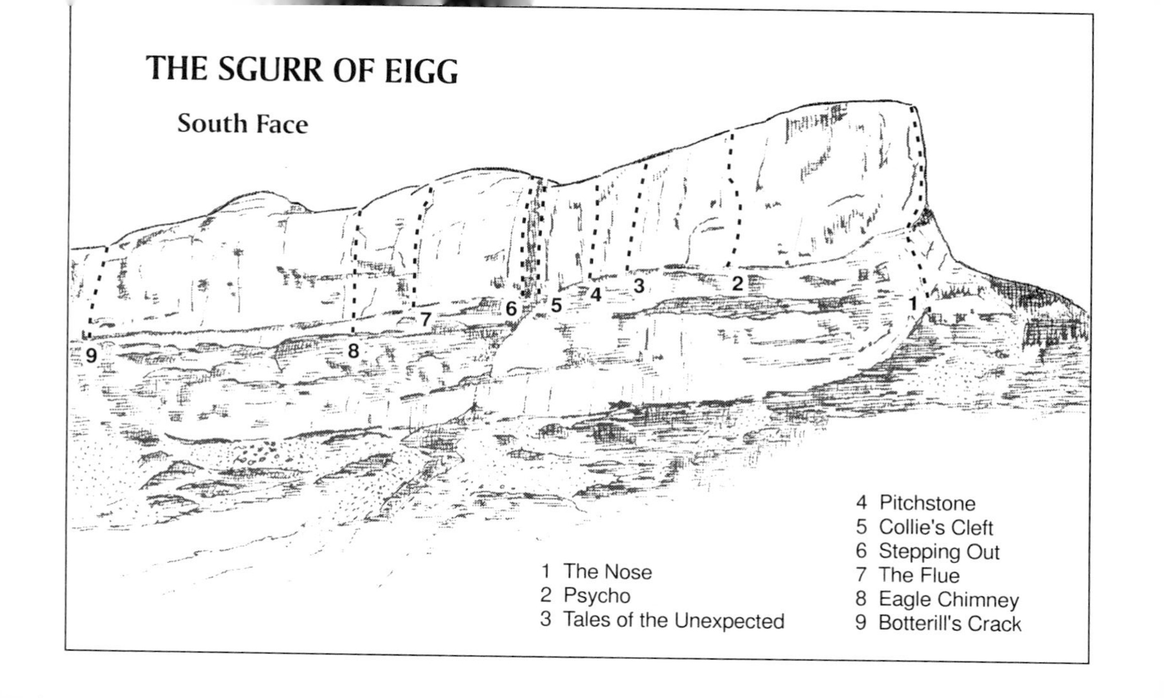
THE SGURR OF EIGG
South Face
1
2
3
4
5
6
7
8
9
1 The Nose
2 Psycho
3 Tales of the Unexpected
4 Pitchstone
5 Collie's Cleft
6 Stepping Out
7 The Flue
8 Eagle Chimney
9 Botterill's Crack

3 Tales of the Unexpected 50m HVS 4c ** (1986)
To the right of Collie's Cleft is a heather groove. Further right still are two dark weep lines with a grey wall in between. This direct and impressive route climbs the centre of the grey wall at a surprisingly friendly grade. Start at a small cairn on the ledge and climb straight up on good holds.

4 Pitchstone 55m HVS (1967)
To the right of the Collie's Cleft is a heather groove. This route takes a curving line immediately to its right.
1. 30m 5a Start 4 metres right of the heather groove. Trend left to near the heather groove, then ascend a short awkward wall (crux) and move up and right to a spike belay.
2. 25m Easier rock trends right to the top.

5 Collie's Cleft 50m Severe (1967)
This route follows a deep, dank, messy chimney at the back of a huge vertical rift in the Main Wall; it is better suited to botanical pursuits than to rock climbing. Not recommended, but if you must:
1. 20m Climb the vegetated chimney to a ledge.
2. 30m Continue up the steep left chimney to an unpleasant exit.

6 Stepping Out 55m E1 *** (1987)
This fine, intimidating route climbs the edge formed by the west retaining wall of Collie's Cleft and the face to the left. Start below the left wall of the cleft where the basalt band disappears into the ground.
1. 45m 5b Ascend the steep wall for 5m, then move left to gain a thin groove. Climb this, step right, then go straight up, avoiding the more vegetated rock to the left.
2. 10m Scramble to the top.

7 The Flue 65m VS (1967)
This takes the first obvious chimney line west of Collie's Cleft (less well defined in its lower part than Eagle Chimney to its left). Approach from the right or left *via* Long Ledge. Dry conditions are recommended.
1. 30m 4c Gain and climb the messy chimney to a heather ledge.
2. 35m 4a Climb the continuation chimney and slabs to the top.

8 Eagle Chimney 65m VS (1967)
The left-hand of the two prominent chimney lines west of Collie's Cleft. Again, dry conditions are strongly recommended.
1. 30m 4b Climb the sustained chimney, passing a very worrying hanging spike high up on the left wall, to reach a heather ledge.
2. 35m 4a Climb the continuation chimney to the top.

9 Botterill's Crack 40m Severe 4a (1967)
This route is located in the second great fault line to break the continuity of Main Wall. In a bay above the level of Long Ledge (accessed by the obvious heathery gully) is a series of chimneys and grooves. On the right of the bay are two well defined chimneys; the groove-crack line to their left is Botterill's Crack. Two more chimney lines lie further left, starting partway up the left wall of the bay. Climb the groove and narrow chimney-crack above. The threatening wedged block high up can be turned by good holds on the steep right wall.

On the right wall of the cleft two curious large spheroids stare from the rock wall, well seen from the top of Botterill's Crack.

Going for Gold 60m E2 ** (1988)
This route lies midway between Botterill's Crack and the descent gully demarcating the west end of Main Wall (above the left end of Long Cave). Traverse in from the left to reach the highest point of the heather ledge. About 4 metres to the right a corner cuts through the fringe of overhangs girdling the base of the wall above the basalt band. This is the start.
1. 15m 5a Ascend the corner then take a low rightwards traverse (just above the lip) to below an obvious corner-groove (taken by Beyond The Fringe). Continue further right, moving slightly up, to gain a foothold and semi-hanging belay.
2. 45m 5b Move hard right for 3 metres, then go up on good flakes to a slight bay. Ascend the bulging wall above, step right and climb clean rock to a ledge. Climb directly up the steepening rock above with technical finishing moves.

Beyond the Fringe 55m E1 * (1988)
Approach as for Going For Gold, with which it has a common start.
1. 25m 5b Ascend the corner then take a low rightwards traverse for about 4 metres (just above the lip). Move up to gain and climb an obvious corner/groove past a hanging flake, then climb the bulging right wall to a ledge.
2. 30m Easier climbing, trending slightly right, leads to the top.

Through the Barricades 50m E2 ** (1987)
Start at the highest point of the heather ledge, reached by traversing in from the left (Going For Gold and Beyond The Fringe start at a corner 4 metres further right).

1. 20m 5b Climb directly up to and climb a vague groove which presents a weakness in the overhanging rock (there is a big jug high up on the left).
2. 30m Climb slabby rock above to the top.

Purphura 115m E2 (1978)
At the left end of Main Wall is an easy open gully. This route ascends the obvious wide ramp which cuts across the gully wall. The grade is for dry conditions, which are essential as the start of pitch two is a natural watercourse. Start at a grassy groove below a small roof to the right of the gully.
1. 30m 4c/5a Climb the groove to the roof, exit right and ascend slabs to a horizontal fault (overhanging rock above). Move left to a good belay. A cleaner and much better first pitch starts at the edge of the gully, ascends bulging rock, then traverses right on small holds until a direct ascent to the belay can be made.
2. 45m 5b Move up and left across a smooth slatey slab (often wet), then climb slightly down before breaking through tiered overhangs. Follow slabs to a heather bay.
3. 40m Climb easy rock above the bay.

From the slabby section on the first pitch of Purphura, a long narrowing ramp runs out to the right (well seen from below) skirting the base of a striking boss of overhanging columnar rock (a challenge for the 21st Century?). Although attempted, this ramp, which is often wet, is not thought to have been climbed.

Between Main Wall and Big Cave Buttress, several descent or ascent routes are available either side of a small buttress. Care should be taken when descending the gully between Main Wall and the small buttress as it contains much loose rock.

BIG CAVE BUTTRESS

This is the next major rock feature west of Main Wall. There is a large cave at its base and an impressive overhanging grey scoop on its west flank. To date no routes have been climbed on this buttress, although it holds considerable potential.

THE SLAB

This lies above Big Cave Buttress, separated from it by a heather ledge.

Cobra 45m Severe * (1987)
Near the right-hand end of The Slab is an obvious heather patch at half-height, above which the slab rears up into a steep wall. Climb easy rock to the heather patch, then take steep rock trending slightly right, then back left, on good holds.

Adder 35m Very Difficult (1987)
Ascend the line of clean grey rock just left of the heather patch, with a steep finish.

To the west and slightly above Big Cave Buttress lies Minor Buttress, separated from the former by a short gully. A well defined section of path runs below Minor Buttress, linking the spine of An Sgurr to Big Cave. A small sharp-edged tower abuts the eastern flank of Minor Buttress.

Splinter Arete 25m HVS 5b (1986)
An obvious vertical arete between two grooves lies on the right hand side of Minor Buttress. Surmount an overhang (crux), then climb the obvious arete.

CHIMNEY BUTTRESS

This buttress is named after the distinctive grassy chimney splitting the centre of the face above the basalt band. It has only one recorded route, although scope exists for several more.

Golden Brown 35m HVS 5a ** (1987)
Start at the base of the grassy chimney. Ascend the chimney for 4m, then move left over flakes onto the face. Traverse up and left, then climb the steep wall, with a hidden jug at half-height, to the start of a groove. Step right onto a broad rib and climb this on perfect rock.

BEEHIVE BUTTRESS

Lying 1km west of The Nose, Beehive Buttress, with its characteristic domed outline, is the most developed and one of the most attractive crags of An Sgurr. The distinctive Arch Cave and a small finger pinnacle at the lowest point of the crag provide useful identification in misty weather. Descents can be made down either side of the buttress; that to the west, adjacent to a stream gully, involves some scrambling. The best access to most routes is by traversing in from the right along a heather ledge.

1 The Comb 45m VS 4c (1986)
This route climbs the right flank of the buttress, immediately right of an obvious V-chimney. Climb the left wall of the arete for 8m, then step right onto a jutting spike. Climb the easy, enjoyable honeycomb slabs above.

2 Pooh Bear 45m HVS 5a * (1986)
Start 12 metres left of the V-chimney at a small roof-capped corner. Move up and right on underclings into a corner. Climb this and the wall and slab above.

3 The Swarm 45m HVS 5a ** (1987)
Start 4 metres left of Pooh Bear. Climb a band of friable basalt to a horizontal break. Ascend the bulging rock above (crux), then traverse 6m hard left to the centre of a clean grey wall between a shallow open groove on the right and a weep line on the left (well seen from below). Climb this directly to the top on good holds.

4 Over the Top 45m E1 5b ** (1987)
A route of considerable character which masochists will repeat again and again! Start at a honeysuckle plant high above the left end of Arch Cave. Climb up to a curious trench and stomach traverse left (shorts and teeshirt not recommended) until the overhanging rock above relents slightly. Pull over, then traverse right with difficulty to gain and climb a fine rock rib, trending slightly right.

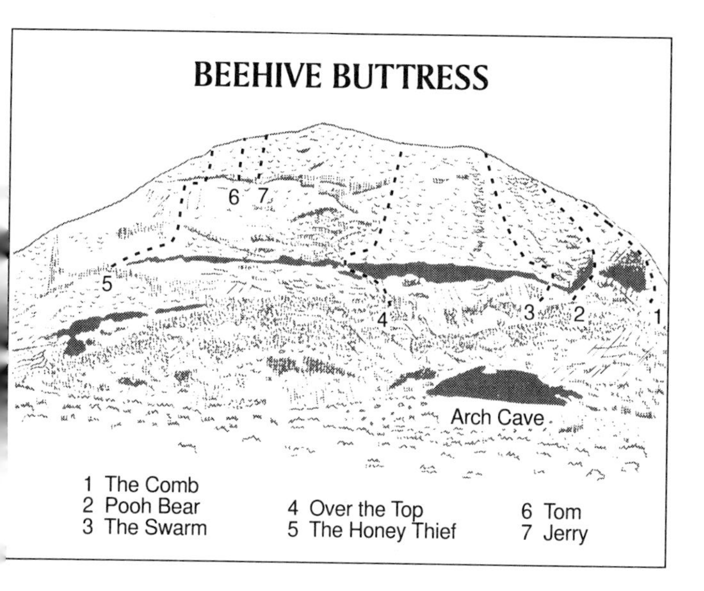

5 The Honey Thief 65m VS * (1987)
An indirect although enjoyable route. Start at the extreme lower left-hand side of the buttress. Ascend heather rightwards, then traverse a ledge back left to the the termination of the basalt band.
1. 40m 4c Take a long diagonal line up and right to a wide waterworn scoop. Go directly up on clean rock to a wide heather ledge.
2. 25m 4b Move right along the ledge for 4 metres, then ascend a superb steep wall on big holds. Finish up slabs.

Further right on this fine upper wall, which can be gained independently from the left, are two short excellent lines on either side of a glassy area of rock. On the left is **Tom** (25m VS 5a ** 1987), and on the right lies **Jerry** (25m HVS 5b ** 1987).

OCEAN WALL

Bounded to its east by a boulder-filled gully, this long slabby wall lies west of Beehive Buttress and extends 250 metres in a north-westerly direction. Its western end is characterised by a steep wall and a big roof (no climbing to date), the centre by a wide heather terrace above mid-height (Le Jardin) below a smooth convex wall, and the east by a great concave slab of perfect rock.

Lego Route 45m VS 5a * (1986)
This route climbs the narrow east-facing flank of Ocean Wall with its distinctive rock structure. Climb a blocky wall to the left of the boulder-filled gully and the easy-angled arete above.

Frozen Ocean 55m E1 ** (1986)
Start west of the boulder-filled gully at an obvious break in the overhangs, where the basalt band merges into the heather. A route of great character, low in its grade.
1. 30m 5a Climb the diagonal weakness trending right, then go up the wall at the first opportunity to gain a left-trending fault which leads to a rock scoop and belay.
2. 25m 5b Traverse up and left by thin cracks to a crumbly flake in a slight recess (crux). Move 3 metres left, then go directly up the wall on good holds to the top.

Earthsea 40m E2 5b ** (1988)
Start left of Frozen Ocean, midway between Frozen Ocean and Echo Beach. Move up and right on a slabby wall, then go back left to easier rock which is followed to the top.

Echo Beach 45m HVS 5a * (1987)
Traverse in left below the clean upper rock shield of Ocean Wall, past Frozen Ocean and Earthsea, to where the ledge narrows just before a short heathery groove. Move up, then make a difficult strenuous move into a small rock scoop (crux). Climb the great slab above, trending slightly right, to the top. Ignore the left-trending ramp high up.

The following four routes start from Le Jardin, a commodious heather ledge near the centre of Ocean Wall. It is possible to approach from the south-west, passing below Frozen Ocean. However this is rather hazardous and an abseil approach is recommended for those not at home on high-angled vegetation.

The Haven 50m Severe (1986)
Start near the right end of Le Jardin.
1. 25m Gain a groove *via* a short wall and traverse left at its top to a ledge and belay.
2. 25m Climb the wall on the right of a vegetated corner to the top.

Paradise Lost 35m HVS 5a * (1987)
Start near the right-hand side of Le Jardin, but left of The Haven, at a cairn. Climb the fine steep wall *via* cracks, traverse right, climb up for 4m then move back left to an easy rock stairway and thence to the top.

To the north-west of Paradise Lost, Le Jardin becomes a narrower ledge again whilst the upper rock tier, although at its lowest, assumes a much smoother convex character. This wall of immaculate pitchstone gives short hard routes of the highest quality. Access to the base is *via* abseil or by a short scramble down at the north-west end of the wall.

Sense of Porpoise 30m E4 6b *** (1994)
Start on Le Jardin, right of centre (just right of an obvious pocket), below an arching overlap. Pull over the bulge with great difficulty, then go up to the right end of the arching overlap. Gain a good flat hold above, then make a very thin move to the base of a left-trending ramp. Move up the ramp, then go up and right on good pockets and thence to the top. Belay well back.

Frolicking with Freddie 25m E3 6a *** (1994)
Start on Le Jardin, in from the left end of the wall, below a short knobbly groove where the skirting roof starts to relent. Move up to and pull strenuously over the bulge (Friend 0 over the lip) into a short groove. Climb this with a difficult exit, then go straight up the face above.

VILLAGE WALL

This is the most westerly of the buttresses on the south flank of An Sgurr, and is separated from Ocean Wall by an area of steep broken ground (not a descent route). Climbing on Village Wall affords a bird's-eye view of the tumbled crofting settlement of Grulin Lochdrach.

First Blood 40m HVS 5a * (1987)
Ascend steep rock *via* a zigzag line to gain and climb a pinkish slab just right of the centre of the face. Trend right near the top.

THE NORTH FACE OF AN SGURR

The cliffs flanking the north side of An Sgurr, although impressive, are neither as high nor as extensive as those to the south and their aspect encourages lingering dampness and turf-filled faults. They effectively terminate at the point where the tourist path gains the spine of An Sgurr, although some small broken buttresses lie further west. To date, only one line (of esoteric interest and unknown vintage) has been climbed. **Zigzag** (Moderate) ascends a wide slab, initially vegetated, at the first obvious break in the ramparts (immediately right of a massive triangular wedge of rock). This route is not recommended in wet weather. Potential for new routes certainly exists on the north face of An Sgurr although they are likely to be in the higher grades and less attractive than those to the south.

CLACH HOSDAIL (Map Ref 454 842)

By far the largest of a cluster of pitchstone boulders to the west of Grulin, Clach Hosdail attains 9m in height and is vertical or overhanging for much of its girth. It provides bouldering on a grand scale. Legend has it that the boulder fell from the cliffs on An Sgurr many eons ago. Nothing so prosaic could of course be true. It was in fact thrown over from Muck by an irate giant.

The easiest route to the dwarf juniper covered top is *via* a narrow ramp in the centre of the east face and a slab above (**Original Route**, Difficult, 1991). The obvious corner-groove on the west face gives an excellent Severe (**Hologram Groove**, 1991). At the junction of the radically overhanging north-east face and the east face a short 5b problem, **The Hang** (1991), will give the short of stature an interesting time. Potential for another half dozen routes exists.

CLEADALE

A tall tapering pillar, topped by a crazy pinnacle, is the most obvious feature of the basalt cliffs to the south-east of Cleadale. It is appropriately named Bidean an Tighearna (*Peak of the House of the Gods*). Its summit can be gained from the moorland plateau above.

LAIG BUTTRESS (Map Ref 478 883)

This is a clean flying buttress on the extreme right of the crags, with a small sphinx-like pinnacle to its right and a little rock amphitheatre behind. It is probable that these two routes have not yet received second ascents.

Grit 45m Severe (1967)
1. 10m From a cairn, climb a groove to a ledge.
2. 20m Climb up right into a corner, then gain an overhanging niche on the left. Swing up left again to a stance and peg belay.
3. 15m Continue to the top.

The Pod 45m VS (1967)
Climb the groove which culminates in a short overhanging corner crack (crux). Continue more easily to the top.

CAMAS SGIOTAIG (Map Ref 472 898)

Host to Traigh na Bigil, the famous 'Singing Sands', Camas Sgiotaig is backed by small, cream-coloured pocketed sandstone crags which give some enjoyable bouldering.

SGORR SGAILEACH (Map Ref 486 912)

Lying at the extreme northern tip of Eigg, this north-east facing columnar sill is pierced by several caves and rises vertically above a boulder beach to a height of 30m. No routes to date have been recorded, but it does have potential. The north-west end offers the cleanest rock.

POLL NAM PARTAN (Map Ref 486 851)

This bay lies north-east of the pier, and is backed by a vertical 20m columnar sill of superficially attractive rock. However, on closer acquaintance it proves to be overgrown and guarded by steep muddy ground and bramble tangles. In summer the air is heavy with the scent of wild garlic.

Mull and Iona

Most of the climbing on Mull is on small cliffs with nothing like the quantity of climbing found on some of the other islands. Quality climbing can be had, however, on a variety of rock types. Within a 25 kilometre radius of Bunessan there are climbs on dolerite, gabbro, gneiss, granite, limestone, quartzite, rhyolite and schist. The cliffs described are all in beautiful settings and have up until now been places of solitude. They are listed from east to west.

Maps
Mull is inconveniently situated at the junctions of three maps, so Ordnance Survey Sheets 47, 48 and 49 are required to cover the whole island. Sheet 48 covers all except two of the crags described.

Access
Two Caledonian-MacBrayne ferries service the island. One sails from Oban to Craignure every 2 hours in summer and takes 40 minutes. There are buses and trains from Glasgow to Oban. The other ferry sails from Lochaline to Fishnish once an hour, taking 15 minutes. It is cheaper but involves more driving if coming from the south. The Lochaline ferry cannot be booked. For further ferry information and bookings contact Caledonian-MacBrayne in Oban (Tel 01631 562285). Buses run from Craignure to Fionnphort (pronounced fin-a-fort), so most crags can be reached (almost) by public transport.

Accommodation
There are numerous hotels and B&B establishments. There is a youth hostel at Tobermory, but unfortunately most of the climbing is at the other end of the island. There are official campsites at:
Newdale, Tobermory (Map Ref 493 544) (Tel: 01688 302306).
Killiechronan, west of Salen (Map Ref 536 413) (Tel: 01680 300403).
Balmeanach, north of Craignure (Map Ref 658 415) (Tel: 01680 300342).
Craignure (Map Ref 723 369) (Tel: 01680 812496).
Fidden, south of Fionnphort (Map Ref 302 213) (Tel: 01681 700213).

Restrictions
There are restrictions to protect nesting birds at several of the cliffs on the island. These are also for the benefit of climbers - who wants to get

covered in guano when there are other clean routes near by? Mull is said to have the highest concentration of eagles in Europe, and climbing past an eyrie could result in a £5,000 fine.

History

Very little climbing has been recorded on Mull, so this section might be a touch inaccurate. Apart from the odd E5, most routes were probably first climbed solo by goats. Ardchrishnish has been seen by every tourist going to Iona and has been climbed on for a number of years. In 1981, Colin Moody visited An Garradh. He rushed back (four years later) with Neil Horn to climb Headless Ridge (VS). Andy Smith and Brian Davison followed the obvious dyke of Drop Out (E3) in 1987. Brian's partners refused to join him on the main face, where he finally climbed Knocking On Heaven's Door (E5) four years after Drop Out, with Andy Nisbet who was suffering from one of his many car crashes. Creach Beinn was observed from the walk in to An Garradh and soon became a well developed high altitude outcrop.

Graham Little wrote enthusiastically about the granite of Erraid in 1989. Over the following two years Stephen Kennedy and friends climbed over a dozen routes there.

Danny Brooks and James Marshall grew up on the Ross of Mull, and worked the fishing boats. They started exploring many coastal crags such as Scoor and Port Bhan. The walk to Port Bhan was made more acceptable by the use of a taxi. At Scoor they climbed White Shite (VS) with Colin in 1991. Danny led Kilvickeon (E2) and Head Butts (E2) the following year. Later, in November, he climbed his first route on mainland Scotland. In 1993 Colin climbed Tystie (E4) and Mark Garthwaite did Better Than A Poke In The Eye (E4), a crack that others had failed on. He came back a week later for the very thin Tweekie Pie (E5), the hardest route on Mull since Ritchie Paterson's 6b at Crissie Burg's in 1985.

The poor summer of 1993 was ideal for the quick drying routes on Iona. The usual pattern was Iona on Saturday and Scoor on Sunday, when the ferry service was poorer. Colin and Billy Hood were drawn to The Good Book (E1) in May. In June, Colin and Stella Adams climbed Jehad (E2) which had been failed on the previous week because of bad rock. John Adams and Steve Scott nipped over for Heretic (E3) the next day. In August, Mark and Davy Gregg did the first route on Eilean Dideal's West Face with Cognative Therapy (E4). The next day standards went up with Yabadabadoo (E5). Grades then stagnated for a week till Mark returned for The Incredible Dr Sex (E6).

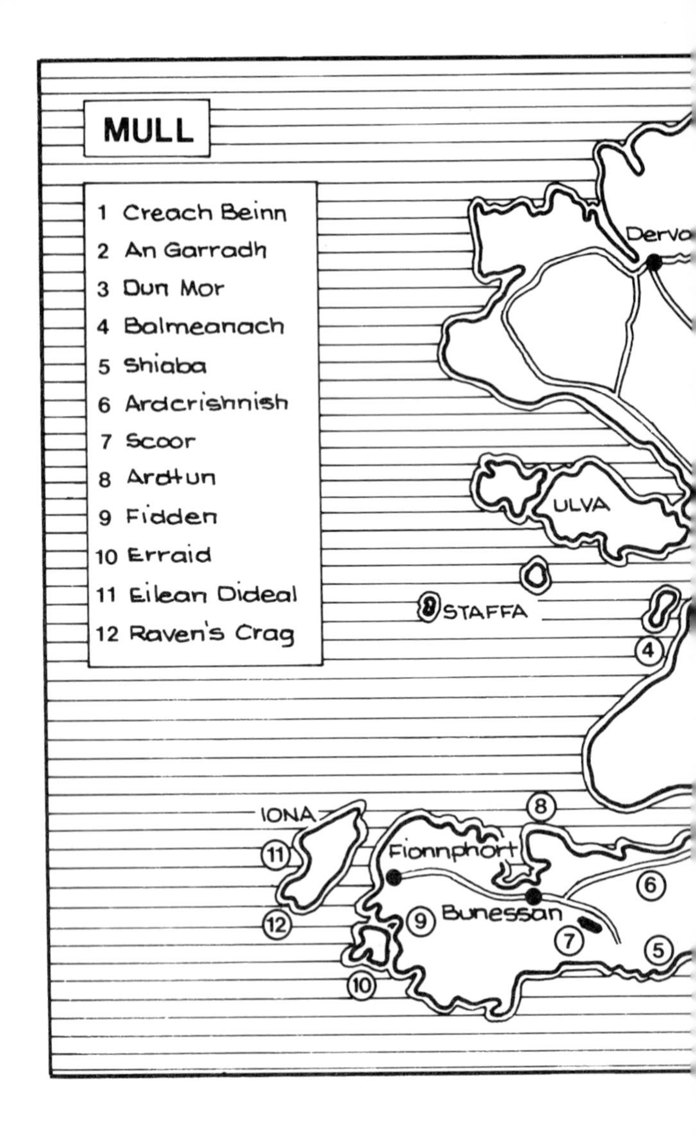
MULL
1 Creach Beinn
2 An Garradh
3 Dun Mor
4 Balmeanach
5 Shiaba
6 Ardcrishnish
7 Scoor
8 Ardtun
9 Fidden
10 Erraid
11 Eilean Dideal
12 Raven's Crag
ULVA
STAFFA
IONA
Fionnphort
Bunessan

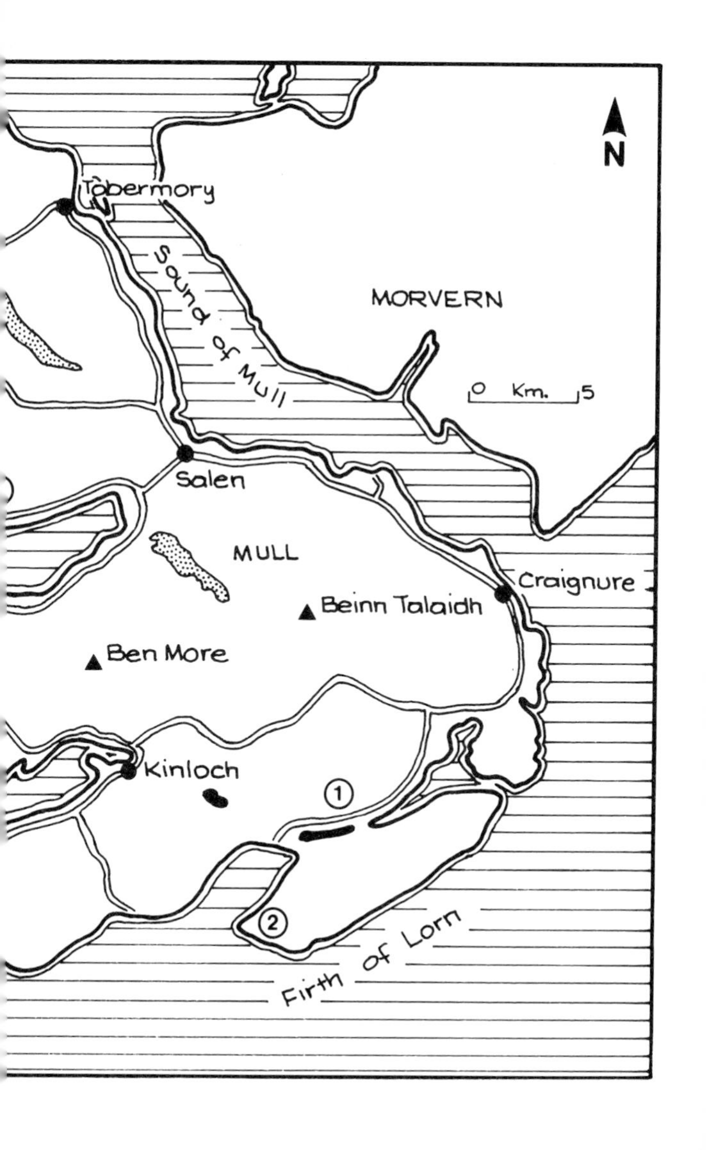

N
Tobermory
Sound of Mull
MORVERN
0 Km. 5
Salen
MULL
Craignure
Beinn Talaidh
Ben More
Kinloch
1
2
Firth of Lorn

In 1994 a few gaps were filled on several crags. Ardtun was rediscovered one wet day in September. Mark Shaw took to The Green Hill enthusiastically. After climbing The Nose of El Cap in 13 hours, Mark Garthwaite was fit enough for Scoor where he climbed See You In Hell Soldier Boy (E6). 1995 saw further development, particularly during a number of evenings at Ardtun.

CREACH BEINN

(Map Ref 637 261)

This gabbro cliff is on the outlying spur of Creach Beinn and lies 350m up the hillside, facing south-east. The routes dry quickly but Sally seeps for a while. The cliff contains an important nesting site; PLEASE DO NOT CLIMB HERE UNTIL 1st AUGUST. Stalking could also limit access. From Craignure follow the Fionnphort road for 10km and turn left for Lochbuie. The road goes over a hill to Loch Spelve. After this is the wooded Loch Uisg. By the side of Loch Uisg is a lodge then a cottage. Park 100 metres past the cottage, at a 1.61 kilometre stone. Climb up the hill until it levels out. The cliff can be seen ahead, about 30 minutes from road to cliff. The first two routes take obvious features on the slabby rock overlooking the burn. This slabby rock is climbable almost anywhere at a reasonable grade.

Balloonski 45m VS 4c (1986)
Start at the wall between two shallow corners. Climb to a ledge below a crack which curves left, then follow the crack to the top.

Instant Relief 55m VS (1986)
Start at the lowest rocks below the corner.
1. 30m Go up to the base of the corner.
2. 25m 4c Climb the corner and go straight over a bulge to easy ground, block belay below a short wall.

Further right is some steep rock. The small buttress left of it is Mild VS. The corner-ramp between these is Mild Severe. The steep rock has an overhanging crack:

Do You Remember Whispering Bob Harris? 45m E1 5b * (1987)
From the Mild Severe corner, traverse right to the overhanging crack. Climb it and continue to the top (or finish up a right-slanting crack, 6a).

Sally 55m VS 4c (1991)
Climb the large corner in the centre of the cliff, trending rightwards. A bit dirty.

Dickie Davies Eyes 55m HVS 5a ** (1987)
1. 35m 5a Start just right of Sally, climb up right (parallel with the edge of the slab) to a small tree in the horizontal fault, then step left to an uncomfortable belay.
2. 20m 4b Move left and climb to the top.

AN GARRADH

(Map Ref 609 204)

This major cliff is located on the Laggan peninsula. The biggest face overlooks Lord Lovat's Bay. It faces south and dries quickly but it is exposed and can be very windy. This can be an intimidating place to climb, but it is in a remote and beautiful area. The massive cliff stretches for over a kilometre and seems to be geologically complex. Most of the rock is rhyolite, occasionally perfect. The eye catching line of Dropout is basalt, Knee Burner feels like gabbro, and the rock right of Fifth Choice is dolerite, worse than the worst Central Belt quarry.

Some maps show the cave as Odin's Cave; the Vikings visited nearby Iona in the 9th and 10th centuries. The cave was one of Lord Lovat's hiding places. He was executed in London in 1747 (1 year after Culloden). In 1926 the cave was filled by a landslide, not the last rockfall in this area.

Access
Follow the description for Creach Beinn to Loch Uisg, then continue to Loch Buie. A path leads along the east side of Loch Buie, past the point to reach Lord Lovat's Bay, in an hour and a half. If a vehicle is being left overnight, please leave a note to calm worried locals (a few walkers have needed to be rescued here in the past).

Warning
Most of the routes were done on sight, so some loose rock should be expected. It is unlikely that any of the routes have been repeated, therefore the grades are unconfirmed. Several climbers have visited the cliff and have no intention of returning, finding the looseness unacceptable. There is also a fair amount of vegetation. Pegs were used on Knocking On Heaven's Door, but none of the other routes need them.

Layout
The main face is steep and impressive, with the dyke line taken by Dropout bounding the right hand side. The face runs westwards into broken grassy ground which terminates at a gully, down which a small burn from the lochan runs. The Western Sector lies west of this gully; Cop Out finishes up the ridge left of the gully, a finish shared with other routes.

East of the main face, the cliff base dips down to give a long ridge - Headless Ridge. Right of this is another face down which the other burn from the lochan runs. This approximates the line of Fifth Choice.

The Boulder Problem 20m VS 4b (1995)
East of Lord Lovat's Bay are some boulders, of which the largest has a broad west face with a prominent off-width crack. There are ample runners after the initial bulge has been climbed.

WESTERN SECTOR

The author believes the rock here is good. Unfortunately some of the belays are on large ledges offering easy escape.

Centipede 90m HVS * (1987)
Left of the gully is a face with three vertical crack lines. Left of this at a lower level is another face with a gully-corner at its left side. Start right of the gully-corner at a niche below a flake chimney.
1. 30m 4c Move up to a corner in the arete left of the chimney. Climb the corner until it is possible to move right into the chimney, and continue to belay on the easy section.
2. 30m 5a Climb the right side of the large flake lying against the face (past a small aspen tree), continue up to an overlap, then step left into a shallow corner. Go up to a flake, step right and continue up the wall to a large ledge.
3. 30m 4b Move right on the buttress to gain the clean-cut corner and climb it.

Third Choice 100m VS * (1987)
The first pitches of this and the next two routes can be interchanged (or easily missed out). The first pitch of Violet is the best. All three routes share a common finish. Start from the lowest point of the wall, below the prominent cracks left of the gully.

1. 40m 4b Climb to the overlap on the right. Pull left onto the slab, move left, then go up the slab to a ledge at the base of the left-hand crack.
2. 30m 4c Climb the crack, move right past the tree and climb the corner.
3. 30m Move right and follow the ridge (the finish of Cop Out).

Violet 95m VS * (1987)
1. 35m 4b Pull onto the slab as for Third Choice. Climb up the slab (Third Choice goes left) to a belay shared with that route.
2. 25m 4c Move right, pull over a bulge, then go up and right to a corner crack. Go up the corner to flakes and traverse right to the crack on Cop Out.
3. 35m Move right and follow the ridge as for Cop Out.

Cop Out 95m VS * (1985)
1. 35m Start as for Third Choice and climb the easy corner on the right.
2. 25m 4c Climb the crack left of the arete.
3. 35m Follow the ridge to the top. A further 60m of climbing can be had on the buttress above at Very Difficult.

Sister Moonshine 70m Hard Severe * (1987)
1. 35m Start in the gully and climb the crack in the left wall.
2. 35m Follow the arete of Cop Out.

MAIN FACE

Juniper Mantle 125m VS (1987)
This 'character-building' route has a touch of seriousness and is best avoided. Start right of the gully.
1. 30m Climb a tongue of rock (avoidable), continue up a fine red slab, then move left to a poor juniper belay and a poor stance.
2. 25m Move right and climb a corner, move right again, then go up to a small oak.
3. 15m Climb the corner to a poor hanging belay off small trees.
4. 35m Step right and climb to a corner.
5. 20m 4b Finish up the corner.

Star Trek 180m E3 * (1987)
At the right-hand side of the main face are two diverging corners in the upper half. This route climbs the steeper right-hand one, with a lot of

grass in the lower pitches. It is possible to finish up the left-hand corner, giving a route at HVS (the finish of The Seductive Finish). Start left of the overhangs at the bottom left-hand side of the main face.
1. 30m 5a Follow a line of weakness up left, then traverse right along a ledge to below a hanging block.
2. 30m 5a Surmount the overhang and continue to a tree.
3. 45m 4c Go up rightwards to a big ledge below the corners.
4. 15m 5a Climb the corner to the bifurcation.
5. 45m 5c Climb the right-hand corner past a ledge at half-height to a large ledge; belay at the back.
6. 15m 4b Climb the corner above.

Knocking on Heaven's Door 210m E5 5c ** (1990)
On the first day the first five pitches were climbed, then on the second an abseil was made to the high point and the last three pitches were climbed. Runners and belays were dubious, even with pegs. The route starts right of centre and trends left until close under the big overhang. At the bottom left of the face is a long overhang. Start at easy-angled slabs midway between this and the dyke (Drop Out).
1. 25m 4c Climb steepening slabs to belay below a small heathery ledge.
2. 20m 5c Gain the ledge, move right to a flake, then step up into a shallow depression. Climb up this, exiting right to a belay ledge.
3. 15m 5a Climb a heathery groove on the left, then continue left to a ledge below a long overhang.
4. 25m 5c Climb a steep groove left of the overhang, then trend right to a ledge and poor belay.
5. 15m 5c Climb a flake at the right end of the ledge, then move back left across the wall to a bottomless groove. Go up this to a flake and step left to a rock ledge about 10m below the right end of the big overhang. The Seductive Finish goes left from here.
6. 15m 5b Go up towards the overhang, then traverse right on smoother rock to a ledge and poor belay.
7. 45m 5c Gain a higher ledge on the right and from its far end, descend about 5m until it is possible to gain the rib on the right. Continue right over a bulge and cross ledges to gain the dyke. Move up this to a good belay.
8. 45m 4c Follow Dropout, climbing up then left to the top.
Variation: **The Seductive Finish** 85m E1 *
This is a less direct finish, on better rock and avoiding the hardest pitch. However, the pitches below merit E4 in their own right.

6a. 20m 5a From the belay under the big overhang, traverse left and slightly up until a ledge appears unexpectedly below and round the arete. It is gained by a sensational small jump. Star Trek goes up and right from here to climb the huge hanging right-hand corner.
7a. 50m 5b After a short descent, go up the left-hand corner on good rock until it deteriorates near the top.
8a. 15m Finish on the left.

Dropout 185m E3 * (1987)
This climb takes the obvious basalt dyke at the right-hand side of the main face; there is some grass.
1. 30m 5a Climb the chimney and belay on the right before the overhangs.
2. 35m 5b Move back left, climb though a second set of overhangs and belay below a third set.
3. 35m 5b Go over the overhang and continue to grass and a tree belay.
4. 60m 5a Continue up the chimney, sometimes on the left wall, to belay in a corner below a big rock scar.
5. 25m 4c Follow a ramp on the left to the top.

April Aphid 225m Severe (1987)
Right of the main face but before Headless Ridge, a line of weakness runs up left between the main wall and a short upper wall. The route has its share of heather and is open to variation.

Headless Ridge 270m VS 4b (1985)
To the left of the main face a ridge starts at a lower level than the base of the cliff. The route is open to variation which might affect the grade. Protection is poor in places and some loose rock gives the climb a serious feel, but escape is easy in several places. Start at the bottom right-hand side of the ridge, move up left past a dead tree to a pinnacle on the ridge. Find a way up the ridge. At the top is a gap between the ridge and the main cliff. Traverse left along the flake to finish.

EASTERN SECTOR

Access Route 60m Very Difficult
This is possibly the easiest way up or down in 1km of cliff. From the start of next route, move left and climb up to join Headless Ridge. Follow this to the top.

Pooh Bear's Delight 60m VS 4c (1987)
Climb the deep-cut chimney right of Headless Ridge to reach horizontal ground. Walk back and climb the short corner.

Fifth Choice 135m Severe (1987)
Right of Headless Ridge is a long face split centrally by a gully, taken by a burn flowing from the lochan. This route climbs slabs to reach the gully, and finishes right of it.
1. 45m From debris, climb a red slab (starting just right of it).
2. 45m Go up an easy ridge to the gully.
3. 45m Climb chockstones in the gully. On the right wall above is a smooth ramp leading up left towards the gully. There are overhangs above the ramp which hide another parallel ramp. Move right to gain the upper ramp and follow it up left to the top.

Another route has been climbed further right, but a fair proportion of it has since fallen down. Historians can find a description of it in the SMCJ 1991.

Knee Burner 45m VS 5a (1987)
About 500 metres east of Headless Ridge, a massive gully cuts inland. This route takes a corner on the east wall. Abseil down the line of the route from a stake (in situ) to a cave. From the cave climb up right, then move up left and climb the corner. The roof of the cave is very sharp and it cut a 9mm rope through to the mantle.

GRIBUN, CREAG MHOR (Map Ref 465 362)

Like Skye, Mull has many impressive basalt cliffs. The following route should be able to cure anyone of a desire to climb basalt.

Loosey Simmons 130m VS 3c (1987)
In the middle of the cliff is a deep gully, ten minutes from the road . Climb the ramp which slants up left from the base of the gully, and finish with a through route. The technique is to climb the route faster than it falls down. Parking below the gully is unwise.

The deep gully, attempted because it is there, has seen off at least three attempts. It is doubtful if any pleasure could be gained from the experience.

BALMEANACH (Map Ref 442 322)

This is an unusual west-facing cliff of quartz conglomerate topped by limestone. The highest section of rock has an overhang at 7 metres which seems to always seep.

From Salen head west, then follow the B8037 along the south side of Loch na Keal past the Gribun cliffs. When the road starts to gain height take a minor road on the right to Balmeanach farm. Follow the footpath to Mackinnon's Cave until the crag comes into sight on the left. It is 15 minutes from the road.

Mur Sans Spits 20m E1/2 5a * (1996)
Start at the right side of the main cliff at a short wide crack. Go straight up to pockets (Friend 3), step up left to an overhang, then go up to a bay. Move left, go up to the top bay, then start up a hollow flake and step right to finish. It may be a good idea to leave a rope *in situ* for the final grassy section.

Mushroom Picking 20m HVS 5a * (1995)
Right of the main face is a corner, and right of the corner is a rib. Climb the right side of the rib. The crux, the bulge high up, is protected by wires in the crack above. The rock below the bulge should be treated with a little care.

Milanda Shelf 15m Severe (1994)
At the right side a fence hangs down the rock. Move up left, and climb the corner just right of the fence; well protected without clipping the fence.

Is it Safe? 20m E4/5 5c ** (1996)
A sustained route with spaced protection. Start just left of Mur Sans Spits. Climb easily to a ledge, make a move up the steep wall, traverse left (damp) to a flake, then climb up to the overlap. Climb directly up steep rock to a good ledge on the right, where the angle relents. Climb up slightly left to the top.

SHIABA (Map Ref 438 181)

In this remote area of quartzite, there are two gullies which have given climbs. The gullies have slabby west faces and overhanging east faces. The routes described are on the slabby faces. The routes are not affected by high tides unless accompanied by gales.

Park at the ruined chapel (see access for Scoor). Walk along the track going round Scoor House, continue to the sheep fank, keeping it on the left. Walk over the hill to the east to reach the deserted village Shiaba. Follow the burn to the beach, then turn left (east) between two small hills until the gullies come into sight. Fifty minutes from the carpark.

WEST GULLY

There should be a belay stake about 3 metres from the east gully and 13m down from the apex. It might be wise to take your own.

Dali's Block 15m Severe (1993)
At the back of the gully is a dripping overhang, and right of this is a huge rectangular block. Move up, step right and climb up to pass the right side of the block and finish up the crack.

The Gardener 15m E1 5b * (1993)
The corner crack right of Dali's Block. Move up, then step left into the corner crack and climb it.

Interflora 15m E1 5b ** (1994)
Right of The Gardener is a clean face. Start at the left side and climb straight up the cracked wall.

Impulse 15m E1 5b * (1993)
Start just right of Interflora. Follow a right-slanting crack to a heather recess, move left, then climb up to finish.

Flower Power 15m HVS 5a (1994)
About 3 metres further right is another right-slanting crack, at its best in spring. Climb the crack to easy ground, then the corner on the left.

Grooved Arete 15m HVS 5a (1993)
Just right of the clean face, climb the easy corner, then the awkward leaning corner in the arete.

Opposite: Tystie, The Slab, Scoor, Mull (Climber, Davie Gregg)

Next page: Eat my Shorts, Horse Wall, Scoor, Mull (Climber, Mark Garthwaite)

To the right of Grooved Arete is a broken face. **Sleepy** (15m Very Difficult *) climbs the shallow left-facing corner, while **Adder Recess** (15m Very Difficult) takes the wall just right. **Snakebite** (15m VS 4b) climbs the arete left of the chimney at the right end of the face, and **Constrictor** (15m Very Difficult) climbs the chimney.

EAST GULLY

Mind The Orchids 25m VS 4b (1993)
At the right side of the face is a shallow chimney (taken by **Webs**, 20m Moderate). Climb the face right of this to a steep finish. There is a large boulder well back for a belay.

ARDCRISHNISH (Map Ref 426 235)

This dolerite sill is obvious as it overlooks the road, so it has received a lot of attention over the years. The climbing is on good solid rock. Some of the harder routes which are rarely climbed might be a bit lichenous until they get more use, and the base of the cliff is a bit of a jungle. The sill faces north, but although a few of the corners are rarely, if ever, dry, many lines dry quickly after rain. A north wind is best to keep the midges down; if the midges don't get you, the ticks will.

Access
From Craignure take the Fionnphort road. Three miles short of Bunessan the white house Ardchrishnish comes into view on the right; the cliff is opposite, above the trees. An old track runs up to a quarry just east of the crag, providing convenient parking. Walk along the flat, then take a steep muddy path up to the east (left) end of the cliff (five minutes from the quarry). Access to the quarry is sometimes blocked to discourage travelling people, in which case park at the road side (still five minutes). It is best to descend the same way, as a descent further west is over boulders and through trees. The routes are described from left to right.

There are a number of short routes at the left of the crag. **We Did** (7m VS 5a) takes the first crack with an undercut start just left of the nose. **Scaber** (6m VS 5a *; route 1 on the diagram) climbs the

Previous page: The Incredible Dr Sex, Raven's Crag, Iona (Climber, Mark Garthwaite)

Opposite: The Mission, Port na Cuilce, Colonsay (Climber, Graham Little)

left-facing corner crack, while Pellet (7m Moderate) goes up to an overhang, then moves right and up. The grassy gully to the right is a scramble.

Twarf's Nightmare 7m E1 5b *
Right of the gully is a clean face with a crack in its right arete. From a grassy ledge, step left and climb the crack with some long reaches.

2 Peace Breaker 7m VS 4c *
Start on the same ledge as Twarf's Nightmare. Follow a corner crack which bears left giving a steep ramp.

Wide Thing 10m VS 4b
Right of a corner is a very wide crack (facing east). Climb the crack, then step left and finish up the corner.

The Lawn 15m Severe
Start right of the wide crack round the front of the face. Move up to a hand crack, then climb it and finish up the arete. It is better than it looks.

Halfers 13m E1 5b *
Move up left to gain the top of a short flake, step up right onto a sloping shelf, then climb a crack which slopes up left.

Root 12m VS 4c
Just right of Halfers is a niche below an oak. Move up left into the niche, gain the oak and climb the corner above.

3 I Do 10m HVS 5a
Climb the black corner crack which is often wet.

Peach Crusher's Wall 10m E1 5b *
Before the chockstone of Chir Mhor is a black cracked wall. Gain the ledge, then go over the bulge and climb the crack. Finish slightly right or left; the right-hand way gives a harder and more sustained route (E2). The wider crack just left is VS 4c.

4 Chir Mhor 10m VS 4c *
Climb the chimney past a chockstone which is defying gravity.

Totally Wired 10m HVS 5a
Climb the corner in the bay, stepping right at the top.

Never Trust a Shunt 10m HVS 5a *
Start at the top of the boulder, climb the jam crack with two small overhangs. A grade easier for English climbers.

5 Late Starter 10m HVS 5a *
Round the arete is a wide, bulging and thrutchy corner crack.

Pocket Slab 10m E2 5b *
Pull over the initial bulge, then go straight up to a big pocket under the overhang. Stand in this, then move right to the arete and some protection above. Climb the arete which is very close to the next route.

Route One 10m Very Difficult
Find the easiest way up the grassy recess.

Squawk 15m VS 4c
The ridge just to the right gives fairly bold climbing.

6 Wisdom 15m VS 4c
The dank corner crack is mossy.

Leaderless 15m HVS 5a *
Climb the arete to a ledge on the right, place wires in the vertical crack on the right. Move up left using a big pocket to finish up a wide crack.

Nothing Really Stunning 13m Severe
Climb the grassy corner, then move out right on the big flakes at the top. The direct finish is a bit harder.

7 John Moore Doesn't 15m E2 5c **
The crack which slants up right across the face is sustained and awkward.

Slugs 13m VS 4c
Climb on top of the large flake, then climb the crack on the left.

8 1,2,3 12m HVS 5a**
The fine-looking flake. The name refers to the sequence of Friends used, but half sizes would also be useful.

Water 12m HVS 5a
A crack line left of easier ground trends right and has a deceptive start.

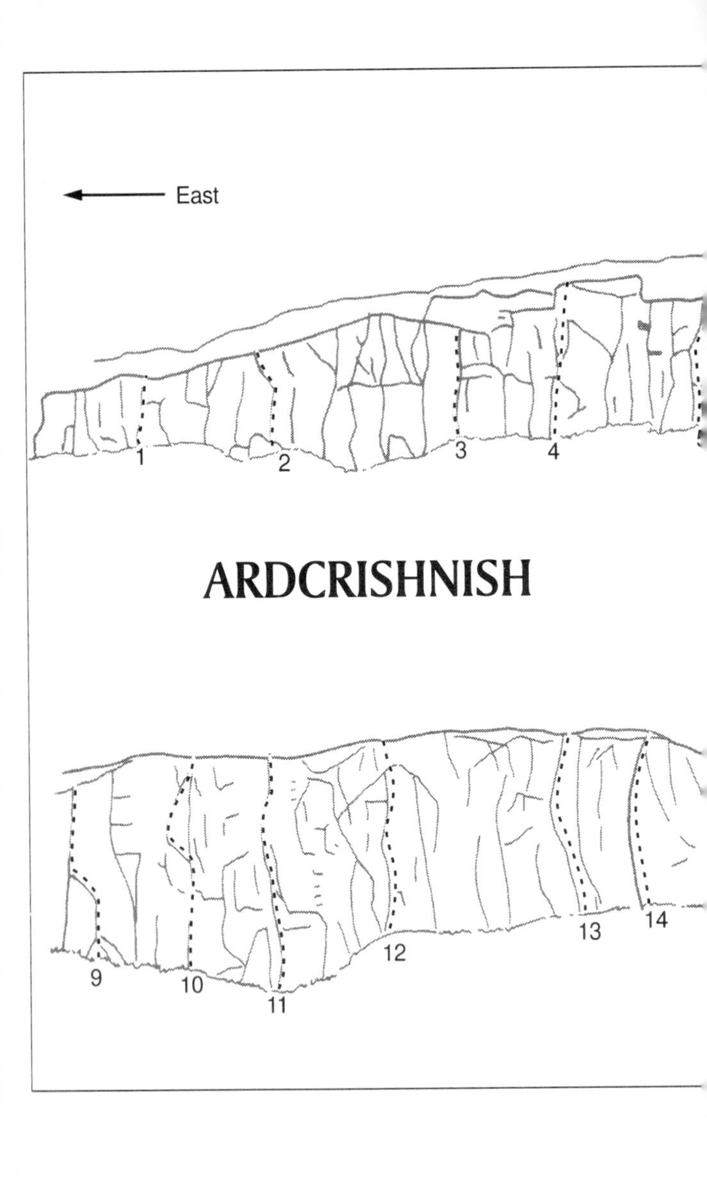
East
1
2
3
4
ARDCRISHNISH
9
10
11
12
13
14

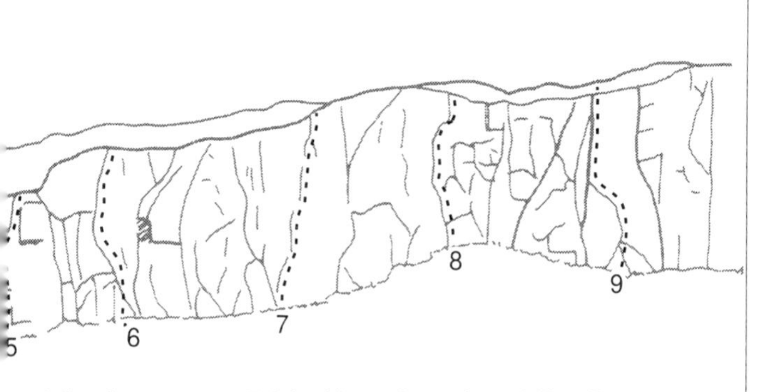

1 Scraber
2 Peace Breaker
3 I Do
4 Chir Mhor
5 Late Starter
6 Wisdom
7 John Moore Doesn't
8 1,2,3
9 Mud
10 Calm Fish Corner
11 Are You Lonesome?
12 Deception
13 First Route
14 The Bastard Son
15 Secret Crack
16 Topic
17 Ritchie's Corner
18 Chattering Tits
19 Honeysuckle Wall

West ⟶

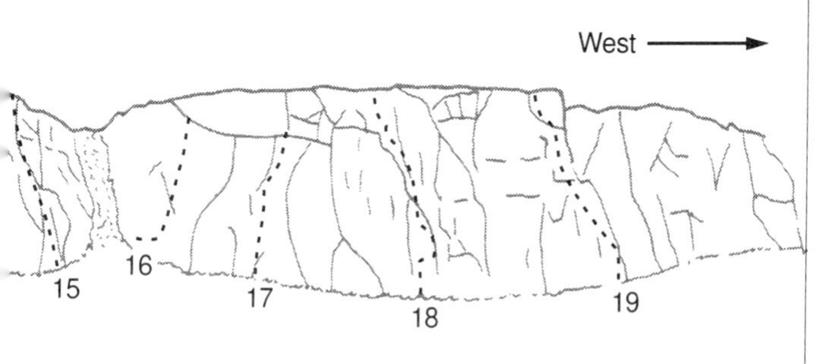

9 Mud 12m HVS 5a
The corner right of the impressive, wild arete is usually wet. The belay is shared with the next route.

The Pond 13m E2 5c **
The crack line has a step left at one-third height. A fine line, but it is often wet; there should be a belay stake 5m back.

10 Calm Fish Corner 15m HVS 5a *
Climb a strenuous crack, then a ramp up left leads to the finishing corner crack; hard for the grade. Belay as for the last route.

Show Some Emotion 15m VS 4c **
Start near the previous route, move out right to the arete and climb it past a small tree; fairly high in the grade. Belay stake in place.

11 Are You Lonesome Tonight? 15m E3 6a *
Climb the corner crack and belay just below the top, or look for a stake.

Viva Las Vegas 15m E3 6a **
Climb the crack below the arete, step right, then climb the corner to the overhang and move left onto the arete. Move up the arete, then pull out left using a one-finger pocket and rockover. Finishing on the right reduces the grade to E3 5c.

I Don't Fancy It 12m Severe
Climb the crack in the large right-facing corner, and step left near the top.

12 Deception 12m E1 5b *
The crack on the front of the buttress just right of the previous route. The flake at the start sounds hollow but seems all right. A belay stake should be 6m back.

13 First Route 13m HVS 5a
This route is round the edge left of the next route. Start up a crack right of a bulging corner, step left onto the face, then climb up to easier ground.

14 The Bastard Son of Dean Friedman 12m E4 6a **
The arching corner crack was climbed on-sight with a rest point. It is graded for a clean on-sight ascent.

15 Secret Crack 10m VS 4b *
Left of the gap are two cracks. Start up the right-hand crack, step left and climb the other one. The direct start is 5a.

Floral Arrangement (10m Severe *) climbs the right-hand crack, while the easy slab with a small birch growing in it is **Birch** (10m Moderate). The gap is a convenient means of access. A VS and a Severe can be found opposite Birch.

16 Topic 10m VS 4b *
Step right pushing past a tree to gain holds on the arete and boldly climb it. A nut at the top protects the second; belay well right at the top of Ritchie's Corner. Down and right is a thin crack and corner; **Hazel Surprise** (10m 5b).

Unidentified Screamers 10m E3 5c
Climb the arete left of Ritchie's Corner keeping on the left side. After the bulge move up right to finish up the arete beside Ritchie's Corner (possibly overgraded).

17 Ritchie's Corner 10m E3 6a **
Climb the corner containing an unhelpful crack.

Venus in Flares 12m HVS 5a *
Gain a ledge below a recess and climb awkward twin cracks.

18 Chattering Tits 10m E2 5b **
This good route is hidden by trees. Step up to an overhang, move up right to a rest on the arete, then step back left to the original crack line. Follow this leftwards to the top.

Still Chattering (10m E1 5b) is a short but technical route up the left-facing corner just right of Chattering Tits. It finishes up **Twin Rocks** (VS 4b) which takes the escapable arete (difficult to protect) just to the right. **Magic Carpet** (15m Moderate) rides the poor ramp line just to the right.

19 Honeysuckle Wall 12m E1 5b *
Start well right. From the shallow corner move up left to the niche below the small birch trees. Climb the bulge and continue to the overhang, go left below it, then climb up to finish.

Fern Forest 12m Severe
A deep corner with an awkward exit which starts well right of the last route.

White Spiral 13m Severe
The pinnacle is detached from the cliff. Start just left of the toe, move up then go right under the overhang to reach a crack on the right side. Climb this and step onto the main cliff.

SCOOR (Map Ref 410 188)

South of Bunessan is an area of schist with a compact group of crags, although the climbing on each is quite different. Beach Wall, Creag Tearmainn and The Dun have blocky holds. Many routes follow cracks, especially on Wave Buttress, while holds on The Slab are usually flakes. Finally, Slochd Wall routes and Hammock climb bubbly rock. The crags face different directions so it should be possible to climb in any available sun and to avoid the wind. The area has a holiday atmosphere with a fine sandy beach. A herd of wild goats is in residence, and there are often eagles around.

The present landowner (who lives in England) has erected 'Private' signs, but climbers have removed sack loads of plastic from the shore so hopefully a confrontation will not occur.

Restrictions
The Pinnacle and part of Creag Tearmainn are nest sites. They will be smelly and unpleasant in the spring and early summer.

Access
From Craignure take the Fionnphort road to the Bunessan suburbs. About 100 metres after the school on the right, turn left for Scoor. Follow this road for 4 km past Loch Assapol to the carpark at the ruined chapel. Walk along the track (not the continuing road to Scoor House); at the third gate the beach is straight ahead. From the gate Wave Buttress can be seen on the island. Left of the island is Beach Wall, while behind it, out of sight, is The Slab. Left of Beach Wall is Dune Wall. To reach The Bay turn right (west) at the beach and follow the coast. Slochd Wall And Creag Tearmainn are easily reached by cutting over the hill just before The Bay. The quickest approach for Slochd Wall and Creag Tearmainn is from the third gate. From the gate gain and follow the fence between two small hills (ahead on the right), continue

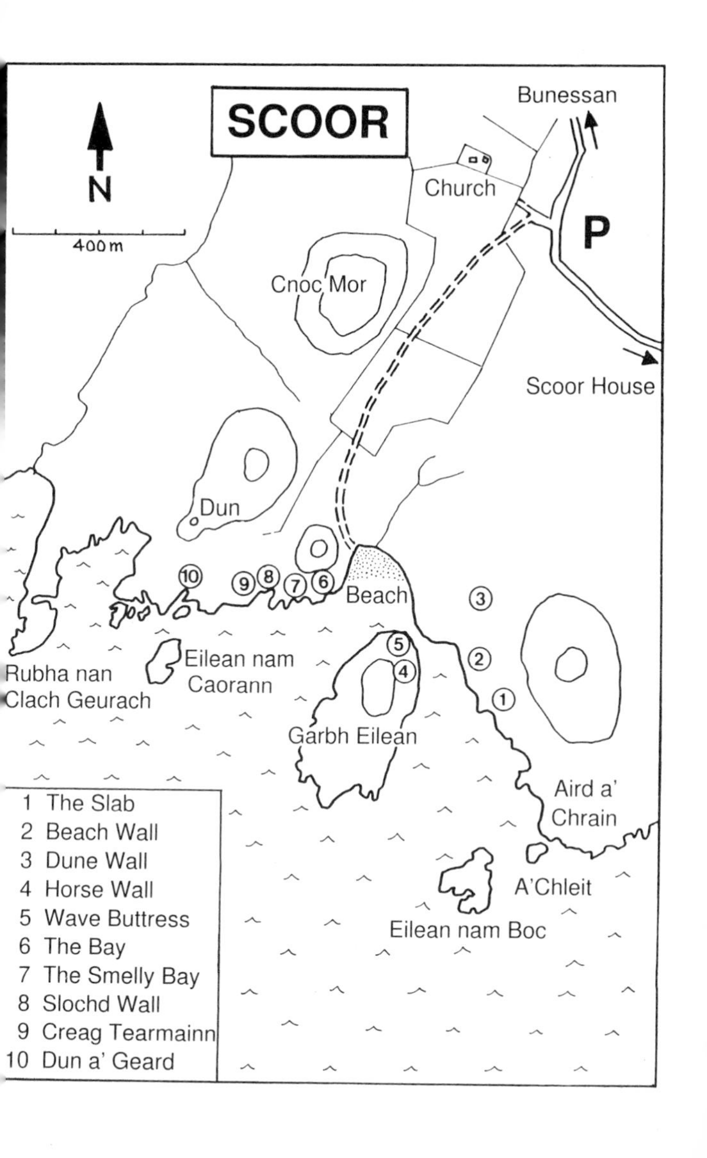
SCOOR
N
400m
Bunessan
Church
P
Cnoc Mor
Scoor House
Dun
Beach
Rubha nan
Clach Geurach
Eilean nam
Caorann
Garbh Eilean
Aird a'
Chrain
A'Chleit
Eilean nam Boc
1 The Slab
2 Beach Wall
3 Dune Wall
4 Horse Wall
5 Wave Buttress
6 The Bay
7 The Smelly Bay
8 Slochd Wall
9 Creag Tearmainn
10 Dun a' Geard

though the bog until Creag Tearmainn comes into sight; Slochd Wall is down on the beach to the left. To get to The Dun and Dun Slab turn right at the end of the fence and go over the hill. The majority of routes are within 15 minutes of the carpark.

THE SLAB

The starts of the first three routes on this west-facing crag are affected by high tides. Protection on The Slab is often behind flakes which might not take a big fall, therefore the adjectival grade is often higher than expected from the numerical grade.

1 Head Butts 15m E2 5b * (1992)
At the right end of the crag is a small overhung niche. Gain this, climb the overhang to the ledge, then continue up the crack in the shallow corner.

2 Tystie 15m E4 5c/6a ** (1993)
Climb the twin thin cracks just left of Head Butts; the crux is near the top.

3 Sawfish Crack 15m E1 5a/b * (1991)
Start 6 metres left of Head Butts, directly below a short left-facing corner. Climb to a triangular overhang, step right and follow the sharp crack which leads to the corner and the top.

4 Pocket Razor 15m Severe * (1991)
Further left is a shallow corner crack (Choughless). Start up this, then move out right to finish up the corner of Sawfish Crack.

5 Choughless 15m VS 4c ** (1991)
The shallow corner crack gives a fine route.

6 Everything Flying By 20m E1 5a/b ** (1992)
Left of the upper half of Choughless are three thin vertical cracks. Move up left to gain and climb the left-hand crack, which is very close to the next route.

7 Seal Show 20m HVS 5a ** (1992)
In the middle of the slab are two obvious faults which start as shallow chimneys. Follow the right-hand fault, stepping right at the top; fairly high in the grade.

8 Greased Lightning 25m E1 5a (1993)
Climb the left-hand fault to a finish past the rock-scarred recess. A bold lead since some of the flakes are a little dubious; belay well back.

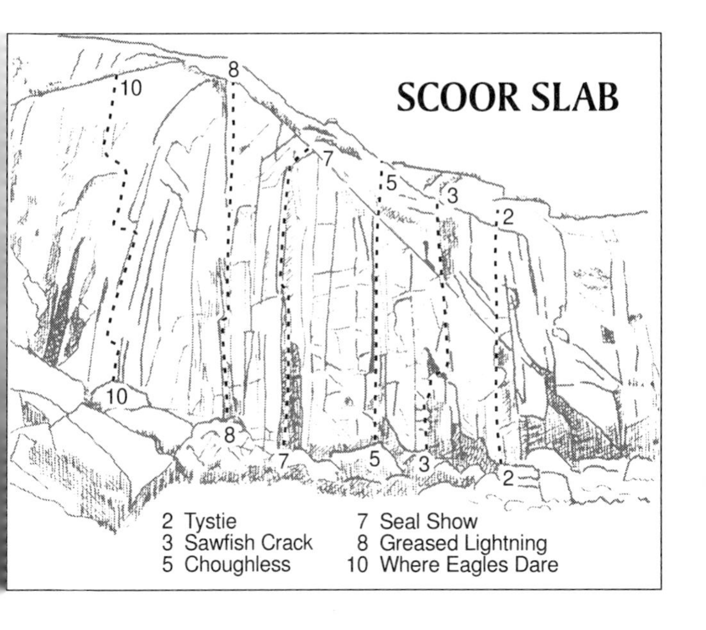

9 Turnstone 25m E2 5b * (1994)
This route is perhaps overgraded. Left of the left-hand fault is a thin crack, and left of this is an easier crack which can be gained from the top of the highest boulder. Climb up passing a block at 7m, then climb up and go over the bulge at two small overlaps to reach a flake. Follow the flake right to join Greased Lightning at the rock-scarred recess. Finish straight up and belay as for Greased Lightning.

10 Where Eagles Dare 25m E1 5a *** (1992)
A fine intimidating wander. Start 7 metres left of the left-hand fault, just left of Turnstone and 3 metres right of where the cliff base angles up more steeply. Climb a crack for 4m, then step left and follow another crack to the small overhangs. Step left and climb the open chimney, then hand traverse left across the wall to a sapling and go up to the top. Belay well back.

Hit and Run 25m E2 5b ** (1993)
A good route which crosses Where Eagles Dare. The start is bold, but it is low in the grade. Start 3 metres left of Where Eagles Dare and climb the crack directly to below the right-hand side of the crescent-shaped overhang. Step right to join Where Eagles Dare, follow it up the open chimney and continue up right to the top. Belay well back.

Mink 15m VS 4b * (1992)
This route climbs the ridge high in the boulder field left of the slab. Start up the right edge and finish up the left edge, then traverse the neck to regain the boulder field. Although the crux is low down, this is a bold route to lead and second. Perhaps it is best soloed.

BEACH WALL AREA

This short west-facing wall and the rocks beside it overlook the east end of the beach, at the left end of which is a large ivy.

Kilvickeon 20m E2 5b ** (1992)
West of The Slab is a boulder field, and west again is a ridge. Start left of the ridge base. Climb a steep flake, move up right to a foot ledge, then move left to gain and follow the ridge.

Bluebell Blues 20m E1 5b * (1993)
Move up the wall left of Kilvickeon to gain the bottom of the ramp which slants up left. Climb the ramp and continuing corner, then move right to finish.

Runout 15m VS 4b * (1992)
Left of Kilvickeon is a recessed area, and left again is another ridge. Climb this ridge to a bulge, then climb a left-slanting crack on the left; strong arms are useful.

Slyvester 15m E2 5c * (1993)
Climb the wide crack to the right of Tweekie Pie.

Tweekie Pie 15m E5 6b/c *** (1993)
Climb thin cracks up the wall right of Waves and White Water with the crux at the top, protected by RPs. There is a stake in the bracken; if top-roping the route into submission, beware of the sharp flake at the top.

Waves and White Water 15m HVS 5a *** (1991)
Climb the corner crack containing a burn.

Fungy 15m HVS 5a * (1991)
Climb the most prominent crack on the long wall left of Waves and White Water, finishing up a wide corner crack.

Better Than a Poke in the Eye 10m E4 6a * (1993)
Left again is an ivy. Climb the right-slanting crack to the right of it.

DUNE WALL

This is the short west-facing wall left of Beach Wall. From a distance, black lichen gives an impression of wetness but the wall dries quickly. If natural belays are absent, use the stake well up from Wallcreeper.

1 Dunechough 10m VS 4c *
This route climbs cracks on the right-hand side of the wall. Climb up to a small overhang, step right and follow the flakes.

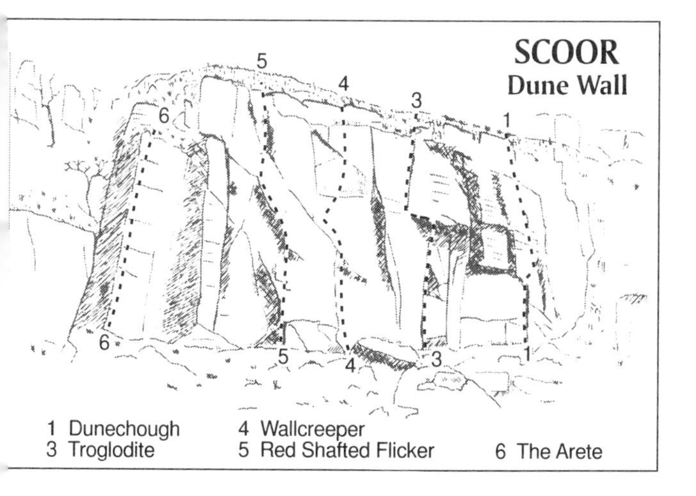

1 Dunechough
3 Troglodite
4 Wallcreeper
5 Red Shafted Flicker
6 The Arete

2 Thorns 10m HVS 5a *
Start as for Troglodite, then move up right and climb the crack.

3 Troglodite 10m HVS 5a **
Climb the crack to the overhang, step left and layback to the top.

4 Wallcreeper 10m E2 6a * (1994)
This route climbs the scoops in the centre of the wall. A steep start gains a left-sloping ramp, then mantel out right and make a thin move (crux) to good holds below the top. The crux is protected by Rocks 1 and 2 which are difficult to place, especially for the short.

5 Red Shafted Flicker 10m E1 5b * (1994)
Climb the shallow corner-flake.

6 The Arete 10m HVS 5a
This route is open to variation.

EILEAN GARBH

This is the island joined to the beach with several short walls. The rock nearest the sands is Wave Buttress. Moving right to left from Wave Buttress, slightly higher are Milk Tray and Black Isle, lower again is the quartz seam, then the nice steep Horse Wall and finally Stranded Arete.

Stranded Arete 12m Severe
Follow the coast east then south until a small bay cuts inland with a cliff at the back. Climb the ridge left of the steep wall. Some of the holds move a little, and the route is open to variation.

HORSE WALL

A clean gently overhanging wall, facing east.

Wild Swans 10m E1 5b (1994)
The crack left of Eat My Shorts; hard for the grade.

Eat My Shorts 13m E4 6a ** (1994)
The awkward layback crack at the left side of the wall.

See You in Hell Soldier Boy 15m E6 6b *** (1994)
Start just left of the black-stained wall at good holds. Move up to a short sharp flake, then move left to a very sharp finger jug; shake and gear. Make very thin technical moves up the wall above to reach the diagonal crack. Pull out right to a finger hold, stand in the crack and reach over the top to finish. RPs and HBs 2-5 are essential.

Lauracheval 13m E3 5c ** (1993)
Climb the left-slanting crack on the right side of the wall, starting at the right edge of the dark-stained wall.

Quartz Rib 13m VS 4b *
Climb the rib immediately right of the vertical quartz seam. The climbing is straightforward but protection is lacking.

Black Chimney 13m Severe
Climb the chimney right of the quartz seam, moving left at the top.

Milk Tray 15m HVS 5a (1994)
Right of Black Chimney is a crag at a slightly higher level. At the left side is an ivy; climb the crack on the right.

Black Isle 15m E2 5b * (1994)
Climb the wall to the right of Milk Tray past two pockets, trending left to finish close to Milk Tray.

WAVE BUTTRESS

This short cliff faces the beach (north). Most of the routes should improve with use, and the grades may come down a little.

Un Peu Salle 13m VS 4b *
At the left end of the cliff is a corner. Climb the crack on the slabby left wall to finish up a shallow chimney.

Jungle 10m VS 4c
To the right is another corner. Climb the crack just left of it with a vegetated finish.

Tern 10m Severe
Start just right of the corner, climb flakes and finish up a Y-crack.

Wavey Crack 10m HVS 5a *
A good climb which is worth the grade if holds on the next route are avoided.

Could Be Sanderlings 10m VS 4c
Climb the chimney to the right of Wavey Crack. There are some dubious flakes.

Surfin Santa 10m Severe
The chimney just to the right can be climbed by traditional means.

Shaky Ridge 10m Very Difficult
Further right a flake leans against the cliff. Follow the ridge just to its right, past a recess at mid-height and some suspect flakes higher up.

Merlin's Crack 10m VS 4c
Right again, climb a crack up the short buttress, starting left of the cave.

THE BAY

The Sleeper 12m E3/4 5c ** (1995)
On the right side of The Bay is a short gently overhanging wall. Climb easily up a rib, hand traverse right, then climb the centre of the wall.

Jimmy's Corner 30m VS 4b * (1992)
The lower half of the big corner is a bit bold, probably undergraded. There is often a wet streak which does not affect the grade.

Student Waster 30m E1 5b * (1992)
Left of Jimmy's Corner are twin left-facing corners. Follow the right-hand one until it fades, then step up left and climb twin cracks.

THE SMELLY BAY

This bay is between The Bay and Slochd Wall. The shore west of The Bay is not easy, so approach from the beach at Slochd Wall, scramble east to reach the cliff (or abseil in).

Weasels Ripped My Tips 15m E1 5b * (1995)
At the right side of the cliff is a prominent rib. Climb the left side of the rib and finish easily.

Socks 15m E1 5b * (1995)
Start in the corner left of Weasels Ripped My Tips. Climb up, then move awkwardly left and continue up the face above.

Aromatherapy 15m HVS 5a * (1995)
Climb a shallow chimney between Socks and A Fetid Stench, then take the right-hand of the two cracks above.

A Fetid Stench 15m E2 5c * (1994)
Scramble up the prominent right-facing corner crack, then climb it. There is a stone lodged at the top.

SLOCHD WALL

The routes on this short east-facing wall start from the pebble beach. Access is usually by scrambling down the ridge in front of the crag (or abseil off the boulders).

Fissure Fisher 15m HVS 5a * (1992)
Start at the right end of the crag. Follow a flake up rightwards to a triangular foothold, then climb directly to the top.

Flight of the Kite 15m E1 5a/b * (1993)
Climb the twin cracks left of Fissure Fisher.

A Quiet Shag 15m E1 5a * (1993)
Right of Pretty Choughed are twin cracks one metre apart. Start up the right-hand crack, then step into the left crack with hands level with the overlap. Move up, then go back right and continue to the top. Protection is plentiful but the rock is a touch soft.

Pretty Choughed 15m HVS 4c * (1992)
Climb the steep crack line at the left side of the crag.

Cup Champions 15m E1 5b * (1992)
Follow a shallow groove left of Pretty Choughed and just right of the arete before the crag changes direction. There is a choice of starts.

Dead Oystercatchers Don't Talk 15m Severe 4c (1992)
The face left of Cup Champions is recessed. Left of this an easy ramp runs up right giving a boulder problem start. A nice solo.

CREAG TEARMAINN

The largest crag at Scoor faces east and has some impressively steep sections. At the right-hand side is a slanting gully; this is the usual descent.

Hammock 20m HVS 5a (1991)
Climb the crack 20 metres left of the descent gully and finish up a shallow chimney. Steep with a couple of suspect holds, but well protected.

Spleenwort Groove 25m VS 4b * (1992)
Left of Hammock is a large left-facing corner. This route climbs the groove right of it. Go up to an overhanging flake, move left round this and follow the groove tó top. The climb improves after a vegetated start.

Agrimony 25m VS 4b * (1994)
Climb the large left-facing corner and finish up the wide crack just right of Creels. Like the previous route the start is a bit green.

Creels 35m Severe
Left of Agrimony the cliff overhangs in its upper half. Midway along the base is a shallow corner. Climb up just right of this to the ledge under the impending wall. Move right and escape up the corners. Not recommended.

Kelpie 35m E2 5b/c ** (1992)
Further left the overhanging wall continues, but this and the next route squeeze between the two leaning walls using the same (and only) gap. Below the gap are two corner cracks which stop halfway up. Climb the right-hand crack to the slab, move left, then traverse left on a large square flake. Move straight up to the short chimney which leads to White Shite and follow it rightwards to the top.

White Shite 50m VS 4c ** (1991)
This trade route has had ascents in double figures and follows the obvious white ramp line leading up right. The second could take a big fall if protection isn't placed. This is a fine route for showery weather as only the start and finish get wet.
1. 35m 4c Climb a short corner, then move rightwards following the ramp to a belay after the steep corner crack.
2. 15m 4b Continue along the ramp to the top.

Shag Vision 25m VS 4b (1994)
Start at the same place as Night Watch and follow the obvious line on the main face leading up right. A rope was left in place at the top to allow a haul up the steep grass.

THE PINNACLE

This is in the sea to the left of Creag Tearmainn and has some unusual routes whose starts are tidal. A diet of carrots would help. Descent is down the south face which is Moderate.

Pinnacle Route 20m Very Difficult
Gain The Pinnacle at low tide and climb the north-east ridge; the crux is moving up left from the niche.

Night Rider 30m E1 5a ** (1994)
This route and the next are atmospheric. Start east of Night Vision below the first chockstone. Haul up on a large hold on the main face and move easily up right to an intimidating step onto The Pinnacle. A move up the short slab gains a line of flakes which lead out left into the real world. Climb up, step right to follow a crack up left, then climb another crack on the right to the top of The Pinnacle. Finding a runner before the step would reduce the grade to HVS 5a.

Night Vision 20m VS 4b * (1992)
From the base of Pinnacle Route go down into the gully between The Pinnacle and the Creag Tearmainn (tidal), move along the gully under a chockstone to a second, lower chockstone and the start of the route. Move up the main face, then bridge across, climb though the hole and follow a corner crack to the top of The Pinnacle. Descend down the south face.

Night Watch 25m VS 4c (1994)
Start just west of Night Vision, climb the slabby west face of the chockstone, then move up left over boulders to reach a deep crack left of a short corner. Climb the crack, then go over a bulge to reach the top of The Pinnacle.

I Would Drive 500 Miles 15m E1 5b ** (1994)
Descending to Dun Slab, a wall is seen on the right. Just right of centre of the wall a thin crack goes up right to give the line of this route.

DUN SLAB

The slab faces the Dun (west) and is reached by walking over the hill from Creag Tearmainn to the stony beach.

Jack in a Box 25m HVS 5a * (1993)
Climb the clean crack left of the W-shaped overlap and finish level with the bush on Therapy. The first ascent started from the beach, climbing through a hole in the boulders; no spring was used.

We Like Sheep 25m VS 4c (1996)
Climb the crack to the left of the next route to a ledge. Climb through the middle of the W-shaped overlap to finish up the last part of That's Fast for a Snail.

That's Fast for a Snail 25m HVS 5c (1994)
Climb the left-slanting crack which runs past the right-hand side of the W-shaped overlap; bush belay.

Therapy 25m VS 4c * (1993)
At the right side of the face is a large flake. Start up its left side, step left and climb the crack line to a bush belay.

DUN A' GEARD

This is the Iron Age dun west of Creag Tearmainn. Below it is a short face next to a cave; this is opposite Jack in a Box and faces east.

One Foot on the Arete 10m E2 5c (1994)
Climb the arete beside the next route, with the crux at the base. Some of the holds are common to the next route.

One Foot in the Grave 10m E1 5b * (1993)
Climb the obvious corner.

Cog's Crack 10m E3 6a ** (1994)
Climb the striking crack two metres right of the previous route.

Doonagear 10m HVS 5b *
Start round the corner right of Cog's Crack and gain a scoop *via* undercut rock. Climb the left-hand crack above, moving right to finish.

ARDTUN

This north-facing dolerite sill is set back from the sea and has high midge rating. Three sections of the sill have been explored, with crack climbing and the odd chimney. The routes are described left to right.

Access
Arriving in Bunessan from the east, follow the road down the hill, then turn right, go over the bridge and go left round the coast for just over a kilometre. Turn down to the left and park near a left-hand bend before the last two houses. Head north-west (boggy) to skirt past the north side of the cairned mound (Dunan Mor), then continue past a boulder to reach a small grassy hill (the only grassy hill). The cliff is directly below (15 minutes from the road). An easy gully just to the east gives access. Below the sill is steep grass, below this is basalt which falls into the sea. To get to Ardtun East continue east, gain and cross the fence, and continue for 300 metres. The base of the crag is covered by bracken.

To reach Creag Eilean an Duilisg from the parking spot, head north-east keeping left (north) of the craggy hill (Torr Mor) to reach the stony beach east of the crag (20 minutes), or continue east from the top of the East Crag.

CREAG EILEAN AN DUILISG (Map Ref 386 246)

This is like a mini Kilt Rock with a tame approach. Care is needed with some of the finishes.

Nest Trundling 15m HVS 5a * (1996)
Climb the obvious twin cracks well left of Teb.

Collie Dolphins 15m HVS 5a * (1996)
Hand jam up the crack right of Nest Trundling, stepping left at the top to avoid the grass.

Teb 18m E1 5a/b ** (1996)
The twin cracks just left of Poorwill.

1 Poorwill 20m HVS 5a ** (1995)
At the left side of the crag is an overhang 5 metres up. Climb twin cracks right of the overhang.

2 Duck Xing 20m E1 5a/b * (1995)
Right of Poorwill are twin cracks; climb the crack just right of them.

3 Kea 20m HVS 5a * (1995)
Right of Duck Xing is a single crack which gives the route, starting up a flake.

4 Gobhar-athair 20m HVS 5a ** (1995)
Twin cracks lead to a bulge, then climb a short wall.

5 Hirondelle 20m E1 5b ** (1995)
At the dry stane dyke, climb the steep crack directly; a nice sustained route.

6 Geadh-glas 20m E1 5b ** (1995)
Follow twin cracks until they merge and bend right, then follow slabby rock to the top.

7 Nutcracker 20m E1 5a/b * (1995)
Climb the crack just left of Nightjar.

8 Nightjar 20m VS 4c ** (1995)
The cliff base is higher below a left-facing corner crack. Climb the corner to a slabby finish.

9 Chicken of Depression 20m E1 5a * (1995)
Gain a platform, follow wide cracks, then climb the crack over a couple of bulges. The moves are good, but it is still slightly friable.

10 Chickens in the Mist 20m HVS 5a * (1995)
Climb to a ledge, then follow twin cracks and finish up the right-hand crack past some loose holds.

11 Jonathan Livingston Dodo 20m E1 5a (1995)
Pleasant climbing, but spoiled by the last moves past loose rock. Start left of the 5m pillar. Climb twin cracks to a short chimney (without using the chockstone). Climb the chimney, move out left and carefully continue to the top.

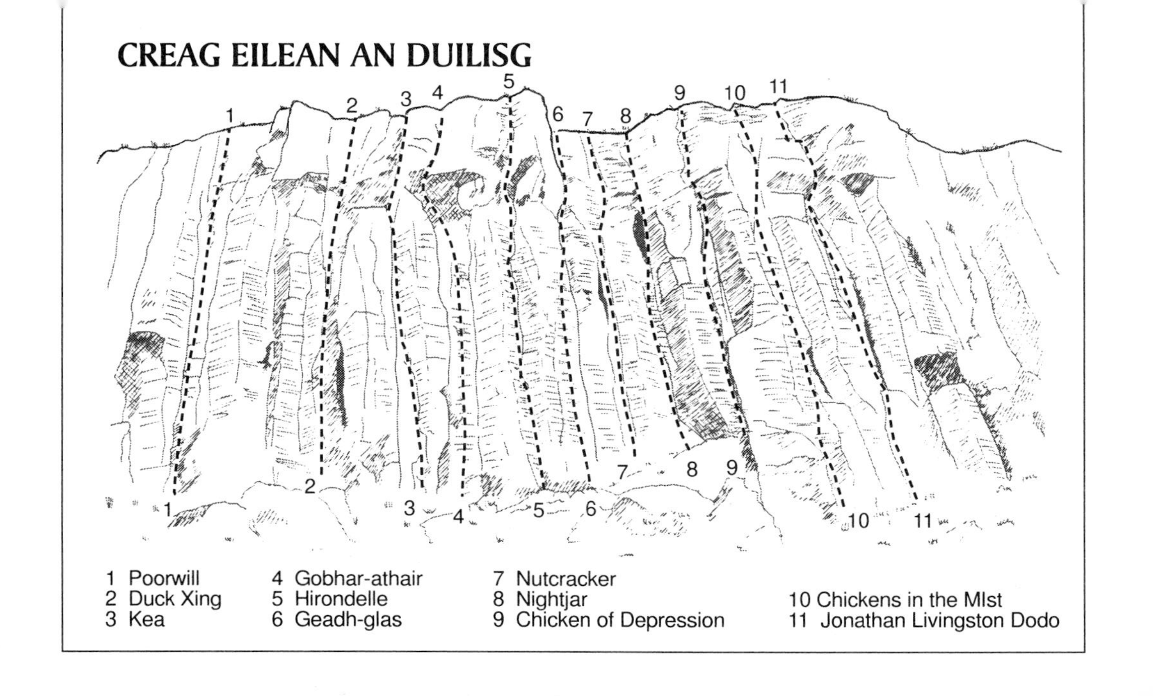
CREAG EILEAN AN DUILISG
1 Poorwill
2 Duck Xing
3 Kea
4 Gobhar-athair
5 Hirondelle
6 Geadh-glas
7 Nutcracker
8 Nightjar
9 Chicken of Depression
10 Chickens in the MIst
11 Jonathan Livingston Dodo

Chouca 15m HVS 5a * (1996)
Right of Jonathan Livingstone Dodo is a 5m pillar and right again are short fallen pillars. Climb the right-bending corner to the right of these.

Donald Duck 20m E1 5a/b ** (1996)
Left of the waterfall left of Doo Stew are three shallow corner cracks. Climb the middle one using flake holds, then step right and finish up a crack.

Doo Stew 20m E1 5a * (1995)
Well to the right is another area of clean rock. Right of the burn is a 6m pillar, just right of it is a larger pillar. Climb twin cracks on the right of the large pillar; the left one is a hand crack and right crack is very thin. Climb a bulge and continue to the top. A belay stake is 12m back.

Spug Korma 20m E1 5b ** (1995)
Right of Doo Stew is a left-facing corner crack. Climb this, step right and continue easily to the top. Belay at the stake.

Stukie Pate 20m HVS 5a * (1995)
Starting right again, climb a crack and step right to a platform, then bridge up the wide crack. Belay at the stake.

Scrambled Sea-Eagle Egg 20m HVS 5a * (1996)
Right of the previous route is a shallow chimney. Climb this using the crack on the right. Near the top, pull out left and step up to the platform. Step right and climb the shallow corner to the belay stake.

ARDTUN EAST (Map Ref 383 247)

1 Ascent Route Severe
At the left end is a large chockstone; climb over this.

2 Walkabout 12m VS 5a **
Climb past ferns just left of Four Legged Friend, then follow twin cracks .

3 Four Legged Friend 12m HVS 5a/b **
The corner crack 4 metres left of Oot Ma Rays has a couple of loose flakes, but they don't want to come out.

4 Oot Ma Rays 13m VS 4c **
There are some large boulders at the cliff base. Climb the shallow corner crack above them, finishing past a bulge.

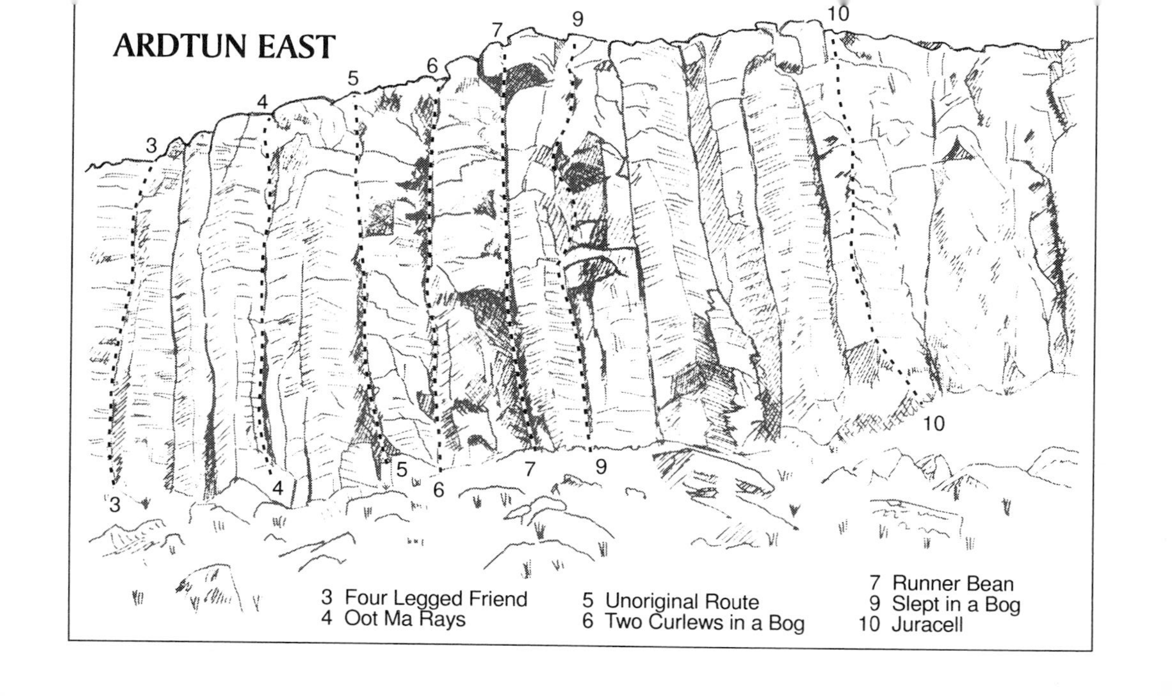
ARDTUN EAST
3 Four Legged Friend
4 Oot Ma Rays
5 Unoriginal Route
6 Two Curlews in a Bog
7 Runner Bean
9 Slept in a Bog
10 Juracell

5 Unoriginal Route 13m HVS 5a **
Climb the wide corner crack 3 metres right of Oot Ma Rays.

6 Two Curlews in a Bog 13m HVS 4c *
Climb a deep, wide crack just to the right. There is a large wobbly flake on the right near the top. Small wires are useful for the cracks beside the main crack.

7 Runner Bean 14m HVS 5a **
The wide crack passes an overhang at 4m and leads to a pull over a bulge at the tallest part of this section of cliff.

8 Two Peas in a Pod 14m VS 4b **
Enter the chimney behind Runner Bean, move up it, then wriggle out over a chockstone to finish as for Runner Bean. Fortunately the graffiti is hidden from view. If the chockstone disappears the climb might become a lot harder.

9 Slept in a Bog 14m E1 5b **
Climb the crack just to the right over two bulges.

10 Juracell 12m HVS 5a **
Start beside a grassy crack at the right side of a pillar, aboiut 7 metres right of Slept in a Bog. Move up left and climb the cracked arete. High in the grade.

11 Mental Block 10m VS 4c **
Climb the north side of the small pinnacle 5 metres right of Juracell, then step onto the face and climb the crack.

12 Rock Around the Block 10m HVS 5a **
Start just right of the pinnacle and climb the crack

A wide corner crack with some hollow blocks 10 metres to the right is Severe, while a line at Very Difficult can be found over the blocks to the right. **Gannet** (VS **) takes the twin cracks just to the right, and **Puffball** (VS 4c **) takes an offwidth crack formed by the left side of a pillar 4 metres right again. **Straight Jacket** (Severe *) is a narrow climb behind Puffball, starting at the right-hand side of the pillar.

THE GREEN HILL (Map Ref 376 247)

Jacket Required 8m Severe
Climb a crack in a right-facing corner; there is a block 2m up just right of the route.

Splash 10m VS 4c *
Further right is a pillar. Climb twin cracks on the right side of the pillar to a ledge on the left, then continue to the top.

Pushing up the Camelot 10m HVS 5a *
Further right is a grassy pillar. Climb twin cracks 4 metres to its left, of which the left-hand crack is wider.

Pancakes at Iochdar 12m VS 4c *
Climb the recessed twin cracks.

Kinloch Bound 12m Severe
Climb another set of twin cracks, 6 metres left of Rally Fever.

Another for Hector 12m VS 4c *
Yet more twin cracks left of Rally Fever.

Rally Fever 12m HVS 5a *
Start past a grassy ledge and bulge just left of Windjammer, then climb twin cracks.

Windjammer 13m HVS 5a *
Climb the corner crack just left of the next route.

Sons of the Hounds Come Here and Get Flesh 13m HVS 5a *
Climb a corner crack above a flake embedded in the turf.

Quest 14m E1 5b ***
Climb yet another set of twin cracks; access is a bit scary.

Terminal 14m E2 5b **
Climb the twin cracks just right again, finishing on the left one.

DUNAN MOR (Map Ref 373 242)

This is the nearest cliff to the road, under (west) of the dun. It is about five minutes from the road.

The Gannet in the Gansey 10m E4 5c **
Left of the other routes is a ruined sheiling, 12 metres left of which is a prominent clean arete (the grade is a guess). Climb the arete; placing runners in the crack on the right would be an obvious temptation, which would reduce the E grade.

Jacob's Creep 10m HVS 5a *
Climb the arete left of Fly Past keeping right of the small overhang, then step left and climb the arete.

Fly Past 10m VS 4c
Climb the obvious crack past the left side of the roof.

Domino 10m HVS 5a *
Start just right of the dry stane dyke. Start up the crack, move left above the bulge to gain and climb the crack coming from the roof.

FIDDEN (Map Ref 306 224)

This is a south-east facing granite crag. From Fionnphort, take the road south towards Knockvologan for 1km. After passing a roadside crag on the right, the road bends left then back right. From the right bend walk boggily east for 10 minutes. The rock looks vegetated on the approach as the cleaner face is hidden from view.

Slainte Bha 10m VS 5a
Start right of Count Jugular. Climb the wide crack, move left round the overhang, step right above it and continue to the top. Belay well back.

Count Jugular 10m Severe 4b
Climb the right-hand corner and belay well back.

Happy New Year 15m HVS 5a **
Start up Count Jugular, traverse left below the overhang, then pull up onto the slab. Climb the short steep corner to the top.

Happy New Year 15m HVS 5a **
Start up Count Jugular, traverse left below the overhang, then pull up onto the slab. Climb the short steep corner to the top.

Merry Noel 15m HVS 5a **
A counter diagonal to Happy New Year, starting from the lochan. Either climb the overhanging left-slanting crack at 5c, or move up right to join the end of the crack. Continue up towards the tree, then move right. Continue right by an exposed hand traverse, then climb the short crack.

Glad Tidings 12m Severe
Climb the broken arete left of Merry Noel, finishing up the wide chimney.

ERRAID (Map Ref 294 192)

There is a granite crag with two tiers on this small tidal island. The rock is good and the area is pleasant, with a beach five minutes away. From Fionnphort, take the road south to park at Knockvologan. Follow the track down the hill, bearing right to reach the sand (or sea at high tide), and walk (or wade) over to Erraid.

Cross the island to reach the beach at Traigh Geal, then follow the east side of the bay to reach the upper tier in about 35 minutes. The lower tier is directly below and can be affected by rough seas. A more direct approach can be taken, but the moor is fairly featureless and navigation is not easy without a compass.

LOWER TIER

The routes are mainly in a bowl. Access is either to scramble from the east side, or to clamber through the arch at the back of the bowl. At high tide come in from the west, just behind Sentinel. The first three routes are left of the arch.

1 Sentinel 12m HVS 5a **
This is the prominent crack line at the left-hand side of the bowl. Climb cracks to a wide ledge, then step back left and climb the crack. A left-hand start gives a more sustained route.

2 Daylight Robbery 10m Severe *
The next crack to the right has a difficult start.

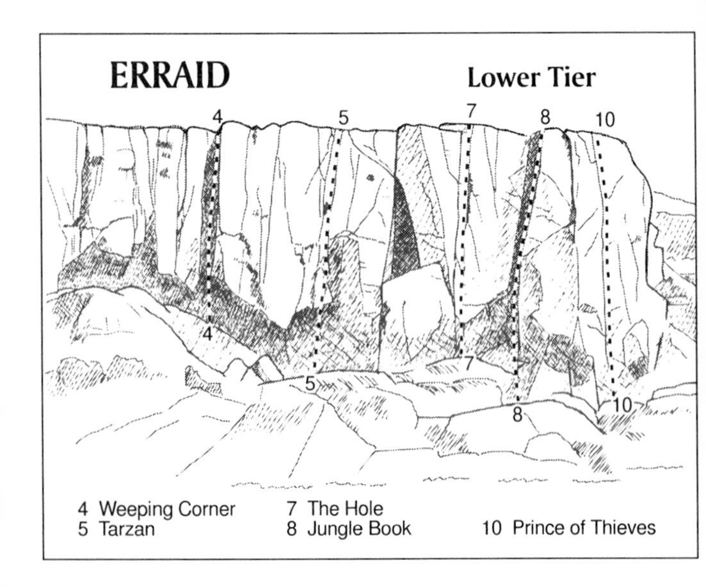

4 Weeping Corner 7m HVS 5a
The black left-facing corner to the right of the arch gives an awkward struggle.

5 Tarzan 10m HVS 5a *
Right of the undercut section, a hard start leads to easier cracks.

6 Jane 10m VS 4c
A difficult crack leads to a big ledge, then climb a corner crack.

7 The Hole 8m HVS 5a **
Climb steep cracks left of the deep corner.

8 Jungle Book 8m VS 4b *
Climb the deep corner.

The next three routes lack independence but offer good climbing. They are only climbable at low tide.

9 Spiral Arete 10m HVS 5a
Start up a short corner and slab to the right of the arete. Spiral back up left and finish up a short corner; possibly undergraded.

10 Prince of Thieves 10m E2 5b
The crack right of the arete gives a sustained route.

11 Moody's Blues 10m E2 5b *
Gain a ledge, climb a thin crack and pull out left to the ledge on Prince of Thieves. Reach out right to a deep crack and continue to the top.

UPPER TIER

The wall tends to overhang five degrees or so. Left of the central crack are two crack lines which stop at a ledge at two-thirds height.

Walls Without Balls 12m E1 5b *
The crack left of the left-hand crack line has a problematical start.

Stealth 12m E1 5c *
The right-hand crack line has another hard start.

Oliver 13m VS 4c *
Start to the right of the central crack at the base of a ramp. Follow a crack up left, then continue straight up.

Fagan 10m HVS 5a *
Gain the base of the ramp and climb the crack above.

A couple of short routes have been climbed right of Fagan. There is also a Very Difficult route left of Walls Without Balls where the crag changes direction.

IONA

This island is considerably older than Mull and quite different in character. There are many small outcrops of gneiss scattered around.

PORT BHAN, TOLKIEN CRAG (Map Ref 264 244)

This fine south-west facing cliff of gneiss has a sandy base. To get there, turn left off the ferry and head south, following the road which turns west heading for the golf course on the west coast. Follow the track across the course to the shore. Turn right (north) and follow the fence, go over a style and cross a field to a second sandy beach. This takes about 30 minutes from the ferry.

The Shire 15m Very Difficult (1993)
Climb the easy-angled blunt arete at the right-hand side.

Cracks of Mordor 15m VS 4b (1993)
Start left of The Shire and climb straight up to twin cracks, then follow them to the top. The wall just to the left is also VS.

Gollum 15m HVS 4c * (1991)
Climb a short wall and a slab to the grey corner, then follow it to a niche and the top.

Smaug 25m E1 5a ** (1993)
Start just left of Gollum. Climb the wall to a small overhang, then move right onto the arete. Climb up and left above the overhang to a small ledge, then continue to a larger ledge above. Move up and right to a horizontal break and a large ledge and go over a bulge to the top. The overhang can be climbed direct; a long reach is useful.

My Preciousssss 25m HVS 5a * (1991)
Climb a break up and right to a small roof, then move round the side of this and follow the groove to the top.

Bilbo and Friends 25m Severe * (1991)
Follow the ramp line before the overhanging wall up right to a ledge, then move left and climb a groove.

Yan's Route 25m HVS 5a * (1993)
Start up the previous route and at 4m go left across the steep wall to a jug and sloping crack; finish straight up.

EILEAN DIDIL (Map Ref 261 242)

This is the island seen on the left when approaching Port Ban. The west end of the island terminates at an overhanging wall. A ramp north of the cliff gives access by scrambling. The north face is big but green, while the south face is clean but does not run to good lines. The west face is a nice cliff, steep and colourful. Being a sea-cliff and not getting much sun, it is often wet. The edge between the south and west faces has been soloed.

Cognitive Therapy E4 6a ** (1993)
Climb the obvious line on the right-hand side of the crag, heading for the short shallow left-facing corner at top.

McQUARRIE'S ROCK (Map Ref 260 242)

This is the island west of Eilean Didil; the two are separated by a boulder-filled cleft. The central crack line on the slab facing Eilean Didil is Very Difficult. Other routes have been climbed beside it.

SOUTH FACE

At the left side of the face are two grooves which are both Very Difficult.

Jackie's Line 10m HVS 5a * (1993)
Climb the right-slanting crack on the right of the grooves.

Fada 10m E1 5a * (1993)
The wall right of Jackie's Line gives a poorly protected climb.

The Day of the Frog 10m HVS 5a (1993)
Climb the weakness left of the corner.

Access Route 10m Difficult
The corner at the right side of the face.

There are two routes on the west face. The obvious crack in the small corner is VS 4c, and the steeper crack to its left is HVS 5a.

THE SOUTH COAST OF IONA

Access
Turn left (south) at the ferry slip, and follow the road which leads west to the golf course. Follow the fence left (south) to meet a rough road which goes up the hill to Loch Staonaig, round the west side of the loch. Continue south round the hill (Maol nan Uan). Druim an Aoinidh then comes into view in the west; head for a point just left (south) of the cairn. The stony beach of Port nan Struth will be seen below. Moal na Ciche is to the left (east) of it, and Aoineadh nan Struth is to the right (west), at the most westerly tip of Iona. Allow a little under an hour.

The climbing is on gneiss, but a few routes climb the darker (and softer) amphibolite. Although many routes were done on sight, a couple of falls have resulted from holds breaking (on precleaned routes!).

RAVEN'S CRAG (Map Ref 255 220)

The main face runs in a straight line, is gently overhanging and faces south-west. Three rocks stand proud of the main face; The Menhir stands guard over the left end, roughly centre is The Pulpit, and the gap behind it is filled with large boulders. Right of The Pulpit is an overhanging prow; The Altar. At the right end of the main cliff the rock turns to face east and diminishes in height. All of the routes on this cliff were climbed after the first of June, because of the raven's nest.

THE MENHIR

Welly Route Difficult
The easiest way up the block, descending by the same way. Belays might not exist at the top.

MAIN WALL

The routes here get the sun in the afternoon. They are described from left to right.

1 Eric the Red 20m E2 5b * (1993)
Climb the right-facing corner crack to the right of The Menhir to a ledge. Finish up a short wall left of the corner crack above.

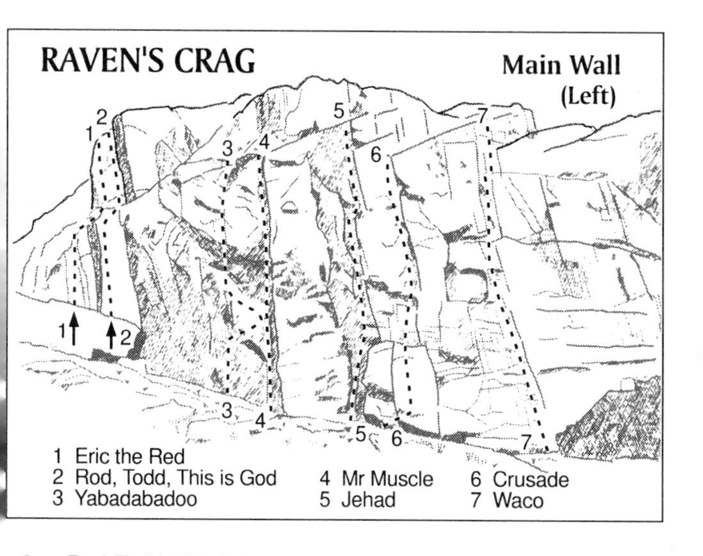

2 Rod, Todd, This is God 20m E4 6a ** (1994)
Climb the thin crack in the red wall, protected by RPs, just right of Eric the Red. Finish up the corner crack.

3 Yabadabadoo 20m E5 6a ** (1993)
This route follows the left-hand crack line in the dark band of rock. A bold start leads to a small sloping ledge and gear, then move up right to the pocket on Mr Muscle (Friend 2½ runner). Move back left and climb the crack through roofs.

4 Mr Muscle 20m E5 6b ** (1993)
The right-hand crack line in the dark band of rock. Climb straight up to a pocket (Friend 2½ runner). Difficult moves lead to a roof (small Friend in the undercut slot), then go right to a jug on the lip and up the wall.

5 Jehad 20m E2 5b * (1993)
Climb the central corner system, trending slightly right and passing a large flake which runs out left from mid-height. A fine line, but spoilt by some dubious dark rock. A nest appeared on the route in 1994, but it didn't affect the grade.

6 Crusade 20m E2 5b * (1993)
Right of Jehad is a small pinnacle halfway up the cliff. This route climbs the crack on the left side of the pinnacle. Start below the crack and climb a green slab that stands proud of the cliff base, then continue up the crack, stepping left at the top of the pinnacle to finish up another crack.

7 Waco 20m E2 5b * (1993)
Start just left of the shallow cave, climb the short right-facing corner and continue straight up.

8 Cul Dreimne 20m E2 5b * (1993)
This is a pleasant route but slow to dry. Start right of the shallow cave, step left off the boulder and climb steeply up to easier ground. Continue to a steepening and climb the slanting crack on the left to finish up the short wall.

THE PULPIT

The routes here are often a bit unbalanced with steep starts and easier finishes. They are in the sun in the afternoon.

Shower Ridge 15m VS 4b
The left arete. Start from the base of the large flake boulder, then move right onto the arete and climb it.

Elastration 15m HVS 5a (1993)
Climb the wide crack just to the right. There is a liberal coating of lichen, but the holds are clean.

Communion Wine 15m E1 5b (1993)
Left of Pleasant Slab is a crack leading to the centre of an easy slab. A steep colourful start gains the crack. Climb the crack and easy slab to reach a flake line, then follow this, step right and continue to the top.

Pleasant Slab 20m E3 5c (1993)
The offwidth crack; a Camelot 4 is of limited use.

A Wing and a Prayer 20m E2 5b (1994)
Climb the crack of Passage until just short of the big shelf. Traverse left until below a flake crack (Rock 4 on the left), then climb up to the flake and continue to the top.

Passage 20m VS 4c/5a ** (1993)
This pleasant route takes the obvious ramp which cuts across the face. Climb the crack and follow the ramp to the right until it finishes conveniently at another crack which leads to the top.

Parable 20m E1 5b * (1993)
A good route which cuts through the previous climb. Start just left of the left-slanting crack, step up and right and follow the crack to the ramp. Climb in the same line over the bulge at a notch and continue to the top.

Fire and Brimstone 20m E3 5c * (1994)
This route takes the red wall *via* a fine start, but the second half is a disappointment; easy for the grade. Right of the crack of Parable is a short black crack at head height. Climb past the crack to reach the small ramp. Follow the ramp up right until it ends, then pull out left and carry on up, trying to avoid Scripture.

Scripture 20m E1 5b * (1993)
Start up a bulging crack and follow it up the arete to a finish shared with Passage.

Apocrypha 20m E1 5b * (1993)
Just right of the previous route are two seams of dark rock. Climb the right-hand one, then continue up the corner on large flakes.

Pulpit Groove 20m E2 5b (1994)
On the right-hand side of The Pulpit is a left-slanting groove. Climb this to the platform, then take the steep crack just right of Apocrypha.

THE ALTAR

Complete Abstinence 12m E1 5a (1994)
Start at the back of the recess between The Pulpit and the next route. Follow a shelf boldly rightwards, then climb up to finish.

The Incredible Dr Sex 12m E6 6b *** (1993)
The stunning arete of the pinnacle. Start just left of the arete, move up right to a jug and runners on the arete. Move up and slightly right to small flat holds, then make hard moves to gain and use the undercut on the right. Gain the next break and runners, then more hard climbing leads direct to the top.

Smoke Yourself Thin 10m E4 6a * (1994)
Start just left of Monologue. Move up to then climb the left-leaning shallow groove and continue up, stepping right at the top.

Monologue 10m HVS 5a
Climb a vein on the right side of the pinnacle to the niche left of overhangs and continue to the top.

Inverted-V 10m E2 6a (1994)
Climb up to and through the overhangs right of Monologue.

MAIN WALL

Left of the nest is a short face bounded on the left by a left-facing corner (just right of a bay). The corner gives a Severe route, finishing up a short open chimney.

1 Brush Off 13m HVS 5a
Climb the arete left of the nest, starting on the right-hand side. Gain the large sloping ledge and continue up the arete.

2 The Bantry Boat 20m E2 5b * (1995)
Below the nest are two corners. Climb the left-hand one, move right brushing past the nest, then a steep wall and easier climbing leads to the top.

3 Smoking the Toad 20m E5 6b *** (1994)
Start on the shelf at the obvious crack in the middle of the red wall, right of the nest. Make a series of long reaches on good holds to a peg. Hard moves above lead to a shake out under the roof and gear. Pull through the roof and finish direct. The peg was placed in 1993 and should probably be replaced with a stainless steel one.

4 Prodigy 25m E4 6a *** (1993)
This route climbs the right-hand side of the red wall. Climb the grey crack, step left and climb a ramp to a small overhang. Move up right to the main overhang, traverse left under it to the lip, then climb up and over.

5 Skinhead 20m HVS 5a (1993)
Right of the nest is a steep face climbed by the last two routes. Climb the wide corner crack right of it, just left of the quartz seam.

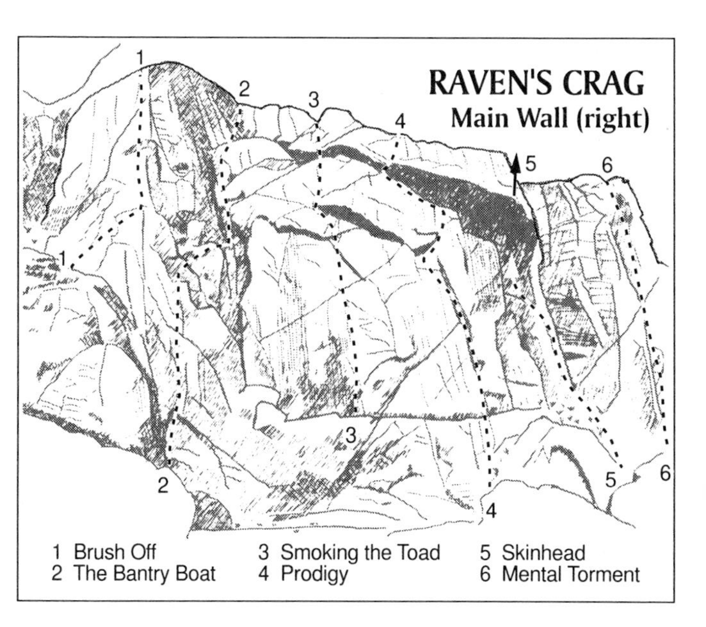

EAST FACE

6 Mental Torment 20m E2 5b ** (1993)
Climb the corner at the left side of the face; worthwhile and easy for the grade.

Don't Bang the Drum 15m VS 4b (1993)
Climb the right-slanting corner crack formed by a flake, then step left and climb the slabby wall.

At One 15m VS 4b (1993)
Gain the shelf, follow it left and climb the slabby corner.

Melter 10m HVS 5a
Climb the left-slanting arete which marks the right edge of the overhanging wall, and pull over a bulge to finish.

There are a number of unnamed routes further right. A crack running leftwards through a gap in the overhang is Very Difficult. A VS route goes past the shelf to a ledge under the overhang, then climbs straight up. The wide crack is HVS 5a, as is the left-facing corner just to the right. The steep arete is VS 4b, and the weakness in the slabby wall is Very Difficult.

AOINEADH NAN STRUTH (Map Ref 253 223)

The approach is described in the previous section. There are climbs on three cliffs: firstly, the cliff on the south-west tip of Iona, starting from a sloping shelf - Ireland Wall; secondly, a smaller cliff further north which also starts from a sloping shelf - Labrador Wall; and thirdly the area between, which is beside a deep gully - Gully Wall.

IRELAND WALL

Heretic 25m E3 6a ** (1993)
This route climbs the fine crack at the bottom of the shelf from a tidal start. Move up and right to gain the crack; belay well back.

The Good Book 30m E1 5b ** (1993)
Climb the corner crack from another tidal start.

Chinatown 25m E3 5b (1993)
Climb the crack in the black seam on dubious holds.

Vatican City 20m Severe
Step onto a shelf and move left to gain the crack line. Climb the crack, then the flake on the right. Finish up the corner crack just left of Sash Vert.

Sash Vert 20m VS 4c
The start is shared with the next route. Climb up past a green band of rock to the overhang, move up left and finish up an easy corner.

The Shelf 25m Difficult
Start below the overhang, step up and follow the easy shelf rightwards to finish up a corner.

GULLY WALL

This is reached by scrambling down from the top of Labrador Wall (just north of The Black Streak), traversing south from the base of Labrador Wall at low tide or abseiling in. There is a convenient shelf at the base which only gets wet with big waves. The routes are south-west and west-facing.

The Black Streak 12m Very Difficult
Climb the obvious line at the left side.

A Vicious Streak 15m Severe
Climb the crack left of The Quartz Crack (which is also Severe), move right and finish up a corner.

Drunken Biker's Route 15m Very Difficult *
Climb an easy corner to a bulge, avoid it by moving left and continue up.

The Man of Riou 15m VS 4c
Start right of the arete. Climb up and step left onto a steep ramp, and continue to the top.

L'homme d'Iona 20m HVS 5a * (1993)
Climb up to the overhung corner. From the top of the corner swing out left and climb to the top.

LABRADOR WALL

The first four routes are on the short south-west facing wall at the bottom of the shelf, and the other routes face west.

Chargold 10m VS 4c
Climb the deceptive crack at the left-hand side, starting up dark rock.

Magnetic Wall 12m E1 5b *
Go up to a niche and climb the bulge on the left to gain and follow a left-slanting crack.

The short steep crack on the right is E1 5b, and the corner crack right of the face which leads up left is Severe. There is another Severe 4 metres further right. Right again is an easy descent gully, and right of this is an easy ramp (Moderate).

Looking Around 12m Severe *
This route and the following two are between the easy ramp and an easy shelf on the right. Pull onto a shelf right of the corner, move up and left and climb the corner.

Checking Out 12m VS 4b *
Start just right of the arete to the right. Climb steeply up, then step left and follow the arete.

Another Day 12m HVS 4c
The recessed wall just left of an overhanging bay is strenuous with a dearth of protection

Quack 12m HVS 5a
Climb the right-facing corner crack right of the easy shelf.

Force 5 10m E1 5a
Climb the depression to an overhang, then follow the steep flake out left. There is another cliff to the right (Difficult).

OTHER CLIFFS

Climbs have been found on the basalt of the Carsaig Arches (Map Ref 497 185) on the south coast, but they should be avoided. Hundreds of problems have been climbed on dolerite, mainly between Ben More and the wilderness to the west. Some of the longer routes were led. Dun Mor (Map Ref 462 404) to the north has half a dozen well protected 15m routes from Moderate to Severe, and faces south. Some sills east of Ardchrishnish have been looked at, but they are disappointing. There are some basalt columns at Ulva (Map Ref 435 380) which have given eight south-facing 15m routes in the Difficult to VS range and more are possible. At Knockan (Map Ref 402 239) there are several short routes on dolerite.

Some gabbro cliffs around Loch Ba have also been climbed on, but like Creach Beinn they have nests which should not be disturbed until August. There are several gabbro buttresses above Craig (Map Ref 297 589) in Glen More which have given a few climbs.

Two climbs were done on schist at Scoor beach proper (Map Ref 420 186), but they don't compare well with the routes described. Also on schist a few short climbs have been soloed west of Uisken (Map Ref 386 183).

On granite, many problems have been climbed near Fionnphort. Several routes have been climbed between Kintra and Bunessan, up to 20m long, but the cliffs on this coastline are often difficult to locate.

There has been a fair amount of activity on the gneiss of Iona. The north face of Dun I (Map Ref 284 253) was climbed on sight, otherwise the route might have been worth repeating. A dozen routes were climbed on the east coast, south of the village. A 30m Very Difficult was also climbed just south of the Spouting Cave. A roadside crag near Loch Beg (Map Ref 524 295) is used for top-rope instruction. The belay was once a tree.

Colonsay

Colonsay and its close neighbour Oronsay to the south (linked at low tide), lie to the north-west of Jura and Islay and offer a diversity of scenery unequalled on any other Scottish island of comparable size. The island, generally blessed with good weather, is very rocky with many miniature mountains and lonely coves. There are also some superb beaches, from the popular Kiloran Bay in the north-west to the more secluded white sands in the south-east. Colonsay has all the ingredients for an adventurous family holiday with ample opportunity for the frustrated rock jock to sneak off and enjoy some very good cragging. The maps that cover the island are the Ordnance Survey 1:50,000 Sheet 61 and the 1:25,000 Sheet 375 (NR 38/39/49)

Access

There is a vehicle and passenger ferry from Oban, operated by Caledonian MacBrayne, telephone Oban (01631) 562285 or Gourock (01475) 650100. The crossing time is 2 hours 10 minutes. Once on the island, a postbus service is available, but a bicycle is the ideal form of transport. For a long stay it may be worth taking a car.

Accommodation

There is a hotel at Scalasaig (telephone: 019512 316). A number of holiday cottages and a variety of flats in Colonsay House are available for rent, the latter being situated amidst delightful gardens (telephone: 019512 312). Camping is discouraged.

The only shop (and Post Office) is in Scalasaig.

Rock Climbing

Although Colonsay will never become a major rock climbing centre, the island does possess a wealth of small attractive crags offering numerous one-pitch routes on a wide variety of rock types. It is also perfect for long sea-level traverses interspersed by the occasional swim.

The routes done to date represent a tiny proportion of the potential. The first route recorded on Colonsay was in 1985 and John Spencer climbed a few routes and enjoyed a lot of bouldering in the late 1980s. However, Graham Little and friends discovered the diversity of its potential in 1993, putting up routes on a number of contrasting crags.

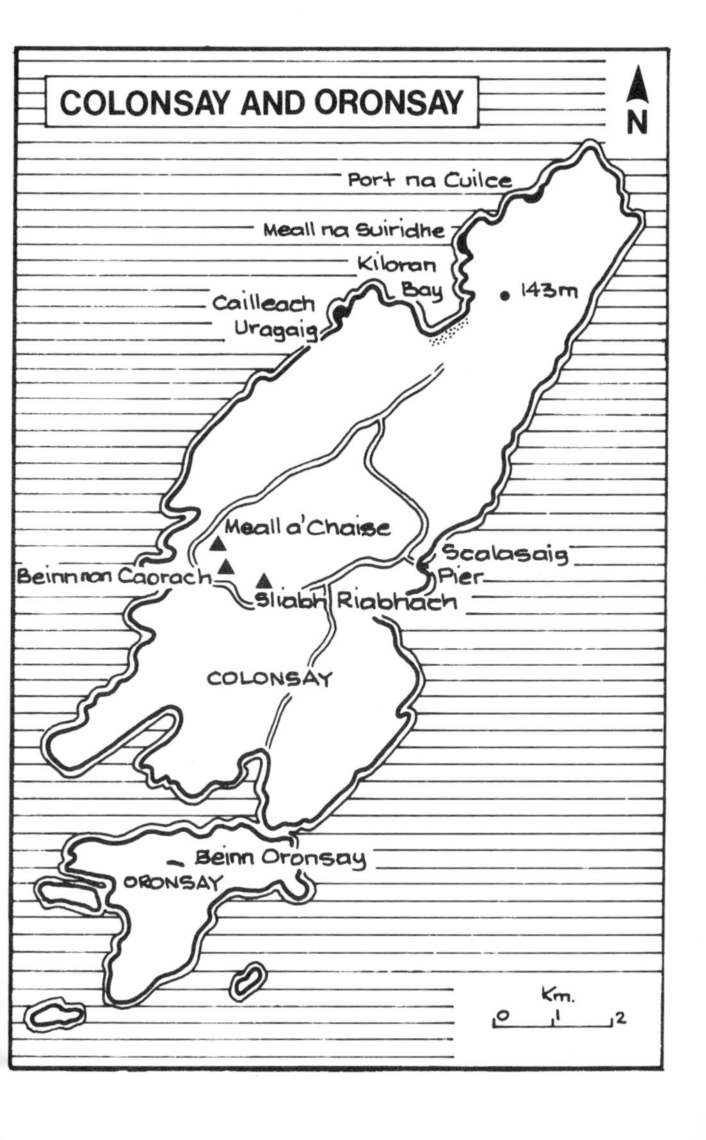
COLONSAY AND ORONSAY
N
Port na Cuilce
Meall na Suiridhe
Kiloran
Bay
143m
Cailleach
Uragaig
Meall a'Chaise
Scalasaig
Pier
Beinn non Caorach
Sliabh Riabhach
COLONSAY
Beinn Oronsay
ORONSAY
Km.
0
1
2

PORT NA CUILCE (Map Ref 415 002)

A 25m west-facing wall of steep cracked slate lies in the secluded bay of Port na Cuilce in the far north-west of the island, commanding an excellent view over to Mull. The rock is superficially loose but once descaled, it is fundamentally sound (give or take the odd fragile edge).

The Mission 25m E2 5b * (1993)
This interesting route takes the line of the striking diagonal flake crack and the cracked wall above. Start at the obvious 3m white cross. Climb the sharp-edged diagonal flake crack to near its end where a thin vein of quartz cuts it to create an X. Move up the wall to gain big flake holds, then go directly up the rusty wall to make the crux moves on to a small rock ledge and thence to the top.

MEALL NA SUIRIDHE (Map Ref 402 993)

This grassy headland, to the west of the track leading from Kiloran Bay to Balnahard, is cut by a narrow cliff-flanked rift. The most striking feature of this rift is a radically overhanging wedge of rock (The Fang), well seen from the track.

Thrift Is a Virtue 25m Very Difficult (1993)
West of The Fang, on the south side of the rift, lies a crag at a more amenable angle, increasing in height towards the sea. This route tackles the high, narrow slab with sea-thrift at its top (this slab should not be confused with the wider slab to the right, more liberally covered in sea-thrift). Climb the slab staying close to its right edge.

At the north-west extremity of the headland, beyond The Fang, lies a 20m vertical wall. It can be accessed at any state of the tide by descending rock steps to the south, then traversing back round on rock shelves to below the wall.

Walking on Sunshine 20m E1 5b *** (1993)
This route climbs a direct line on excellent rock near the left (northern) edge of the wall. Start at a plinth abutting the base of the wall. Climb just left of the diagonal crack for 4m to a fat flake. Step left to two small horns of rock, then go straight up, largely on side holds, to a tiny ledge below the slight groove in the headwall. Climb this strenuously to the top.

CAILLEACH URAGAIG (Map Ref 382 981)

This low headland can be reached from the cottage of Duntealtaig by a vague path. It has an interesting jumble of coves, arches and crags.

Grooved Slab in the Dark with Bendy Boots 20m VS 4b (1990)
Climb the centre of the clean grooved slab on the south side of the headland (on the north side of Port nam Fliuchan).

ARCH CRAG

This impressive little crag forms the south wall of an obvious shingle cove and the outer face of the leg of a natural arch. To the left of the arch the cliff has suffered a major rockfall and is still unstable, whereas the leg of the arch is composed of sound, vertical or overhanging clean rock with the odd loose flake high up.

The Jagged Edge 30m HVS 4c * (1993)
This route takes the clean hanging edge immediately right of the arch (the left edge of the outer face). Pull over overhanging flakes, then go up the exposed edge to an arete and flake runners below the final steepening. Move left and up to a grass ledge and thence to the top.

Waiting for God 35m VS 4b (1993)
Start as for The Jagged Edge and take an easy slab ramp leading up diagonally right. At its termination step down and right at a big shaky flake, then ascend a short steep groove to traverse back left to easier ground. Take a slight groove running out right with an exposed finish (rope drag may dictate a belay before the finishing wall).

Limpet Groove 25m VS 5a (1987)
Start at a crack leading into a groove on the right edge of the overhanging central section of the wall. Climb the crack (crux; not accessible at high tide), then go up an easier groove. Above a horizontal break, the final section is on strangely eroded lichenous rock.

Beachcomber Slab 15m VS 5a (1993)
This route lies on the opposite side of the cove from Arch Crag on a black slabby face. Start at a polished wall below a shallow groove, left of a black hanging arete. Get off the ground (crux), then climb shallow groove-cracks to an overlap. Traverse left below the overlap to easier ground.

MEALL A' CHAISE (Map Ref 363 945)

Above the cottage south of Port Mhor an iron fence leads up the hill, terminating at the base of the crag. Left of the fence the crag forms a steep smooth slab, and to the right the crag is steeper with a prominent thin crack running from left to right.

Limpet Hammer Groove 25m VS 4b * (1987)
At the right edge of the slab, above the fence, is a shallow groove. Climb the groove which gradually becomes less well defined.

Reservoir Slab 15m Severe ** (1987)
Behind the cottage is a wide gully containing a disused reservoir (Map Ref 361 944). The east flank of the gully is formed by a long clean quartzite slab. This can be climbed by a variety of routes, all at about the same grade.

BEINN NAN CAORACH (Map Ref 363 940)

The north-west face of this fine miniature mountain presents a long 30m crag with a number of groove and corner lines. Vegetation and loose rock detracts from this otherwise attractive wall.

Caorach Corner 30m Severe 4b (1985)
Climb the west-facing inverted corner (if you can identify it!).

SLIABH RIABHACH (Map Ref 367 936)

Route 367936 30m Very Difficult (1993)
This is the narrow grey pillar at the back of the second grass bay to the south of Gleann Raonabuilg (cairn). Climb a steep wall, blocks and a final overhang by its right edge, in three short pitches.

BEINN ORONSAY (Map Ref 352 981)

This south-facing edge lies to the north of the Priory and attains a height of over 30m, not bad for an inland cliff on an island with a highest point of only 93m. The highest section of the edge lies immediately above the Priory and has a distinctive, open book corner at its centre, which is slabby and vegetated.

Hairy Habit Groove 30m HVS 4b (1993)
This route tackles the steep groove immediately right of the open book corner with a pinnacle 3m up on its right side. Climb the groove throughout with the crux at half-height gaining a small grassy ledge. Copious drapes of hairy lichen add character to the route and mask many excellent holds - a truly esoteric experience!

Priory Slab 30m Severe * (1987)
The obvious clean slab on the left of the open book corner with a distinctive slim rib at its start. Climb the rib and slab above to a grassy patch, then go up an easy-angled slabby groove, trending right to finish.

List of First Ascents

THE SGURR NAN GILLEAN REGION

1836	17 Jul	The Tourist Route	Prof.J.D.Forbes, D.Macintyre
1873		Nicolson's Chimney	A.Nicolson
1880		Pinnacle Ridge	C. and L.Pilkington
Winter: W.L.Wood and party, 1947			
1887		Original Route	C.Pilkington and party
1890		Slingsby's Route	W.C.Slingsby and party
1896		Naismith's Route	W.W.Naismith and party
1896		Second-Third Gully	Dr Collier and party
1898		Black Chimney	J.MacLay and party
1898		Forked Chimney	W.W.Naismith and party
1898		Naismith's Route	W.W.Naismith, A.Mackay
1898		King's Cave Chimney	W.W.King, G.B.Gibbs, J.MacKenzie
1898		Knight's Peak, North Face	W.W.King and party
1905	Apr	Raeburn's Route	H.Raeburn and party
1905		Third-Fourth Gully	R.Lamb and party
1906		Shadbolt's Chimney	L.G.Shadbolt, A.C.MacLaren
Variation: K.Tarbuck, G.Collin 3 Jun 1932			
1907		Sligachan Gully	A.P.Abraham, H.Harland
1908		North Chimney	W.W.King and party
1909		Am Basteir Chimney	J.Martin, R.Mackenzie, K.P.Scoones
1911	Sep	Second Pinnacle	J.M.A.Thomson and party
1911	Sep	MacLaren's Chimney	A.C.MacLaren, L.G.Shadbolt
1911		Archer Thomson's Route	J.M.A.Thomson, H.O.Jones
1911		South Buttress	L.G.Shadbolt, A.C.MacLaren
Direct Start: E.L.Wigham, C.E.W.Johnson 30 May 1946			
1911	Sep	Sligachan Buttress	J.M.A.Thomson and party
1918		Left Rib	R.W.Lamb, M.G.Bradley
1919		Flutings Climb	R.Lamb, E.E.Roberts
1920	Jun	Knight's Peak, North Face	G.D.Abraham, H.Harland, G.Summers
1920	Aug	Luscher's No.1 and No.2	Dr Luscher
1927	24 Jun	West Face Direct	F.W.Giveen, C.H.Cooper, D.R.Orr
Winter: K.Bryan, N.Robb, 30 Dec 1962			
1934	Aug	Naismith's Route Direct	J.K.W.Dunn, J.G.Wilson
1937	26 Jun	Murray's Climb	W.H.Murray, J.K.W.Dunn
1949	Jun	Smith's Climb	C.M.G.Smith, R.C.Putman
1953	10 May	North Buttress	E.A.Wrangham
1956	Jun	Tooth Chimney	W.M.MacKenzie
1960	18 Aug	West Wall	T.W.Patey, C.J.S.Bonington
1960	18 Aug	King's Cave Wall, etc	C.J.S.Bonington, T.W.Patey
1963	11 Jul	Thor	A.James, G.Reid
1963	12 Jul	Fria	A.James, G.Reid
1965	31 Jan	The Winter Traverse	T.W.Patey, B.Robertson
1965		Braehead Climb	H.M.Brown, J.Matyssek, J.R.Tomlinson
1967	Aug	August Rib	C.J.Rumball, J.Rumball

1968	Jun	Aslan's Tongue	H.M.Brown, D.J.M.McNabb
1969	17 Jun	Sidetrack	Mr and Mrs Adams, I.S.Clough
1969	17 Jun	Blasphemy Chimneys	Mr and Mrs Adams, I.S.Clough
1980	10 Apr	Cheek of the Devil	P.Hunter, S.Drummond
1980	3 May	Rat Trap	S.Drummond, P.Hunter
1980	4 May	Opal Creamer	P.Hunter, S.Drummond
1986	22 Feb	Lament	B.S.Findlay, G.Strange
1986	28 Feb	North-West Face Route	P.Langhorne, Miss J.Douglas
1983	Feb	White Wizard	K.Hopper, C.Rowland
1989	12 Jul	Rainbow Warrior	S.Hill, T.Dickson
1993	31 Mar	Just a Boy's Game	C.Threlfall, P.McGuire
1993	4 Jun	Eagle's Eyrie	R.McLaughlin, P.Stone
1994	22 Feb	Doctor's Chimney Right	C.Threlfall
1994	15 May	Elizabeth	R.McLaughlin, P.Stone
1994	15 May	Raptor	P.Stone, R.McLaughlin

SGURR A' MHADAIDH, SGURR A' GHREADAIDH AND SGURR NA BANACHDICH

1895 Waterpipe Gully — J.Kelsall, A.W.Hallitt
Winter: B.S.Findlay, G.Strange 24 Feb 1986; Complete ascent - C.Downer, D.Scott 28 Feb 1986

1896 North-West Buttress — N.Collie and party

1898 North-West Ridge, Sgurr a' Ghreadaidh — W.W.King, G.B.Gibbs, Dobson
Winter: M.Don, R.J.C.Robb 10 Jan 1976

1898		Banachdich Gully	G.B.Gibbs, W.W.King, J.MacKenzie
1906		Window Buttress	N.Collie
1907		The Spur and Summit Gullies	A.P.Abraham, G.Bartrum, A.H.Binns, H.Harland
1907		Slanting Gully	A.P.Abraham, G.Bartrum, A.H.Binns, H.Harland
1908		Hidden Gully	F.Greig
1908	Sep	Branching Gully	W.Garden, J.R.Levack, W.Reid
1909		Black Chimney	G.Barlow and party
1910		Vanishing Gully	G.Barlow, E.W.Steeple, A.H.Doughty, H.E.Bowron
1910		Eagles' Gully	E.W.Steeple, G.Barlow, H.E.Bowron, A.H.Doughty
1911		Two Pitch Gully	N.C.Madan, H.E.L.Porter
1911		Archer Thomson's Route	J.M.A.Thomson, H.O.Jones, L.G.Shadbolt
1914		Bishop's Climb	H.Bishop, C.D.Yeomans
1914		North Gully	H.Bishop, H.P.Cain, C.D.Yeomans

Winter: S.Kennedy, N.Morrison 20 Feb 1983

1918 Jul Pye and Mallory's Route — D.R.Pye, G.H.L.Mallory, R.Mallory, L.G.Shadbolt

1929 Jul North-East Gully — P.M.Barclay, J.A.Ramsay
Winter: D.Rogerson, M.Eastwood 17 Feb 1978

1937	Jul	South Gully	W.M.MacKenzie, A.M.MacAlpine, F.A.Oxley
Winter: M.Fowler, T.Saunders 1 Mar 1986			
1939	4 Jun	Gauger's Gully	W.L.Woods, P.Greeman, W.H.Rae
1947	Jul	Overhanging Gully	W.A.Greenwell, P.D.Roberts
1949	20 Sep	Deep Gash Gully	H.G.Nicol, A.S.Parker
Winter: M.Fowler, J.Lincoln 2 Feb 1991			
1950	Jul	Foxes' Folly	D.Leaver, A.Smee
1950	9 Aug	Goat's Gully	T.Shaw, C.M.Dixon
Winter: C.Threlfall, A MacRuary 26 Dec 1993			
1951	4 Jun	Fox Trap	C.M.Dixon, W.D.Brooker
1952	22 Jun	Shining Cleft	G.H.Francis, J.F.Adams, E.A.Wrangham
1952	15 Aug	Hidden Gully Buttress	J.Evans, T.Evans
1952	15 Sep	Centre Gully	H.G.Nicol, I.H.Oliver, A.Grieve
1953	Jun	Toolie Grooves	J.R.Marshall, C.L.Donaldson, G.Hood
1955	12 Jun	An Dorus Buttress	W.P.L.Thomson, A.G.Mitchell, S.Martin
1956	5 Aug	Dyke and Buttress Route	P.R.Stafford, A.C.Gilby
1957	19 Jul	Upper Window Buttress	A.D.Marsden, R.Redfern
1958		Aesculapius	H.MacInnes, J.A.Hartley, M.C.Munday, Miss M.E.Elliot
The Hygeia Variations: H.Insley, J.Hartley 1958			
1958	30 May	Sanguinary Cracks	D.J.Temple, I.S.Clough
1958	Sep	Mantrap	N.Drasdo, C.M.Dixon
1960	Apr	Thunder Rib	R.Smith, G.Milnes
1960	18 Aug	Whispering Wall	T.W.Patey, C.J.S.Bonington
1962	11 Sep	Durham Slabs	K.Moseley, R.Wilson
1963	28 Jul	Moon Raker	I.A.MacEacheran, I.Kennedy
1964	27 Aug	Goliath Buttress	J.Harwood, D.W.Robbins
1965	Jun	Diamond Buttress	G.Martin, N.Smythe, D.Boston
1965	30 Jun	Hamish's Chimney	W.Poole, R.Gaff
1965	22 Jul	Pincer	J.Harwood, H.Small
1965	23 Jul	Gail	J.Harwood, H.Small
1965	23 Jul	Ceo	H.Small, J.Harwood
1965	24 Jul	Virgin Arete	J.Harwood, H.Small
1966	21 Aug	Clap Trap	D.Chapman, J.R.Sutcliffe
1967	14 May	Thor	C.Boulton, A.C.Cain
1968	16 Jun	Scimitar	J.Harwood, R.A.High
1968	12 Jul	Vixen Groove	B.K.E.Edridge, D.C.Forrest
1969	24 Jun	Gargantua	J.Estcott, G.Hardie
1970	10 Jul	Footrot	B.Taplin, D.Bain
1970	10 Jul	Verucca	B.Taplin, D.Bain
Direct Start: B.Taplin, M.Chalwin 6 Jul 1970			
1970	23 Jul	Widow's Eye	R.O'Donovan, B.Marshall
1971	14 May	Fosdyke	A.J.Gilbert, D.A.P Steel
1972	Sep	Megaton	C.Boulton, P.Nunn, R.Toogood
Pitch 3 onwards: M.Boysen, P.Braithwaite, P.Nunn Apr 1974			
1974	May	Resolution	C.Rowland, S.Rowland

Year	Date	Route	Climbers
1976	3 Jun	Trapist	G.Evans, J.Harwood
1976	3 Jun	Simplicity	G.Evans, J.Harwood
1976	3 Jun	Gauche	G.Evans, J.Harwood
1976	28 Aug	Quark	C.Boulton, P.Nunn
FFA: T.Prentice, C.Fraser, 1984			
1977	24 Sep	Gael Force	H.Henderson, R.G.Ross
1978	17 Feb	The Hose	I.Dalley, T.Anderson
1979		The Smear	J.Duff, D.Scott
1980	Apr	Drainpipe Gully	C.Rowland
1980	Apr	Edgeway	C.Rowland, S.Rowland
1980	Apr	The Rent	C.Rowland, S.Rowland
1980	18 May	Val	D.McCallum, R.Milne
1980	May	Revelation	B.Ledingham, M.Richardson, J.Smith
1980	May	Retribution	A.Livesay, P.Nunn, C.Rowland
1980	6 Jun	Nearer My God to Thee	J.R.Mackenzie, D.Butterfield
1980	Sep	Sinistra Crack	G.Reilly, A.Paul
1981		Waterpipe Slabs	C.Rowland, K.Hopper
1986	1 Mar	Icicle Factory	M.Fowler, T.Saunders
1986	2 Mar	White Wedding	T.Saunders, C.Watts, M.Fowler
1990	14 Jul	Hearthammer	G.Nicoll, K.Noble, A.Chamings
1992	20 Jun	Black Slab	J.R.Mackenzie, G.Cullen
1992	20 Jun	Soft Options	G.Cullen, J.R.Mackenzie
1993	14 Oct	North-North-West Spur	C.Threlfall, P McGuire
1994	22 Mar	Stag Gully	C.Threlfall, J.Gregory, S.Hallay
1994	27 Dec	Stag Buttress	C.Threlfall, P.McGuire
1995	2 Jan	Central Buttress	C.Threlfall, B.Rogers
1995	28 Mar	Stepped Buttress	C.Threlfall, P.McCue

COIRE LAGAN

Year	Date	Route	Climbers
1880		Gully E, Sgurr Thearlaich	C.Pilkington
1880	18 Aug	Inaccessible Pinnacle, East Ridge	C. and L.Pilkington
1886		Inaccessible Pinnacle, West Ridge	A.H.Stocker, A.G.Parker
1887		North Ridge, Sgurr Sgumain	C.Pilkington and party
1890		Collie's Ledge, Sgurr Sgumain	J.N.Collie
1896		Collie's Climb	J.N.Collie, Howell, W.W.Naismith
1898		King's Chimney	W.W.King and party
1906	Jun	South Crack	H.Harland, A.P.Abraham, A.H.Binns
1906		West Buttress	G.D.Abraham, A.P.Abraham and party
1907		Abraham's Climb	G.D.Abraham and party
Winter: W.D.Brooker, C.M.Dixon, J.W.Morgan 2 Apr 1952			
1908		An Stac Chimney	Goggs and Russell
1908		Gully A, Sgurr Thearlaich	E.W.Steeple, G.Barlow, A.H.Doughty
Winter: R.O'Donovan 11 Apr 1970			
1908		Gullies B, C and D, Sgurr Thearlaich	H.B.Buckle, G.Barlow, A.H.Doughty

1909		Baly's Route	Prof E.C.C.Baly
1920		Final Tower Direct	E.W.Steeple, G.Barlow
1921		Routes I and II	A.S.Pigott, J.Wilding
1924	Jul	West Trap Route	J.H.B.Bell, F.S.Smythe
1925	4 Aug	Frankland's Gully	C.D.Frankland, M.M.Barker, H.V.Hughes
Winter: P.Cairns, B.Ledingham, C.Rowlands 1 Mar 1981			
1932	27 Jun	Wood-Johnson's Route	E.Wood-Johnson, C.J.A.Cooper, J.Levers
1937		Stone Shoot Face	W.M.MacKenzie, A.M.MacAlpine
1937	2 Aug	Barber's Route	B.K.Barber, M.Burton, G.Eisig, H.B.Law
1947	Aug	Lagan Route	D.Thomas, G.Goddard
1948	24 May	Jeffrey's Dyke	R.Jeffrey, Mrs Jeffrey, J.H.B.Bell, Mrs Bell, C.M.Allan
1950	15 Jul	Central Route	D.D.Stewart, D.N.Mill
1951	13 Jul	Sunset Slab	J.D.Foster, B.C.Blake
1951	13 Jul	Superstition	J.D.Foster, J.R.Stead, B.L.Blake
1952	25 Aug	Western Drainpipe Direct	T.W.Waghorn, P.G.White, C.J.Breeze
1952	25 Aug	Western Drainpipe Ridge	P.G.White, T.W.Waghorn, C.J.Breeze
1955	29 Jul	Mistaken Crack	G.S.Beattie, W.K.Davies, K.A.Sturrock
1956	23 Aug	Sally's Climb	H.Barrs, J.E.Jackson
1957		Prometheus	H.MacInnes, J.M.Alexander, I.S.Clough (3 p.a.)
1957		Prokroustes	H.MacInnes, I.S.Clough (3p.a., 1 bolt)
1957	21 Sep	Direct Route	D.D.Stewart, A.Colquhoun, P.Vaughan
1958		Oedipus	H.MacInnes and party (aid)
1958	May	Introduction	I.S.Clough, D.J.Temple
1958	29 May	Theseus	J.M.Alexander, T.R.Wilkinson (3 p.a.)
1958	9 Jun	Penitentiary Grooves	H.MacInnes, I.S.Clough (aid)
FFA: D.Dinwoodie, B.Lawrie 1971			
1958	27 Jun	Hermaphra and Ditus	H.MacInnes, M.C.Munday
1958		Priam	H.MacInnes and party
1958	1 Sep	The Slant	A.H.Greenbank, J.Wilkinson, D.Murray
1959	28 Apr	Willit	J.McLean, I.S.Clough
1959	28 Apr	Lost Hope	J.McLean, I.S.Clough
1960	14 Aug	Lower Rib	C.J.S.Bonington, T.W.Patey
1962	11 Sep	Hadrian's Wall	K.Mosley, R.Wilson
1964	30 Jun	Yellow Groove	I.S.Clough, D.J.Temple, M.Battle, B.Fein
1964	11 Aug	Varicose	J.Harwood
1965		Lethe	W.Smith, J.MacLean
1965	Aug	Laceration	I.MacEacheran, J.Renny
1968	24 Jun	Frostbite	M.J.Guillard, J.R.Irvin
1968	23 Jun	Purple Haze	M.J.Guillard, J.R.Irvin
1970	12 Jun	Reluctance	A.Robertson, W.Tauber
1971	12 Jun	Grannie Clark's Wynd	J.S.Shade, W.Tauber
1978	Feb	The Twister	C.Rowland, S.Rowland

1979	11 Jun	Styx	J.R.Mackenzie, D.Butterfield, G.Lipp

Original line first climbed in 1957 by H.MacInnes and party with 1 p.a.

1988	3 May	The Klondyker	A.Tibbs, D.Bearhop
1994	22 May	The Cutter	G.Nicoll, M.Crowther
1994	2 Jul	Raynaud's	M.McLeod, C.Moody
1994	5 Aug	Vanishing Beads	C.Moody, A.Petrie
1994	5 Aug	Raven's Rib	C.Moody, A.Petrie
1994	5 Aug	Mud Wrestler	C.Moody, A.Petrie
1994	5 Aug	Huffy Messiah	C.Moody, A.Petrie
1994	5 Aug	Up the Down Stoneshoot	C.Moody, A.Petrie
1994	5 Aug	Starless Bay	C.Moody, A.Petrie
1994	5 Aug	Flap Cracker	C.Moody, A.Petrie

SRON NA CICHE AND COIRE A' GHRUNNDA

1891		Thearlaich-Dubh Gap	J.N.Collie, J.MacKenzie, W.W.King
1906		Cioch Gully	H.B.Buckle, G.Barlow
1906		Collie's Route	J.N.Collie
1906		Western Gully	J.N.Collie
1907		Central Gully	A.G.Woodhead, E.W.Steeple, H.E.Bowron
1907		Amphitheatre Arete	J.N.Collie
1907		Zigzag Route	J.N.Collie
1907		Cioch Direct	H.Harland, A.P.Abraham
1908		West Central Gully and Arete	G.Barlow, H.B.Buckle
1909		Median	E.W.Steeple, H.E.Bowron
1909		East Wall and Central Gully Arete	G.Barlow, H.B.Buckle, A.H.Doughty
1911		Archer Thomson's Route	J.M.A.Thomson and party
1911		Zigzag	L.G.Shadbolt, A.C.McLaren, E.S.Reynolds
1911		Chimney and Crack	J.M.A.Thomson, H.O.Jones, Miss B.C.Jones
1912		The Girdle Traverse of Sron na Ciche	E.W.Steeple, G.Barlow
1912		West Gully	E.W.Steeple, G.Barlow, A.H.Doughty
1912		West Gully	Herford, Laycock
1912		Central Gully	Herford, Laycock
1912		East Gully	Herford, Laycock
1912		Direct Route	E.W.Steeple, G.Barlow, A.H.Doughty
1912		Chimney Route	E.W.Steeple, G.Barlow
1912	Jun	Engineer's Slant	D.L.Reid, Sale, Brown
1913		Eastern Gully	E.W.Steeple, G.Barlow
1914		Trap Face Route	J.B.Burrell, C.N.Cross

Variation: A.C.Cain, B.L.Dodson, Jul 1950

1915		Wallwork's Route	W.Wallwork, H.M.Kelly, J.Wilding
1918		Mallory's Slab and Groove	G.H.L.Mallory, D.R.Pye, L.G.Shadbolt
1918	Aug	Crack of Doom	D.R.Pye, L.G.Shadbolt

Direct Approach: B.Ritchie, C.D.Milner June 1936

Direct Finish: A.S.Pigott, J.Wilding Jun 1921

1919		Bower's Climb	G.S.Bower, J.B.Meldrum

1919		Cioch West	C.F.Holland, H.R.C.Carr, Miss D.E.Pilley

Cioch West Variation: J.G.S.Smith 1951

1920		Parallel Cracks Route	E.W.Steeple, G.Barlow, A.H.Doughty

Direct Start: J.Harwood, H.Small, D.Robbins Jul 1963

1920		Far South Buttress	E.W.Steeple, G.Barlow
1920		Green Recess Chimneys	E.W.Steeple, G.Barlow
1920		Central Buttress	E.W.Steeple, G.Barlow
1920		Trap Dyke Route	E.W.Steeple, G.Barlow
1920		White Slab	E.W.Steeple, G.Barlow

Direct Finish: R.O'.Donovan, M.Chalwin 26 Jun 1970

1920		South Crag Gully	E.W.Steeple, G.Barlow
1920		Owl Chimney	E.W.Steeple, G.Barlow
1920		Stack Buttress Direct	E.W.Steeple, G.Barlow
1920		Red Wall Variant	E.W.Steeple, G.Barlow
1920		North Crag Gully and Black Knight's Wall	E.W.Steeple, G.Barlow
1920		Slab Buttress	E.W.Steeple, G.Barlow
1921		Central Route	E.W.Steeple, G.Barlow
1924	Jul	Owl Buttress, Left	E.W.Steeple, G.Barlow
1932	19 Jun	West Ridge of the Cioch	C.J.A.Cooper, E.Wood-Johnson, D.Levers
1932	22 Jun	Central Slabs	E.Wood-Johnson, C.J.A.Cooper, D.Levers
1932	25 Jun	Owl Buttress, Right	D.Levers, C J.A.Cooper, E. Wood-Johnson
1932	22 Jul	Amphitheatre Wall	A.Horne, H.V.Hughes
1936	Aug	A.B. Route	A.Armitage, Miss H.Broadbent
1937	Jul	Left Edge Route	W.MacKenzie, A.MacAlpine
1944		Arrow Route	I.Allan
1946	19 Jul	Diamond Slab	A.Allsopp, R.G.Morsley

Direct Finish: J.Harwood, P.Thomas 12 Aug 1964

1946	Jul	Apex Route	J.Wilkinson, D.W.Jackson, H.Ironfield
1947	May	Girdle Traverse of South Crag	V.J.Wiggin, E.Wood-Johnson
1947	17 May	Hangover Route	D.H.Haworth, G.J.Ritchie
1947	21 May	Crack of Double Doom	D.H.Haworth, I.E.Hughes
1947	21 May	Doom Flake	D.H.Haworth, I.E.Hughes
1947.	Aug	East Wall Route	R.E.Davies, C.B.Machin
1949	Jun	Rib of Doom	C.M.G.Smith, A.Cleland
1949	9 Jun	Caravan Route	G.W.S.Pigott, A.S.Pigott
1949	11 Jul	Integrity	D.H.Haworth, I.E.Hughes
1950	14 Apr	White Slab Direct	G.H.Francis, J.M.Bowen

Oxford Variation: G.H.Francis, R.H.Hobhouse, P.F.Mitson 28 Aug 1950

1950	Jul	Commando Crack	A.C.Cain, B.L.Dobson
1951	16 May	Quiver	J.Hammond, R.Morden
1952	29 Jun	Petronella	G.H.Francis, E.A.Wrangham
1952	11 Sep	Boomerang	D.D.Stewart, D.N.Mill
1953	21 Jun	Magic Casement	M.M.Miller, G.H.Francis (aid)
1953	Jul	Jack O'Diamonds	D.Leaver, C.E.N.Wilson

Year	Date	Route	Party
1953	Jul	Coronation	D.D.Stewart and party
1955	13 Jul	Angel's Pavement	M.North, M.Grundy, J.Roberts
1956	16 Jul	Bastinado	J.Cunningham, J.Allan, W.Smith (1 p.a.)
Variation: D.Dinwoodie, C.McLean 25 Jul 1983			
1956	16 Jul	Trophy Crack	P.Walsh, H.MacKay
1957		Schadenfreude	R.D.Hinds, H.MacInnes, H.D.Parker, J.D.Small
1957		Kinloss Gully	I.Clough, R.Wilkinson (3 p.a.)
1957		Vulcan Wall	H.MacInnes, D.J.Temple, I.S.Clough (aid)
The Chambre Finish: G.Latter, D.Cuthbertson Summer 1982			
1957		Creag Dhu Grooves	H.MacInnes, I.S.Clough (aid)
FFA: G.Reagan, A.McHardy 1977			
1957	1 Apr	Intermediate Traverse	A.D.Marsden, M.McNamara
1957	8 Jun	Strappado	H.MacInnes, A.D.Marsden, I.S.Clough
1957	Jul	Central Route	D.Leaver, J.Gott
1957	21 Sep	Cioch Grooves	I.G.McNaught-Davis, G.H.Francis
1958	1 Jun	Depravity	H.MacInnes, I.S.Clough, D.Pipes
1958	1 Jun	Grand Diedre and Direct Start	H.MacInnes, I.S.Clough, D.Pipes
1958	4 Jun	Boreas Grooves	H.MacInnes, I.S.Clough, D.Pipes
1958	27 Jul	Crembo Cracks	D.Gregory, R.Hutchison (1 p.a.)
1958	30 Jul	Lambda	R.C.Mason, T.Shallice
1958	30 Jul	Mu	R.C.Mason, T.Shallice
1962	6 Aug	The Plunge	B.W.Robertson, E.Cairns (aid)
1963	Jul	Lumps	A.McKeith
1964	May	Pearly Gates	A.C.Wilmott, R.Ratcliffe
1964	20 Jun	Shangri-La	I.S.Clough, A.Nicholls
1964	27 Jun	Searcher	I.S.Clough, A.Nicholls
1965		The Asp	J.McLean and party
1965		Con's Cleft	J.McLean and party
1965	Jun	W.C.Route	I.S.Clough, Mrs N.Clough
1965	Jul	Trojan Groove	I.Heys, K.Roberts
1965	Jul	Spartan Groove	I.Heys, J.Firth
Direct variation: P.Hunter, Miss S.Drummond 8 Aug 1980			
1965	9 Aug	The Snake	W.Sproul, J.Renny, J.Hall
1968	20 May	Mega Route	J.R.Dempster, J.I.Wallace
1979	26 Feb	Little Gully	R.O'Donovan, M.Chalwin
1970	13 Jun	Fidelity	K.V.Crocket, D.M.Jenkins
1970	27 Aug	The Whet	M.G.Geddes, J.C.Higham, Miss A.C.Lamb
1976	5 Aug	Sundance	B.Dunn, A.Paul
1977	21 Jun	Dilemma	M.Fowler, P.Thomas
1977	21 Jun	The Nipple	M.Fowler, P.Thomas
1977	13 Aug	Oneshotbang	C.Higgins
1978		Overhanging Crack	M.Hamilton, G.Cohen
1978		Atropos	M.Fowler, P.Thomas
1979	May	Enigma	M.Hamilton, D.Mullin
1979	24 May	The Stag	S.C.Allen, P.Darbyshire
1980	4 May	Cuckoo Groove	R.Atkinson, D.Formstone

Year	Date	Route	First ascent
1980	16 May	Strappado Direct	P.Hunter, C.Lees
Pitch 1: G.Szuca, C.Moody 13 Jun 1988.			
1980	17 May	Vanity	M.Priestman, A.Kassyk
1980	17 May	Krugerrand	P.Hunter, C.Lees
1980	17 May	Hang Free	D.McCallum, R.Milne
1980	18 May	Spock	P.Hunter, C.Lees
1980	Aug	Atlantis	K.Leinster, A.Paul
1980	9 Aug	Acapulco Wall	P.Hunter
1981	18 May	Ghost Riders	C.Dale, S.Cox
1982	Summer	Confession	D.Cuthbertson, G.Latter
1982	Summer	Zephyr	D.Cuthbertson, D.McCallum
1982	Summer	The Team Machine	D.Cuthbertson, G.Latter
1982	Summer	Magic	D.Cuthbertson, G.Latter
1983	24 May	The Conjuror	R.Anderson, M.Hamilton
1983	Jul	Erotica	D.Dinwoodie, G.Livingston
1984	28 May	Vagabond Crack	B.Molyneux, R.Reeve
1985	2 Jun	Piety	N.Horn, C.Moody
1985	Jun	Stormy Petrel	S.Hill
1987	17 Jun	Presdigitateur	R.Wightman, J.Topping
1988	2 May	Gonzo Jamming	G.Jones, A.Waters
1988	2 May	Stormwatch	G.Jones, A.Waters
1988	13 Jun	Pocks	G.Suzca, C.Moody
Pitch 2: C.Moody, N.Smith 7 Jun 1992			
1990	22 Jul	Tennatte	G.Szuca
1990	22 Jul	Uhuru	K.Howett, T.Prentice
1990	23 Jul	Why	G.Szuca, A.Connolly
1990	24 Jul	Protect and Survive	G.Szuca
1990	25 Jul	Hindsight	G.Szuca, A.Connolly
1992	17 May	Victoria Buttress	J.Tout, J.Andrew
1992	17 May	Victoria Sponge	J.Tout, J.Andrew
1992	Jun	Banana	D.Griffiths, M.Roy
1992	16 Jun	Mistral Buttress	N.Horn, C.Moody
1992		The Highlander	G.Farquhar, G.Latter
1994	25 May	Slabby Wall Crack	D.Shepherd, J.Anderson
1994	31 Jul	Helen	S.Hill, C.Moody

CORUISK AND THE EAST SIDE OF THE MAIN RIDGE

Year	Date	Route	First ascent
1600		An Dorus Gully	Marauding MacLeods
1896		South-East Ridge	J.N.Collie, E.B.Howell
1897		Brown's Climb	W.Brown and party
1910		South-East Gully	E.W.Steeple, G.Barlow
1912		North-East Gully	C.O'Brien, E.L.Julian
1912		O'Brien and Julian's Climb	C.O'Brien, E.L.Julian
Winter: B.Davison, A.Nisbet 16 Mar 1996			
1913		Sgurr Thearlaich, North-East Ridge	H.Raeburn and party
1913		Raeburn's Route	H.Raeburn, V.B.Meldrum, the Wallwork brothers
1913		Eag Dubh Gully	E.W.Steeple, G.Barlow, A.H.Doughty

1913		Second-Third Gully	E.W.Steeple, G.Barlow, A.H.Doughty
1913		First-Second Gully	E.W.Steeple, G.Barlow
1915	Apr	The Chasm	E.W.Steeple, G.Barlow

Summer: E.W.Steeple, G.Barlow, A.H.Doughty Aug 1919

1920		South-East Ridge Direct	W.A.Morrison, D.H.Menzies
1920	Aug	Terrace Gully	G.Barlow, A.H.Doughty
1922		Terrace East Buttress	E.W.Steeple, G.Barlow
1924	Jul	Terrace West Buttress	E.W.Steeple, G.Barlow
1939	Jun	Slab Route	J.E.Byrom, P.Wigglesworth
1948	May	Western Buttress	R.S.Dodson, B.W.Smith, H.Booth
1949	Jun	Original Route	C.M.G.Smith, R.C.Putman
1949	23 Oct	Shelf Route	J.D.G.Davidson, F.R.Brooke
1950	Jul	Aladdin's Route	J.W.B.Barnes, H.Swift, D.Rich
1950	24 Jul	North-East Buttress	W.D.Brooker, C.M.Dixon
1950	1 Aug	Fluted Buttress	W.D.Brooker, C.M.Dixon
1950	7 Aug	Hourglass Crack	C.M.Dixon, T.Shaw
1951	6 Aug	Crack of Dawn	W.D.Brooker, C.M.Dixon
1951	12 Aug	Forgotten Groove	W.D.Brooker, C.M.Dixon
1953	13 Aug	Thunderbolt Shelf	T.W.Patey, W.D.Brooker
1953	15 Aug	South Twin	T.W.Patey, W.D.Brooker
1953	15 Aug	North Twin	T.W.Patey, W.D.Brooker
1953	15 Aug	Midget Ridge	T.W.Patey, W.D.Brooker
1953	15 Aug	Clouded Buttress	T.W.Patey, W.D.Brooker
1954		Gemini	C.M.Dixon, R.Cra'ster
1954	3 Jun	Black Cleft	C.M.Dixon, J.E.Monks
1954	4 Jun	Lost Arrow	C.M.Dixon, J.E.Monks
1954	4 Jun	The Bow	C.M.Dixon, J.E.Monks
1954	5 Jun	Pinnacle Face	R.Cra'ster, C.M.Dixon
1957	Sep	Ladders	R.Smith
1957	Sep	Left Edge	R.Smith, H.Kindness
1958	25 Jun	Chemist's Constitutional	L.J.Morris, W.Bonthrone
1958	27 Jun	St Andrew's Crack	L.J.Morris, W.Bonthrone, M.J.Hill
1958	22 Aug	Dawn Grooves	R.W.P.Barclay, W.D.Brooker
1959	19 Jun	Sue's Chimney	W.Bonthrone, Miss S.M.Bell, W.S.Yeaman
1960	21 May	Central Groove	D.J.Bennet, D.A.Bennet, R.Cameron
1960	14 Aug	King Cobra	C.J.S.Bonington, T.W.Patey
1961	May	Mayday	K.Bryan, M.Slesser
1962	Apr	Warsle	Mrs M.Wallace, M.Slesser
1962	May	Diagonal	K.Bryan, M.Slesser
1962	19 May	Coruisk Slabs	T.M.Lauren, J.Highet
1964	May	JMCS Buttress	B.Barclay, R.Chalmers
1965	30 May	Bee Cee Crack	B.Sproul, B.Cuthbert
1966	1 Jun	Rongwrong	R.A.Hobbs, P.L.Jackson
1966	25 Aug	Tenderfoot	D.Chapman, J.R.Sutcliffe
1966	25 Aug	Rebound	D.Chapman, J.R.Sutcliffe
1968	16 Jun	Peridot	J.Harwood, R.A.High
1968	17 Jun	Magpie Cracks	J.Harwood, R.A.High
1968	19 Jun	Leviathan	J.Harwood, R.A.High

1968	Jul	Dwindle Wall	J.R.Mackenzie, R.Lambert
1968	17 Jul	The Happy Wanderer	J.R.Mackenzie, R.Lambert
1969	19 Jul	Skye Ride	R.Lambert, J.R.Mackenzie
1968	19 Jul	Phaeton	J.R.Mackenzie, R.Lambert
1969	Jun	Cocoa Cracks	J.Barraclough, J.B.Cooper
1969	Jun	Tinn Lamh Crack	J.Barraclough, J.B.Cooper
FFA: J.Harwood 1972			
1971	3 Jun	Hanging Slab	J.A.Austin, D.G.Roberts
1974		Mongoose Direct	J.Lamb, P.Whillance
Direct pitch: M.Fowler, P.Thomas 20 Jun 1977			
1977	12 Aug	Populace	N.Muir, A.Paul
1983	24 Jun	Lightfoot	M.Hamilton, R.Anderson, P.Whillance
1990	18 May	James's Crack	T.Walkington, A.Cunningham
1990	19 May	Assault Course Bimbo	T.Walkington, A.Cunningham
1990	20 May	Peterless Crack	T.Walkington, A.Cunningham
1990	20 May	Bryantless Crack	T.Walkington, A.Cunningham
1990	21 May	Witchless Corner	T.Walkington, A.Cunningham, M.Smith
1992	28 Jun	King Cobra Direct	B Davison, H.Day
1994	24 May	Beached Whale	D.Shepherd, J.Andrew
1995	4 Mar	Exiguous Gully	M.Fowler, A.Cave

MARSCO AND THE BLA BHEINN AND CLACH GLAS GROUP

1896		Naismith's Route	W.W.Naismith, J.A.Parker
1905	Apr	Pinnacle Ridge	W.I.Clark, T.E.Goodeve, H.Walker
1907		South-East Buttress	H.MacRobert, R.A.Brown, W.A.Morrison
1907		Consolation Gully	A.P.Abraham and party
1907		Arch Gully	A.P.Abraham and party
1914	Jun	C-D Buttress	J.C.Thomson, J.R.Young
1914	Jun	South-East Route	J.C.Thomson, J.R.Young
1915	Jun	Central Buttress	W.N.Ling, E.Backhouse
1920	Jun	B Gully	G.D.Abraham, H.Harland, G.Summers
Winter: S.Kennedy, D.Ritchie 12 Jan 1991			
1943	19 Jul	Odell's Route	N.E.Odell
1953	22 Aug	Central Buttress	E.A.Wrangham
1958	12 Jun	Penelope	H.MacInnes
1961	24 Aug	Chock-a-Block Chimney	T.W.Patey, R.Harper
1967	21 Jul	The Horn	D.D.Stewart, D.J.Bennet
1968	15 Jun	The Great Prow	T.W.Band, P.W.F.Gibbon, N.S.Ross, W.Tauber
Twilight Slab Variation: A.J.Kennedy, G.Rooney 6 Jun 1975			
1968		Left-Hand Buttress	J.Greenwood, I.S.Clough
1968		Trundle Buttress	A.Silvers, D.J.Waller
1968	20 Jun	The Snark	J.Harwood, R.A.High
1968	20 Jun	The Boojum	J.Harwood, R.A.High
1968	Sep	Belinda	I.S.Clough, J.Greenwood, A.Silvers, D.J.Waller
1968	Sep	Central Pillar	H.MacInnes, M.C.MacInnes

1968 Sep Birthday Groove — I.S.Clough and party (as above)
Winter: D.Ritchie,M.Shaw 15 Mar 1996
1968 Sep Virgo — I.S.Clough and party (as above)
Winter: D.Ritchie, I.Stevenson 23 Dec 1995
1968 Sep Judas — I.S.Clough and party (as above)
1968 Sep Escalator Direct — I.S.Clough and party (as above)
1968 Sep The Outsider — I.S.Clough and party (as above)
1968 Sep The Hem — I.S.Clough and party (as above)
1968 Sep Canopy — I.S.Clough and party (as above)
1968 Sep Scorpion — I.S.Clough and party (as above)
1968 15 Sep The Horn Direct — I.S.Clough and party (as above)
FFA: P.Thomas, M.Fowler 19 Jun 1977
1968 16 Sep Route One — H.MacInnes, M.C.MacInnes
1968 16 Sep Sidewinder — I.S.Clough, A.Silvers, J.Greenwood, D.J.Waller
1968 18 Sep Sickle — I.S.Clough, D.J.Waller, A.Silvers, J.Greenwood
1968 19 Sep Clough's Cleft — H.MacInnes, M.C.MacInnes
1969 Hawse Pipe Chimney — H.MacInnes, M.C.MacInnes
1969 Access Gully — H.MacInnes, M.C.MacInnes
1969 Loss Leader — H.MacInnes, M.C.MacInnes
1969 May Creep — I.S.Clough, H.MacInnes
1969 May Bargain Offer — M.Boysen, S.Alcock
1969 May Jib — M.Boysen, D.Alcock
Chimney Start, FFA: M.Fowler, P.Thomas 19 Jun 1977
1976 1 Jun Teflon — J.Harwood, G.Evans
1977 19 Jun Stairway to Heaven — M.Fowler, P.Thomas
1979 3 Apr April Fools — P.Hunter, C.Lees
1980 Far East Buttress — A.C.Cain
1980 Cubs' Corner — A.C.Cain, B.Scout
1980 Skye Ride — C.Rowland, K.Hopper
1980 Seilg Gully — C.Rowland, K.Hopper
1980 Cuckoo Waltz — C.Rowland, K.Hopper
1980 3 May Slow Riser — P.Hunter, C.Lees
Right-Hand Finish: J.Cooper, N.Smith 9 Aug 1995
1981 Hand Jive — C.Rowland, J.Smith
1981 Streetwise Dancer — C.Rowland, J.Smith
1981 Alpha Groove — C.Rowland, K.Hopper
Direct Finish: C.Rowland, J.Smith 1981
1981 Tapered Buttress — P.Nunn and party
1983 7 Aug Eventide — M.McLeod, C.Moody
1987 19 Jul Rosie's Stash — C.Moody
1988 1 Jun Cunning Stunts — J.R.Mackenzie, E.Jones
1990 26 May Rites of Passage — J.R.Mackenzie, G.Cullen
1990 27 May Black Magic — J.R.Mackenzie, G.Cullen
1990 27 May Flights of Fancy — M.Haltree, M.Frew, S.Price
1994 Jan Escape from Colditz — M.Lates and partner
1994 Jan Sailaway — D.Bissett and partner
1994 8 Jan The Crucifix — D.Litherland, M.Moran

1994	8 Jan	South-East Gully	D.Litherland, M.Moran
1994	May	Mistaken Identity	R.McLaughlin, P.Stone
1995	26 Jan	The Big Ramp	M.E.Moran, J.Singh
1995	5 Mar	Serious Picnic	A.Cave, M.Fowler, C.Jones, D.Rcerz
1995	9 Mar	A1 Gully	D.Bunker, K.Law, M.E.Moran, A.Nolan
1995	7 Aug	Heart but no Sole	J.Cooper, N.Smith
1995	28 Aug	Zeke	N.Smith, J.Cooper
1996	14 Feb	Thrutcher's Groove	P.Bass, M.Lockley, M.Welch

STRATHAIRD

SCHOOLHOUSE BUTTRESS

1987	12 May	Schoolhouse Buttress	W.F.Alexander, J.Ashbridge
1992	22 Jun	Schoolhouse Rock	J.R.Mackenzie, G.Cullen
1992	22 Jun	Wafer Wall	G.Cullen, J.R.Mackenzie
1994	25 Jul	Apiary Arête	S.Park, L.Whitmarch, L.Varney, A Ballard
1994	29 Jul	Bee Keepers Bother	S.Park, L.Whitmarch, L.Varney
1994	29 Jul	'Orrible Crack	L.Whitmarch, S.Park, L.Varney

SUIDHE BIORACH

1987	11 Jul	Fertility Right	D.N.Williams, W.Jeffrey
1987	11 Jul	Fertility Left	D.N.Williams, W.Jeffrey
1992		Jamie Jampot	R.MacDonald
1992		Crack of Zawn	R.MacDonald
1992		Altar Ego	D.Partridge, R.MacDonald
1993		India	N.Smith, D.Partridge
1993		Veritas Splendour	S.Hill
1993		Transept	D.Partridge
1993	18 Sep	The Golden Fleece	C.Moody, N.Smith
1993	18 Sep	Hairy Beast	N.Smith, C.Moody
1993		The Fringe	M.Lates
1993		Right Fright	S.Bally
1993		Digitalis	D.Partridge
1993		Hairy Beast	N.Smith
1994	17 Sep	Suidhe nan Eun (Tyrolean)	A.Matthewson, A.Tibbs, A.Hume
1994		Mother's Pride	D.Partridge, R.MacDonald
1994		Arc of the Covenant	D.Partridge
1994		Tree Route	D.Partridge
1994		Angel of Sharkness	M.Philp, N.Smith
1995	11 Jun	Green Green Green	C.Moody, M.Shaw
1995	8 Jul	Plenty of Onomatopoeia	M.McLeod, C.Moody
1995	8 Jul	Rusty Old Wire	M.McLeod, C.Moody
1995	9 Jul	Fault Finding	I.Taylor, C.Moody
1995		Pick Pocket	N.Smith, M.Philp
1995		Rum Doodle	N.Smith, M.Philp, R.Lupton

MINGINISH

RUBH' AN DUNAIN

All routes by S.Hill, W.Simkiss, P.Pugh, C.Biggar in 1985 and 1986. The same party climbed several other routes in the this area.

NA HURANAN

Climbs have been done on this escarpment since at least the 1970s.The following routes may not be first ascents.

1995	28 May	Krishando	K.Seewraj, A.Bulgin
1995	28 May	Freezer	K.Seewraj, A.Bulgin

TALISKER STACKS

1970s		The Corkscrew	R.O'Donovan
1971	3 Jun	West Ridge	B.Taplin, D.Sharpe
1993	29 May	The Lesser Stack	K.Milne, S.Richardson

FISKAVAIG

1971	20 Aug	The Struan Face	B.Taplin and party

DUIRINISH

MACLEOD'S MAIDENS

Before 1950		The Middle Maiden	F.A.Evans
1959	26 Apr	The Old Lady	I.S.Clough, J.McLean
1992	30 May	The Outer Maiden	G.Muhlemann, E.Grindley, S.Richardson

WATERSTEIN AND NEIST

1961	26 Aug	The Green Lady	T.W.Patey, F.Harper
1977	17 Dec	Two Step	M.Geddes, D.N.Williams
1977	17 Dec	Side Step	D.N.Williams, M.Geddes
1980		Waterstein Arete	M.Fowler, C.Watts; S.Vietoris (solo)
1981	26 Apr	New Order	B.Kerr, D.N.Williams
1981	22 Aug	Supercharger	E.Grindley, C.Grindley, W.Jeffrey, D.N.Williams
1981	28 Dec	Lightning Corner	T.Furnis, W.McCrae
1981	29 Dec	Breakfast in America	D.Armstrong, P.Whillance
1981	30 Dec	California Dreaming	W.McCrae, D.Armstrong
1981	30 Dec	Ice Diamond	T.Furnis, P.Whillance, D.Armstrong
1981	30 Dec	Wind and Wuthering	P.Whillance, D.Armstrong
1981	30 Dec	Cold Turkey	D.Armstrong, P.Whillance
1982	2 Jan	Cold Comfort Corner	P.Whillance, D.Armstrong
1982	2 Jan	Frigid Air	D.Armstrong, P.Whillance
1982		North-West Arete	M.Hall (solo)
1983	1 May	The Murray Mint	M.Hamilton
1983	1 May	Grooveless Bodily Harm	M.Hamilton, K.Spence, R.Duncan
1983	1 May	Fisherman's Friend	M.Hamilton, R.Anderson
1983	2 May	Hot Blast	M.Hamilton, R.Duncan
1983	2 May	Sea Enemy	M.Hamilton, R.Duncan
1983	21 May	Fat Man's Folly	R.Anderson, M.Hamilton

1983	22 May	Starfish Enterprise	M.Hamilton, R.Anderson
1983	22 May	Jellyfish Roll	M.Hamilton, R.Anderson
1983	22 May	Sealy Dan	R.Anderson, M.Hamilton
1983	22 May	Seagulls	B.Kerr, D.Bartle
1983	22 May	Temptation	B.Kerr, D.Bartle
1983	23 May	Cool Breeze	M.Hamilton, R.Anderson
1983	23 May	Freeze Dried	M.Hamilton, R.Anderson
1983	23 May	Prawn Broker	M.Hamilton, R.Anderson
1983	12 Nov	Bay City Roller	M.Hamilton
1983	12 Nov	Westcoastin'	D.Dinwoodie, C.MacLean
1983	12 Nov	Westagain	C.MacLean, D.Dinwoodie, M.Hamilton
1983	13 Nov	Neisty Beisty	D.Dinwoodie, C.MacLean
1983	13 Nov	Wild West	M.Hamilton, A.Ross
1984	Jun	Joint Experience	N.Smith, G.Bisset, S.Reid
1987	Apr	Patricia	J.Robertson, S.Wallis
1987	Apr	Bernard's Dilemma	J.Robertson, S.Wallis
1987	Jun	Death Pirate	G.Livingston, P.Moores
1988	13 Jun	Neist an' Easy	L.Steer, W.Birkett
1988	13 Jun	Golden Mile	L.Steer, W.Birkett
1989	27 May	Temgesic	G.Szuca, M.Limonci, D.Heffernan
1989	27 May	Flake Route	P.Hyde, D.Heffernan
1989	27 May	Karen	G.Szuca, M.Limonci
1989	27 May	Abrakebabra	G.Szuca, M.Limonci
1989	27 May	Hanging Groove	P.Hyde, D.Heffernan, A.Stewart
1989	27 May	Bost	P.Hyde, D.Heffernan, A.Stewart
1989	1 July	The Cruiser	M.Worsley, G.Urquhart
1990	23 Sep	Flash Dance	A.Holden, M.Hudson
1990	24 Sep	Ruby Groove	A.Holden, R.Holden
1990	25 Sep	Gannet Crack	A.Holden, R.Holden
1990	25 Sep	Natural Look	M.Hudson, A.Holden
1990	26 Sep	Conductor's Arete	M.Hudson
1990	26 Sep	Dulux Corner	M.Hudson, P.Brown
1990	Sep	Wish You Were Here	G.Armstrong, G.Szuca
1990	Sep	Brass Monkeys	G.Armstrong, G.Szuca
1990	Sep	Gritstone Reminiscence	G.Armstrong, G.Szuca
1990	Sep	Nothing Special	G.Armstrong, G.Szuca
1990	Sep	Monkey Hanger	G.Armstrong, G.Szuca
1990	Sep	Sore Phalanges	G.Armstrong, G.Szuca
1990	Sep	Smeg	G.Armstrong, G.Szuca
1991	2 Jun	Horny Corner	C.Moody, B.Taylor
1992	20 May	Sheep Tick	D.Gregg, G.Szuca, A.Wren
1992	20 May	Route With A View	M.Garthwaite, G.Szuca
1992	21 May	Heavenley's Pleasure	M.Garthwaite, D.Gregg
1992	21 May	Myopic	G.Szuca, A.Wren
1992	21 May	Panorama	A.Wren, G.Szuca
1992	21 May	Primeline	G.Szuca, A.Wren
1992	21 May	Gruinard Mutant	G.Szuca, A.Wren, D.Gregg
1992	18 Jun	Tinderbox	N.Horn, C.Moody
1992	18 Jun	Solar Furnace	N.Horn, C.Moody

1992	20 Jun	Luscious	M.McLeod, C.Moody
1992	20 Jun	Disturbing the Wildlife	M.McLeod, C.Moody
1993	24 Apr	Trilobite Groove	C.Moody, B.Taylor
1993	24 Apr	The Ratagan Strangler	C.Moody, B.Taylor
1994	24 May	Warmer Cleaner Better	I.Taylor, C.Moody
1994	6 Aug	Agfa	C.Moody, A.Petrie
1994	6 Aug	Tourist Attraction	C.Moody, A.Petrie
1994	6 Aug	Cameras Clicking	C.Moody, A.Petrie
1994	12 Oct	Baywatch	D.N.Williams, P.Duggan
1995	15 Apr	Sonamara	D.N.Williams, S.Abbott, L.Taylor
1995	12 Jun	Sunken Howker	C.Moody, M.Shaw
1995	12 Jun	Camera Obscura	C.Moody, M.Shaw
1995	1 July	Wall Street	S.Abbott, D.N.Williams
1995	1 July	Shocks and Stares	D.N.Williams, S.Abbott
1995	16 Jul	Insider Dealing	D.N.Williams, S.Abbott
1995	16 July	Venture Capital	S.Abbott, D.N.Williams
1995		Inanimate Objects Fight Back	G.Smith, A.Wainwright
1995		Perfectly	D.Holmes, A.Cave, C.Waddy
1996	6 Apr	Blockbuster	W.Jeffrey, D.N.Williams
1996	4 May	Powerbroker	S.Abbott, D.N.Williams
1996	6 May	Terminal Bonus	S.Abbott, D.N.Williams
1996	18 May	All Quiet on the Western Front	C.Moody, B.Taylor
1996	18 May	How the West was Won	B.Taylor, C.Moody
1996	18 May	The Umpire Strikes Back	C.Moody, B.Taylor
1996	21 May	Gene Therapy	D.Musgrove, D.Borthwick
1996	16 Jun	A Fistful of Dollarite	W.Jeffrey, D.N.Williams
1996	16 Jun	Security Risk	W.Jeffrey, D.N.Williams, A.Holden

TROTTERNISH

THE OLD MAN OF STORR AREA

1898	1 Sep	"A small pinnacle near the Old Man"	A.W.Russell, H.Raeburn
1955	18 Jul	Old Man of Storr, Original Route	D.Whillans, J.Barber, G.J.Sutton
1960	19 Aug	The Cathedral	C.J.S.Bonington, T.W.Patey
1967	Sep	Old Man of Storr, Portree Face	G.B.Lee, P.Thomson
1988	25 Jun	Old Man of Storr, Staffin Face	M.Fowler, D.Tunstall, J.Lincoln
1995	28 Dec	Deeply Digestible Gully	M.Fowler, S.Sustad
1995	29 Dec	Aperitif	S.Sustad, M.Fowler
1995	29 Dec	The Main Course	M.Fowler, S.Sustad
1995	29 Dec	Blue Moon Gully	S.Smith, P.Pritchard

CARN LIATH

1989	3 Jun	The Notch, Original Finish	W.Jeffrey, D.N.Williams
1990	7 May	Mummy's Church	M.Hudson, D.Hudson
1990	7 May	Sixties Special	M.Hudson, D.Hudson

1991	1 Aug	Staffin Cowboy	M.Hudson, R.Brown
1991	2 Aug	White Criterion	M.Hudson, R.Brown, P.Brown
1991	6 Aug	Western Arete	M.Hudson, D.Hudson, R.Brown
1991	8 Aug	Prospect of Rona	M.Hudson, R.Brown
1991	21 Oct	The Blade	M.Hudson, R.Brown
1992	24 May	Cracked Rib and Slab	R.Brown, D.Hudson
1992	26 May	One in Thirteen	M.Hudson, A.Holden, R.Brown
1992	26 May	Hearts Highway	M.Hudson, A.Holden
1992	5 Jul	K.I.P.	D.Brown, R.Brown
1992	8 Aug	Thief	M.Hudson, R.Brown
1992	8 Aug	Bad Man Zone	A.Holden, D.Hudson
1992	9 Aug	Rogue's Rake	R.Brown, D.Hudson
1992	9 Aug	Dirtsman	M.Hudson, R.Brown, D.Hudson
1993	2 Apr	The Judge	D.Brown, R.Brown
1993	2 Apr	Swizzler	D.Brown, R.Brown
1993	4 Apr	Another Notch	D.Brown, R.Brown
1993	6 Apr	Dagger Crack	M.Hudson, J.Pearce
1993	1 Jun	Arbocranker	A.Holden, M.Hudson
1993	2 Jun	The Negatron	A.Holden, R.Brown
1993	18 Jul	England's Dreaming	R.Brown, M.Hudson
1993	18 Jul	Crack-U-Like	M.Hudson, R.Brown
1993	18 Jul	Rocks-R-Us	M.Hudson, R.Brown
1993	31 Oct	The Big Easy	D.Brown, D.Ferguson
1993	31 Oct	Cream Crackers	D.Brown, D.Ferguson
1993	1 Nov	Captain Cacky and Commander Energy	D.Ferguson, R.Carter
1993	1 Nov	Marking Time	D.Brown, R.Brown
1994	19 Jun	Change in Perspective	D.Ferguson, J.Brooke-Jones, R.Brown
1994	19 Jun	Jenga	D.Ferguson, J.Brooke-Jones, R.Brown
1994	19 Jun	Sandbagger	D.Ferguson, R.Brown
1994	19 Jun	Perce Strings	D.Pattullo, A.Kopack
1994	15 Oct	The Forty Nine Steps	D.Brown, R.Brown
1994	16 Oct	Silence of the Lambs	D.Brown, R.Brown
1994	16 Oct	Bengal Lancer	M.Hudson, A.Holden
1994	8 Nov	Fifties Special	M.Hudson, R.Brown
1995	25 Jun	Knickerhead	D.Ferguson, R.Brown
1995	26 Jun	Donkey	D.Ferguson, J.Brooke-Jones, R.Brown
1995	28 Aug	The Mace	R.Brown, J.Holden
1995	9 Sep	Brick House	M.Hudson

SGURR A' MHADAIDH RUAIDH

1987	16 Jul	Inaccessible Pinnacle, N and S ridges	D.N.Williams

THE QUIRAING

1970s		The Needle	K.Bridges, M.Bridges

KILT ROCK AREA (ELLISHADDER WALL TO FALLEN PILLARS)

1970s		Ellishadder Pinnacle	P.Lord, A.N.Other
1983	31 Apr	Road to Ruin	E.Grindley, R.Swinden, D.N.Williams

1983	1 May	Internationale	R.Swinden, E.Grindley
1983	28 May	Clandestine	D.N.Williams, C.A.Hill
1983	May	Wide Eyed	E.Grindley, C.Grindley
1983	Jun	Footloose	E.Grindley, R.McHardy
1983	Jun	Fancy Free	R.McHardy, E.Grindley
1983	9 Jul	Grey Panther	E.Grindley, D.N.Williams, P.Hunter, W.Jeffrey
1983	10 Jul	Sporran	W.Jeffrey, D.N.Williams, P.Hunter
1983	10 Jul	Edge of Beyond	P.Hunter, W.Jeffrey
1983	11 Jul	Jamboree	D.N.Williams, W.Jeffrey, P.Hunter
1983	11 Jul	Romper	D.N.Williams, W.Jeffrey
1983	12 Jul	The Pioneer	P.Hunter (unseconded)
1983	13 Jul	Tartan Terror	P.Hunter, D.N.Williams
1983	13 Jul	Secret Service	D.N.Williams, P.Hunter
1983	16 Jul	Jammy Dodger	D.N.Williams, P.Hunter
1983	16 Jul	Skyeman	P.Hunter, D.N.Williams
1983	16 Jul	The Electric Bagpipe	D.N.Williams, P.Hunter
1983	16 Jul	Ruination	P.Hunter (unseconded)
1983	18 Jul	Brazen	P.Hunter, D.N.Williams
1983	21 Jul	Pied Piper	P.Hunter, D.N.Williams
1983	30 Aug	Killer Whale	W.Birkett, D.Lyle
1984	28 May	Drop the Pilot	W.Birkett, B.Wightman
1984	28 May	The Tempest	B.Wightman, W.Birkett
1984	17 Aug	Mushroom Billy	T.Walkington, W.Birkett
1984	19 Aug	Received with Thanks	W.Birkett, T.Walkington
1985	28 May	Over The Rainbow	W.Birkett, B.Wightman
1985		Bob Bob Stack	B.Wightman, W.Birkett (both solo)
1987	6 Apr	Stormwatch	G.Farquhar
1987	15 Apr	Iron Crow	D.Dinwoodie, B.Lawrie
1987	16 Apr	Mystery Cat	D.Dinwoodie, B.Lawrie
1987	16 Apr	High Noon	D.Dinwoodie, B.Lawrie
1987	16 Apr	Fish Tail Cracks	D.Dinwoodie, B.Lawrie
1987	17 Apr	Toll Dubh	D.Dinwoodie, B.Lawrie
1987	17 Apr	Demon Lover	D.Dinwoodie, B.Lawrie
1987	25 Apr	Brightside Crossing	G.Farquhar, G.Ettle
1987	16 May	The Great Deep	D.Dinwoodie, D.Hawthorn
1987	17 May	Blasphog	D.Dinwoodie, D.Hawthorn
1987	18 May	Bocan Mor	D.Hawthorn, D.Dinwoodie
1987	May	Sheer Sear	G.Latter
1987	8 Jun	Black Crow King	C.Waddy, G.Percival
1987	9 Jun	Fe Fi Fo Fum	C.Waddy, G.Percival
1987	10 Jun	Ill Wind	C.Waddy, G.Percival
1987	13 Jun	Actually Hyperbole	R.Wightman, J.Topping
1989	27 Aug	Ragged Robin	C.Moody
1989	27 Aug	The Danglers	M.McLeod, C.Moody
1990	20 May	The View	E.Grindley, G.Libeks
1990	28 Jul	Bandasky	C.Moody, B.Taylor
1990	1 Dec	Confiture	C.Moody
1990	1 Dec	Marmelada	C.Moody

1991	13 Apr	Cak	A.Smith, B.Davison
1991	13 Apr	F.B.C.	B.Davison, C.Moody, A.Smith
1991	14 Apr	Entrevennes	C.Moody, B.Davison
1992	25 May	Y Bilidowcar	N.Carson, D.Carson
1993	2 Jun	Frisky After Whisky	L.Steer, C.Hannah
1994	30 Jul	Easter Island	M.McLeod, C.Moody
1995	9 Jul	A Haggis Called Wanda	C.Moody, I.Taylor

STAFFIN AND STAFFIN SLIP BUTTRESSES

1984	18 Aug	Dustbin Jimmy	W.Birkett, T.Walkington
1985	26 May	Sailin' Shoes	B.Wightman, W.Birkett
1987	18 May	Dawn of Time	D.Dinwoodie
1987	12 Aug	Staffin Classic	W.Birkett, E.Grindley
1988	24 Apr	Lats in Space	E.Grindley, I.Sykes
1988	30 Apr	Captain Patience	C.Downer, G.Libeks, E.Grindley, S.Suthorn, A.Pounder, I.Blakeley
1988	30 Apr	Dial Card	I.Blakeley, A.Pounder, E.Grindley, S.Suthorn
1988	30 Apr	The Facilitator	I.Blakeley, G.Libeks, C.Downer, E.Grindley
1988	30 Apr	The Latvian	C.Downer, G.Libeks, S.Suthorn
1988	8 May	Green Vote	E.Grindley, I.Sykes
1988	May	East Chimney Crack	J.Hargreaves, W.Birkett
1988	29 May	The Sheriff's Black Dog	C.Downer, G.Libeks, E.Grindley
1988	29 May	Gorbachev	E.Grindley, G.Libeks, S.Suthorn
1988	29 May	Experimental Learning	I.Blakeley, C.Downer
1988	29 May	The Beast of Bolsover	C.Downer, G.Libeks
1988	30 May	Lat up a Drainpipe	G.Libeks, E.Grindley, S.Suthorn
1988	30 May	Woman of the Eighties	I.Blakeley, R.Kenyon, C.Downer
1988	Jun	Silly Pollack	L.Steer, W.Birkett
1988	Jun	Silly Pollack Two	W.Birkett, L.Steer
1988	Jun	Living Hell	W.Birkett, L.Steer
1989	27 May	Birdman of Bewaldeth	C.Downer, I.Blakeley
1989	27 May	Lusting after Glenys Kinnock	I.Blakeley, C.Downer, G.Libeks, R.Williamson
1989	27 May	Easy Day for a Lady	G.Libeks, E.Grindley, R.Williamson
1989	28 May	Swillington Common	I.Blakeley, G.Libeks, C.Downer
1990	3 May	The Avon Man	E.Grindley, G.Libeks
1990	10 May	Lateral Thinking	W.Jeffrey
1990	28 May	Staffin Follies	G.Cullen, J.R.Mackenzie
1990	9 Jun	Sasha	E.Grindley, G.Libeks
1992	15 Jun	Post Marital Blues	N.Horn, C.Moody
1992	15 Jun	The Swelling	N.Horn, C.Moody
1992	21 Jun	Tremour	G.Cullen, J.R.Mackenzie
1992	21 Jun	Earthquake	J.R.Mackenzie, G.Cullen
1994	14 May	Hand Jive	W.Jeffrey, D.N.Williams
1994	17 Sep	Prometheus	C.Thorpe, W.Birkett
1994	17 Sep	Heracles	W.Birkett

FLODIGARRY AREA

1989	7 May	Rock Island Line	D.N.Williams, W.Jeffrey
1989	28 May	Buoy Racer	W.Jeffrey, D.N.Williams
1989	10 Sep	Slab and Tickle	D.N.Williams, W.Jeffrey
1989	8 Oct	Tresspassers Will be Prosecuted	E.Grindley, G.Libeks
1989	19 Nov	Karl Marx's Lament	E.Grindley, G.Libeks
1989	19 Nov	Rightward Drift	E.Grindley, G.Libeks
1990	22 Apr	Stalking Horse	D.N.Williams, E.Grindley
1990	22 Apr	One Armed Bandit	D.N.Williams, E.Grindley
1990	3 May	Election Chimney	D.N.Williams, P.Duggan, C.Clark
1990	3 May	Floating Voter	D.N.Williams, P.Duggan
1990	3 May	Swingometer	D.N.Williams, P.Duggan
1990	13 May	No No Hervo	E.Grindley, D.N.Williams
1990	13 May	Black Beauty	D.N.Williams, E.Grindley
1990	13 May	Councillor Dubh	E.Grindley, D.N.Williams
1990	19 May	House of Horrors	E.Grindley, G.Libeks
1990	26 May	Lucy in the Sky	D.N.Williams, W.Jeffrey
1990	26 May	Spantastic	D.N.Williams, W.Jeffrey
1990	6 Jul	Newspaper Taxis	D.N.Williams, P.Duggan
1990	6 Jul	Head in the Clouds	D.N.Williams, P.Duggan
1991	8 Aug	Lipstick	D.N.Williams, P.Duggan
1994	1 May	Castaway	D.N.Williams, I.Sykes
1994	1 May	Brinkmanship	I.Sykes, D.N.Williams
1994	14 May	Gutter Politics	D.N.Williams, E.Grindley, W.Jeffrey
1994	14 May	Men in Suits (both starts)	E.Grindley, W.Jeffrey, D.N.Williams
1994	14 May	Reach for the Sky	W.Jeffrey, D.N.Williams, E.Grindley
1995	13 Apr	Captain Nemo	S.Abbott, D.N.Williams

KILMALUAG AREA

1981		Double Dragon	R.Bates, P.Agnew
1990	2 Jun	Stac Buidhe, Original Route	E.Grindley, G.Libeks, D.N.Williams
1990	9 Sep	Goofus Band	E.Grindley, D.N.Williams
1991	11 May	Minnie the Moocher	E.Grindley, D.N.Williams
1991	8 Jun	Stacan Goblach (both stacks)	G.Muhlemann, S.Richardson
1991	8 Jun	Stac Buidhe, North Ridge	G.Muhlemann, S.Richardson
1995	25 Jun	Stac Buidhe, South-west Face	A.Holden, M.Hudson

RUBHA HUNISH

1986	11 Jun	South Stack, Willie Hunish	J.Hargreaves, W.Birkett
1987	4 May	Middle Stack, Original Route	J.Hargreaves, F.Snallam, W.Birkett
1987	5 May	North Stack, Original Route	W.Birkett, J.Hargreaves, F.Snallam
1987	7 May	Opening Gambit	W.Birkett, J.Hargreaves, F.Snallam
1989	6 May	Whispering Crack	W.Jeffrey, D.N.Williams
1989	27 May	The Red Barron Flies	K.Milne, H.Buxton
1989	Jun	Fly Man	I.Barron, S.Kennedy, C.Grindley

1991	9 Sep	Northern Lights	W.Birkett, A.Sheehan
1992	31 May	Middle Stack, Eilean Groove	S.Richardson, G.Muhlemann
1993	31 May	Northern Exposure	W.Birkett, C.Thorpe
1993	25 Sep	South Stack, Maol Groove	S.Richardson, G.Muhlemann
1993	25 Sep	Split Stack, Trodday Wall	G.Muhlemann, S.Richardson
1993	26 Sep	North Stack, Shiant Corner	S.Richardson, G.Muhlemann
1994	29 May	Minch and Tatties	D.N.Williams, W.Jeffrey
1996	31 May	Friends in the North	N.Robinson, W.Birkett (alt)

BORNESKETAIG

1984	2 Apr	The Mitre	J.Moffat, C.Dale
1984	2 Apr	King Canute	J.Moffat, C.Dale
1992	1 Jun	Mitre Groove	S.Richardson, G.Muhlemann

STACK OF SKUDIBURGH

1995	6 Nov	Landward Face	R.Brown, A.Holden
1995	6 Nov	Seaward Face	M.Hudson, I.Willeboordse

THE MOUNTAINS OF LEWIS AND NORTH HARRIS

1930		Central Gully, Sgurr Scaladale	M.Botterill
1933		North Rib of the Pala Glas	W.Ewing, G.R.Symmers
1938	Jul	Irens' Route	H.J.Irens, F.Solari, A.Kinnear
1948	28 Jul	Amphitheatre Buttress	R.G.Folkard, M.deV.Wills
1948	29 Jul	No.3 Buttress	R.G.Folkard, M.deV.Wills, Miss J.Fox
1948	30 Jul	No.1 Buttress, Sron Ulladale	R.G.Folkard, M.deV.Wills, Miss J.Fox
1948	30 Jul	Amphitheatre Approach	R.G.Folkard, M.deV.Wills, Miss J.Fox
1948	4 Aug	South Buttress	R.G.Folkard, M.deV.Wills
1948	4 Aug	No.1 Rib	R.G.Folkard, M.deV.Wills, Miss J.Fox
1948	5 Aug	Central Buttress, Mealisval	R.G.Folkard, M.deV.Wills, Miss J.Fox
1952		No.1 Buttress, Teinnasval	G.S.Johnstone, Mrs. S.Johnstone
1952		No.2 Buttress, Sgaoth Ard	G.S.Johnstone, Mrs. S.Johnstone
1952		Lochan Crag, Glen Skeaudale	G.S.Johnstone, Mrs. S.Johnstone
1952		No.1 Buttress, Sgaoth Iosal	G.S.Johnstone, Mrs. S.Johnstone
1952		Pinnacle Buttress, Sgaoth Iosal	G.S.Johnstone, Mrs. S.Johnstone
1952		Coire Dubh Slab, Clisham	G.S.Johnstone, Mrs. S.Johnstone
1954		Central Rib, Sgurr Scaladale	N.Tennent, M.Tennent
1958		The Direct Route	G.J.Fraser, Miss E.M.Baldwin
1959		West Buttress, Sgur Scaladale	A.Powling, D.Yates
1961	May	Great Gully	R.B.Evans, L.A.Hawarth, Mrs. A.Evans
1961	May	Tyke	R.B.Evans, L.A.Hawarth, Mrs. A.Evans
1961	May	The Gangway	R.B.Evans, L.A.Hawarth, Mrs. A.Evans

1961	May	South Buttress	R.B.Evans, L.A.Hawarth, Mrs. A.Evans
1961	May	Midgard	R.B.Evans, L.A.Hawarth, Mrs. A.Evans
1961	May	Windwhistle	R.B.Evans, L.A.Hawarth, Mrs. A.Evans
1961	May	Miny	R.B.Evans, L.A.Hawarth, Mrs. A.Evans
1961	May	Miolnir	R.B.Evans, L.A.Hawarth, Mrs. A.Evans (1pa)
FFA: A.Macfarlane, B.Davison, 1990			
1965	15 Aug	Inversion	M.A.Reeves, J.Ball
1965	23 Aug	Gollum	M.A.Reeves, B.Reeves
1965	26 Aug	Smeagol	M.A.Reeves, J.Ball
1966	Jul	Haudes	H.Small, J.W.Graham
Variation Finish: P.Macdonald, I.G.Rowe May 1969			
1967	28 May	Prelude	M.A.Reeves, J.Grieve
1967	31 May	Aurora	J.Grieve, M.A.Reeves, E.Jones
1967	1 Jun	Eureka	J.Grieve, E.Jones
1967	5 Aug	Direct Route, Sron Scourst	M.Slesser, D.J.Bennet
1968	May	Golden Gully	R.Sharp, W.Sproul
1968		North Buttress, Creag Dubh Dibidale	J.Ball, Mrs. H.Ball
1968		South Buttress	J.Grieve, M.Reeves
1969		1948 Route	W.Sproul, W.Sharpe
1969	May	The Scoop	D.Scott, G.Lee, J.Upton, M.Terry
A tremendous achievement, with 30 hours of very hard aid climbing spread over several days. The route was included in Hard Rock to make ticking the whole lot rather difficult!			
1969	May	Iron Butterfly	P.Macdonald, I.G.Rowe
1969	May	Stone	K.Spence, J.Porteous
FFA: M.Fowler, A.Meyers 1981			
1969	8 Jun	Islivig Direct	R.Sharp, W.Sproul
1969	8 Jul	West Buttress	A.Powling, D.Yates
1969	11 Jun	Sundowner	R.Sharp, W.Sproul
1969	6 Aug	Herbivore	P.T.Newll, C.G.Winfield
1970		Via Valtos	A.W.Ewing, W.Sproul
FFA: R.Archbold, G.Cohen			
1970		Solitude	J.Ball, M.Reeves
1970	4 Jun	Lochlan	D.C.Forrest, J.McEwan
1970	13 Aug	The Scroll	J.Ball, M.Reeves
1970	15 Sep	The Parker	M.H.Moar, G.Lawson
1971	3 Oct	Original Route, Flannan Buttress	G.M.Wallace, J.Crombie
1971	24 Oct	Direct Route, Ardroil Buttress	G.M.Wallace, J.Crombie
1971		Sidewinder	D.Scott, G.Lee, D.Hennick
1972		The Nose	D.Scott, G.Lee, D.Hennick
Two more impressive aid climbs which have yet to be completely freed.			
1972	1 Jun	Footpad	B.Clarke, J.Macdougall
1972	3 Jun	Joint	B.Clarke, K.Tremain
1972	3 Jun	Reefer	T.Fletcher, I.Sommerville
1972	3 Jun	Twenty Minute Buttress	T.Fletcher, I.Sommerville
1972	4 Jun	Flannan	T.Fletcher, J.Macdougall
1972	4 Jun	Nosferatu	B.Clarke, K.Tremain

1974		Joplin's Wall	G.Cohen, R.Archibold
1974		Election Special	B.Newton, M.Tighe
1974		The Eyrie	M.Tighe, B.Newton, J.Pollard
1977		Knucklehead	P.Lloyd, T.King
1980	8 Jul	Little Bo Peep	M.Fowler, A.Strapcans
1980	8 Jul	King Lear	M.Fowler, A.Strapcans
1980	20 Jul	Panting Dog Climb	M.Fowler, A.Strapcans
1980	Jul	Macbeth	M.Fowler, A.Strapcans
1980		Wee Gommie	S.Vietoris, C.Watts
1981	Jun	Take Two	C.Watts, S.Vietoris
1981		Flakeway to the Stairs	C.Watts, S.Vietoris
FFA: A.Macfarlane, B.Davison, April 1990			
1981	30 Jun	Panorama	M.Fowler, A.Meyers
1981	1 Jul	The Big Lick	M.Fowler, A.Meyers
1981	2 Jul	Little Red Rooster	M.Fowler, A.Meyers
1981	2 Jul	Grey Rib	M.Fowler, A.Meyers
1985	May	Beyond the Ranges	D.Cuthbertson, P.Moores
1987		The Scoop, Free Version	J.Dawes, P.Pritchard
1987		Knuckle Sandwich	J.Dawes, P.Pritchard
1987	1 Sep	Ventus	M.Tighe, A.Scouler
1987	1 Sep	Con John	J.Stevenson, A.Birrel
1987		Spike Fright	J.Sykes, I.Sutherland
1989		Pairc	A.Macfarlane
1989		Moskill Grooves	B.Moon, J.Dawes, P.Pritchard
1989		The Chisel	C.Waddy, B.Drury, J.Biddle
1989		Kismet	C.Waddy, R.Rogers
1989		White Dwarf	C.Waddy, R.Rogers
1989		Cuinas	C.Waddy, R.Rogers
1989		Palace of Swords Reversed	C.Waddy, R.Rogers
1989		Big Luigi	C.Waddy, J.Biddle
1989	8 Jul	Antipodean Exile	A.Macfarlane, D.MacGimpsey
1989	8 Jul	Macbeth Variation	A.Macfarlane, D.MacGimpsey
1989	14 Jul	Borealis	A.Macfarlane, D.MacGimpsey
1989	26 Aug	King Billy	A.Macfarlane, D.Stelfox
1990	Apr	Hitch Hiker	A.Macfarlane, B.Davison
1990	19 May	Herbivore Direct	B.Davison, A.Macfarlane
1990	Jun	All about Lewis	C.Rumsey
1990	Jul	Sideshow	A.Macfarlane, D.MacGimpsey
1991	28 Apr	Cold Start	A.Macfarlane, J.Norgrove
1992	13 Mar	Leodhas	A.Macfarlane, P.Macfarlane
1992		Crackhead	C.Waddy, A.Donson
1992		The Second Coming	C.Waddy, R.Rogers
1992		The Orphan	C.Waddy, A.Donson
1992		The Missing Link	C.Waddy, A.Donson
1993		Central Grooves	S.Meyers, G.Lovick
1994		Premonition	C.Waddy, G.Smith
1995	4 Jun	Dominus Vobiscum	C.Waddy, A.Wainwright
1996	13 May	Peatsmoke	J.L.Bermudez, J.Walker, N.Wilson

THE LEWIS SEA-CLIFFS

1970s		Broken Rib	I.Sutherland, I.Sykes
1970s		Director's Corner	I.Sykes, I.Sutherland
1970s		President's Chimney	M.Tighe, J.Paterson
1970s		Immaculate Crack	I.Sykes, I.Sutherland
1970s		Claymore	I.Sykes, I Sutherland
1970s		Spike Fright	I.Sutherland, I.Sykes
1970s		The Black Crack	Lochaber M.C.
1974	Jun	Newton's Law	B.Newton, M.Tighe
1974	Jun	Star of the Sea	M.Tighe, B.Newton
1974	Jun	Moac Wall	M.Tighe, B.Newton, D.Kirtley, J.Pollard
1975		Anonomous	M.Tighe and party
1975		Cormorant Corner	M.Tighe, I.Sutherland, I.Sykes
1975		Shag Crack	M.Tighe, I.Donaldson
1978	.May	Flannan Slab	M.Tighe, J.Paterson
1978	May	Sunset Rib	M.Tighe, J.Paterson
1978	Jun	Flannan Direct	M.Tighe, C.Davies
1979	May	Atlantic Crossing	M.Tighe, J.Paterson
1979	May	Flannan Chimneys (Left and Right-Hand)	M.Tighe, J.Paterson
1979	May	Flannan Crack	M.Tighe, J.Paterson
1979	May	Mick's Corner	M.Tighe, J.Paterson
1979	May	Scooby Rhu	M.Tighe, J.Paterson
1979	May	Chicken Run	M.Tighe, J.Paterson
1979	May	Chicken Run Direct	M.Tighe, J.Paterson
1980s		Let's go down to the Water Line	M.Tighe and party
1980s		Motion Control	M.Tighe, B.Newton (1 p.a.)
FFA: G.Latter, D.Cuthbertson 5th May 1985			
1983	May	Spiney Norman	M.Tighe, J.Paterson and party
1983	May	Hidden Gem	M.Tighe, J.Paterson and party
1985	5 May	The Painted Wall	D.Cuthbertson, G.Latter
1985	5 May	Whisky Galore	D.Cuthbertson, G.Latter
1985	6 May	Hundred Pipers	D.Cuthbertson, G.Latter
1985	5 May	The Magician	J.Moran, D.Pearce
1985	7 May	Dauntless	G.Latter, D.Cuthbertson
1985	5 May	Penny Whistle	J.Moran, D.Pearce
1985	7 May	The Dreaded Dram	D.Cuthbertson, G.Latter
1985	5 May	The Sorcerer	J.Moran, D.Pearce
1985	7 May	Into the Sea	D.Cuthbertson, G.Latter
1985	7 Jun	Queen's Freebie	D.Cuthbertson, P.Moores
1985	7 Jun	Limka	P.Moores, D.Cuthbertson
1985	7 Jun	Campa Crack	D.Cuthbertson, P.Moores
1985	7 Jun	Pink and Black	G.Latter
1985		In the Pink	L.M.C.
1985	Oct	The Vee	M.Tighe, J.Paterson
1985	Oct	The Zed	M.Tighe, J.Paterson
1985	Oct	A Night at the Opera	D.Cuthbertson and another
1985	Oct	Heel Hooker's Wall	D.Cuthbertson, T.Paisley

1986		Friends	M.Tighe, E.Nichols, B.Newton
1986	Jun	Twelve Years On	M.Tighe, I.Donaldson, J.Mathieson
1986	16 Sep	Whimp's Chimney	M.Tighe and party
1986	16 Sep	Cor Blimey Corner	M.Tighe and party
1986	16 Sep	Cuthron	M.Tighe and party
1986	16 Sep	Tickled Pink	M.Tighe and party
1986	16 Sep	Photographer's Corner	M.Tighe and party
A direct version of this route has been climbed by S.Abbott and party 1986			
1986	16 Sep	Sally's Dilemma	M.Tighe and party
1987	Jun	Red Ramp	M.Tighe, B.Newton and party
1987	Jun	Bay Back Crack	M.Tighe, B.Newton and party
1987	Jun	Sea Storm	M.Tighe, B.Newton and party
1987	Jun	Ken's Dilemma	M.Tighe, B.Newton and party
1987	Jun	The Taroin Chimneys	M.Tighe, B.Newton and party
1987	Jun	Taroin Grooves	M.Tighe and party
1988	7 May	Coloured Rain	M.Tighe, J.Stevenson
1988	7 May	Shadows in the Sun	M.Tighe, I.Sutherland, B.Newton
1988	8 May	Scoosh Case	J.Stevenson, I.Sutherland
1988	8 May	Hitman	M.Tighe, B.Newton
1988	Jun	If All Else Fails	D.Cuthbertson, L.Clegg, C.Henderson
1988	Jun	Moscow Mule	D.Cuthbertson, L.Clegg, C.Henderson
1988	Jun	Singapore Sling	D.Cuthbertson, L.Clegg, C.Henderson
1988	Jun	Suffering Bastard	D.Cuthbertson, L.Clegg, C.Henderson
1988	Jun	Killer Fingers	D.Cuthbertson, L.Clegg, C.Henderson
1988	Jun	Salty Dog	D.Cuthbertson, L.Clegg, C.Henderson
1988	Jun	The Screaming Ab Dabs	D.Cuthbertson, L.Clegg, C.Henderson
1988	Jun	In the Shop on the Hill	L.Clegg, D.Cuthbertson, C.Henderson
1988	Jun	Hughy's Cocktail	L.Clegg, D.Cuthbertson, C.Henderson
1989	Apr	Original Route	B.Davison
1989	Apr	Bones	B.Davison
1989	May	Solitude	B.Davison
1989	May	Ruth's Lazy Days	D.MacGimpsey, C.Allen
1989	17 May	Limpet Crack	A.Cunningham, B.Davison
1989	17 May	Neptune	B.Davison, A.Cunningham
1989	17 May	Dalbeg Buttress	B.Davison, A.Cunningham
1989	18 May	Wave Watcher	B.Davison, A.Cunningham
1989	19 May	Underneath the Arches	A.Cunningham, B.Davison
1989	19 May	Simple Jim	A.Cunningham, B.Davison
1989	19 May	Beam me up Scotty	B.Davison, A.Cunningham
1989	19 May	Kling On Corners	B.Davison, A.Cunningham
1989	20 May	The Black Hole	B.Davison, A.Cunningham
1989	21 May	DiLithium Crystals	A.Cunningham, B.Davison
1989	21 May	Captain's Log	A.Cunningham, B.Davison
1989	21 May	Sea Shanty	A.Cunningham, B.Davison
1989	21 May	Sea Monster	A.Cunningham, B.Davison
1989	21 May	Briny	B.Davison, A.Cunningham
1989	21 May	Salty Old Sea-Dog	B.Davison, A.Cunningham
1989	22 May	Old Salt	B.Davison, A.Cunningham
1989	24 May	Damp Down	B.Davison, A.Cunningham

1989	24 May	Neptune a Calling	B.Davison, A.Cunningham
1989	25 May	Warp Drive	B.Davison
1989	25 May	It's No Good Captain She's Breaking Up	B.Davison
1989	18 Jun	Hang It	A.Macfarlane, B.Marshall
1989	18 Jun	Thuggery	A.Macfarlane, D.MacGimpsey, B.Marshall
1989	20 Jun	Druid	A.Macfarlane, D.MacGimpsey
1989	5 Jul	Celtic Swing	A.Macfarlane, D.MacGimpsey
1989	5 Jul	Harr	A.Macfarlane, D.MacGimpsey
1989	15 Jul	The Milky Bar Kid	A.Macfarlane, D.MacGimpsey
1989	23 Jul	Navy Cut	A.Macfarlane, D.MacGimpsey, B.Marshall
1989	23 Jul	No Fags for Christmas	B.Marshall, D.MacGimpsey, A.Macfarlane
1989	Jul	Tea for Two	D.MacGimpsey, A.Newey
1989	Jul	Flying Teapot	A.Macfarlane, D.MacGimpsey, B.Marshall
1989	23 Jul	Outlaw	A.Macfarlane, D.MacGimpsey, B.Marshall
1989	30 Jul	Mr Big Comes Clean	A.Macfarlane, D.MacGimpsey, B.Marshall
1989	13 Aug	Cloud Burst	B.Davison, A.Nisbet
1989	13 Aug	State of Mind	A.Macfarlane, D.MacGimpsey
1989	24 Aug	Mongrel	A.Macfarlane, D.MacGimpsey
1989	28 Aug	Gleaning the Bone	A.Macfarlane, D.Stelfox
1989	28 Aug	Red Hand Gang	D.Stelfox, A.Macfarlane
1989	Aug	Robbery Under Arms	A.Macfarlane, D.MacGimpsey
1990		Celtic Rag	P.Mallon, C.McCartney
1990		Don't Break my Raybans	C.McCartney, P.Mallon
1990		Born to Fly	C.McCartney, P.Mallon
1990	13 May	Sunday Stroll	B.Davison (solo)
1990	13 May	Down Under	B.Davison, A.Macfarlane
1990	17 May	New World	B.Davison (back rope solo)
1990	17 May	Island of no Return	B.Davison
1990	17 May	New Addition	B.Davison (solo)
1990	17 May	First Born	B.Davison (solo)
1990	21 May	Endurance	B.Davison, A.Macfarlane
1990	24 May	Clean Hand Gang	B.Davison (back rope solo)
1990	24 May	Jessie James	B.Davison (back rope solo)
1990	16 Jul	A Prophet's Doom	A.Macfarlane, D.MacGimpsey
1993		Things are Looking Up	G.Latter, R.Campbell
1993		Look Back In Anger	R.Campbell, G.Latter
1993		Don't Look Now	G.Latter, R.Campbell
1993		Gannet Crack	M.Tighe, E.Sherstone
1993		Am Burrach	R.Campbell, G.Latter
1993	May	Gloss	N.Dalzell, J.Ashdown
1993	May	Lagalibility	N.Dalzell, J.Ashdown
1993	May	Black Foot	N.Dalzell, J.Ashdown

1993	Jun	I'll Try Up Here Again	M.Tighe, E.Shereton
1993	Jun	The Dark Crystal	S.Mayers, G.Lovick
1993	Jun	The Crystal Maze	S.Mayers, G.Lovick
1993	Jun	Distant Voices	M.Tompkins, S.Mayers
1993	6 Jun	Dry Dock	C.King, R.Kenyon
1993	Jul	Shadow Dancer	S.Mayers
1993	Jul	Pinky	G.Lovick, S.Mayers
1993	Jul	Perky	G.Lovick, S.Mayers
1993	Jul	Hullaballoo	S.Mayers
1993	Jul	Here Today, Gone Tomorrow	S.Mayers, G.Lovick
1993	Jul	Brutal Reality	S.Mayers, G.Lovick
1996	23 May	Blessed are the Weak	G.Huxter, unseconded
1996	24 May	Prawn in the USA	H.Jones, G.Huxter
1996	24 May	It's HVS Glen, ...	H.Jones, G.Huxter
1996	25 May	The Alchemist	N.Clement, G.Latter
1996	27 May	The Storm	G.Huxter, unseconded
1996	29 May	Paranoid Slippers	G.Farquhar, R.Campbell, N.Clement
1996	29 May	It's Raining Rocks!	G.Latter, N.Clement
1996	29 May	The Prozac Link	H.Jones, G.Huxter
1996	29 May	Grant's Bad Hair Day	H.Jones, G.Huxter
1996	6 Sep	Ladies Who Lunch	G.Huxter, K.Pyke
1996	7 Sep	Romancing the Moose	K.Pyke, G.Huxter
1996	7 Sep	Corner Climb	G.Huxter, K.Pyke
1996	8 Sep	Conundrum	G.Huxter, K.Pyke
1996	8 Sep	Rick Campbell's Motorway Adventure	G.Huxter, K.Pyke
1996	8 Sep	Crab Sunday	K.Pyke, G.Huxter
1996	9 Sep	Goodbye Ruby Tuesday	G.Huxter, K.Pyke
1996	10 Sep	First Born	K.Pyke, G.Huxter
1996	11 Sep	Chew the Route	K.Pyke, G.Huxter
1996	13 Sep	Parting Shot	G.Huxter, K.Pyke

NORTH UIST

All the routes were climbed in 1993, mostly by C.Jex. Other contributors were G.Jackson, D.Sharman, T.Habgood, R.Thomsett and T.Clements.

SOUTH UIST

The climbs on Leac Shleamhuinn were soloed by J.R.MacKenzie on 29th July 1992. The climbs on the nearby cliffs, and that on Ben Corodale, were climbed by B.Davison in May 1994.

MINGULAY

1993	30 May	Grey Rib	C.Bonington, M.Fowler (alt)
1993	30 May	No Puke Here	M.Fowler, C.Bonington (alt)
1993	31 May	The Silkie	G.E.Little, K.Howett (alt)
1993	31 May	Voyage of Faith	G.E.Little, K.Howett (alt)

1993	31 May	Stugeron	C.Bonington, M.Fowler (alt)
1993	31 May	Pressure Band	M.Fowler, C.Bonington (alt)
1993	1 June	Liverbird	C.Bonington, M.Fowler (alt)
1993	1 June	With a View to a Shag	G.E.Little, K.Howett
1993	1 June	Easy Day for a Shag	K.Howett, G.E.Little
1993	1 June	From the Hole to Heaven	G.E.Little, K.Howett
1995	31 May	Ossian Boulevard	A.Cunningham, G.Nicoll, R.Reid (alt)
1995	31 May	Taxing Macphee	K.Howett, G.E.Little (alt)
1995	1 June	Fifteen Fathoms of Fear	G.Nicoll, A.Cunningham (alt)
1995	1 June	Children of Tempest	G.E.Little, K.Howett (alt)
1995	1 June	Done Mingulay	A.Cunningham, G.Nicoll (alt)
1995	1 June	Dun Moaning	K.Howett, G.E.Little
1995	2 June	Crystal Daze	K.Howett, G.E.Little (alt)
1995	2 June	Okeanos	G.Nicoll, A.Cunningham (alt)
1995	2 June	Under the Pink	G.E.Little, R.Reid (alt)
1995	2 June	A Word With the Bill	A.Cunningham, G.Nicoll (alt)
1995	2 June	Lost Souls	K.Howett, G.E.Little (alt)
1995	2 June	Oh No, Norman's Back Tomorrow!	A.Cunningham, G.Nicoll, R.Reid (alt)
1995	2 June	Port Pillar	G.Nicoll, A.Cunningham, R.Reid (alt)
1996	26 Jun	The Wreck of the Edmund Fitz	L.Hughes, G.Nicoll
1996	26 Jun	Black Slab	G.Nicoll, F.Fotheringham
1996	26 Jun	Rubha Soul	K.Pyke, G.E.Little
1996	26 Jun	The Power of the Sea	K.Pyke, G.E.Little (alt)
1996	26 Jun	Morning Glory	G.E.Little, K.Howett (alt), K.Pyke
1996	26 Jun	Rory Rum the Story Man	K.Howett, G.Ridge
1996	26 Jun	Here We Go	A.Cunningham, F.Fotheringham, J.Lowther
1996	26 Jun	Don't Forget the Rope	A.Cunningham, F.Fotheringham
1996	26 Jun	Alzheimer's Grooves	F.Fotheringham, A.Cunningham
1996	26 Jun	Oh, No Archies Going Around...	A.Cunningham, F.Fotheringham
1996	26 Jun	Depth Charge	S.Muir, J.Lowther
1996	27 Jun	A Few Fathoms More	G.E.Little, K.Pyke (alt)
1996	27 Jun	Loose Living	G.E.Little, K.Pyke
1996	27 Jun	Lament to the Abyss	S.Muir, A.Cunningham, F.Fotheringham

PABBAY

1995	18 May	Warm Up	R.Gantzhorn, R.Witt
1995	18 May	Steife Brise	J.Fisher, A.Seeger
1995	9May	U-Ei	R.Gantzhorn, S.Wacker (alt)
1995	19 May	Spit in Paradise	R.Witt, J.Fischer
1995	19 May	Shortbread Fingers	Seitz, Bohnacker
1995	19 May	Orang-Utang Klaus	A.Seeger, K.Lotze
1995	19 May	Pat und Patachon	Seitz, Bohnacker
1995	19 May	Telefonmann	A.Seeger, K.Lotze
1995	19 May	Geniestreich	J.Fischer, A.Seeger
1995	19 May	Katzenklo	R.Gantzhorn
1995	19 May	Es gibt Reis Baby	J.Fisher, A.Seeger
1995	19 May	Das is doch die Situation Hier	A.Seeger, K.Lotze
1995	19 May	Leftie	R.Witt, Seitz

1995	30 May	The Priest	G.E.Little, K.Howett (alt)
1995	30 May	Spring Squill	A.Cunningham, G.Nicoll (alt)
1995	30 May	Oh No, Norman's in Reverse!	G.Nicoll, A.Cunningham (alt)
1995	30 May	Corncrake Corner	G.Nicoll, A.Cunningham (alt)
1995	30 May	Spooky Pillar	A.Cunningham, G.Nicoll (alt)
1996	23 Jun	Stretch it Out	A.Cunningham, F.Fotheringham
1996	23 Jun	Squat Thrust	F.Fotheringham, A.Cunningham
1996	23 Jun	Blo' na Gael	A.Cunningham, F.Fotheringham
1996	23 Jun	Wind Against Tide	A.Cunningham, F.Fotheringham
1996	23 Jun	Out of the Womb	S.Muir, L.Hughes (alt)
1996	23 Jun	Winos in a Barren Land	K.Howett, G.E.Little
1996	23 Jun	The Craik	K.Howett, G.E.Little
1996	23 Jun	The Abridged Version	G.E.Little, J.Lowther, K.Howett
1996	23 Jun	Wiggly Wall	G.Nicoll, M.Crowther, J.Lowther
1996	23 Jun	Illegal Alien	G.Nicoll, M.Crowther
1996	23 Jun	The Immigrant	G.Nicoll, M.Crowther
1996	23 Jun	Human Cargo	G.Nicoll, M.Crowther, L.Hughes
1996	23 Jun	Bogus Asylum Seekers	G.Nicoll, L.Hughes
1996	23 Jun	Wee Free	G.Ridge, K.Pyke
1996	23 Jun	Corncrake Chorus	K.Pyke, G.Ridge
1996	23 Jun	Hoofer's Route	K.Pyke, G.Ridge
1996	24 Jun	Zen and the Art of Corncrake	A.Cunningham, F.Fotheringham
1996	24 Jun	Squeeze Job	A.Cunningham, F.Fotheringham
1996	24 Jun	The Ramp	F.Fotheringham, A.Cunningham
1996	24 Jun	The Complete Works	G.Nicoll, M.Crowther, J.Lowther
1996	24 Jun	Geovannie	L.Hughes, S.Muir
1996	24 Jun	Wetter Than a Day at the Beach	L.Hughes, S.Muir
1996	24 Jun	Nothing to Declare	G.Nicoll, J.Lowther
1996	24 Jun	Customs and Exercise	G.Nicoll, J.Lowther
1996	24 Jun	In the Pink	G.E.Little, K.Howett, J.Lowther
1996	24 Jun	Prophesy of Drowning	K.Howett, G.E.Little (alt)
1996	24 Jun	Bint There Dun It	G.Ridge, K.Pyke
1996	24 Jun	Sugar Cane Country	K.Pyke, G.Ridge
1996	24 Jun	As Sound as Mr JA	K.Pyke, G.Ridge

RUM

1931/32		East Ridge, Hallival	D.L.McCallum, M.B.Nettleton
1933		Oxford Groove	R.C.S.Bow, M.B.Nettleton, F.A.Pullinger, A.C.Cunliffe
1935	Jun	Askival Slab	OUMC party
1938	28 Jun	Ogilvie's Ridge	I.Ogilvie, J.Ward, P.Holloway
1945/6		Bill's Finish	Junior Mountaineering Club of Yorkshire (JMCY)
1945/6		No. 1 Gully	JMCY
1945/6		North Corner	JMCY
1945/6		One-Two Buttress	JMCY
1945/6		Peretz Corner	JMCY

1945/6		Slab and Groove	JMCY
1945/6		South Corner	JMCY
1945/6		The Creep	JMCY
1947	5 Aug	Demolition Crack	H.G.Nicol, I.H.M.Smart, C.G.M.Slesser
1947	5 Aug	Hallelujah Heave-Up	I.H.M.Smart, C.G.M.Slesser, H.G.Nicol, G.J.F.Dutton
1947	5 Aug	Woden's Walk	I.H.M.Smart, H.G.Nicol, C.G.M.Slesser
1947	6 Aug	Fat Man's Evasion	H.G.Nicol, C.G.M.Slesser
1947	6 Aug	Ptarmigan Crack	G.J.F.Dutton, I.H.M.Smart
1947	6 Aug	Giant's Staircase	J.G.Parish, H.G.Nicol
1947	7 Aug	Edinburgh Climb	H.G.Nicol, I.H.M.Smart, C.G.M.Slesser
1947	8 Aug	Shearwater Arete	J.G.Parish, H.G.Nicol
1947	8 Aug	Shearwater Chimney	J.G.Parish, H.G.Nicol
1947	8 Aug	Avalanche Avenue	J.G.Parish, H.G.Nicol
1947	8 Aug	Bachelor's Choice	H.G.Nicol, J.G.Parish
1947	9 Aug	Airy Mary	H.G.Nicol, G.J.F.Dutton
1947	9 Aug	Jawbone Crack	H.G.Nicol, G.J.F.Dutton
1947	9 Aug	The Whited Crack	C.G.M.Slesser, I.H.M.Smart
1947		Sloping Ledge	Unknown
1948	May	Archangel Route	M.Ward, W.H.Murray
1948	May	Atlantic Ridge	M.Ward, W.H.Murray
1948	May	Bloodstone Crack	M.Ward, W.H.Murray
1950	18 Jul	Woden's Crack	D.Stewart, D.Bennet, S.Paterson
1950	18 Jul	Cracked Rib	D.Stewart, D.Bennet, S.Paterson
1950	20 Jul	Botany Crack	D.Stewart, D.Bennet
1950	20 Jul	Zigzag Route	D.Stewart, M.A.Mycroft
1950	22 Jul	Central Rib	D.Stewart, D.Bennet
1950	Jul	Demolition Crack Variation	D.Stewart, D.Bennet, S.Paterson
1951	28 Jun	Rolling-Pin Route	A.Waites-Fairbairn, E.Wrangham
1951	2 Jul	Archangel Variation Start	A.Waites-Fairbairn, E.Wrangham
1951	2 Jul	Right-Central Gully	A.Waites-Fairbairn, E.Wrangham
1951		Cambridge Arete	A.Parker, J.Young
1957	14 Jun	Shearwater Rib	C.Jorgensen, H. and D.Stembridge
1959	5 Jul	Perdita's Traverse	A.Littlejohn, A.Clark
1959	6 Jul	Variation Finish Bachelor's Choice	A.Littlejohn, A.Clark
1959	10 Jul	Groove and Chimney	A.Littlejohn, A.Clark
1959	10 Jul	Riona	A.Littlejohn
1959	10 Jul	Sentry's Sortie	A.Littlejohn, A.Clark
1960	1 Jun	Fist and Finger Stack	H.Brown, N.Hunter
1960	1 Jun	Sgorr an t-Snidhe	H.Brown
1960	22 Jun	Rangail Route	I.Southern, H.Brown, W.Harrison
1960		Perdita's Groove	A.Littlejohn
1961	23 Jun	Chuckiestane Groove	A.Littlejohn, A.Dinwoodie
1961	18 May	Consolation Crack	A.Littlejohn, E.Nisbet
1961	18 May	Right-Hand Buttress Direct	A.Littlejohn, E.Nisbet
1961	19 May	Red Brick	E.Nisbet, A.Littlejohn
1961	21 Jun	Yellowstone Chimney	A.Littlejohn
1961	22 Jun	Curving Chimney	A.Littlejohn, A.Dinwoodie

1961	22 Jun	Gothic Crack	A.Littlejohn, A.Dinwoodie
1961	22 Jun	Jun Jigsaw	A.Littlejohn, A.Dinwoodie
1961	23 Jun	Right-Hand Chimney	A.Littlejohn, A.Dinwoodie
1966	19 Jun	Zigzag	J.Matyssek, H.Brown
1966	20 Jun	Campion Slab	H.Brown, J.Matyssek and party
1966	20 Jun	No. 1 Arete	J.Matyssek, H.Brown, J.Patterson
1966	20 Jun	Right Corner	J.Matyssek, H.Brown, S.Menmuir
1966	20 Jun	Right Corner Chimney	H.Brown, W.Simpson, J.Yule
1966	20 Jun	Seoras	J.Matyssek, H.Brown
1966	19 Jun	Gargoyle Chimney	J.Matyssek, H.Brown and party
1966	19 Jun	Flake and Crack Route	J.Matyssek, H.Brown
1966	20 Jun	Face Route	J.Matyssek, T.Izatt, S.Crockatt
1966	20 Jun	Fork Slab	J.Matyssek, H.Brown
1966	18 Aug	Helen's Horror	M McCallum, H.Steven
1966	22 Aug	Midge	M.McCallum, A.Littlejohn
1966	23 Aug	Midgeless	M.McCallum, A.Littlejohn
1966	23 Aug	Moly	A.Littlejohn, M.McCallum
1966	30 Aug	Lotos	M.McCallum, A.Littlejohn
1966	30 Aug	Ashes	A.Littlejohn, M.McCallum
1966	31 Aug	Amaranth	A.Littlejohn, M.McCallum
1966	31 Aug	Asphodel	A.Littlejohn, M.McCallum
1966	31 Aug	Corner Crack	M.McCallum, A.Littlejohn
1967	18 May	Rose-Root Slab and Crack	J.Matyssek, H.Brown
1967	18 May	Western Isles Buttress	J.Matyssek
1967	19 May	Sunny Side	J.Matyssek, H.Brown
1967	19 May	Frustration	J.Matyssek, H.Brown
1967	19 May	Diamond Corner	J.Matyssek, H.Brown
1967	21 May	Calder Chimney	I.Clough, J.Greenwood
1967	22 May	Breeze	J.Matyssek, H.Brown
1967	22 May	Broad Buttress	J.Matyssek
1967	22 May	Narnia Arete	H.M.Brown, A.T.Rollo
1967	22 May	Choochter Rib	I.Clough, K.Ross
1967	23 May	Fylde Crack	I.Clough, N.Clough
1967	23 May	Grunt	I.Clough
1967	23 May	Grease Crack	I.Clough, K.Ross
1967	23 May	Striding Edge	I.Clough, J.Greenwood
1967	24 May	Claymore	J.Matyssek, H.Brown
1967	24 May	Dribble	I.Clough
1967	24 May	Amble Arete	N.Clough, K.Ross
1967	24 May	Eyrie Arete	I.Clough, N.Clough, K.Ross
1967	24 May	Fluch	I.Clough, K.Ross
1967	24 May	Fuarr	J.Greenwood, N.Clough
1967	25 May	Layback Crack	I.Clough
1967	24 May	The Ramp	I.Clough
1967	25 May	Tyke Arete	I.Clough
1967	26 May	The Candle	I.Clough, K.Ross
1967	26 May	Trap Chimney	I.Clough, J.Greenwood
1967	May	Stac nam Faoileann	I.Clough and party
1970	Jun	Very Well	M.H.Moar, J.D.Roberts-James

Year	Date	Route	First ascensionists
1974	8 Apr	Atlantic Slab, Askival North-West Face	S.R.Bateson, T.Little
1974	8 Apri	Haddie	S.R.Bateson, T.Little
1974	10 Apr	Thumbs	A.Nisbet, S.R.Bateson
1974	12 April	Fingerless	A.Nisbet, S.R.Bateson
1975	20 Mar	Asgard	N.Hill, D.Brown
1975	20 Mar	Skrymir	N.Hill, D.Brown
1975	20 Mar	The Pink	N.Hill, D.Brown
1975	21 Mar	Trundle	N.Hill, D.Brown, C.Matthews
1975	21 Mar	Valhalla	N.Hill, D.Brown, C.Matthews
1975	28 May	Black and Tan	C.Ross, A.J.Young
1975	28 May	Christopher	H.Brown, C.Ross
1976		Rouma Route	Unknown
1979	Jun	Guillotine	R.Barton, D.Morris
1980	25 Mar	Iso-Amylase	W.Wright, J.Rose
1980	25 Mar	The Rozzer	J.Rose, W.Wright
1980	28 Mar	Morning Tide	W.Wright, G.Eadie
1980	28 Mar	Ocean of Mercy	W.Wright, G.Eadie
1980	Apr	Gemme	D Goldie, S.Pearson, R.Pitt, D.Forrest
1982	25 Mar	The Wandering Botanist	D.Bearhop, A.Tibbs
1982	29 Mar	Satisfaction	A.Tibbs, D.Bearhop
1982	30 Mar	Aficionado	D.Bearhop, A.McLintock
1982	30 Mar	Rose-Root Slab and Crack Variation	A.Tibbs, H.Irvine
1983	Apr	Big Boots and Trainers	K.Connor, D.Bannernman
1983	Apr	Tidal Exit Cracks	K.Connor, D.Bannernman
1983	1 May	Black Day	J.Fotheringham, R Allan
1984	5 May	Relish	G.S.Nicoll, J.Banks
1984	5 May	Salad Days	G.S.Nicoll, J.Banks
1984	30 Jun	Malindarra	G.E.Little
1985	18 May	Orval Pinnacle	G.E.Little

D.Bathgate and H.MacInnes reached the summit via abseil, lasso and Tyrolean traverse in 1977

Year	Date	Route	First ascensionists
1986	2 Jun	Hagar	A.Kirk, A.Lumsden
1986	2 Jun	Lucky Eddy	G.Swinton, J.Mitchell
1986	8 Jul	Ankle	H.M.Brown
1989	Aug	Half-a-Gale Slab	K.V.Crocket, A.Walker
1989	27 July	The Witness	A.Matthewson
1990	16 July	Allivalhalla	N.Reid, J.Mitchell
1990	16 Jul	Nice 'n' Easy	J.Mitchell, N.Reid
1990	18 Jul	Bishop's Groove	J.Mitchell, E.Mitchell
1990	18 Jul	Cullie's Route	M.Dunlop, A.Bain
1990	18. Jul	Fugazi	E.Mitchell, J.Mitchell
1990	18. Jul	Grendel	J.Mitchell, E.Mitchell
1990	18 Jul	Moss Slab	A.Bain, M.Dunlop

Direct Start: A.Bain, J.Mitchell, N.Reid 16 Jul 1995

Year	Date	Route	First ascensionists
1990	18 Jul	Pandora's Box	J.Mitchell, N.Reid
1990	18 Jul	Slab Direct	J.Mitchell, N.Reid
1990	18 Jul	Troll Corner	N.Reid, J.Mitchell

1990	18 Jul	Breeze Variation	A.Bain, M.Dunlop
1990	18 Jul	Western Ridge	A.Bain, M.Dunlop
1991	16 Jul	Pineapple Wall	M.Beetham, C.Smart, M.Wakeman, R.Weare
1991	16 Jul	Rum and Pineapple	M.Beetham, C.Smart, M.Wakeman, R.Weare
1992	31 Mar	Honky Tonk	A.Tibbs, C.Dale
1994	23 Jul	Archangel Superdirect	A.Tibbs, D.Bearhop
1994	23 Jul	Doric	S.Pearson, A.Kassyk
1994	23 Jul	Peer Gynt	A.Hume, A.Matthewson
1994	23 Jul	Return Call	S.Pearson, A.Kassyk
1994	23 Jul	The Dwarfie	A.Hume, A.Matthewson
1995	16 Jul	Wander	D.Bryson, C.McGregor
1995	16 Jul	Dog Day Sunrise	C.McGregor, D.Bryson
1995	17 Jul	Left Edge	J.Mitchell, A.Bain, N.Reid
1995	17 Jul	Atlantic Highway	J.Mitchell, A.Bain
1995	17 Jul	Vanishing Point	N.Reid, D.Bryson
1995	17 Jul	Atlantic Breeze	C.McGregor, D.Bryson
1995	18 Jul	Slab and Arete	K.Burns, A.Bain
1995	18 Jul	Feersum Endjinn	D.Bryson, C.McGregor
1995	18 Jul	Across the Lines	A.Bain, K.Burns
1995	18 Jul	Doric Direct	I.Robertson, N.Reid
1995	21 Jul	Phew!	I.Robertson, A.Bain
1995	21 Jul	Heartwork	C.McGregor, D.Bryson
1995	21 Jul	The Light Fantastic	C.McGregor, D.Bryson
1995	21 Jul	Breenge	D.Bryson, C.McGregor
1995	21 Jul	Cruise Control	D.Bryson, C.McGregor
1995	21 Jul	A Bit on the Side	N.Reid, I.Robertson, A.Bain
1995	21 Jul	Rum Doodle	N.Reid, I.Robertson
1995	21 Jul	On the Greener Side	A.Bain, I.Robertson
1995	21 Jul	Shadowlands	D.Bryson, A.Bain
1996	6 Jun	Golden Rib	M.Hudson, J.Burleigh

EIGG

1967	11 Apr	Grit	I.Clough and party
1967	11 Apr	The Pod	I.Clough, C.Greatwich
1967	12 Apr	Botterill's Crack	I.Clough, J.Davidson, C.Greatwich
1967	13 Apr	Collie's Cleft	I.Clough, C.Greatwich
1967	14 Apr	Eagle Chimney	I.Clough, C.Greatwich
1967	18 Jun	The Flue	D.S.Nicol, P.Gunn
1967		Pitchstone	H.MacInnes, I.Clough (alt)
1970		The Nose	C.Boulton, K.Jones
1978	25 May	Purphura	P.Moores, S.Whaley
1986	21 Jul	The Comb	G.E.Little, D.Saddler
1986	21 Jul	Pooh Bear	D.Saddler, G.E.Little
1986	22 Jul	Lego Route	G.E.Little, D.Saddler
1986	22 Jul	Frozen Ocean	G.E.Little, D.Saddler (alt)
1986	23 Jul	Splinter Arete	G.E.Little, D.Saddler
1986	23 Jul	Tales of the Unexpected	G.E.Little, D.Saddler

1986	25 Jul	The Haven	G.E.Little, D.Saddler (alt)
1987	16 Apr	First Blood	G.E.Little, D.Saddler
1987	16 Apr	Paradise Lost	G.E.Little, D.Saddler
1987	16 Apr	Echo Beach	D.Saddler, G.E.Little
1987	17 Apr	The Honey Thief	G.E.Little, D.Saddler (alt)
1987	18 Apr	The Swarm	G.E.Little, D.Saddler
1987	20 Apr	Cobra	D.Saddler, G.E.Little
1987	20 Apr	Adder	G.E.Little, D.Saddler
1987	22 May	Through the Barricades	D.Saddler, G.E.Little, R.Wilson (alt)
1987	23 May	Stepping Out	G.E.Little, D.Saddler, R.Wilson
1987	23 May	Psycho	D.Saddler, G.E.Little (alt)
1987	24 May	Over the Top	D.Saddler, G.E.Little, R.Wilson
1987	24 May	Golden Brown	G.E.Little, D.Saddler, R.Wilson
1987	24 May	Tom	D.Saddler, R.Wilson
1987	24 May	Jerry	D.Saddler, G.E.Little, R.Wilson
1988	1 Apr	Earthsea	G.Latter, G.E.Little
1988	2 Apr	Purphura, direct start	G.E.Little, G.Latter
1988	3 Apr	Beyond the Fringe	G.Latter, G.E.Little (alt)
1988	3 Apr	Going for Gold	G.E.Little, G.Latter (alt)
1991	24 May	Original Route	G.E.Little
1991	24 May	Hologram Groove	G.E.Little
1991	24 May	The Hang	G.E.Little
1994	21 Aug	Sense of Porpoise	K.Howett, G.E.Little
1994	21 Aug	Frolicking With Freddie	G.E.Little, K.Howett

MULL

CREACH BEINN

All routes on Creach Beinn were done by C.Moody with various partners: D.Donoghue, A.Smith, B.Davison and A.Petrie.

AN GARRADH

1985	7 Apr	Headless Ridge	N.Horn, C.Moody
1985	27 Oct	Cop out	N.Horn, C.Moody
1987	18 Apr	Violet	C.Moody, D.Hayter
1987	18 Apr	Juniper Mantle	D.Hayter, C.Moody
1987	8 May	Fifth Choice	C.Moody, D.Richie
1987	26 May	Drop Out	A.Smith, B.Davison
1987	27 May	Star Trek	B.Davison, A.Smith
1987	27 May	Sister Moonshine	A.Smith, B.Davison
1987	28 May	Mincing Loiterer	C.Moody, B.Davison, A.Smith
1987	4 Jun	Third Choice	C.Moody, M.McLeod
1987	11 Jun	April Aphid	C.Moody, N.Horn
1987	11 Jun	Knee Burner	N.Horn, C.Moody
1987	12 Jun	Pooh Bear's Delight	N.Horn, C.Moody
1987	13 Jun	Centipede	N.Horn, C.Moody
1990	30 Apr	Seductive Finish	B.Davison, A.Nisbet
1990	1 May	Knockin on Heaven's Door	B.Davison, A.Nisbet
1995	11 Nov	The Boulder Problem	C.Moody, D.Mitchell

CREAG MHOR

1987	3 Sep	Loosey Simmons	C.Moody

BALMEANACH

1994	8 Aug	Milanda Shelf	C.Moody, D.M.McLean
1995	17 Sep	Mushroom Picking	C.Moody, M.Bennett
1996	21 May	Mur Sans Spits	C.Moody, D.Ritchie

ARDCHRISHNISH

Routes climbed by Cameron Bell, Danny Brooks, Rob Burney, Brian Davison, Drew Gallacher, Mark Garthwaite, Neil Horn, Colin Lambton, Morris McLeod, Colin Moody, John Offord, Ritchie Patterson, Allan Petrie, Dave Ritchie, Mark Shaw, Andy Smith, Bruce Taylor, and probably others.

SHIABA

All routes at Shiaba were climbed by Colin Moody with Neil Horn and Mark Shaw.

SCOOR

1991	Aug	Pocket Razor	D.Brooks, J.Marshall
1991	28 Sep	Choughless	C.Moody D.Brooks, J.Marshall
1991	28 Sep	Sawfish Crack	C.Moody J.Marshall, D.Brooks
1991	5 Oct	White Shite	C.Moody, J.Marshall, D.Brooks
1991	Oct	Waves and White Water	D.Brooks, J.Marshall
1991	Oct	Fungy	D.Brooks, J.Marshall
1991	20 Oct	Hammock	D.Brooks, C.Moody
1991	20 Oct	Seal Show	C.Moody, D.Brooks
1992	Mar	Kilvickeon	D.Brooks (unseconded)
1992	Mar	Runout	J.Marshall, D.Brooks
1992	12 Jul	Student Waster	C.Moody, A.Petrie
1992	16 Aug	Kelpie	C.Moody, D.Brooks
1992	19 Aug	Everything Flying By	C.Moody, D.Brooks
1992	5 Sep	Jimmy's Corner	D.Brooks, C.Moody
1992	9 Sep	Dead Oystercatchers	C.Moody, D.Brooks
1992	9 Sep	Pretty Choughed	D.Brooks, C.Moody
1992	18 Oct	Cup Champions	C.Moody, D.Brooks
1992	18 Oct	Head Butts	D.Brooks, C.Moody
1992	18 Oct	Spleenwort Groove	D.Brooks, C.Moody
1992	25 Oct	Night Vision	D.Brooks, C.Moody
1992	25 Oct	Fissure Fisher	C.Moody, D.Brooks
1992	Nov	Where Eagles Dare	D.Brooks, S.Morris
1993	Jan	Jack in a Box	D.Brooks, S.Morris
1993	Feb	Bluebell Blues	D.Brooks (unseconded)
1993	13 Jun	A Quiet Shag	C.Moody, N.Horn
1993	13 Jun	One Foot in the Grave	N.Horn, C.Moody
1993	14 Jun	Greased Lightning	N.Horn, C.Moody
1993	14 Jun	Tystie	C.Moody, N.Horn
1993	17 Aug	Therapy	C.Moody, J.Marshall, D.Brooks, A.Pedley
1993	22 Aug	Flight of the Kite	D.Brooks, C.Moody
1993	22 Aug	Hit and Run	C.Moody, A.Pedley

1993	29 Aug	Better Than a Poke in the Eye	M.Garthwaite (unseconded)
1993	29 Aug	Slyvester	M.Garthwaite, C.Moody
1993	5 Sep	Lauracheval	M.Garthwaite, G.Szuca
1993	5 Sep	Tweekie Pie	M.Garthwaite (unseconded)
1994	17 Apr	Milk Tray	C.Moody, B.Davison, A.Smith
1994	17 Apr	Red Shafted Flicker	C.Moody, B.Davison, A.Smith
1994	17 Apr	Black Isle	B.Davison, C.Moody, A.Smith
1994	17 Apr	That's Fast for a Snail	B.Davison, C.Moody, A.Smith
1994	19 Apr	Cog's Crack	B.Davison, A.Smith
1994	19 Apr	I Would Drive 500 Miles	A.Smith, B.Davison
1994	19 Apr	One Foot on the Arete	B.Davison, A.Smith
1994	12 Jul	Turnstone	C.Moody, M.Shaw
1994	18 Jul	A Fetid Stench	C.Moody, M.Shaw
1994	31 Aug	Night Watch	D.Brooks, C.Moody, M.Shaw
1994	31 Aug	Shag Vision	C.Moody, D.Brooks M.Shaw
1994	1 Sep	Agrimony	C.Moody, D,Brooks M.Shaw
1994	2 Sep	Night Rider	D.Brooks, C.Moody, M.Shaw
1994	25 Sep	Wallcreeper	C.Lambton, C.Moody M.Roser
1994	25 Sep	Eat My Shorts	M.Garthwaite, C.Moody
1994	15 Oct	Wild Swans	C.Moody, M.Garthwaite
1994	15 Oct	See You in Hell Soldier Boy	M.Garthwaite (unseconded)
1995	2 Sep	The Sleeper	C.Moody, D.Ritchie
1995	24 Sep	Aromatherapy	C.Moody, M.Shaw
1995	24 Sep	Weasels Ripped my Tips	C.Moody, M.Shaw
1995	24 Sep	Socks	C.Moody, M.Shaw
1996	31 Mar	We Like Sheep	T.Charles-Edwards, C.Moody

CREAG EILEAN AN DUILISG

All routes were climbed by Colin Moody with various partners:
Mark Shaw, Tom Charles-Edwards, Dave Ritchie and Michael Tweedly.

ARDTUN EAST

The routes were climbed by Danny Brooks, Derek McGlone, Colin Moody and Mark Shaw.

THE GREEN HILL

The routes were climbed by Donald Cameron, Colin Moody and Mark Shaw.

DUNAN MOR

The routes soloed by Tom Charles-Edwards.

FIDDEN

The routes were climbed by Danny Brooks, James Marshall, Sean Morris and Michael Tweedly.

ERRAID

Routes climbed by Colwyn Jones, Stephen Kennedy and Dave Ritchie.

IONA (NORTH)

1991	Oct	Gollum	D.Brooks, G.Hutter, J.Marshall

1991	Oct	My Precioussss	J.Marshall, G.Hutter, D.Brooks
1991	Oct	Bilbo	D.Brooks, G.Hutter, J.Marshall
1993	15 Feb	The Shire	D.Brooks, J.Ferrie, Y.Taylor
1993	15 Feb	Cracks of Mordor	D.Brooks, J.Ferrie, Y.Taylor
1993	15 Feb	Yan's Route	Y.Taylor, J.Ferrie, D.Brooks
1993	15 Feb	Smaug	D.Brooks
1993	5 Aug	Jackie's Line	B.Vaucher
1993	5 Aug	The Day of the Frog	B.Vaucher
1993	5 Aug	Fada	C.Moody, B.Vaucher
1993	27 Aug	Cognative Therapy	M.Garthwaite, D.Gregg

IONA (SOUTH)

1993	1 May	L'homme d'Iona	C.Moody, W.Hood
1993	2 May	The Good Book	C.Moody, W.Hood
1993	12 Jun	Passage	C.Moody, N.Horn
1993	12 Jun	Parable	C.Moody, N.Horn
1993	12 Jun	Apocrypha	C.Moody, N.Horn
1993	12 Jun	Don't Bang the Drum	N.Horn, C.Moody
1993	12 Jun	At One	C.Moody, N.Horn
1993	19 Jun	Chinatown	S.Scott, J.Adams
1993	19 Jun	Pleasant Slab	J.Adams, S.Scott
1993	19 Jun	Scripture	C.Moody, S.Adams
1993	19 Jun	Jehad	C.Moody, S.Adams
1993	20 Jun	Heretic	J.Adams, S.Scott
1993	21 Aug	Mental Torment	C.Moody, D.Brooks, J.Marshall, A.Pedley
1993	21 Aug	Skinhead	C.Moody, J.Marshall
1993	28 Aug	Waco	D.Gregg, M.Garthwaite, C.Moody
1993	28 Aug	Cul Dreimne	D.Gregg, M.Garthwaite, C.Moody
1993	28 Aug	Yabadabadoo	M.Garthwaite, D.Gregg
1993	30 Aug	Mr.Muscle	M.Garthwaite, D.Gregg
1993	30 Aug	Prodigy	D.Gregg, M.Garthwaite
1993	4 Sep	Eric the Red	G.Szuca, C.Moody, M.Garthwaite
1993	4 Sep	The Incredible Dr Sex	M.Garthwaite (unseconded)
1993	26 Sep	Crusade	C.Moody, A.Petrie
1993	26 Sep	Communion Wine	C.Moody, A.Petrie
1993	26 Sep	Elastration	C.Moody, A.Petrie
1994	11 Jun	A Wing and a Prayer	C.Moody, B.Davison, A.Smith
1994	11 Jun	Pulpit Groove	B.Davison, C.Moody, A.Smith
1994	11 Jun	Inverted-V	B.Davison, C.Moody, A.Smith
1994	12 Jun	Complete Abstinence	C.Moody, S.Kennedy
1994	20 Aug	Fire and Brimstone	C.Moody, M.Shaw
1994	24 Sep	Smoke Yourself Thin	M.Garthwaite, C.Moody
1994	24 Sep	Smoking the Toad	M.Garthwaite, C.Lambton
1994	24 Sep	Rod, Todd, this is God	M.Garthwaite, C.Lambton
1995	22 Jul	The Bantry Boat	C.Moody, T.Charles-Edwards

COLONSAY

Routes on Colonsay were first climbed by D.Curtis and B.Howard (1985), J.A.Spencer and J.Sadler (1987,90) and G.E.Little, J.Skidmore and J.Finlay (1993).

Index of Routes

Note: Entries refer only to the pages on which the route descriptions are given